multiple intelligences
reconsidered

Studies in the
Postmodern Theory of Education

Joe L. Kincheloe and Shirley R. Steinberg
General Editors

Vol. 278

PETER LANG
New York • Washington, D.C./Baltimore • Bern
Frankfurt am Main • Berlin • Brussels • Vienna • Oxford

multiple intelligences
reconsidered

Joe L. Kincheloe, editor

PETER LANG
New York • Washington, D.C./Baltimore • Bern
Frankfurt am Main • Berlin • Brussels • Vienna • Oxford

Library of Congress Cataloging-in-Publication Data

Multiple intelligences reconsidered / edited by Joe L. Kincheloe.
    p. cm. — (Counterpoints; v. 278)
Includes bibliographical references and index.
1. Multiple intelligences. 2. Gardner, Howard. Multiple intelligences.
I. Kincheloe, Joe L. II. Series: Counterpoints (New York, N.Y.); v. 278.
BF432.3.M86   153.9—dc22   2003026734
ISBN 0-8204-7098-8
ISSN 1058-1634

Bibliographic information published by **Die Deutsche Bibliothek**.
Die Deutsche Bibliothek lists this publication in the "Deutsche
Nationalbibliografie"; detailed bibliographic data is available
on the Internet at http://dnb.ddb.de/.

Cover art "Fluid" by Matthew F. Dougherty (mfdartist@yahoo.com)
Cover design by Lisa Barfield

© 2004 Peter Lang Publishing, Inc., New York
275 Seventh Avenue, 28th Floor, New York, NY 10001
www.peterlangusa.com

Printed in the United States of America

to J. B. Kincheloe

CONTENTS

PART III
Themes and Issues

PART I

INTRODUCTION

Chapter 1

Joe L. Kincheloe

TWENTY-FIRST-CENTURY QUESTIONS ABOUT MULTIPLE INTELLIGENCES

When we first read Howard Gardner's theory of multiple intelligences (MI) in 1983, we were profoundly impressed by the challenge he issued to traditional psychology, particularly psychometrics. We believed that Gardner stood with us in our efforts to develop psychological and educational approaches that facilitated the inclusion of students from marginalized groups whose talents and capabilities had been mismeasured by traditional psychological instruments. Gardner's theory appeared to assume a wider spectrum of human abilities that were, for some reason or another, excluded from the domain of educational psychology and the definition of intelligence. We taught multiple intelligences theory to our students in hopes of exposing and overcoming some of the ways particular students were hurt by these exclusionary disciplinary practices. As Gardner has continued to develop his theory over the last twenty years, those of us associated with this book grew increasingly uncomfortable with many of his assertions and many of the dimensions he excluded from his work. A few years ago we decided it was time to undertake a comprehensive questioning of the theory and Gardner's work surrounding it. *Multiple Intelligences Reconsidered* is the result of that project.

Our point here is not to issue some reductionistic validation or repudiation of Gardner's work. We are more interested in raising questions about the nature of mind, self-production, intelligence, justice, power, teaching, and learning arising from a careful confrontation with his scholarship. At times our questions may be harsh and our conclusions biting. We do not mean for such unsparing criticism to be taken as a personal attack. We respect Gardner, the work he has produced, and the constructive passions he has elicited from a variety of individuals. Our sharpness is a manifestation of our own deep concern for the profound issues raised by Gardner's contributions of the last two decades. In this context we are not issuing an *ad hominem* attack and assume it will not be received that way.

Gardner, Multiple Intelligences (MI), and the Public Distrust of Science

Gardner's *Frames of Mind* was received enthusiastically by sectors of a public intuitively unhappy with psychometrics' technocratic and rationalistic perspective on human ability. Within the narrow boundaries of the American culture of scholarship, Gardner became a celebrity. Teachers emerging from a humanistic culture of caring and helping were particularly taken with the young scholar, many traveling all over the country to hear him speak. MI, such teachers maintained, provided them with a theoretical grounding to justify a pedagogy sensitive to individual differences and committed to equity. Though Gardner consistently denied the political dimension of MI, liberal teachers and teacher-educators viewed it as a force to democratize intelligence (Traub 1998). Living in a Eurocentric world, many interpreted Gardner as arguing that cognitive gifts are more equally dispersed throughout diverse cultural populations than mainstream psychology believed. They took MI as a challenge to an inequitable system.

Frames of Mind struck all the right chords:

- Learning is culturally situated.
- Different communities value different forms of intelligence.
- Cognitive development is complex, not simply a linear cause-effect process.
- Creativity is an important dimension of intelligence.
- Psychometrics does not measure all aspects of human ability.
- Teaching grounded on psychometrically inspired standardized testing is often deemed irrelevant and trivial by students.

Numerous teachers, students, parents, and everyday citizens deemed these ideas important. And, we agree, they are—especially in light of the positivist reductionism and standardization of the twenty-first-century educational standards movement. As with most popular theories, the time was right. MI resonated with numerous progressive impulses that had yet to retreat in the face of the right-wing educational onslaught coalescing in the early 1980s.

Throughout this book, various authors explore different dimensions of this sociopolitical theme. Searching for alternatives to the psychometric educational psychology establishment, various individuals held MI close to their hearts. In this context most of the critiques of MI emerged from more conservative analysts, arguing that theory shifted educational priorities away from development of logic, in the process producing a trivialized, touchy-feely mode of education. In *Multiple Intelligences Reconsidered,* we provide a progressive critique, maintaining that despite all its democratic promise Gardner's theory has not met the expectations of its devotees. The reasons for this failure are multidimensional and complex, as the authors of this volume carefully delineate. One aspect of the failure, we will argue, comes from Gardner's inability to grasp the social, cultural, and political forces that helped shape the initial reception of MI. Even when he has addressed what he describes as a "dis-ease" in American society, Gardner (1999a) fails to historicize the concept in a way that provides him a larger perspective on the fascinating relationship between American sociocultural, political, and epistemological dynamics of the last two decades and MI theory.

Gardner is entangled in this sociocultural, political, and epistemological web whether he wants to be or not. Not so, he maintains, contending that his is a psychological and pedagogical position—not a social, cultural, political, or epistemological one. In a naïve decontextualized and psychologized *modus operandi* he asserts that the psychological and pedagogical domains are separate from all these other denominators. This is a profound analytical error on Gardner's part. The epistemology (ways of knowing) traditionally employed by Gardner's psychometric predecessors and contemporaries is the epistemology of MI. As Richard Cary (1999) puts it in his chapter on visual-spatial intelligence: "Although MI theory is more appealing and democratic at first glance, it remains a stepchild of positivism's exclusively quantitative methodologies and of grand narrative psychology." Indeed, there is less difference between Gardner and the psychological establishment than we first believed. As in so many similar domains, Gardner has been unwilling to criticize the power wielders, the gatekeepers of the psychological castle.

In her chapter in this volume Kathy Berry (1999) extends this point:

> [Gardner's] works, as scholarly and beguilingly penned as they are, have seduced the field of education into yet another Western logo-centric, psychological categorization. Under the guise of educational/school reform, his theory of MI has spawned a host of other supportive theories, practices, disciples, and critics. . . . Once labeled, however, whether in the singular or the plural, intelligence acts as an economic, social, political, and cultural passport for some and for others, a cage. . . .

The authors in this volume are especially concerned with the democratic and justice-related dimensions portended in Gardner's early articulation of MI. Taking our cue from the concerns of many people of color, the poor, colonized individuals, and proponents of feminist theory, we raise questions about the tacit assumptions of MI and its implications for both education and the social domain. Informed in part by Kincheloe & Steinberg's (1993) notion of postformalism, we raise questions about knowledge production and power in the psychological domain in general and MI in particular (Weil 1998; Berry 1999; Kincheloe, Steinberg, & Hinchey 1999; Kincheloe, Steinberg, & Villaverde 1999; Cannella 1997 and 1999; Horn 1999 and 2000; Steinberg 2001; Malewski 2001; Pushkin 2001). Postformalism is especially interested in modes of cognition that recognize the complicity of various academic discourses, psychology in particular, in the justification and maintenance of an inequitable status quo and an ecological and cosmological alienation from the planet and universe in which we reside (see Marla Morris's chapter here). As Morris puts it:

> If we are to talk about a naturalistic intelligence, we need to understand that intelligence does not mean anything goes, just because a scientist works with or in nature. I argue that an ecological sensibility springs from a sensitive, ethical, and holistic understanding of the complexities of human situatedness in the ecosphere.

Gardner seems either unable or unwilling to trace the relationship of MI to these issues (Johnson 1999; Weil 1998 and 2001). Danny Weil's chapter in this volume carefully delineates the social alienation, the absence of situatedness that Gardner so summarily dismisses from his work.

Thus, as postformalists we deploy our power literacy to reveal MI's ideological inscriptions. In this context we examine the multiple and complex ways power operates to shape psychological descriptions of human abilities and behaviors. For example, what is labeled intelligence can never be separated from what dominant power groups designate it to be. Thus, what Gardner attributes solely to the authority of a Cartesian science always reveals the fingerprints of power. What psychologists such as Gardner designate as intelligence and aptitude always holds political and moral significance. Kathleen Nolan illustrates this ideological dynamic clearly in her chapter on linguistic intelligence. While Gardner's notion of linguistic intelligence at first glance appears to value a more equitable classroom, it tacitly privileges the language of the dominant culture as superior and the language of marginalized groups as inferior. As Nolan puts it:

> While Gardner does acknowledge different socially constructed discourses, his assimilationist goals and his emphasis on the cognitive process of language development lead to the evaluation of subordinated discourses within the context of the dominant ideology.

Indeed, what postformalists and any other cognitive theorists designate as intelligence and aptitude produces specific consequences. The important difference between postformalism and Gardner's psychology involves postformalists' admission of such ramifications and their subsequent efforts to shape them as democratically, inclusively, and self-consciously as possible. Gardner, concurrently, dismisses the existence of such political and moral consequences and clings to the claim of scientific neutrality.

The editor and authors of *Multiple Intelligences Reconsidered* take seriously these political and moral consequences of both Gardner's work and the knowledge produced by his psychological tradition. Indeed—surprising as it may be to some of his devotees—there are aspects of Gardner's MI theory that are:

- antidemocratic;
- supportive of an abstract individualism;
- epistemologically naïve;
- subversive of community;
- insensitive to race and socioeconomic class issues;
- patriarchal;
- Western colonialist;
- Eurocentric.

Despite all of these concerns the editor and authors of this book still believe there is value in Gardner's work. In many of the chapters authors seek the kinetic potential of Gardner's ideas in the sociopsychological and educational domain. In this context we seek to retain the original democratic optimism of Gardner's theories, confront him and his many sympathizers with powerful paradigmatic insights refined over the past twenty years, and move the conversation about MI forward with a vision of a complex, rigorous, and transformative pedagogy.

Coming to Terms with Power

In a nation where information produced for schools and media-constructed knowledge for public consumption are misleading, ideologically refracted, edited for right-wing political effect, and often outright lies, the notion of learning to become a scholar takes on profound political meanings—whether we like it or not. Do we merely "adjust" students to the misrepresentations of dominant power or do we help them develop a "power literacy" that moves them to become courageous democratic citizens? In a post-9/11 era, Lynn Cheney's American Council of Trustees and Alumni report, "Defending Civilization: How Our Universities Are Failing America and What Can Be Done about It," symbolizes our power-knowledge concerns. This so-called Cheney Report lists several examples of unpatriotic actions from higher education.

Educators calling for historical study of what led up to the terrorist attacks on the World Trade Center and the Pentagon are labeled anti-American agents. It is apparent from the Cheney Report and many other sources that numerous political leaders in the United States view the notions of rigorous analysis and democratic pedagogy advocated in this book as unsavory activities (see Kincheloe 2001a). While the stakes were already high, dominant power wielders have upped the ideological ante in the twenty-first century. In raising these concerns we are not arguing that Gardner has supported this type of ideological management. We are contending that Gardner has fallen prey to false dichotomies in his work, separating the political from the psychological and educational. Indeed, he has been unwilling to address the relationships connecting dominant power, psychological theory, and teaching and learning. In this era of American democracy such political decontextualization can be dangerous. This fragmentation has exerted a profound influence on the character and value of Gardner's work. These dynamics are addressed throughout *Multiple Intelligences Reconsidered*.

The power concerns developed here played little role in Gardner's educational experiences in developmental psychology and neuropsychology at Harvard:

> I was born in Scranton, PA in 1943, the son of refugees from Nazi Germany. I was a studious child who gained much pleasure from playing the piano: music has remained very important throughout my life. All of my post-secondary education has been at Harvard University. I was trained as a developmental psychologist and later as a neuropsychologist. For many years, I conducted two streams of research on cognitive and symbol-using capacities—one with normal and gifted children, the second with adults who suffered a form of brain damage. (Gardner 1999c)

Such an educational and research background protected Gardner from emerging concerns with the relationship between psychological knowledge production and power. In writing about motivation and learning in *Frames of Mind*, for example, he addresses the development of a general, universal theory of motivation. Such theorizing takes place outside the consideration of motivation's contextual, cultural, and power-related specificity (Gardner 1983, 286). A student, for example, from a poor home in the southern Appalachian mountains whose parents and extended family possess little formal education will be situated very differently in relation to educational motivation than an upper-middle-class child of parents with advanced degrees. The poor child will find it harder to discern the relationship between educational effort expended and concrete rewards attained than will the upper-middle-class child. Such perceptions will lead to different levels of performance shaped by relationship to dominant power in its everyday, lived-world manifestations. Such motivational and performance levels have little to do with innate intelligence, whether of a linguistic, visual-spatial, or mathematical variety. Gardner has not made these types of discernments in his MI theorizing.

Thus, power theory (see Fiske 1993; Kincheloe & Steinberg 1997) has eluded Gardner. Sociopolitical reflection is not an activity commonly found in the history of developmental psychology and neuropsychology. Indeed, such concerns have been consistently excluded as part of a larger positivistic discomfort with the ethical and ideological. Such political dynamics reveal themselves in *Intelligence Reframed*, as Gardner (1999b, 218) writes of Western civilization as a story of progress toward both democracy and respect for the individual. Democracy has been achieved in the United States and the civilized West, Gardner assumes, as he cautiously avoids confronting democratic failures in these domains outside the tragedy of the Third Reich. He explores business involvement with education in *The Disciplined Mind* but expresses little concern with corporate power's capacity to shape the ideological purposes of schools (Gardner 1999a, 237). And, as Kathy Berry writes in her chapter in this volume, he never considers the effects of these political forces on the very definitions of intelligence employed by psychologists and his own MI theory.

Danny Weil in his chapter confronts Gardner on these absences, marveling at Gardner's erasure of issues of social justice and democratic citizenship. Though

Gardner labels himself an educational progressive, Weil astutely continues, he ignores the powerful dictum of John Dewey—the father of Progressive Education—that such a pedagogy refuses to make schooling a vehicle of conformity and control. In light of Weil's concerns and the historical democratic pronouncements of the Progressive tradition, Gardner's description of MI-produced "masters of change" appears thin and impotent. Such an individual "acquires new information, solves problems, forms 'weak ties' with mobile and highly dispersed people, and adjusts easily to changing circumstances" (1999b, 2).

Gardner's masters of change are mere technicians to be fed into the new corporate order of the globalized economy. They are not empowered scholars who understand the larger historical and social forces shaping the macro-structures that interact with the complexities of the quest for democracy and the production of self. There is no mention here, for example, of

- the impact of 500 years of European colonialism;
- the continuing anticolonial movements of the post-1945 world; and
- Western neoliberal/neoconservative efforts to "reclaim" cultural, political, and intellectual supremacy over the past twenty-five years (Gresson 1995 and 2004; Kincheloe, Steinberg, Rodriguez & Chennault 1998; Rodriguez & Villaverde 2000)

Such macro-forces exert profound influences on how we view the roles of Western psychology and education or where we stand or are placed in relation to them. MI and its masters of change stand outside history. They are passive observers of the great issues of our time.

Studying Gardner's work, we perceive no indication that he has ever imagined a critique of his work in light of the issues of power. In *Frames of Mind* he asserted that he could envisage two types of modifications of MI: he could be convinced to drop one or two of the intelligences, or he could be persuaded to add some new ones (1983, 296). In this power vacuum Gardner is not unlike many other upper-middle-class Americans in that he cannot imagine how dominant-power–inscribed psychologies and educational practices can harm individuals—especially those marginalized in some way by the dynamics of, say, race, class, or gender. As I have spoken about or written elsewhere, growing up in the rural Appalachian mountains of Tennessee, teaching on Native American reservations, and studying schooling in various poor inner-city schools, I am painfully aware of how these practices hurt particular individuals in specific ways. Gardner's naïve acceptance of the benefits of school for all came across clearly in *Frames of Mind:*

> [T]he overall impact of a schooled society (as against one without formal education) is rarely a matter of dispute. It seems evident to nearly all observers that attendance at school for more than a few years produces an individual—and, eventually a collectivity—who differs in important (if not always easy to articulate) ways from members of a society that lacks formal schooling. (1983, 356)

Gardner would be well served to familiarize himself with literature that documents the way school often serves to convince many individuals from marginalized backgrounds that they are unintelligent and incompetent. The most important curricular lessons many of these students learn is that they are not "academic material." The individuals we are talking about here are young people who may be profoundly talented but, because of their relationship to the values and symbol systems of schooling, are evaluated as incapable of dealing with the higher cognitive processes of academia. Wasn't it some of these individuals that MI theory was supposed to help? Weren't we supposed to see valuable talents in individuals who were overlooked by a monolithic mode of defining intelligence?

Writing Defensively

Though he never anticipated the power-related critique of his work, Gardner knew that something about MI was out of synch with many progressive intellectual impulses of the late twentieth and early twenty-first centuries. On one level Gardner recognizes the cultural blinders he wears and is quick to let readers know that he knows. Yet he never addresses the effects of such blinders and their implicit power dynamics on this psychological theorizing. For example, Gardner in *The Disciplined Mind* lays out a universal curriculum—though he equivocates with the ambiguous caveat that such a course of study is "not privileged"—based on the true, the beautiful, and the good. To illustrate "the true" he proposes the curriculum include a study of Darwin's theory of evolution. For "beauty" he selects Mozart. And for "the good" he chooses the study of the Holocaust. Intrinsically, there is nothing wrong with these choices of topics.

I would hope most students in Western societies knew something about them—especially the horrors and the sociohistorical context of the Holocaust as well as the debate about the lessons learned from the nightmare. But Gardner knows their selection represents a larger tendency throughout his work to ignore, time and again, the study of groups possessing the least status and the most negative dominant cultural representations of their intellectual ability. Outside of an abbreviated reference to African drumming, African Americans and Africans in general and Latinos living in the United States and Latin American peoples in general, are absent in Gardner's work. In his examples of genius he stays quite close to those who test highly on IQ tests. We find this fidelity to dominant and unrepentant modes of psychometrics disturbing.

Indeed, the disturbance is magnified by Gardner's awareness of what he is doing. After delineating his curriculum in *The Disciplined Mind,* he writes:

> It is not difficult to anticipate a response to this trio of topics: How can one call this an education for all human beings? It is time-bound (the modern era); it is place-bound (Western Europe and places influenced by it); and it is even linked to the author's personal concerns. (1999a, 18)

He answers his own question in the next few lines.

> Within the West, there are numerous other scientific theories of importance (New-
> tonian mechanics and plate tectonics, to name just two examples); other singular
> artistic achievements (the works of Michelangelo or Rembrandt, Shakespeare or
> George Eliot); other morally tinged historical events (the French and Soviet revo-
> lutions; the American struggle over slavery). And within other cultural traditions,
> there are abundant examples of the true (these would include folk theories about
> healing or traditional Chinese medicine); the beautiful (Japanese ink and brush
> painting; African drum music); and good and evil (the precepts of Jainism, the sto-
> ries of Pol Pot and Mao's Cultural Revolution; the generosity of the bodhisattvas).
> (1999a, 19)

A quick examination of this response is in order. In this quotation and throughout Gardner's work there is no questioning of the supremacy of Western scientific
thinking and therefore:

- no need to historically contextualize it;
- no reason to seek the ways it reflects the cultural blinders of the place and time
  of its development;
- no motive to scrutinize its moral and ethical insensitivity;
- no concern with exploring what many have pointed out as its inherent logical
  flaws—its "rational irrationality";
- no justification for studying its linguistic construction;
- no cause to explore the ways it tends to uphold the status quo and the interests
  of the powerful; and
- no need to analyze its tendency to pathologize the different and the marginalized.

As far as artistic achievements are concerned, aren't all of the musical forms that
are labeled American, such as blues, jazz, gospel, country, rock, pop, and rap (see
Yusef Progler's chapter for an expansion of these musical concepts), either African
American creations or appropriations/direct derivations of African American
music?, etc. As far as "morally tinged historical events" are concerned, aren't all historical events inseparable from moral context? For those who would ask if the reference to the "American struggle over slavery" covers the issue of including
African Americans in Gardner's curriculum, many mainstream historical chronicles
of this theme omit African American voices. It is often portrayed as a debate
among white people about the country's "race problem." Toni Morrison writes of
this absence of blackness in American writing. Her words resonate in relation to
Gardner's progressive and liberal scholarship:

> One likely reason for the paucity of critical material on [blackness in America] is that,
> in matters of race, silence and evasion have historically ruled literary discourse. Eva-
> sion has fostered another, substitute language in which the issues are encoded, fore-
> closing open debate. The situation is aggravated by the tremor that breaks into dis-
> course on race. It is further complicated by the fact that the habit of ignoring race is

understood to be a graceful, even generous, *liberal* gesture. To notice is to recognize an already discredited difference. . . . (Morrison 1993, 9–10)

Gardner's silence and defensiveness about these concerns are well displayed by his dismissal of the benefits of the postmodern paradigm shift in the sciences. Painting with a broad brush, Gardner labels that which passes for postmodernism as relativistic. As Gaile Cannella deftly explores in her chapter in this volume, Gardner confuses postmodernism's questioning of psychology as final truth with a threatening form of nihilism. Writing defensively, Gardner asserts that "I do not believe in singular or incontrovertible truth, beauty, or morality . . ." (1999a, 23). But throughout his work he undermines such a claim by tacitly assuming that there are "proper" ways of producing truth (the scientific method of Descartes, Newton, and Bacon) and that some cultures have higher claim to truth, beauty, and morality than others (white Europe vis-à-vis Africa and African America). Indeed, where is the role of cultural critique or power analysis in his MI curriculum? We would like to see once the inclusion of a debate within or between particular fields of study.

Gardner teases us with the possibility that critique and "disagreement across cultures and subcultures" might be important (1999a, 35). But he retreats with the conclusion that inculcating the best knowledge of the Western academic disciplines is the correct way to educate our world. Our point here is not to allege that Gardner has no business making judgments about the best ways to produce knowledge or build a curriculum. We all make these assessments—indeed, we need to openly discuss and debate how to make them. Instead, our purpose is to point out that in the name of inclusivity and progressive psychology and education Gardner's MI theory exhibits disturbing patterns of exclusion that are consistent with more regressive and ethnocentric versions of Western scientific work. We are assessing Gardner by the criteria of the traditions with which he overtly identifies and the groups to which he has appealed.

Between the Rock and the Hard Place

Gardner's work rests in an awkward locale between paradigms, between an objectivist positivism and an antipositivist understanding of the role of subjectivity in all knowledge production. He consistently promotes the idea that his multiple intelligences are value-free, objective constructs of science but preaches a pedagogy that eschews positivistic demands of a standardized curriculum assessed by the administration of standardized tests. Empirical psychologists, Richard Cary asserts in his chapter, view Gardner's work as soft science devoid of rigorous quantitative data, while, concurrently, proponents of more postmodern pedagogies see him too often in collusion with his positivistic colleagues in psychology. From this counter-Cartesian perspective Gardner does not move the study of cognition to an unprecedented domain. He covertly inscribes old ways of knowing with a new veneer of excitement.

MI is a child of a Cartesian psychology that fails to recognize its own genealogy. Gardner uses the intelligences to pass along the proven verities, the perennial truths of Western music, art, history, literature, language, math, and science. The notion of constructing a meta-analysis of the ways cultural familiarity occludes our ability to see the plethora of assumptions driving work in these domains does not trouble Gardner's psychic equilibrium. If Gardner were interested in performing a cultural meta-analysis of his theories, he would begin to see them as technologies of power that reproduce Western and typically male ways of making meaning. Gardner seems oblivious to the epistemological, cultural, and political coordinates of his work. As Kathy Berry argues in her chapter, he doesn't sense that the classification systems and cognitive frameworks of MI routinely exclude "the knowledge and values of women, non-white races, non-Christians, and local and premodern ways of knowing."

In the descriptions of what counts as intelligence and curricular knowledge in Gardner's eight domains resides a battle over cultural politics. Whose science, literature, music, history, art, etc., gains the imprimatur of the labels classical and canonical? When patterns of racial, cultural, gender, and class exclusion consistently reveal themselves in Gardner's work, why would nonwhite and non-European individuals and groups not be suspicious of it? Again, Gardner's reading of expressions of such concerns is naïve. In *Intelligence Reframed,* for example, he states that MI has been disparaged "as racist and elite . . . because it uses the word intelligence and because I, as its original proponent, happen to be affiliated with Harvard University . . ." (1999b, 149). We assure Gardner that if he were a professor at some small college who developed the "theory of multiple talents" and had exerted comparable levels of influence on the fields of psychology and education, we would still criticize his exclusionary scholarship. Gardner the progressive is trapped on a terrain littered with cultural, political and epistemological land mines.

In his contradictory paradigmatic position Gardner operates to normalize/universalize European cultural expressions. Excluded from his intelligences are the practices that most inhabitants of the earth view as wise, insightful, and intelligent. When compared with some of the alienating and environmentally destructive practices produced by the Western sciences, many of these practices should not be dismissed so cavalierly. Gardner might consider these modes of alienation and destruction when arguing for K–12 curricular fidelity to the disciplines and what is excluded by his definitions of the various intelligences. Much work is required by Gardner to acquaint himself with the contradictions that result from this paradigmatic schizophrenia. A rigorous understanding of these issues could lead to a much more coherent, inclusive, and intellectually challenging version of the eight domains.

From our subjective perspective Gardner would be well served by contextualizing, analyzing, and understanding the ways of thinking, knowing, and seeing that produced the disciplines and methods of knowledge production in which he is embedded. Such activities are not the remote, esoteric domains of ivory-tower philosophers. Many individuals in Western societies and around the world have come to recognize that these understandings affect academic institutions and everyday life, the complex mundane world where people are empowered or beaten down by ways of seeing that are tacitly inscribed by these paradigmatic dynamics. When psychologists and educators don't rigorously understand such processes, they participate in the sorting functions of testing and schooling that too often privilege the privileged and oppress the poor and the "culturally different." Writing about Gardner's cosmos of intelligences in his chapter here, Danny Weil puts it succinctly: "Formal educational psychological theories serve as gatekeepers for the dominant social and economic order and the power relations inherent in it." Peter Appelbaum makes a similar point in his critique of logical-mathematical intelligence, arguing that Gardner's view of mathematics excludes everything but the most Western logic-based dimensions of the discipline. Ways of seeing math and logic that fall outside this narrow conception of logic do not exist in Gardner's mathematics.

The Critical Complex Challenge to Gardner's Psychological Modernism

The critical complex, counter-Cartesian perspective we bring to this analysis of Gardner's MI posits that valuable sociopolitical and pedagogical outcomes can be derived from understanding:

- the etymology of knowledge production;
- the development of a power literacy with its insight into the relation between power and knowledge;
- the social production of self;
- the historical context of the disciplinary processes of psychology;
- cosmological meaning-making;
- ecological sensitivity;
- the value of multiple cultural perspectives, especially the insights derived from cultures traditionally marginalized;
- the effects of European colonialism and the knowledges produced in anticolonial movements; and
- premodern knowledges and values that have been rejected by Western modernism.

Gardner rejects the importance of these understandings. The purpose of elementary and secondary education, he maintains, involves mastering and "appropriately" joining particular disciplines (Gardner 1999a, 219). The adverb *appropriately* here signifies an absence of critique or analysis of the critical complex points listed above. What is the value of a MI-based education if it doesn't prepare democratic citizens in an era of disinformation to challenge unstated assumptions within academic and media-generated knowledges? What does it provide if it doesn't encourage students and teachers to think about the genesis of their belief structures and attitudes toward self, others, and the world? In Gardner's psychological paradigm, such critical educational orientations are unacceptable. Since democracy is already established and power complicity in the production of knowledge is irrelevant in Gardner's cosmos, these modes of thinking are "inappropriate."

Gardner accepts the interpretative strategies of psychological science although, as Richard Cary observes in his chapter here, Gardner avoids strict modes of controlled observation. He can't seem to admit that he is involved in an interpretive theory-making activity rather than empirical research. In this same context Marla Morris asserts in her chapter that, epistemologically speaking, Gardner's MI is a realist theory which claims it is providing an accurate description of correspondence between the intelligences and their theoretical description. A realist correspondence theory that is scientifically produced denies that it is inscribed by the researcher's own sociopolitical location in the web of reality. In Gardner's conception the eight intelligences are universal (the same qualities are possessed by individuals from all over the world) and objective (no values are involved in generating them). Gardner's intelligences are consistent, intractable entities that have always existed, exist now, and will always exist in their present form.

Thus, in a bizarre way, Gardner in the name of innovation and reform reinforces mainstream rationalities and Eurocentric ways of thinking. From our critical complex orientation we want to push the boundaries of Cartesian rationality, to discover and create new ways of making meaning, new modes of intelligence that can help change ourselves and the world in a just, egalitarian, and smart manner. While by no means advocating the abandonment of rationality—that would be silly—we are calling for a reassessment of what has passed as reason in traditional Western scientific and psychological scholarship. We are not satisfied that this is the ultimate expression of human genius. We believe there is an irrationality, a madness, operating in particular dimensions of mainstream psychology's view of intelligence and reason. Indeed, a key feature of producing reason and intelligence involves excluding those others who are "unreasonable" and "unintelligent." As we have examined these individuals throughout the history of psychology, they consistently seem to be those people who, in terms of culture, race, sexual orientation, gender, or economic status, are different from the psychologists creating the classification system. Gardner has yet to deal with these concerns.

Popularity and Inadequacy

It is not unusual to hear Gardner referred to as an academic superstar and a genius while seeing MI theory labeled as a rallying cry for school reform and a concept so popular that it is now a cultural commonplace. "Howard is the guru and *Frames of Mind* is the bible" (Traub 1998), a critic of progressive education recently proclaimed. MI pulls everything together in education, educators often exclaim. Educational leaders are often heard to say that MI democratically cultivates diverse human gifts. We cannot help but find it fascinating that in light of such adoration,

Gardner has rarely had to justify his views of mind and society, the nature of the individual, and the process of identity formation. A broader theoretical view would seem to be demanded from such an important intellectual figure. As I explore in my chapter on personal intelligence, Gardner's notion of the self in this context is underanalyzed and problematic.

Outside of addressing the psychometric monolithic definition of intelligence, Gardner is reluctant to ask questions about the basic assumptions of the Cartesian-Newtonian scientific tradition and its use within the psychological and educational sciences. The critique of Gardner's work in MI provides a classic case study involving the use of social theory and the paradigmatic consciousness developed over the past few decades to expose where more traditional modes of knowledge production are lacking in the psychological, social, and educational sciences. In our critical complex analytical context we understand that Gardner's, our own, and all intellectual work is embedded in and inseparable from larger webs of meaning. Particular cultural, linguistic, and ideological conventions shape the way we tell our stories, in this case, about intelligence (Gergen 1997; Kincheloe & Weil 2001). We can be more aware or less aware of these important dimensions that shape our view of the world and our action within it. Gardner chooses to be less aware.

At one point Gardner admits that the Cartesian view of mind is rationalistic and conceived outside of historical context. His strategy, however, is not to examine the process of knowledge production used in psychology but to retreat to a facile Darwinian position, arguing that mind and intelligence have "evolved" and must be understood in the context of their evolution. Thus, the question of the historical social construction of both the concept of intelligence and the emergence of psychology is avoided (Gardner 1983; Traub 1998). On numerous occasions Gardner moves into a conceptual zone where the questions we raise here about knowledge production in psychology haunt those who enter. But Gardner eludes the inquiring specters, focusing his attention on whether or not the mind is a single coherent domain (Sempsey 1993). Such an issue exists in a cosmos separate from concerns with the intricacies of social construction and the assumptions of Eurocentric psychology.

Culture, Values, and Subjectivity: Gardner's "Neutral" Scholarship

Gardner never gets to the formulation of the relationship between mind and culture, with all of the complex interactions of power, values, moral issues, emotions, and social structures involved. He never addresses his attention to the ways culture facilitates or subverts the power of mind to realize its potential. He makes references to the social placement of mind and self but doesn't possess the historical or philosophical background to imagine what such a process might involve (Gardner 1999b, 158). For example, when discussing innovative methods of evaluating intelligence in *Intelligence Reframed,* Gardner asks:

Why settle for an IQ test or an SAT, on which the items are at best remote "proxies" for the ability to design experiments, write essays, critique musical performances, or resolve a dispute? Why not instead ask people to *do* the things—either in person or on-line? As long as we do not open the Pandora's box of values and subjectivity, we can continue to use established insights and technologies judiciously. (1999b, 209)

Of course, it is these values and subjectivities that rest at the very heart of the relationship between mind and culture. Such pronouncements indicate that Gardner does not exactly know what we are referencing when we raise issues of the social construction of and cultural context in which definitions of mind and intelligence are formulated.

Obviously, we profoundly differ with Gardner around the perception of the meaning of the relationship between mind and culture. Though we all claim the label "progressive," we differ on questions regarding the purpose of our psychological/educational scholarship, the values we embrace in the process, and our political relationship with dominant power. As we observe the implementation of educational policies that are based on a grotesquely simplistic definition of "good scholarship" (the top-down–standards movement shaping American education in the first decade of the twenty-first century, for example) and a disregard of the well-being of numerous marginalized students, we are distressed. Indeed, in this context we are taken aback by Gardner's avoidance of the Pandora's box of values and subjectivity. Gardner's refusal to connect his work on MI to the political and educational attack on the victims of poverty and racial/ethnic prejudice manifests a specific value position. He cannot claim neutrality in this cultural context.

As we read Gardner's repeated references to this type of value neutrality, we marvel at the value assumptions he makes throughout his work. His assumption that American democracy is a completed project, chugging along successfully in the twenty-first century is a profoundly value-laden ideological statement issued from a position of privilege. In the same vein his equation of multiculturalism and multicultural curricula with low standards and scholarly inaccuracy is semiotically disturbing and racially problematic:

I call for educators "to learn and propagate the best that is known and thought in the world." I also want students to have information that is as accurate as possible. So long as these two criteria are met, I believe that multicultural curricula and approaches are beneficent. When, however, multiculturalists abandon high standards in their selection of work, or favor inferior work just because of its appealing provenance, I part company with them. (199a, p.58)

Why would Gardner want to raise issues of accuracy and standards in the context of multiculturalism? Like a lawyer who brings up inadmissible evidence in a parenthetical comment to the jury, Gardner plants the implication that multiculturalism is characterized by nonwhite advocates possessing low cognitive abilities and a disregard for curricular accuracy.

Gardner continues:

By the same token, I have no sympathy for those who choose to rewrite history, so that credit for discoveries is given, without convincing evidence, to individuals or groups that happen to have a certain accent, cultural background, or political attitude. (1999a, p.58)

The coding here is clearly racial, particularly African American, as Gardner makes oblique reference to the dominant culture's hysteria concerning black historical scholarship attempting to correct centuries of Eurocentric research placing Africans and African Americans in an inferior position as mysterious inhabitants of the "dark continent."

Again, Gardner inscribes his "value neutrality" in relation to the multiculturalists, never contextualizing the historical distortion that motivates their corrective actions:

Let me phrase my point positively. I want all students to develop a sense of high standards; I want all students to strive for accuracy and to use evidence properly; I want all students to respect a range of groups and cultures, but not to do so uncritically.

It is possible to have a precollegiate education that is multicultural and that meets these criteria, though that is not a necessary outcome of multicultural education. It is *not* possible to have a postmodern curriculum that meets these criteria—indeed, the criteria have no legitimacy in the eyes of postmodernists. (1999a, 58)

Historical distortion and low scholarly standards are the province of the multiculturalists—not the generations of Europeans who erased nonwhite peoples from the story of humanity. Bad scholarship and historical distortion can be found in all ideological schools of thought. In light of the revelations in 2002 about the poor scholarship and plagiarism of mainstream celebrity-historians Doris Kearns Goodwin and Stephen Ambrose, this point is made even clearer. And, in addition, to claim that postmodern scholars do not strive for high scholarly standards, accuracy, and proper use of evidence is a biased and narrow charge. Just because such scholars have raised questions about the complexity of tacit value inscriptions and neutrality claims of various definitions of standards, accuracy, and proper use of evidence does not mean that such scholarship should be summarily labeled poor.

We argue that scholarship that raises such questions and adeptly answers them with carefully compiled evidence is a prime manifestation of good scholarship with profound social value. Indeed, the analysis we are engaged in here could be labeled a form of postmodern exposé. Everyone involved in this book strives to be accurate, maintain high scholarly standards, and use evidence in a fair manner. Our claim is that such pursuits may not be as transparent as scholars such as Gardner might assert. For example, is one conducting high-quality and accurate scholarship and making proper use of evidence when one has already judged and excluded the accomplishments of individuals from particular racial and cultural traditions? The editor and authors of this volume assert that the answer to this question is no. Claims of value neutrality are dangerous and frequently come back to bite the claimant.

Gardner and the Problem of Cultural and Socioeconomic Class Specificity

Gardner's work is beset by the same flaw that undermines so many other psychologists operating within the parameters of the modernist, Eurocentric, socioeconomic class-inscribed paradigm: the failure to recognize that what is represented as universal features of mind is shaped by cultural and class factors. Thus, a degree of complexity is added to the study of mind that Gardner ostensibly recognizes but fails to act upon in his delineation of the eight intelligences. Jay Lemke in his chapter expands this concept:

> I do doubt that we can usefully reduce the domains of intelligent human behavior to a small number, and I mainly fear that every attempt to do so that claims the universal validity of objective science may in time become part of political projects to unjustly advance the values and interests of some social and cultural groups in the world at the expense of others.

Donald Blumenthal-Jones in his chapter on bodily-kinesthetic intelligence extends Lemke's point as he discusses the possible inclusion of the intelligence of car mechanics. Given the socioeconomic position of car mechanics vis-à-vis dancers, actors, and athletes, Blumenthal-Jones questions why their intelligence is not addressed by Gardner:

> We must seriously examine Gardner's selection of "geniuses" and note that he has privileged certain kinds of physical behavior and ignored others. Highly skilled car mechanics do not make the list of special-abilities people. Why is this? It is not disingenuous to note that Gardner's list of intelligences and his lists of exemplars within intelligences are replete with high-culture icons. This makes the genius criteria automatically suspect since he does not create these lists from a broad spectrum of cultural possibilities but, rather, echoes the prejudices of the culture.

Lemke is right on target in his assertion about the use of such scientific universalizations, and Blumenthal-Jones is insightful with his example of the inseparability of Gardner's universal intelligence with cultural status. We maintain that Gardner's implicit privileging of dominant European over African frames of mind and high-socioeconomic–status over low-socioeconomic–status occupations are prime examples of this value-laden, pseudo-objective, elitist dynamic at work. Such cultural and class insensitivity places Gardner's theorizing on the same paradigmatic plane with the decontextualized psychometric g-theory he ostensibly wants to subvert.

Cultural and socioeconomic class contexts and the complications of human consciousness are abandoned in this mode of positivist scientific scholarship. The psyche is studied in the same manner as physical reality—of course, the complexity of the psyche's cultural/class embeddedness and the consequences of consciousness such as the human capacity for self-direction are dismissed. Humans cannot be reduced to the ontological status of igneous rocks or sulfuric acid. Another angle on this process that demands understanding in psychological scholarship involves the tendency of modernist Eurocentric epistemology to exclude the culturally constructed mind's role in shaping what psychologists observe the mind to be. Such procedures have allowed scientists of all stripes to assume that their mental pictures of the world were accurate, objective reflections of reality. In the case of his view of the mind, Gardner travels this epistemological path, maintaining throughout his journey that his picture of the mind with its eight intelligences is an accurate, objective, culturally and socioeconomically neutral reflection of psychic reality.

Here Gardner falls into the epistemological trap of the Cartesian notion of the abstract individual—"abstracted" from the cultural/class context that helped produce him or her. Intelligences are contained within this abstract individual's head—not a product of larger cultural and social processes on any level. Taking our cue from the enactivist cognitive science of Francisco Varela and Humberto Maturana—the Santiago School—we maintain that cognition and learning cannot be appreciated outside of the context of coemergence. Coemergence involves the idea that individual intelligence and collective intelligence arise together, one being impossible without the other. Enactivists are dedicated to the analysis of context and the numerous, interrelated, and complex ways individuals are produced while at the same time they produce their sociocultural and historical surroundings (Maturana & Varela 1987; Sumara & Davis 1997; Fenwick 2000). Indeed, individuals do not spontaneously spring into being, as in the old theory of spontaneous generation with its maggots automatically emerging from rotten meat. Cultural context and the social interactions taking place within it produce individuals in a manner that transcend the governance of any one person.

Thus, the specificity of culture and socioeconomic class shapes the biological structures of individual minds. This dynamic exerts not only a dramatic influence on the attempt to make universal generalizations about the mind but also on how we see the world in general and the mind in particular. Seeing himself as an autonomous individual, Gardner claims that he has eliminated his own cultural and historical subjectivity from his theory of MI. Thus, what he purports to present is a transcultural, transhistorical view devoid of the biases of his time or place. In a world that is changing dramatically, there are ever-increasing global challenges to European Cartesianism and its epistemological colonialism and socioeconomic disparity. Because of the consciousness these challenges construct, we believe that Gardner's social and cultural blinders will become increasingly apparent to observers. Such awareness will cause his work to be viewed more and more as a form of Eurocentric elitist psychological parochialism in the years to come. The weight of global history is working against MI theory.

The Vision Quest: Cosmological and Epistemological Alienation

Gardner's decontextualization of his psychological theory is so profound that it undermines a vision of human possibility. In this context, Gardner's theory is cosmologically, epistemologically, and ontologically alienated, producing cognitive and educational constructs that offer little hope for those interested in producing a better future for human beings. In his cosmological alienation, Gardner provides—despite his naturalistic intelligence—little insight into ways of addressing the ecological transformation of the earth with its destruction of life systems and its challenge to the continuation of human existence. In the same alienated mode Gardner's work is punctuated by an epistemological lack of consciousness that consistently moves him to substitute claims of scientific evidence for what in actuality is logical reasoning. Gardner's assumptions about MI are not tested empirically against fact; paradigmatic consensus shapes what will be viewed as evidence and what will be dismissed. Thus, manifestations of intelligence recognized by Eurocentric psychology count; those not recognized do not. Biological context is taken into consideration; social, cultural, political, and economic contexts are not. These hidden forces working to shape MI theory must be exposed.

Richard Cary is especially helpful in our understanding of this epistemological alienation. Analyzing Gardner's use of biological evidence to "prove" the validity of visual-spatial intelligence, Cary questions what such data have to do with supporting Gardner's "version" of such intelligence:

> Gardner reviews scientific research that has established the location of visual-spatial intelligence and that it operates as a biological process. So what? This information contributes little to our understanding of how a visual-spatial intelligence operates in the culture and why we should value it in our daily experience.

Thus, in the name of proving to the guardians of the discipline of psychology his fidelity to data produced via positivist epistemology, Gardner references information that has little to do with his purpose: delineating the nature and use of the multiple intelligences. As Cary concludes, he hides the hermeneutic nature of the epistemology he employs. In this context we return to Gardner's epistemology of naïve realism, deployed in this case to hide his actual epistemological approach. In a further attempt to conceal his epistemological alienation, Gardner uses postmodernism as a straw man. Distorting the position, Gardner piously argues that despite the postmodern insistence that there are no standards for producing or judging knowledge, there must be standards for scientific work. In this context Gardner fails to understand that the epistemological fragmentation of the traditional psychological paradigm undermines the quest for a deeper understanding of the complexity of interrelatedness. Such an understanding would profoundly contribute to Gardner's appreciation of the multiple forces that are operating to construct society's—and thus his—own views of intelligence. In this context he would be far better equipped to provide a socially helpful and much thicker description of intelligence as a multidimensional concept. This is where scholarly standards and the quality of knowledge production could be profoundly improved. Indeed, this is the meat and potatoes of scholarly standards.

Gardner's epistemological foundations shape a form of knowledge production that separates individuals/students/research subjects from the cosmos surrounding them. These individuals stand alone as *things*-in-themselves abstracted from their multiple relationships with the structural forces of the lived world. Gardner fails to confront and grapple with the complexity of these all-important relationships. Indeed, these social, cultural, philosophical, ideological, economic, linguistic, and historical relationships shape minds, their abilities, the recognition and validation of their abilities, and research on their abilities. Stated bluntly, the exclusion of these dynamics is a manifestation of epistemological reductionism, of low standards of psychological scholarship. As a manifestation of epistemological alienation, an entire range of concepts, knowledge traditions, and lexicons is removed from Gardner's scholarship. Especially in light of his claim that postmodernism has "no standards," we are not impressed with Gardner's version of rigorous scholarship.

Ontological Alienation: "Don't Need Nothin' from Nobody"

One aspect of our excitement about MI in 1983 involved our belief that it could help provide cognitive insight into what human beings could become. In our social imagination we could transcend the Enlightenment category of abstract individualism and move toward a more textured concept of the relational individual. While abstract individualism, a self-sufficient ontology, seems almost natural in the Western modernist world, such is not the case in many non-Western cultures and has not been the case even in Western societies in previous historical eras. In ancient Greece, for example, it is hard to find language that identified "the self" or "I"—such descriptions were not commonly used because the individual was viewed as a part of a collective who could not function independently of the larger social group (Allen 2000). In the "common sense" of contemporary Western society and the unexamined ontological assumptions of Gardner's psychology, this way of seeing self is hard to fathom.

Enlightenment ontology sees the natural state of the individual as solitary. The social order in this modernist Eurocentric context is grounded on a set of contractual transactions between isolated individual atoms. In other works I have referred to Clint Eastwood's "man with no name" cinematic character who didn't need "nothin' from nobody" as the ideal Western male way of being—the ontological norm (Kincheloe 1993). Operating in this context, Gardner's intelligences reflect cognitive psychology's tradition of focusing on the autonomous development of the individual monad. In our critical complex ontology, a human being simply can't exist outside the inscription of community with its processes of relationship, differentiation, interaction, and subjectivity. Indeed, in this critical complex ontology the relational embeddedness of self is so context dependent that psychologists can never isolate a finalized completed "true self." Since the self is always in context and in process, no final delineation of ability can be determined—whether it is IQ or assessment of MI.

One can quickly discern the political consequences of such an Enlightenment, Cartesian ontology. Human beings in Western liberal political thought become abstract bearers of particular civic rights. If individuals are relational, context-embedded beings, however, these abstract rights may be of little consequence. A critical complex ontology insists that individuals live in specific places with particular types of relationships. They operate or are placed in the web of reality at various points of race, class, gender, sexual orientation, religion, physical ability, geography, and other continuums. Where individuals find themselves in this complex web holds dramatic power consequences. Their location shapes their relationship to dominant culture and the cognitive psychology that accompanies it. In other words the intelligence—whether described as "*g*," musical, bodily-kinesthetic, or linguistic—psychology deems them to possess profoundly depends on this contextual, power-inscribed placement. A prime manifestation of Gardner's ontological alienation involves his lack of recognition of the dramatic effect of these dynamics on the very topics he has written about over the previous two decades.

Gardner's stable, autonomous self that either has or does not have particular forms of intelligence is becoming a psychological anachronism. While in no way dismissing the power of human beings to affect their own destinies, to possess human agency, or to change social conditions, we argue that one's ontological condition must be re-examined in light of the sociological, cultural-studies, cultural-psychological, and critical-analytical work of the past few decades. Much of what Gardner and his fellow psychologists consider to be free will and expressions of innate intelligence are manifestations of the effects of particular social, cultural, political, linguistic, ideological, and economic forces. While we can make decisions on how we operate as human beings, we are never completely independent of these structuring forces, whether we are Howard Gardner or Michel Foucault. It is important to note here that Gardner claims that his development of MI took place outside of these dynamics. He claims that his work avoids cultural values and morally inscribed issues, and because of such diligence, he has presented us with the truth. We believe that in this ontological context, Gardner must take a closer look at who he is and the structuring forces that have shaped his view of the world, the mind, and the self.

Gardner, MI, and the Purposes of Education

In an article in *Phi Delta Kappan* in the mid-1990s, Gardner wrote about his dedication to one of our most important concerns—stimulating a conversation about the purposes of education and schooling. In this piece he emphasized the importance of this consideration in his work with MI and of his belief that MI has stimulated these types of inquiries. Such focus on the purpose of education, he contended, will move schools to teach for understanding rather than the rote mastery of test-based isolated data—a concern we share with Gardner. Intoxicated with the popularity of MI among so many educators, Gardner boasted that MI concerns with understanding, educational purpose, and pedagogical personalization were creating a revolution in schooling around the world (Gardner 1995;

Barr & Tagg 1995; Cantu 1999). Answering a right-wing critic of *The Disciplined Mind,* Gardner reiterated his commitment to the analysis of educational purpose, writing that insufficient conversation about American education "has focused on why we should educate students at all" (Gardner 1999c). What is difficult for us to understand is that after all this expression of concern, Gardner studiously avoids any discussion of the social, cultural, political, ideological, and economic purposes of schooling in a democratic society.

This issue is profoundly important in understanding what is missing in Gardner's psychoeducational analysis. When examining his construction of the purpose of schooling, the abstract individual again rears her socially decontextualized head. The purpose of education he offers involves individuals achieving their potentials. While readers may find nothing wrong with this particular goal, it is what Gardner omits in this discussion that is so troubling. When we understand the self as contextually embedded and relational, we begin to discern the multitude of forces that impede particular individuals from attaining their potential—whatever exactly this means. A student's socioeconomic, cultural, and linguistic background must be addressed even to reach the starting line of this process. If it is not, then she cannot be blamed for not having the mental ability—the potential—to learn what is taught.

Just as important, our emphasis on educational purpose, while certainly concerned with individual development and the contextual factors shaping that process, also addresses larger civic, democratic, ecological, justice-related, and power-based issues. Gardner fails to question the ways schools are used to "regulate" students for the political needs of business and government. From the school crusades of the mid-nineteenth century to the present, power wielders have attempted to use schools to domesticate students in order to perpetuate the status quo. Such social regulation is a central feature of the twenty-first-century–standards movement that Gardner so vehemently opposes—but for reasons other than this political one. As Danny Weil argues in his chapter, Gardner simply ignores the existence of racism, class bias, sexism, and homophobia, and their relationship to both individual achievement in school and the social purposes of American education in general. Gardner seems unconcerned with the ways these forces shape the field of psychology or the ways they structure what goes on in classrooms across the country.

In relation to this question of educational purpose Gardner seems callous to the construction of the curriculum and its discursive, ideological, and disciplinary dimensions. The concept of problematizing what we learn, asking where it comes from, why we learn A but not B, is irrelevant in Gardner's world. He displays disconcerting confidence in what has been established as the true, the beautiful, and the good in dominant Western culture, operating as if the concepts have not been saturated by the power relations of ethnocentric, patriarchal, and class-elitist ways of seeing. Does he not understand that the anger various groups around the world and within this society direct at high-status educators of his stripe emerges precisely from these types of assumptions and exclusions? After carefully studying his pronouncements on the purpose of MI-grounded schooling, we conclude that Gardner wants to educate obedient subjects for the American global empire.

In this context Gardner couches his speculations on educational purposes within his fidelity to the traditional academic disciplines. In his response to Mary Eberstadt's conservative critique of *The Disciplined Mind,* Gardner writes: "Formal schooling has several purposes, of course, but I believe its most fundamental purpose should be the inculcation of the major ways of thinking that have been crystallized in the disciplines" (1999c).

Gardner makes this disciplinary argument in an era when the sanctity of disciplinarity has been successfully called into question. In my recent work on bricolage (Kincheloe 2001b), I have referred to the ruins of disciplinarity and the need to move to a more rigorous and challenging form of scholarship. Once the understanding of the limits of "objective science" and its "universal knowledge" escaped from the genie's bottle, there was no return to the confines of modernist scholarship. Gardner is part of a larger attempt of many politicos and scholars to recover what they perceived to "be lost" in the implosion of the disciplines, namely:

- the value-laden products that operate under the flag of objectivity;
- the avoidance of contextual specificities that subvert the stability of its structures; and
- the fragmenting impulse that moves the disciplines to fold their methodologies and the knowledge they produce neatly into disciplinary drawers.

My argument here is that progressive scholars must operate in the ruins of the disciplinary temple, in post-apocalyptic social, cultural, psychological, and educational sciences in which certainty and stability have departed for parts unknown.

Gardner accepts the way complex knowledges are compartmentalized in the traditional disciplines, creating in the process a sense that truth exists in disciplinary canons. This subdivision fragments important topics, such as intelligence, rendering it the exclusive domain of psychology—not sociology, cultural studies, history, linguistics, literary studies, philosophy, anthropology, education, and psychoanalysis, to name a few disciplines. Indeed, Gardner's acceptance of disciplinary ways of thinking, researching, and validating knowledge is unshakable. He unequivocally accepts school curricula teaching such knowledge and standardized tests measuring how well students have memorized it. In *Intelligence Reframed* Gardner reports research results illustrating standardized test score improvement in MI schools. Such educational improvement, Gardner argues, is beyond dispute because it is "based on empirical data, which an impartial party cannot dismiss" (1999b, 113). Gardner simply cannot imagine critique by observers who question the value of schools teaching the unassailable empirical truths of disciplines to uncritical, passive students.

Conclusion: A Debate Outside of History

Too often, Gardner's discussion of educational purpose degenerates into a discussion of what methods we should employ and what knowledge we should transmit. Even when he asks the question *"what* should be taught and *why?,"* his answers are weak and socially, historically, and linguistically decontextualized:

> [I]t is helpful to lay one's curricular cards on the table. Here are my cards. Education in our time should provide the basis for enhanced understanding of our several worlds—the physical world, the biological world, the world of human beings, the world of human artifacts, and the world of self. (1999b, 158)

Gardner operates as if he never registered for an introductory course in the social, historical, and philosophical foundations of education. Historically, how have schools been used? Do schools exist to reproduce or challenge a society? What philosophical assumptions are operating in the development of particular curricular and instructional practices? Should schools teach traditional European values or expose students to a range of cultural values from around the planet? What is the relationship between schools and the economic structures of the society? In what ways are schools implicated in political struggles? Is education in a democratic society different from education in a totalitarian society? Is social regulation a proper role of democratic schooling? None of these are questions that Gardner asks.

By not asking these questions, by not exploring the ways power shapes educational purpose and the knowledges validated by dominant culture, Gardner omits a huge piece of the psychoeducational puzzle. Without this piece, students are left vulnerable to the sociopolitical and cultural forces that produce disinformation in the contemporary informational landscape. In this ideological vacuum Americans in general are undermined in the effort to situate themselves in various sociopolitical, cultural, philosophical, and economic domains. In many cultures education has focused its purpose on the effort to establish oneself in the world (O'Sullivan 1999). This is certainly not the intent of Gardner's education or a factor in shaping MI theory. Gardner's vision is truncated; his sense of the sociohistorical is naïve. Without substantial rethinking and reconstitution, MI theory and the schooling it informs have reached a conceptual dead end.

References

Allen, M. (2000). Voice of reason. *www.curtin.edu.au/learn/unit/10846/arrow/vorall.htm*

Barr, R., & Tagg, J. (1995). From teaching to learning—A new paradigm for undergraduate education. *Change, 27,* 6, pp. 12–25.

Berry, K. (1999). Destabilizing educational thought and practice: Postformal pedagogy. In Kincheloe, Steinberg, & Hinchey (1999), pp. 330–348.

Bloomquist, L. (1999). A reflection on information technology from a humanities perspective. *www.bloomquist.on.ca/publications/itarticles/pico%20epilogue.html*

Cannella, G. (1997). *Deconstructing early childhood education: Social justice and revolution.* New York: Peter Lang.

——. (1999). Postformal thought as critique, reconceptualization, and possibility for teacher education reform. In Kincheloe, Steinberg, & Villaverde (1999), pp. 145–164.

Cantu, D. (1999). An Internet-based multiple intelligences model for teaching high school history. *www.mcel.pacifica.edu/jahc/jahc113/k12113.cantuindex.html*

Fenwick, T. (2000). Experiential learning in adult education: A comparative framework. *www.ualberta.ca/~tfenwick/ext/aeq.htm*

Fiske, J. (1993). *Power plays, power works.* New York: Verso.

Gardner, H. (1983). *Frames of mind: The theory of multiple intelligences.* New York: Basic Books.

——. (1995). Reflections on multiple intelligences: Myths and messages. *Phi Delta Kappan, 77*(3), 200–209.

——. (1999a). *The disciplined mind: Beyond facts and standardized tests, the K-12 education that every child deserves.* New York: Penguin Press.

——. (1999b). *Intelligence reframed: Multiple intelligences.* New York: Basic Books.

——. (1999c). My views on education, unfiltered. *www.pzweb.harvard.edu/whatsnew/policyrev1.htm*

Gergen, K. (1997). The place of the psyche in a constructed world. *Theory and Psychology, 7*(6), 723–746.

Gresson, A. (1995). *The recovery of race in America.* Minneapolis: University of Minnesota Press.

——. (2004). *America's atonement Racial pain, recovery rhetoric, and the pedagogy of healing.* New York: Peter Lang.

Griffin, D. (1997). *Parapsychology, philosophy, and spirituality: A postmodern exploration.* Albany: State University of New York Press.

Hinchey, P. (2001). Purposes of education—educational standards: For whose purposes? For whose children? In Kincheloe & Weil (2001), pp. 745–772.

Horn, R. (1999). The dissociative nature of educational change. In Kincheloe, Steinberg, & Hinchey (1999), pp. 855–878.

——. (2000). *Teacher talk: A postformal inquiry into educational change.* New York: Peter Lang.

Johnson, A. (1999). Teaching as sacrament. In Kincheloe, Steinberg, & Villaverde (1999), pp. 105–116.

Kincheloe, J. (1993). *Toward a critical politics of teacher thinking: Mapping the postmodern.* Westport, CT: Bergin & Garvey.

——. (2001a). *Getting beyond the facts: Teaching social studies/social science in the twenty-first century* (2nd ed.). New York: Peter Lang.

——. (2001b). Describing the bricolage: Conceptualizing a new rigor in qualitative research. *Qualitative Inquiry, 7*(6), 679–92.

Kincheloe, J., & Steinberg, S. (1993). A tentative description of post-formal thinking: The critical confrontation with cognitive theory. *Harvard Educational Review, 63*(3), 296–320.

——. (1997). *Changing multiculturalism.* London: Open University Press.

Kincheloe, J., Steinberg, S., & Hinchey, P. (eds.). (1999). *The post-formal reader: Cognition and education.* New York: Falmer.

Kincheloe, J., Steinberg, S., Rodriguez, N., & Chennault, R. (1998). *White reign: Deploying whiteness in America.* New York: St. Martin's.

Kincheloe, J., Steinberg, S., & Villaverde, L. (eds.). (1999). *Rethinking intelligence: Confronting psychological assumptions about teaching and learning.* New York: Routledge.

Kincheloe, J., & Weil, D. (eds.). (2001). *Standards and schooling in the United States: An encyclopedia.* 3 vols. Santa Barbara, CA: ABC-CLIO.

Lester, S. (2001). Working with knowledge—Learning for the twenty-first century: Raising the level. In Kincheloe & Weil (2001). pp. 1121–1136.

Malewski, E. (2001). Administrative leadership and public consciousness: Discourse matters in the struggle for new standards. In J. Kincheloe & D. Weil (Eds.) *Standards and schooling in the United States: An encyclopedia.* Santa Barbara, CA: ABC-CLIO.

Maturana, H., & Varela, F. (1987). *The tree of knowledge.* Boston: Shambhala.

May, T. (1993). *Between genealogy and epistemology: Psychology, politics, and knowledge in the thought of Michel Foucault.* University Park, PA: Penn State Press.

Morrison, T. (1993). *Playing in the dark: Whiteness and the literary imagination.* New York: Vintage.

O'Sullivan, E. (1999). *Transformative learning: Educational vision for the 21st century.* London: Zed.

Pushkin, D. (2001). Science—To standardize, or too standardized? What becomes of our curriculum? In Kincheloe & Weil (2001), pp. 855–878.

Rodriguez, N., & Villaverde, L. (2000). *Dismantling White Privilege.* New York: Peter Lang.

Sempsey, J. (1993) The pedagogical implications of cognitive science and Howard Gardner's MI theory (a critique). *www.netaxes.com/~jamesiii/gardner.htm*

Steinberg, S. (2001). *Multi/intercultural conversations: A reader.* New York: Peter Lang.

Sumara, D., & Davis, B. (1997). Cognition, complexity, and teacher education. *Harvard Educational Review, 67*(1), 75–104.

Traub, J. (1998). Howard Gardner's campaign against logic. *The New Republic,* 26 October.

Varela, F. (1999). *Ethical know-how: Action, wisdom, and cognition.* Stanford, CA: Stanford University Press.

Weil, D. (1998). *Towards a critical multi-cultural literacy: Theory and practice for education for liberation.* New York: Peter Lang.

——. (2001). Florida state standards—Florida's advanced academic standards for the assessment of critical and creative thinking. In Kincheloe & Weil (2001), pp. 429–480.

The editor and the authors would like to thank Aostre Johnson for her valuable criticism of the chapters in this book.

PART II

THE EIGHT INTELLIGENCES

Chapter 2

Kathleen Nolan

THE POWER OF LANGUAGE: A CRITIQUE OF THE ASSUMPTIONS AND PEDAGOGICAL IMPLICATIONS OF HOWARD GARDNER'S CONCEPT OF LINGUISTIC INTELLIGENCE

So if you really want to hurt me, talk badly about my language.
—GLORIA ANZALDUA, *"How to Tame a Wild Tongue"*

Introduction

When Howard Gardner's theory of multiple intelligences found its way into the conversations of elementary and high school teachers, many expressed optimism. The concept of multiple intelligences offered a framework for developing new and more creative ways of tapping into students' potential. There was hope that a framework based on a theory of multiple intelligences could lead to more mean-ingful curricula and innovative teaching methods and better forms of assessment. Particularly for teachers of poor and working-class students of color, there was hope that such a framework could lead to a better quality of education and more educational opportunities.

However, while Gardner's theory might lead to better teaching and assessment practices, it does not ameliorate inequities and differential access for poor and working-class students of color. In fact, a framework based on Gardner's theory, like many neoliberal educational policies, may appear to support a more equitable and inclusive classroom, but in actuality it only serves to reproduce the inequities found in schools and the social and class structures. This is because Gardner's theory in practice obfuscates the asymmetrical power relations in our society and maintains a harmful focus on the decontextualized cognitive processes of individual students. Further, in addressing the needs of diverse student populations, Gardner adheres to an assimilationist model of multicultural education, which ultimately negates the value of students' home cultures and languages.

I am particularly concerned with the notion of "linguistic intelligence," which Gardner himself calls a "pre-eminent instance of human intelligence" (1983, 79). Language use, I argue, serves as the primary gatekeeper in schools. Historically, schools have made all sorts of incorrect assumptions about the intelligence of children from subordinated groups based on their use of language, limiting their educational opportunities and often crushing their self-esteem. In this chapter, I will delineate some of the problems of isolating the notion of linguistic intelligence and integrating the concept into an educational philosophy or practice. I am a teacher of English as a second language (ESL) who has also taught English and composition classes in high school and community college. Thus, the notion of identifying students as linguistically intelligent frightens me immensely. If there are those who can be determined linguistically intelligent, then clearly there are others who would be considered less linguistically intelligent, or even linguistically dull or inept. Two essential questions emerge from this: what standards are used to determine one's linguistic intelligence, and how might such determinations lead to patterns of exclusion and alienation for certain students?

Gardner does situate his "intelligences" in a cultural context, thus offering a level of sensitivity to cultural and linguistic differences. However, as Kincheloe and others in this volume have pointed out, Gardner does not consider the dynamics that exist between dominant cultural groups and subjugated groups. A close look at Gardner's definition of linguistic intelligence will illustrate that his notions of intelligence are drawn from an objectivist examination of the brain. Although he claims to recognize cultural differences, his measures of linguistic intelligence (lexical, syntactic, phonological, semantic and pragmatic—the last two including "inputs from other intelligences" [1983, 81])—are embedded in the "grand narratives" of Western tradition, or, put another way, the discourses of the dominant classes. The real danger here is that the dominant discourse is framed as "correct" and "natural"; thus, those who are positioned outside the dominant culture (and consequently, the dominant discourse community) will inevitably be judged as less intelligent, at least in the area of language.

The near-invisibility of African Americans and Latinos in Gardner's work is particularly telling, and a practice of distinguishing students as linguistically intelligent (or unintelligent) could be detrimental to these groups. African American and Latino students, particularly members of the working class, inevitably belong to subjugated discourse communities, and given that their (subjugated) worldviews are both constituted and expressed through language, conscientious educators should be wary of any educational theory that implies an immediate connection between one's language use and one's intelligence.

In sum, a critical interrogation of Gardner's notion of linguistic intelligence and its implications for educational practice necessitates a discussion of several

)cial, and educational theories. To start, Gardner's own assumptions of language must be located in particular linguistic and social frameworks. Next, drawing on the research and experience of scholars who hold a critical perspective, I hope to provide an alternative view of language that reveals the problems with Gardner's notion of linguistic intelligence.

A Brief Description of Gardner's Linguistic Intelligence

Simply put, linguistic intelligence is "sensitivity to the spoken and written word and the ability to master languages and the capacity to use language to accomplish certain goals" (Gardner 1999, 41). In *Frames of Mind* (1983), Gardner introduces the notion of linguistic intelligence by presenting a correspondence between the writer T. S. Eliot and a student. In this correspondence, Eliot critiques a poem written by the student and, in doing so, provides what Gardner sees as linguistic intelligence exemplified. Gardner continues by providing other examples of European poets' reflecting on their own construction of a poem. Gardner writes: "In the poet's struggles over the wording of a line or a stanza, one sees at work some central aspects of linguistic intelligence" (Gardner 1983, 75).

On the semantic level, which focuses on the meaning or connotation of words, Gardner states that "the poet must be superlatively sensitive to the shades of meanings of a word" (75), and he adds that "words must capture the emotions or images that have animated the initial desire to compose" (76). A good poet (and thus a linguistically intelligent person) must also be sensitive to phonology, or the musical interaction between words. Next, Gardner suggests that it is necessary to have the capacity to follow the rules of grammar while knowing how to break those rules on selected occasions. This means having an aptitude for the pragmatic function of language. Gardner also identifies some rhetorical aspects of language, which he associates with linguistic intelligence. He mentions the ability to use language to convince others, to explain, and also to speak about language (that is, to engage in metalinguistic activity).

While one may argue that the skills Gardner points to do appear to constitute a certain aptitude for using language, we must be cautious. The notion of "meaning," for example, is not nearly as straightforward as Gardner implies, and if one identifies "the capacity to follow the rules of grammar" as a sign of linguistic intelligence, a critical analysis would beg the question, whose grammar?

Finally, Gardner identifies the memorizing of verse as a form of linguistic intelligence. Here, he extols the talents of "illiterate" Africans who "were more successful at remembering stories than schooled Africans or schooled New Yorkers" (92). With this example, Gardner recognizes a non-Western discourse community with its own values, traditions and worldviews; however, as he often does, he chooses to focus on a distant cultural group, leaving unexamined the relations of power between this group and any other.

In a more recent volume (1991), Gardner actually draws on the work of Shirley Brice Heath in order to provide a discussion of the values held within subordinated discourses in relation to the art of storytelling. He writes that within the poor black community of Trackton, storytelling is highly valued, and the ability to tell a "tall tale" is especially treasured. In the impoverished white community of Roadville, on the other hand, story telling is used to recount actual events, and fabrications are frowned upon. Finally, in the middle-class white community of Gateway, imaginary tales are enjoyed so long as they have been explicitly marked as fantasy. Unfortunately, Gardner stops there in his discussion of cultural difference. He offers no statement on the need to validate the culturally specific linguistic talents of students from subordinated communities. He ends only by implying that the closer one's "scripts" are to those valued in school, the easier one will assimilate these new scripts.

How One Becomes "Linguistically Intelligent": The Ideological Nature of Language

Before unpacking the ideological nature of language, it is important to situate Gardner's own understanding of language. Gardner's notion of linguistic intelligence is consistent with a view of language that, I argue, is rooted in Cartesian rationalism and Leibniz's conception of universal grammar (Bakhtin 1973; quoted in Walsh 1991). In more recent times, as Catherine Walsh (1991) indicates, the objectivist tendency to view language as an abstract system minimally connected to the social context in which it is produced can be identified with the work of Leonard Bloomfield. "For Bloomfield, culture and experience were thought to be minor. Language was conceived of as a scientific system, as an abstract objective, grammatical form extracted from history and from day-to-day use" (38).

The work of linguist Noam Chomsky is associated with this school of thought. Chomsky's distinction between "competence" and "performance" embodies the disconnection of self from society. "Competence" indicates "the tacit understanding of the rule system of language"; while "performance" refers to "the use of this rule system in social communication" (38).

On the surface, the competence-performance distinction may seem to imply that language production is embedded in social life and that there exists an interaction between the self and society. However, in actuality, Chomsky's theory posits a dichotomous relationship between the individual and her surroundings. This is because Chomsky emphasizes the universal structures of language, which he contends are "part of the genetic endowment of humans, requiring little more than minimal stimulation from the environment" (Hakuta 1986, 83). In taking this view, Chomsky places little importance on the existence of an a priori sociolinguistic environment that influences the production of all utterances (to use a Bakhtinian term).

Chomsky's work appeals to Gardner in two ways. First, Gardner builds on the Chomskian theory that language exists as an independent function in the brain.

This supports Gardner's theory of (distinct) multiple intelligences. Yet Chomsky's work also provides Gardner with a theoretical basis from which to claim the primacy of innate mental faculties that determine linguistic, as well as other, capabilities. Gardner writes:

> Chomsky's work is important because it suggests that children are born with certain quite specific kinds of mental representations, which develop along narrowly constrained lines. There are structures dedicated to language, and these unfold in a prescribed manner—much like a physical organ growing—during the first years of life. (1999, 70)

A critical perspective of language challenges Chomsky's linguistic theories and, subsequently, Gardner's notion of linguistic intelligence. The influential work of M. M. Bakhtin helps elucidate this critique. Bakhtin focuses his analysis on the "utterance," the "real" unit of speech communication (Wertsch 1991). The concept of the utterance is an extension of what Saussure called the *parole* (speech act), and thus could be confused today with the Chomskian notion of performance (Walsh 1991). However, there is an important difference. Bakhtin insists that speech, unlike *parole* or performance, cannot exist outside the form of an utterance, which comes from a particular speaking subject within a particular social context. He views the utterance as "made specifically social, historical, concrete and dialogized . . . [and] a living dialectical synthesis is constantly taking place between the psyche and ideology, between the inner and the outer" (Bakhtin 1981, 433).

Put another way, instead of adhering to the Cartesian notion of a split between mind and world, which would locate meaning and language within the wiring of our brains (Kent 1994), a critical perspective of language acknowledges that "each human individual stands at a unique intersection of discourses and relationships: a 'position' embedded in historical, political, cultural, social, and interpersonal contexts, that largely determines mind" [3]; quoted in Cummins 1996.

Thus, the linguist's analysis of a word or sentence abstracted from its context or actual use could not adequately provide an account of the utterance. An analysis of the utterance requires an approach that transcends linguistics, and Bakhtin took on this task. Two concepts that are central to Bakhtin's analysis are those of "voice" and "dialogicality" (Wertsch 1991). Walsh provides a description of "voice" that elucidates the historical and cultural specificity of all utterances and shows how meaning is constructed differently in different contexts. She is worth quoting at length:

> as language is generally viewed as a common denominator of a people—a sociocultural unifier or composite force that brings together individuals for the purpose of meaningful interaction—language does not preclude a commonality of experience, equal relations of power, or a sharing of purpose. It is rather through language that individuals fashion a "voice," a "speaking consciousness" as Bakhtin (1981) has called it, that is rooted in their collective history, struggles, and lived experience, and in their

relation to one another, to society, and the ideological and material forces that surround them. "Voice" is never singular or unitary but reflects a connection of individuals to realities that are sometimes multiple and contradictory. As such, the voice or voices of individuals frequently reveal much about the conditions and relations that position and surround them. (4)

It is important to expand on the notion of "meaning" within this conceptualization of "voice," as one of Gardner's stated criteria for the determination of linguistic intelligence is a sensitivity to meaning. Bakhtin (1981) maintains that an utterance always "takes meaning and is shaped at a particular historical moment in a socially specific environment [and] cannot fail to brush up against thousands of living dialogic threads, woven by socio-ideological consciousness" (276). "Meaning," in this sense, has a contextual specificity and is always contested; it is "open to dispute, charged with value, already enveloped in an obscuring mist" (276).

Within the dominant ideology—in the school setting, for example—there is the erroneous assumption that words have literal meaning, in the sense that they are removed from a sociohistorical and ideological context. "The notion of literal meaning is thus part of a modern 'linguistic ideology' that privileges a particular view of language and language activity" (Wertsch 1991, 85). While Gardner does acknowledge different socially constructed discourses, his assimilationist goals and his emphasis on the cognitive process of language development lead to the evaluation of subordinated discourses within the context of the dominant ideology.

In the school setting, we assume parallel realities and common linguistic understanding. Yet as the discourse of students who are marginalized by their class, race, or ethnic or linguistic backgrounds is interpreted within the dominant school-based discourse, these students are misunderstood (Walsh 1991). Walsh provides a cogent example that illuminates the complexities of "meaning." She conducted a study in which she asked a group of young students to define the word "respect." The group of students was made up of white (Anglo) children and Puerto Rican children. Interestingly, all of the Puerto Rican children spoke of concrete relationships of authority within their definitions. For example, they spoke of the need to respect their parents and their teachers. For the white children, on the other hand, "respect" had to do with appropriate treatment due to them (conveying the children's own sense of entitlement). "Respect" was not associated with age, status or cultural dominance (Walsh 1991). We can see here how "meaning" is dependent on the worldviews and values of the children in a specific temporal and spatial context.

The Bakhtinian notions of "the utterance" and "voice" are related to the currently fashionable term "discourse." Many scholars in disciplines associated with language, such as, sociolinguistics and composition, have turned to the terms "discourse" and "discourse communities" in order to emphasize the social and ideological nature of language (Foster 1992). Linguist James Gee suggests that in order to understand how the production of language is embedded in a social context, we should think in terms of discourses instead of language or dialects. Gee defines a discourse as:

a socially accepted association among ways of using language, of thinking, feeling, believing, valuing and of acting that can be used to identify oneself as a member of a socially meaningful group or "social network" or to signal (that one is playing) a socially meaningful "role." (Gee 1990, 143)

This definition illuminates several important elements of discourse. First, a discourse community suggests a shared understanding among its members about language and the way it is used. It also maintains that discourses are inherently ideological in that they are based on shared social theories or assumptions about the world and the relationships that exist within it.

The term "discourse" is helpful here because, while knowledge of a language or a dialect may not imply an understanding or a sense of connectedness to the values attached to that language or dialect, membership in a particular discourse community does entail a connectedness to the history, values, and viewpoints of that community. However, a particular variation of language (a class-based dialect, for example) would constitute a discourse, in Gee's use of the word. In fact, many scholars use such terms as "language," "social language," "dialect," and "vernacular" in ways that would fall under Gee's definition of discourse.

Gee, similarly to Walsh's delineation of "voice," posits that discourses are defined in opposition to other discourses. This leads us to the crucial notion that "Discourses are intimately related to the distribution of social power and hierarchical structure in society" (144). In other words, each discourse holds a certain status, which is determined within the ideology of the dominant discourse.

Wertsch (1991) views the asymmetrical relations among discourses in terms of "privileging." For him, privileging indicates that a "social language" (discourse) "is viewed as being more appropriate or efficacious than others in a particular sociocultural setting" (124). Wertsch distinguishes "privileging" from "dominant" because he believes that domination is too closely tied to the study of social structure and implies a deterministic view of relationships between social languages. Although I do not agree with Wertsch that language should (or can) be isolated from social structure, his notion of privileging is helpful in that it suggests both the hierarchical relationships between discourses and the possibilities of human agency and resistance (ideas that will be discussed later in this chapter).

As I posited in the introduction, a critique of Gardner's theory of multiple intelligences from a critical perspective necessitates not just a delineation of the social nature of language but also its organization into various discourses and the asymmetrical power relations that exist between them. In order to grasp fully the perniciousness of Gardner's concept when used to measure one's language abilities, we must examine the real and hidden powers of the dominant discourse. It is through the language of the dominant discourse that even liberal, well-meaning (yet ultimately patronizing) educators in the field of language come to believe, on the one hand, that the dominant discourse is natural, good, and correct, and, on the other hand, that subjugated discourses are inferior or deviations of "standard" forms. But how does the discourse of the dominant group get constructed as superior to those of subordinated groups? Walsh (1991) posits that the Gramscian notion of hegemony is central to understanding the linguistic (and other) struggles of subjugated groups. The notion of hegemony suggests not only the power of repressive force but domination through ideological control. In this framework, subjugated people accept their own subjugation as they internalize the dominant ideology.

In the construction of a "correct, standard language"(which is generally not referred to as a dialect despite the fact that it is simply another dialect), other dialects must be disparaged, so that they are labeled nonstandard, corruptions, or incorrect. In fact, the word "dialect" itself, holds a connotation of something substandard. However, the work of linguist William Labov (1972), illustrates both the richness and the logic inherent in perhaps the most often denigrated language, so-called Black English Vernacular (BEV). Unfortunately, his work has gone largely ignored by educational policy-makers. His work, beginning in the 1960s, countered the "deficit theories" of the day, and although some strands of language pedagogy have acknowledged his work, mainstream teaching practices still privilege dominant discourses while silencing subordinated ones, and one's intelligence is still often judged on one's command of the "standard" dialect.

James Gee (1990) explains that Labov demonstrated not only that BEV was logical and governed by rules, but that much middle-class speech is overly verbose and disorganized. Gee provides an example of the dominant culture's misconceptions of Black English. In this example, an African American child utters, "My puppy, he always be following me" (10). Gee contends that in school, this child's utterance would most likely be considered incorrect for deviating from "standard" grammatical structures. Nevertheless, Gee goes on to explicate the grammatical logic of the child's utterance, demonstrating that the child was consistent with rules that govern her own dialect. For example, the verb "be following" in BEV indicates an action that is regularly repeated. In the "standard" dialect, the verb would be replaced with "follows" in this sentence. If at another time the child said, "My puppy following me," the classroom teacher would likely argue that the child is inconsistent and does not even know the rules of her own dialect (that is, if the teacher even believed that the child could have her own rule-governed dialect). Again, however, this would be a misconception. The child's second utterance simply indicates a different verb tense. In other words, the child is stating that the puppy is following her presently.

It is not in the scope of this chapter to give a detailed analysis of Black English. Nevertheless, the important points are that naïve social beliefs about language lead to inaccurate and harmful assessments of children from subjugated groups, and so-called non-standard dialects are just as (if not more) logical than the so-called standard dialect (Gee 1990). Put another way, the essential point here is that one's primary dialect is not an indicator of one's level of intelligence or linguistic intelligence; it is, instead, an indicator of one's social and cultural position (Bernstein 1975), and if power relations were to shift, a more accurate assessment of "non-standard" dialects would inevitably emerge.

Gee presents another relevant example of how rhetorical conventions valued in one discourse community may not be valued in another. Specifically, the linguistic (and cultural) capital with which white middle-class children come to school is highly valued within the context of the school-based discourse, while the linguistic and cultural capital of, say, a Black child is deemed incorrect. In this example, a young Black girl shares a story with her classmates during "sharing time." Her story, reflecting her own rich cultural background, is less linear and perhaps more exaggerated than conventional stories. The teacher, treating the conventions of the sharing-time discourse as natural (implying a correct way to tell a story), assumes that the little girl has a speech deficit. However, the little girl has no deficit whatsoever. In fact, Gee would argue, she probably even has an advantage, or a talent, in the areas of creative writing and storytelling. Nevertheless, in the course of the child's interaction with her teacher, the child's self-image is harmed.

While Gardner offers a similar discussion of storytelling (p. 34), there is one very important difference. Gardner does not expose the asymmetrical power relations between different discourses, nor does he argue the need to understand, validate, and integrate into the school setting the linguistic capacities of children from subordinated discourse communities.

I now turn back to Gardner's description of linguistic intelligence. Frankly, I am left only with questions. For instance, what does it mean to have "a sensitivity to shadings of meaning and what they imply" (76) when meaning, as we have seen, has a cultural and sociohistorical specificity and is always contested? And how can we determine a child's (linguistic) intelligence based on her use of grammar or her rhetorical skills if we are unaware of the grammatical rules and rhetorical conventions of the child's discourse? Gardner's notion of linguistic intelligence does not take these questions into account, and in disregarding them, his notion of linguistic intelligence can serve to further marginalize students from subordinated groups.

I am not arguing that children from marginalized groups should not be exposed to and learn the rules and conventions of dominant discourses. Indeed, they can and should. Yet, for many reasons, these rules and conventions cannot be forced upon children as the "correct," "natural," and "intelligent" forms of discourse without crushing the identities and self-esteem of these children.

In the following section, I will discuss the crucial differences between Gardner's understanding of multicultural education and a critical understanding of multicultural education, and I will explore how identities are formed within these two models. Finally, I will present a brief discussion of the pedagogical implications of Gardner's work.

Linguistic Intelligence, Multiculturalism and Dominant Culture

Gardner's work has long been associated with progressive education, and he considers himself a follower, in many respects, of John Dewey. In addition, Gardner's work has been used to demonstrate the importance of multicultural education. Indeed, his work certainly does address the importance of recognizing different learning styles, and it also acknowledges that students enter the classroom from various socioeconomic and cultural backgrounds. One might conclude from this that Gardner adheres to a progressive form of multicultural education—one that validates the linguistic and cultural capital of students from nondominant groups by using teaching and assessment methods that reflect and affirm their experiences, worldviews, and learning styles. However, there is a contradiction in Gardner's work. While he acknowledges various learning styles and cultural differences, he does not appear to place much value on the capacities of children from subordinated groups. In fact, his notion of multicultural education is quite conservative, and, I argue, is consistent with an assimilationist approach. The purpose of this type of multicultural education is to assimilate children from subordinated groups into the dominant culture.

Gardner reveals his own conservatism in his discussion of two well-known educators, Allan Bloom and E. D. Hirsch. Gardner maintains (1991) that, while both of these educators assert the importance of transmission of the Western canon in American schools, there is a clear difference in their positions. Gardner criticizes Bloom for "endorsing an explicit political, ideological, and educational agenda framed according to Western neo-conservative values" (190). Gardner thus finds Bloom's perspective problematic and "distinctly elitist" (190). Contrarily, Gardner avoids referring to Hirsch's work as ideological and elitist, and he maintains that Hirsch's emphasis on the transmission of cultural literacy has merit. He writes that "Ignorance of such common [cultural] references proves devastating, particularly for minority students who might wish to be integrated into the historically dominant culture" (189).

Gardner does criticize Hirsch's work and its applications for leading to the teaching of cultural references as if they were a list of vocabulary words. Echoing a more progressive viewpoint, he argues that these applications do not create opportunities to apply new knowledge and increase motivation. Nevertheless, Gardner does not critique the notion of transmitting cultural literacy into students from subordinated groups. Indeed, he extols the idea. Thus, Gardner's work lends itself to an unproblematic understanding of multicultural education that rests on the assumption that there is a common culture, and it is the school's job to transmit this culture (i.e., the dominant culture) into students. And although he recognizes differences, Gardner disregards the ideological nature of education and the potential harm done to children from subordinated discourse communities during the process of assimilation.

As a teacher, I have seen how such buzz words as "multiculturalism"—or "multiple intelligences," for that matter—are framed as the keys to equality and inclusiveness. However, by promoting such ideas as multiculturalism within a neoliberal framework, educators only mask the inequalities and injustices done to students from subordinated cultures. In other words, schools practice what Freire (1970) might call false generosity. Schools feign to be sensitive to the "other" while insisting that the "other" will be engaged within the context of the dominant culture and language, thus reproducing their subordination.

The literature on multiculturalism stresses the need to appreciate cultural differences and acknowledge student "voice," yet the underlying assumption is that the celebration of other cultures will take place in "standard" English (Macedo & Bartolome 1999). Macedo and Bartolome articulate a critical understanding of multiculturalism when they argue that:

> promising the "other" a dose of tolerance so we can get along, not only eclipses real opportunities for the development of mutual respect and cultural solidarity but also hides the privilege and paternalism inscribed in the proposition "I will tolerate you even though your culture is repugnant." (35)

It is frightening that it is within this framework of "inclusion" and "tolerance" that the linguistic and cultural capital of students from subjugated groups is devalued or considered inferior to that of students from the dominant classes.

This is not to say that a critical multicultural education model simply dismisses the importance of acquiring dominant discourses. A critical multicultural education calls for the selective appropriation of dominant discourses—language and interaction styles—for the purpose not only of surviving in the mainstream but, more important, of challenging it (Leistyna 1999). This is where Gardner's work falls short.

So what happens to children from marginalized discourse communities when educational policies and practices reflect Gardner's work? I argue that in adhering to an assimilationist model of multicultural education and not making explicit notions of power and ideology, Gardner's work, particularly his notion of linguistic intelligence, is likely in practice to alienate students from marginalized discourse communities. In order to fully understand the process of alienation that occurs within educational practices grounded in theories such as Gardner's, we must begin with the premise that human subjectivities are constituted through language. That is to say, language, with the conventions and values inherent within it, shapes our thoughts and our identities. This is why, as I have already suggested, one's identity is intimately connected to the discourse(s) in which one is positioned. At the same time, however, the dominant discourse works to construct other discourses and the values embedded within them as inferior. Thus, for children from marginalized discourse communities, identity negotiation can be a difficult and traumatizing process when they confront the dominant discourse at school. For these children, learning the school-based discourse involves complicity with values and social practices that often conflict with the values and social practices of their own discourses (Gee 1990). Moreover, in order for a child from a marginalized discourse community to gain access to the dominant school-based discourse, she must accept the dominant ideology that frames her own culture and language as inferior. Thus, in school, the child struggles between maintaining her own sense of self-worth and learning to "speak and write correctly."

In order to help preserve children's sense of self-worth, educators must start by rejecting the humanist understanding of subjectivity, which is predicated on the notion of a unified, rational, self-determining consciousness (Giroux 1997). This notion of subjectivity disregards both the economic and social constraints placed upon individuals and the discursive construction of their identities. For example, the dominant educational and political discourse of the day is full of terms such as "at risk," "disadvantaged," or even "culturally deprived." These labels assigned to children from marginalized groups locate the problem (some labels more subtly than others) within the marginalized group members, thus constructing them as the cause of their own subordinated position. Much of the time, such discourse is internalized by group members; at other times it may be covertly or overtly resisted. However, such resistance, which is often an individual or collective effort by students to maintain their linguistic and cultural identities, serves to frame them as "unmotivated," "disruptive," or even "unreachable."

Gardner's notion of linguistic intelligence, like his whole theory of multiple intelligences, is grounded in the problematic humanist/liberal framework of the autonomous subject. One telling example of this is his delineation of the notion of "motivation." In *The Disciplined Mind,* Gardner takes up the matter of motivation in an attempt to move "beyond cognition." When I came across this section, I wondered whether Gardner might be addressing some external factors that influence students' level of engagement in academic work. I was eager to find out what he believed motivated students. I was disappointed once again. He writes: "researchers now believe that learners are best served when their motivation is intrinsic: when they pursue learning because it is fun and rewarding in itself, rather than because someone has promised them some material benefit" (Gardner 1999, 76). Gardner maintains that positive early experiences do enhance motivation, which admits some level of external cause; however, he also posits that "The theory of multiple intelligences suggests another factor: people may be most motivated to learn when they undertake activities for which they have some talent" (76–77).

I think many teachers hold the same understanding of motivation that Gardner does; they are the ones who seem to love to complain about students who are not motivated, who just sit there and refuse to participate or do not submit their written assignments. Like Gardner, these teachers fail to consider the great risks a child must take in order to speak, to give her opinion, or share her experiences, particularly when that child is from a marginalized discourse community. Based on Gardner's understanding of motivation, a child who does not speak in class or submit written assignments must lack intrinsic motivation, or worse, is probably just not inclined toward language. Her talents must lie elsewhere. Perhaps she is good with her hands.

I do not know if there is such a thing as intrinsic motivation. Our drive to do anything is so connected to our experiences in the world. *Something* influences our level of motivation—a smile, a kind remark, possibilities for a better job in the future. I suppose some children do have more innate linguistic talent than other children (it is not my intent to argue otherwise), and perhaps these children do exhibit high levels of motivation based purely on their aptitude for language. Chicana scholar Gloria Anzaldua, certainly someone who is gifted with words, tells how as a young girl she used to make up long stories to tell her sister late at night while they were in bed. She did this so her sister would not tell her parents that she was staying up late to read (Olson & Worsham 1999). Here talent and motivation seem to have some connection but only in the most intimate of contexts. In school, when children from marginalized discourses are required to produce language, the judgments about their linguistic abilities that (even if unspoken) are already in the classroom serve to undermine their motivation. In effect, children are judged twice. When their linguistic capital is devalued in the classroom, they are silenced, and, when they sit in silence, they are viewed as unmotivated, not inclined toward language.

Teachers, unaware of the social and discursive forces that have constructed certain children as linguistically unintelligent, often accept students' refusal to participate, in essence giving them "permission to fail" (Ladson-Billings 2002). To illustrate this point, Gloria Ladson-Billings shares a story of a young African American child who, sitting among her white classmates, refuses to write a sentence. In a sense, the child's refusal to write could be viewed as an act of resistance or at least an effort to preserve her own cultural and linguistic identity and sense of self-worth. Yet it is not likely to be perceived by the teacher as such. Instead, the teacher assumes the child is not capable or is unmotivated, and, as she has done on previous occasions, she responds by saying, "That's okay. Maybe you'll feel like writing tomorrow."

This type of casual acceptance of the child's opposition to writing perpetuates the cycle of silencing. Gee (1990) writes on this issue: "if you undermine someone's motivation, hurt their self-image, and destroy their trust in teachers and school, they will eventually be less good at and less interested in learning" (9). Put another way, despite what Gardner would have us believe, one's level of motivation is not merely intrinsic, nor does it say much about the linguistic capacities of students from marginalized groups. As resistance, or perhaps fear, is constructed as "a lack of motivation," children become increasingly alienated from school.

Nevertheless, there is a price to pay for children who do not resist. Many times these students experience internal conflicts as they attempt to maintain their cultural and linguistic identities while acquiring the dominant language (see Fordham [1996] for a detailed discussion of African American identity formation in schools and Cummins [1996] for a discussion of issues of identity formation for Latinos). Illuminating the complexities of these issues, Joanne Kilgour Dowdy (2002), a Trinidadian scholar, shares her own experience with identity formation, resistance, and linguistic subordination in a reflective essay on her schooling within the postcolonial Trinidadian educational system. She writes that under her mother's, grandmother's, and teachers' tutelage she was on a journey to becoming a "good girl" according to the colonizer's belief system, which entailed rejecting the Trinidadian language of her people and speaking "proper" British English. Dowdy claims that she survived school by "assuming the best mask ever fabricated—the mask of language" (9), thus enabling her to invent a character to please her teachers. Yet, she remembers that the more she succeeded in playing this role by speaking the Queen's English, the more she felt segregated from her peers. She poignantly describes this as a painful and even humiliating experience.

These are often the only choices we give our students. They must accept that their own discourse, their own ways of thinking and knowing, indeed their whole culture, is not good enough, thus separating themselves from those in their own discourse communities. Or, if they consciously or even unconsciously resist, they are likely to be considered unmotivated or incapable. Even if students manage to create two voices, a dual identity, in order to survive in school, how can teachers accurately assess their language or even know who their students are when the students' language is a mask?

Fortunately for Dowdy, she became adept at code-switching between British English and Trinidadian and, ultimately, was able to assert her Afrocentric identity at school. However, code-switching, while it can be empowering, is merely a survival technique for members of subjugated groups. People who learn to code-switch still must contend with the fact that the language in which they express their innermost thoughts and desires is constructed as inferior. Dowdy argues that what is central to real liberation is for people from subjugated groups to, "have the freedom to go back and forth from the home language to the public language without feeling a sense of inferiority" (13). She believes that liberation will be realized when "she who is marginalized comes to speak more in her own language and people can accept her communication as valid and representative" (13).

Pedagogical Implications

In many ways, Gardner offers educators a liberal framework that is, at least, sensitive to difference. He criticizes the use of biased IQ tests and offers the notion of studying history through multiple entry points, for example (1991). His work also suggests possibilities for enabling, say, a visually oriented learner to develop his or her writing through the use of diagrams and other visual images to generate and organize ideas.

Nevertheless, from a critical perspective, Gardner's work has two main problems. First, his concept of multiculturalism is defined by tolerance for "the other" as long as "the other" is willing to conform to the conventions of the dominant culture. In other words, we can "do multiculturalism" but only within the context of the dominant ideology/ discourse. Thus, Gardner's whole theory is associated with a pedagogy based on the transmission of "cultural literacy" and respect for the grand narratives of Western tradition. What follows from this is what Freire (1970) calls a banking pedagogy, in which knowledge is transmitted from teacher to student instead of being produced collaboratively among students with the guidance of the teacher. Gardner might advocate the use of cooperative learning but not for the purpose of the type of knowledge production and problem-solving that helps students look critically at their worlds and understand their own social locations within the world. Second, Gardner denies the ideological nature of language and the asymmetrical relations of power that exist among various discourses.

Within the language classroom (composition, language arts, and ESL, for example), Gardner's assumptions about language are problematic even if we associate his work with a liberal, process-oriented pedagogy. Writing as cognitive process, according to Patricia Bizzell (1992), actually came into vogue in the 1970s as liberal educators claimed that the shift from product to process would empower working-class students and facilitate initiation into academic discourse. However, Bizzell maintains that writing as cognitive process assumes a relationship between familiarity with the dominant academic discourse and cognitive development. She contends that writing as process becomes an attempt to develop students' cognitive levels by introducing them into the "cognitively superior," "standard" dialect of academic discourse. This focus on writing as process claims to be able to make determinations about one's cognitive abilities based on familiarity with the dominant discourse.

I do not mean to be politically or pedagogically stymied by suggesting that our subjectivities are constituted through language. Put simply, I am not proposing a poststructuralist, decentered "self," for which human agency, resistance, and emancipation do not exist. On the contrary, I would like to suggest that writing and other forms of language-production can be emancipatory practices. As I have already argued, many students from subordinated groups resist accommodating to the dominant ideology and discourse, at least at times, to preserve a sense of self-worth and assert their cultural identities. Although the forms of resistance I have mentioned do often serve to reproduce the social and class structure, within a transformative pedagogy, they need not.

Bakhtin's work strongly suggests the possibilities for human agency and the emancipatory potential of language. Walsh (1991) writes that for Bakhtin (as well as Freire and Gramsci), language is intimately connected to the dialectics of both power and culture. The dialectical and dialogical relationship between self and society indicates that, while it is through language practices that individual consciousness is shaped (not determined) within the dominant ideology, language, in turn, evolves through the actions and deliberations of individuals. Thus, the notion of dialogicality, as well as "voice," suggests the possibilities for tensions and contradictions to emerge as meaning is struggled over. In this framework, the classroom can become a space of cultural production and critique as opposed to cultural and social reproduction. I am not suggesting that this happens easily in schools, especially given the structural constraints placed on the classroom, such as the imposition of standardized tests, mandated textbooks that present an unproblematic and biased view of culture and history, or funding disparities that favor middle- and upper-class students. Nevertheless, teachers can contribute to the creation of a potentially emancipatory space.

First, teachers must emphasize the social nature of language production. Viewing writing as a collaborative project legitimizes students' prior knowledge.

Collaborative projects, when initiated or conceptualized by the students them-selves, are also conducive to the generation of new ideas. When collaborative pro-jects are carried out in combination with the use of literature that reflects the students' cultural and historical perspectives, there is potential for students to de-velop a critical voice. However, writing becomes an emancipatory practice only when the teacher is explicit about not just the social but also the ideological nature of language. This means that the composition or language arts teacher needs to ex-plain to students how language is used to construct the subordinated students' own discourse as "incorrect" and the dominant discourse as "superior" and "cor-rect." Put another way, it is the teacher's responsibility to help students understand that "discourse communities are organized around the production and legitima-tion of particular forms of knowledge and social practices at the expense of oth-ers" (Chase 1988, 13). By doing this, teachers help students to see the logic of their own discourses while they learn to critically engage the dominant discourse. That is, students can benefit from learning the dominant discourse but must be able to interrogate the assumptions embedded within it.

In addition, a critical pedagogy, I argue, calls for the inclusion of subordinated discourses in the classroom. Students must be allowed to express themselves and generate new ideas in their own language, whether it be Spanish or Black English or any other subordinated discourse. Unlike the practices that would emerge from Gardner's notion of linguistic intelligence, a critical pedagogy that validates subor-dinated discourses does not penalize children for not following the grammatical rules or conventions of the dominant discourse. Nor would it judge students' lexi-cal choices removed from an understanding of the child's own discourse. This type of validation of subordinated discourses encourages students to write and speak, thus supporting the "amplification of voices that participate in the productive act" (Freire 1987, 55; quoted in Walsh 1991).

While these suggestions for writing and speaking as emacipatory practices in no way constitute a comprehensive explication of a critical pedagogy of language, they do hint at alternatives to the type of language pedagogy supported by Gardner's work. Put simply, if educators really wish to practice inclusion, encour-age students to speak and write in an academic setting and help them develop a critical understanding of their world, we cannot rely solely on practices informed by Gardner's notion of linguistic intelligence. While Gardner acknowledges the social nature of language, he expects the school to espouse a "common culture," that is, the dominant culture, and it is within this context that students will be judged in terms of their language use. Thus, the idea of identifying students as lin-guistically intelligent or unintelligent further silences and alienates students from subordinated groups regardless of their language strengths, and it buttresses the erroneous notion of the linguistic and cognitive superiority of the dominant dis-course. I am only suggesting that, as teachers, we can do better than that for our students.

References

Anzaldua, G.(ed). (1987). How to tame a wild tongue. In *Borderlands: The new mestiza* (pp. 53–64). San Francisco: Aunt Lute Books.

Bakhtin, M. (1973). *Marxism and the philosophy of language*. Trans. Matejka & R. Titunik. Cambridge, MA: Harvard University Press.

——. (1981). *The dialogic imagination*. Austin: University of Texas Press.

Bernstein, B. (1975). *Class, codes, and control*. Boston: Routledge & Kegan Paul.

Bizzell, P. (1992). *Academic discourse and critical consciousness*. Pittsburgh, PA: University of Pittsburgh Press.

Chase, G. (1988). Accommodation, resistance and the politics of student writing. *College Composition and Communication 39*, 13–22.

Cummins, J. (1996). *Negotiating identities: Education for empowerment in a diverse society*. Ontario, CA: California Association for Bilingual Education.

Kilgour Dowdy, J. (2002). Ovuh Dyuh. In L. Delpit and J. Dowdy (eds.), *The skin that we speak* (pp. 3–14). New York: New Press.

Fordham, S. (1996). *Blacked out: Dilemmas of race, identity, and success at Capital High*. Chicago: University of Chicago Press.

Foster, D. (1992). *A primer for writing teachers: Theories, theorists, issues, problems*. Portsmouth, NH: Boynton/Cook Publishers.

Freire, P. (1970). *Pedagogy of the oppressed*. New York: Seabury Press.

——. (1987). The Imortance of the Act of Reading. In P. Freire & D. Macedo (Eds.) *Literacy: Reading the Word and the World*. South Hadley, MA: Bergin and Garvey.

Gardner, H. (1983). *Frames of mind: The theory of multiple intelligences*. New York: Basic Books.

——. (1991). *The unschooled mind: How children think and how school should teach*. New York: Basic Books.

——. (1999). *The disciplined mind: What all students should understand*. New York: Simon & Schuster.

Gee, J. (1990). *Social linguistics and literacies: Ideology in discourses*. New York: Falmer Press.

Giroux, H. (1997). *Pedagogy and the politics of hope: Theory, culture, and schooling*. Boulder, CO: Westview Press.

Hakuta, K. (1986). *Mirror of language: The debate on bilingualism*. New York: Basic Books.

Kent, T. (1994). Externalism and the production of discourse. In G. Olson and S. Dorbin (eds.), *Composition theory for the postmodern classroom*. Albany: State University of New York Press.

Kilgour Dowdy, J. (2002). Ovuh Dyuh. In L. Delpit and J. Dowdy (eds.), *The skin that we speak* (pp. 3–14). New York: New Press.

Labov, W. (1972). *Language in the inner city: Studies in the Black English Vernacular*. Philadelphia: University of Pennsylvania Press.

Ladson-Billings, G. (2002). I ain't writin' nuttin': Permission to fail and the demands to succeed in urban classrooms. In L. Delpit and J. Dowdy (eds.), *The skin that we speak* (pp. 107–120). New York: New Press.

Leistyna, P. (1999). *Presence of mind: Education and the politics of deception*. Boulder, CO: Westview Press.

Lunsford, A. (1999). Toward a mestiza rhetoric: Gloria Anzaldua on composition and postcoloniality. In G. Olson and L. Worsham (eds.), *Race, rhetoric and the postcolonial* (pp. 43–78). Albany: State University of New York Press.

Macedo, D. & Bartolome, L. (1999). *Dancing with bigotry.* New York: St. Martin's Press.

Olson, G., & Worsham, L. (eds.) (1999). *Race, rhetoric, and the postcolonial.* Albany: State University of New York Press.

Shor, I., & Friere, P. (1987). *Literacy: Reading the word and the world.* Westport, CT: Bergin & Garvey.

Walsh, C. (1991). *Pedagogy and the struggle for voice: Issues of language, power, and schooling for Puerto Ricans.* New York: Bergin & Garvey.

Wertsch, J. (1991). *Voices of the mind: A sociocultural approach to mediated action.* Cambridge, MA: Harvard University Press.

Chapter 3

Yusef Progler

MUSICAL STUPIDITY AND
THE REIGNING MONOCULTURE

Many music educators, such as myself, thought Howard Gardner's theory of multiple intelligences was useful when it first appeared. But over time, some of us became frustrated with its emphasis on separating out the individual components of what in the end needs to be a whole, integrated person. On the heels of hard-won gains in holistic education, the theory of multiple intelligences is recompartmentalizing schooling by suggesting that a different curriculum can be developed for each intelligence, whereas what is needed is a curriculum for the whole person. While Gardner insists that the various intelligences can be merged together in life and education, the discourse of multiple intelligences reifies intelligence into separable entities, each testable and isolatable.

The effects of this became evident when I was a graduate teaching assistant for sociomusicologist Charlie Keil. He noticed that music education teachers in his popular Afro-Latin musical praxis course would resist participatory musicking strategies by asking for scores and notations of the drum parts, positioning themselves as "visual learners" and in need of specialized instruction. In many cases, this went against the participatory consciousness that Charlie was trying to teach by listening, watching, doing, feeling, and grooving in a group. That got me thinking about multiple intelligences in a new way, and whether it was really useful for teaching people how to make music. Since then, some of us have discussed Gardner as being "trapped in a bourgeois ideology" or somehow "caught between paradigms," but to me, Gardner's theory is about reviving the same old visually oriented, elitist musical canons of Western civilization that have alienated most ordinary people from doing their own musicking. Although notation does not play a major role in his "core musical operations," to me, Western music in general, by way of notation, transfers music from the right to the left side of the brain, where it can be read as text, but which disables the primordial musicking instincts that all humans seem to possess.

Besides this, his theory is largely monocultural, with little or no mention, for example, of the musics of the African Diaspora that form the basis for most global pop music today, and with only cursory mentions of other non-Western traditions. While Gardner seems meticulous in making sure that we give equal weight to the mind and body intelligences as separate entities, something that should rightly be applauded, it seems to me that intelligent musicking involves integrated humans in participatory relationships nested in culture and ecology. By looking at the theory of musical intelligence as embodying some of the central assumptions and structures of Western modernity—Cartesian individualism, elitist cultural politics, and an obsession with assessment—I wish to argue that conceptualizing and learning music the modernist way shuts people down at a very early age, which can result in an enculturated form of what I am referring to as musical stupidity.

Autonomous Individualism

Louis Terman's infamous circular definition of intelligence as "what we measure on intelligence tests" has given way to more complex definitions, such as that offered by Howard Gardner (1993b): "intelligence entails the ability to solve problems or fashion products that are of consequence in a particular cultural setting or community." According to Gardner, problem-solving requires goals and plotting routes to achieve them, which can lead to the creation of a "cultural product" (15). While Gardner's view is certainly an improvement over the old circular definitions, it still retains a basic cultural assumption of Western civilization that intelligence is an attribute of the autonomous individual. Gardner frequently relies on the autonomous individual to explain his theories, with little social reality acknowledged beyond a mention of "large numbers of individuals" who may learn by way of the Suzuki method (1993a, 112), or when he wonders whether "individuals in other cultures" felt as isolated as John Lennon did when no one noticed his early talents (115), or when mentioning music cognition, in which "individuals expect that the verbal material will interfere with the melodic material" (117–18), or in discussions of Stravinsky, in which Gardner (1993c) reduces social, political and economic context to "groups of individuals" that "quickly reaches the hundreds" (127).

As a consequence of this fixation on the autonomous individual, Gardner (1993b) advocates "individual-centered schooling" (68). He sees this as an antidote to standards and cultural literacy, which seeks a "uniform view" (69) of one sort or another, a point that Gardner has developed in his numerous debates with conservative cultural critic E. D. Hirsch. To Gardner, education should insure that individuals are able to maximize all of their potentials, and to achieve this Gardner's individual-centered school relies on profiling to assess individual intelligences and tailor instruction accordingly (1993a, xv). This is to be accomplished by developing a fairer set of measurements that do not rely on language and logic as their primary criteria. Gardner seems to have realized that intelligence is context specific and that the earlier quest for "raw" intelligence is misguided. He sums it up this way:

> At the level of the individual, it is proper to speak about one or more human intelligences, or human intellectual proclivities, that are part of our birthright. These intelligences may be thought of in neurobiological terms. Human beings are born into cultures that house a large number of domains—disciplines, crafts, and other pursuits in which one can become enculturated and then be assessed in terms of the level of competence one has attained. While domains, of course, involve human beings, they can be thought of in an impersonal way—because the expertise in a domain can in principle be captured in a book, a computer program, or some other kind of artifact. (xvi)

His "triangle of creativity" investigates the dialectics within the individual, the domain in which they work, and the field of "knowledgeable experts who evaluate works in the domain" (Gardner 1993c, 380). Yet in its sophistication, the discussion still hinges on the autonomous individual as the primary locus of intelligence.

Focusing on the autonomous individual as the locus of intelligence distorts and obscures the nested hierarchy that places individuals in a cultural setting, which, in turn, grows out of a broader ecosystem. The implications of this modernist oversight are developed by Bowers (1995):

> [T]he view of intelligence as an attribute of the individual, as well as the educational practices predicated upon it, reinforce the same deep cultural assumptions that lead us to view every technological innovation as the expression of progress, and to mistakenly interpret the visual sensation of the plenitude of shopping malls as validating the ideal of individual freedom rather than as a metaphor of a culture that is destroying the chances of future generations to live in balance with the Earth's ecosystems. (105)

These latter issues suggest that what we are calling intelligence can sometimes be nested in an "ecology of bad ideas," to use Bateson's phrase (1972, 484). From the realization that intelligence is in a sense immanent, not isolated, Bowers concludes: "If we nest individuals in the symbolic systems of culture, and cultures in the natural systems that are the source of the many sources of energy humans rely upon, then we have a very different way of understanding intelligence" (1995, 126).

The individual-centered view of intelligence is also at odds with the insights formulated decades ago by linguists such as Sapir, Whorf, and Vygotsky, all of whom in their own ways make a strong case that as people use language to express thoughts, the language they use thinks for them as well by way of its metaphors and taken-for-granted modes of understanding. Language can also encode a cultural form of intelligence that is "based on ways of understanding cultural/environmental relationships that are not sustainable," which may also sustain the ecology of bad ideas (Bowers 1995, 115). Once one accepts this, it become possible to see that "the wide range of competing root metaphors that characterize modern culture (masculine versus feminine, anthropocentric versus ecological models, mechanistic versus process, God centered versus secular and individual centered, to identify just a few) makes it possible, even necessary in some instances, to select which root metaphor and accompanying metaphorical language will be used to think and communicate about relevant aspects of the world" (120). With respect to communication, Bowers continues: "The anthropocentrism in the West, with its emphasis on intelligence as essentially a human attribute, as well as the practice of treating communication as a sender-receiver process of sharing information between individuals, has contributed to a form of conscious awareness that recognizes only a limited range of communication" (Bowers 1995, 121). If one considers the ecological view of intelligence put forth by Bowers, then it becomes possible to see that everything communicates information, and that intelligence can be immanent everywhere.

The cult of the autonomous individual creates an ecology of heroism for musicians and artists, sometimes even leading to a form of deification, as we often see in the case of composers such as Bach, Beethoven, and Mozart, which centralizes innovation, progress, and change as essential elements of musical intelligence. Viewing musical intelligence as an attribute of the autonomous individual also downplays the implications of the nested hierarchy of people, culture, and environment. Though Gardner acknowledges that some cultures are more "traditional," in which intelligence can be measured by the adherence of an individual to his cultural traditions, this still imposes an individual-centered Western explanation on the varieties of human experience. To find two brief examples, one could look toward Islamic and indigenous peoples. Qur'anic recitation (which Gardner categorizes as linguistic intelligence) is a complex sound art with specific organizational features, the centrality of which has informed sacred and secular musical practice throughout the Islamic world (Faruqi 1984).

The Qur'an in Arabic is revealed from the Divine, the other-than-human world of the unseen, and for Muslims its recitation as a sound art reproduces that connection to the Divine. Similarly, for many indigenous peoples, musical practices are informed by the environment in which they live, be it a desert, forest or river valley. Sovereignty for sound-making, whether music, chanting, recitation, or prayer, lies not with the autonomous individual in such cultures; it lies within the relationship between people and these other-than-human realities. To position such relationships within the minds of autonomous individuals, or to see them as simple modes of communication among autonomous individuals, is to do deep damage to our understanding of non-Western ways of being, and basing a theory of musical intelligence on this premise limits the possibilities for musicking to a very narrow segment of humanity.

Cultural Politics

In the recesses of discussions on musical intelligence there lurks a struggle over cultural politics. Whose music gets exemplified, normalized, assessed, and venerated is more and more a political struggle. It is no longer tenable to assume that the Western classics are by definition the epitome of humanity's musical accomplishment for all time and across cultures (a premise that Gardner, to some extent, shares with his archnemesis, E. D. Hirsch). While much of the musical-intelligence literature is about implementing this theory, often to justify funding for the fine arts in general, this has led to a utilitarian pairing of a broad range of the arts with other subjects. In many cases, this has also ended up constricting the freedom of art and music teachers by linking them up with the new-standards movement of the last fifteen years (and its funding). During the 1990s, with increased funding for the arts, there had been a resurgence of interest in public music programs gutted by budget cuts in the 1980s. But a lot of these developments are problematic for two reasons: either they link music in a utilitarian relationship with other subjects as a sort of handmaiden to improve performance or increase interest in the academic subjects (the "Mozart effect"), or they assume music as taking on a sort of civilizing mission by promoting the Western canon, implying that the ultimate purpose of school music programs is to train future musicians and patrons for that tradition. Although he is not as rigid and single minded as Hirsch about promoting the Western canon, and despite a few token references to selected non-Western musical traditions, Gardner is still in the thick of cultural and political struggles over the meaning and purpose of art and music in society, as implied by his choice of musical exemplars in Mozart, Stravinsky, and others within the Western canon.

Gardner's attempts to muster cross-cultural validity for his theories often fall short and instead reveal his Eurocentrism (despite his frequent protestations of this epithet). Musical intelligence apparently has several components, which get intertwined with the process of normalizing definitions of music: "there is relatively little dispute about the principal constituent elements of music" (Gardner 1993a, 104). These are pitch and rhythm, with timbre "next in importance." But this is a Eurocentric ranking. For example, to many indigenous peoples, timbre is often the key feature. Pitch, Gardner claims, is more central in "Oriental" societies, which favor "tiny" quartertone intervals. But in Islamic culture, for instance, it is the subtle rhythmic variations that make the music interesting, not the quarter tones, which in any case are taken for granted even though they may sound "odd" and "exotic" to Westerners, whose hearing is severely impaired by cultural acclimation to the twelve-tone scale. Similarly, Gardner's Eurocentric understanding of world musics is also evident in his citing "dizzying" African rhythmic complexity, again centralizing the Western feeling toward those musics as the normative definition.

While Gardner (1993a) admits that his discussion is "partial to Western civilization in the period following the Renaissance" (to be more accurate, he'd need to add elite patriarchal civilization, which found its musical apex in the orchestral forms of the eighteenth and nineteenth centuries), he occasionally casts a cursory "glance around the globe" to search for verification of his theory. Just as in the colonial mode of thought, in which white reign dictates that the natives are useful insofar as their cultures verify Western norms; deviations from those norms are ignored, adjusted, or destroyed. Gardner is not immune from this colonial imperative. For instance, he uses a paragraph on African musics to introduce a discussion on the applicability of Piagetian theory to musical development, followed by (Western) debates on the figural versus formal aspects of music (1993a, 110). At one point, he evokes the rest of the world (115), exclaiming about the "stunning range of attitudes toward the creation of music" (stunning to whom?), and, again, cursorily noting some cross-cultural examples that provide an illusion of multicultural inclusivity and scientific objectivity as a front for what remains a distinctly elitist, Eurocentric discourse.

But even within the norms of the Western canon, Gardner's analysis of music and culture falls short. When he notes that Mozart produced "permanent works in a genre" (1997, 60), he doesn't acknowledge two main points about the great master and his works. First, Mozart loved to improvise, to "play" with music and then later wrote down what sounded good. Second, genres and permanency were created by social sifting processes that left behind only several hundred symphonies out of more than twenty thousand composed. In light of these features of Western musical genius, one would need to ask questions like the following: Why not teach improvisation if the great master was first and foremost an improviser? How did some of these works and not others become "permanent works"? What happened to all the other works? Who decides which ones become permanent works? Though he seems to feel his Eurocentrism, Gardner does not engage his readers in any meaningful discussions to counter it.

Discussions of musical intelligence, which for Gardner seem intertwined with discussions of talent and the great masters of the Western tradition, are further complicated by debates currently raging in musicology and related fields. Two traditional camps, intramusical and extramusical, have been vying for authority in the field. To this mix one might add the recent infusion of cultural studies and feminist theory, not only in the extramusical camp, where they would appear to be at home, but in the intramusical camp, too (e.g., McClary 1991). Here, the music is seen to contain embodied social realities and relationships, cultural assumptions, and gendered or colonial biases. Although the whole notion of whether or not music can capture and communicate emotions and meaning is itself debatable (e.g., Keil & Feld 1994), if, as Gardner suggests, "Music can serve as a way of capturing feelings, knowledge about feelings, or knowledge about the forms of feeling, communicating them from the performer or the creator to the attentive listener" (1993a, 124), then we need to look at the full range of those feelings. For example, in McClary's (1991) reading of one great work of the Western canon, "the point of recapitulation in the first movement of Beethoven's Ninth Symphony unleashes one of the most horrifyingly violent episodes in the history of music" (28), an episode which Adrienne Rich (1973) saw much earlier, as articulated in her poem "The Ninth Symphony of Beethoven Understood at Last as a Sexual Message" (205–6). McClary's work is at the forefront of a new musicology that applies the usual tools of formalist analysis to the great Western canon, but which is not limited to the staid tradition of unquestioning veneration of the masters.

Musicologists have also begun to look closely at the social context of the great masters. Some of these studies focus on patronage and class and how genres were adopted or rejected. So, for example, while "Mozart may have begun to orient himself to a consciously articulated notion of masterpieces at a time when the prevailing winds of musical fashion were still directed away from . . . the 'unmeaning art and contrivance' of J. S. Bach," Beethoven's music "was recognized from the beginning as 'higher' and more 'learned'—as 'connoisseur's' music" (Bowen 1998, 15, citing DeNora 1995). Viennese aristocrats used Beethoven and emerging notions of "serious" music to maintain social distance from the middle class during a time of economic change. "Much of the groundwork for this shift occurred in the private world of aristocratic salons, particularly as activity in these salons centered on Beethoven, who was uniquely celebrated for the expressiveness and complexity of his compositions" (DeNora 1995, 18–19).

Similarly,

> Mozart's music was dragooned into cultural service "as the Kingpin of Salzburg's nationalist cosmopolitanism: the sharing of German culture with the outside world." Therefore, his unredeemed hero, Don Giovanni, was recruited by the Salzburg festival impresarios to play alongside Hofmannsthal's *Jedermann* (his adaptation of *Everyman*), and *The Magic Flute* became "a natural common denominator for Salzburg's Mozart and baroque cults and Third Reich *volkisch* ideology." Far from being the free-floating universal genius he has become since *Amadeus,* Mozart was right in the thick of cultural politics, as in fact his music has always been. (Said 1991, 57–58, citing Steinberg 1990).

This line of inquiry suggests that the artists Gardner and others venerate today, whose works are portrayed as timeless and universal, were intertwined with identity formation that favored different classes of people—and their music—over others. It is not too far of a leap, then, to see that they serve a similar function today, with recent arguments focusing on the moral worth and uplifting qualities of the classics, or of the so-called Mozart effect. But:

> If Beethoven could have been used as a propaganda device by the winning side, if Wagner could have been perverted to support the megalomaniac obscenity of Nazism, if concentration camp doctors could have spent their days performing unspeakable experiments on human beings and pass their evenings peacefully playing Mozart and Haydn quartets, where, then, was the moral authority claimed for the tradition? (Small 1980, 119)

What is now called "classical music" emerged from the vernacular traditions of different regions in Europe. The classics fed the vernacular as they were fed by it. Even the great masters, such as Mozart, were improvisers. And it is ironic indeed that the best of today's performers in this tradition have rarely composed a piece of their own, and improvisation is frowned upon. Instead, preservation has taken precedence over process (Small 1987), and culture has crystallized into civilization

(Keil & Feld 1994, 228). What has happened, in other words, is that later generations have canonized these cultural vernaculars into the "classics" of Western civilization, which was made possible by the composers themselves, who set down their works in visual scores, but which ultimately perpetuates the preservation of centuries-old elite culture.

The cultural politics that created the genres and styles that we venerate today are still at work, and once people realize this, then the classics will "either remain, or they will not, according to the extent to which they are found relevant to the lives of those who hear their music" (Small 1980, 219). Even within the West, the civilized classics are a small part of the sum total of musical possibilities and experiences. And besides, at the dawn of the twenty-first century, if there ever were a "universal" music style, it would certainly have to be those musics derived from the African Diaspora. So, too, would one need to take into consideration the mediating effects of mass culture and the still-lively vernacular musical traditions around the planet. Absent any mention of these factors, one would have to assume that they are either unworthy of consideration or that the Western classics are somehow intertwined with inviolable cultural themes of the West. All of these factors have the end result of alienating most people from attempting to participate in musicking of their own.

Music at the Altar of OWM

In an open letter to a university music department, Keil (1991) defined the parameters of a musical challenge into the twenty-first century: "How about setting a policy that all hiring over the next decade or two will be in the interests of broadening offerings in African-American, Afro-Latin, and World Music, until the rest of the world is at least on an equal footing with the Old White Male (OWM) west?" While history and English departments began dismantling their "OWM shrines" to broaden their perspectives earlier in the century, music departments have remained among the most conservative curators of the OWM tradition. And Keil is not alone in suggesting that there is a quasi-religious dimension to what he calls "OWM worship" (Kingsbury 1991) and that universities are curating the products of a world largely without women (McClary 1991). For any discussion of music, performance, talent, and intelligence to be meaningful, it is "vital to acknowledge the backwardness of musicology with regard to cultural and feminist theory, especially in comparison to literary, film, and performance studies" (Schwartz 1995).

Music at the altar of OWM also remains bound up with notions of the Absolute. Its staunchest proponents insist on the paradoxical position that the music is experienced both individually and as a universal. In other words, OWM worship encompasses everything except social and cultural realities. This is not to say that musicology is without its internal debates on these questions—quite the contrary, as noted above. Although one would not know it reading Gardner and his proponents, interdisciplinary approaches to musicology in the 1980s and 1990s shifted from analysis of structural patterns to methods that take into consideration the so-cial and political context of compositions (Agawu 1997).

Part of the problem here comes back to my earlier point of situating music and intelligence in the mind of the autonomous individual. For Gardner, formally rec-ognized individuals seem to matter most. When discussing music, he limits himself to exceptional individuals, those famous composers of the OWM canon. As the mu-sically intelligent are identified, it is their disciplined acclimation to the norms of OWM worship that will one day mark them as musically competent. This acclima-tion involves identifying the forms and meters and other conventions of the OWM corpus. Gardner is uneasy with the implicit race, gender, and class dynamics inher-ent in venerating the OWM corpus. Although he seems to believe that "music occu-pies a relatively low niche in our culture," he neglects the enormous popularity of pop, rock, rap, and other musics in the West, each with its own musical language and accepted competencies, yet not worthy of mention in the OWM orthodoxy. He is perhaps here just a victim of the discourse he cites, in this case mainstream conser-vative musicology. But, in a sense, this is the key to his whole enterprise. Whose dis-course will rule? While it may seem a noble intention for Gardner to dismantle and problematize the legacy of inequity in biases toward language and math, he does not allow himself to move beyond other stodgy norms of Western modernity.

Gardner (1993a) accords a great deal of weight to composing in his quest for the parameters of musical intelligence. He cites the composer Roger Sessions, who spoke of having "tones in his head," which is another defining feature of mu-sical intelligence. However, Gardner notes that much of this head music is "worth little musically," suggesting that some music is of value and other works not. The question becomes, who decides? Copland, Wagner, Saint-Saëns, and Schoenberg all seem to agree that there is a certain "naturalness of the act of composition," which leads Gardner into the debates on the role of language in music, in which Sessions and Stravinsky are archetypes of the assertion that "language plays no role in the act of composition." But language here seems to mean spoken language, in the compartmentalized realm of linguistic intelligence, which does not rule out the essentialist position that music is a sort of ineffable language, with the com-poser being its earthly translator, and that it is a medium of communication, usu-ally of specific emotions, but which in the end points to problems with the limita-tions of a highly disciplined discourse.

How music communicates, or what its message is, is more of a murky question, and one that ethnomusicologists have reflected upon. In many cases, listeners uti-lize a series of "interpretive moves" to bring alive a piece anew each time they lis-ten to it (Feld 1984). Gardner's lack of awareness of this discussion within musi-cology and its kindred disciplines is suggested by his relying instead on Copland, who insisted that listeners be educated (indoctrinated?) to achieve the skills needed to appreciate the finer points of Western art music, skills which Gardner likens to those of composing (1993a, 102). When Schoenberg says there is nothing in the music except the constant shaping of the original musical idea, Gardner still wants to understand this mysterious innate "musical lexicon," so he turns to another composer, Harold Shapero, who suggests that "the musical mind is concerned predominantly with the mechanisms of tonal memory," elevating melody and harmony over rhythm and texture, further revealing the Eurocentric foundations of Gardner's understanding of music and intelligence.

To this core set of attributes of musical intelligence, Gardner adds "audition," with the ironic reminder that some composers have produced works that can be appreciated entirely visually. But this colludes with the inherent visual bias in Western art music that relies on a written score for realization and articulation. Still other members of Gardner's OWM brigade cite affect and pleasure as defining factors of musical intelligence (1993a, 105). Here he sees, "in its most sophisticated terms, the claim that, if music does not in itself convey emotions or affects, it captures the *forms* of these feelings" (106). Even if one takes this assertion at face value, it means that music may embody all sorts of feelings, which leads Gardner to a discussion of music and emotions in which he cites Sessions on music capturing the "form" of culture-bound abstracted emotions such as fear and despair.

Subsequent to *Frames of Mind* and *Multiple Intelligences,* Gardner's work began to look in more detail at individuals that exemplify his theories of intelligence. In *Creating Minds* (1993c), he profiles seven individuals who exemplify each of his seven intelligences. He chose Stravinsky as the musical mind but cautions that what makes each of the creators great is their particular blend of intelligences. While Stravinsky (along with Gandhi) did not do well in school, Gardner (1993c, 363) emphasizes that this was not due to "any fundamental [presumably biological] intellectual flaw," but simply because of lack of (cultural?) interest. And,

> Stravinsky was interested in the world of children, but certainly did not dote on his own childhood and took no special pleasure in appearing to act like a child. He probably was most reminiscent of a child in his extraordinary litigious nature—his desire to pick, and then to win, every fight and, if possible, humiliate "the enemy" in the process. Like other modern artists, he anchored his work in the most basic elements of the medium—primitive rhythms and harmonies of the sort that had so impressed him when he was a young child. (Gardner 1993c, 366)

Gardner cites Stravinsky's famous assertion that music does not express anything by noting that the composer intended it as a rebuttal to those who would marshal music to nonmusical ends. Stravinsky wanted to replace "emotional self-expression with strictly musical statements" (1993c, 220), apparently contra Wagner and the Romanticists. Although Gardner would not see it as such, Stravinsky seems to have had a real flare for disputation—his "litigious nature," as Gardner puts it—suggesting that he might have had a proclivity toward "contra-personal intelligence." One could make a case for this across cultures, too, as in Talmudic and Qur'anic commentary, or Marxist dialectics. That Stravinsky fashioned himself in opposition to others is evident in his music, which constantly challenged the norms of nineteenth-century Romanticism. The *Rite of Spring* was Stravinsky's most challenging work (1993c, 200), and in it he marshaled forces to "shock, provoke, and challenge." Indeed it did, but though Stravinsky was initially panned for his waywardness, over the years he, too, became part of the OWM canon. This process is lost on Gardner, who seems to read present realities into the past. And the language used to discuss his work is conventional, as in when Gardner uses orthodox OWM language to describe Stravinsky's use of chromaticism for supernatural effects, diatonics for humanness, and "Oriental" strains for the Russia of yore (1993c, 196). This discussion also ignores Stravinsky's control fetish that ended up gutting jazz idioms, as evidenced by his *Ebony Concerto,* stiffly performed from score by Woody Herman's Orchestra.

While he venerates many of the canonical great men of Western music, Gardner reserves his true adulation for Mozart. In *Extraordinary Minds* (1997), he develops Mozart as an exemplar of mastery in a particular domain, one among a few "seminal artists." According to Gardner, Mozart as master had as his goal the complete mastery of the formal musical conventions of his day. Gardner boldly proclaims that Mozart's accomplishments in music "may have eclipsed those of any other human being in the realm of the arts" (55). Yet the master appears to have miraculously operated as a disembodied mind, "almost as if, independent of the events in his personal life and in the wider society, Mozart's brain had been set to produce a certain number of melodies and compositions per unit of time," attributes which characterize his high level of productivity (66). But Gardner gives short shrift to a key aspect of Mozart's approach to composition, as mentioned earlier: his reliance on improvisation. In fact, "Mozart seems to have regarded composition as the provision of something to play" (Small 1987, 51), suggesting his "playfulness" with the music.

Gardner seems to recognize the latter aspects, noting that "Mozart's music retains a simplicity and elegance that we associate with the innocence of childhood" (Gardner 1997, 67), but he fails to see beyond the blinders of OWM worship to discuss Mozart the improviser as well as the composer. And, true to OWM worship, improvisation does not even make the list of attributes for considering musical intelligence. Mozart himself would probably be aghast at how his playful art has been crystallized. The almost mythlike image of Mozart in *Extraordinary Minds* seems somehow closer to Hollywood than to any reality of the past. In fact, Gardner ascribes anachronistic agency to the long-dead master in saying that "Mozart has created our sense of the prodigy" (Gardner 1997, 67). No, he didn't; Hollywood, musicologists, and other scholars involved in OWM worship created Mozart the prodigy. This irony of cultural colonization eludes Gardner, who preaches the enduring popularity of Mozart's compositions "in every society to which they have been introduced" (67), thus dutifully propagating the gospel of OWM to the less fortunate minions of a perfectly colonial worldview.

Talent and Assessment

In one of his introductions to the concept of musical intelligence, Gardner (1993a) refers to "talent," which is "endowed" and a "gift," the "nature" of which is uncertain. But by invoking Bach and Mozart in this context, he is introducing readers directly into the world of Western musical monoculture and by implication setting its standards of taste and talent above others. After a few token cross-cultural references, Gardner suggests that, while "musical achievement is not strictly a reflection of inborn ability but is susceptible to cultural stimulation and training," it also "pays to have adequate or lavish genetic background" (112). To bolster this, he cites musical families from the OWM music tradition. Although he seems to sit on the fence between the nature–nurture debate, Gardner leans toward a "genetic proclivity" and "considerable genetic potential" as a necessary factor to "reach the heights of musical achievement," but which is liable to be unrealized or immature depending on upbringing and social conditions (113), the nature of which are vague. This view continues unabated right into one of his later works (1999), in which he also posits Mozart as the exemplar of beauty.

Despite his protestations to the contrary, Gardner offers no reasoned response to criticisms that his discussion of musical intelligence is elitist. As noted above, he is using the norms of OWM music culture as a baseline from which a few individuals can attain the highest degree of achievement as specialists according to its dictates. As Gardner the cultural spokesman declares, "Ultimately, any individual in our culture who would wish to gain musical competence should master formal musical analysis and representation," albeit "at a cost" (1993a, 111), thus reinforcing one of the key tenets of OWM worship. Although he senses that something is amiss here, in that the development of the formal mode will occur at the expense of the figurative, he is unable to conceptualize the two outside of a duality, pitting differences against each another. So, to Gardner, musical intelligence is an "ability" that can be identified in various quantities: "Leonard Bernstein had lots of it; Mozart, presumably, had even more" (Gardner 1993b, 15). And, in an individual-centered regime of assessment, "tests of musical intelligence would examine the individual's ability to analyze a work of music or to create one" (39). Gardner's insistence that musicality involves "knowing how to perform a piece of music to bring out its deeper structures or its contrasting moods" (1993b, 42) only further reinforces the gospel of OWM.

Gardner (1993b) suggests that it is not necessary for all individuals in a group to master multiple intelligences because, "so long as the individuals 'at promise' in particular domains are located efficiently, the overall knowledge of the group will be advanced in all domains" (29). Besides reinforcing the necessity of keeping the intelligences separate so that educators can locate and measure people for efficiency, the dilemma is to identify as many "at risk" individuals as possible in order to bring them closer to an "at promise" level. But one wonders, in light of all the discussion on the attributes of a musically intelligent or "at promise" individual, what would an "at risk" (musically stupid?) individual be like? One key seems to involve identifying early affective reactions to various domains, at which time more formal introduction into the intelligence can take place (29). This, presumably, must involve measurement, in the belief that a careful regime of testing will better serve pre-existing cultural proclivities by assigning people to what they do best. While

Gardner sees these insights as supporting individual-centered schooling, taken together with his emphasis on testing, such a regime could also lead to a rigid sorting and human profiling, in which cultures "profit" from individual differences and managers "are able to 'staff' our numerous roles and niches more effectively because people exhibit different profiles of intelligence" (1993b, 71). Framed in this way, the theory brings to mind a science fiction story by Orson Scott Card, from the *Monkey Sonatas,* in which children are tested at two and schooled into areas for which they are thought to be best suited, slotting people for life by intelligence.

Descriptions of testing and assessment abound in Gardner's work, as in, for example, his admonition that "one is assessing a complex compound of initial proclivities and societal opportunities" (Gardner 1993b, 222). While he seems to realize that intelligence cannot be measured in the abstract, that there cannot be separate tests for each intelligence, and that forms of performance-based assessment "would be ascertaining the nature and extent of previous experiences in the realm of music" (222), he still insists on measurement, the shared feature of most forms of testing and assessment. Even if teachers use a more subtle assessment regime that evolves over time, with the individual being observed by teachers and others who can examine "their profile of intelligences at work and play" (222), the utility of Gardner's theory is evident in that "individuals charged with assessing promise in the musical domain will be able to draw on findings from this eclectic approach to musical competence" (1993a, 108).

As the above examples suggest, in reading Gardner's work one is struck by his numerous references to locating, measuring, categorizing, testing, and assessing intelligence. Though he distances himself from his psychometric colleagues, he seems to share their proclivity toward assessments and testing. While the measurements of the early psychometricians are now seen for what they were, as racist and repressive mechanisms of social control and validation for white supremacy (Gould 1981; Kevles 1985; Kincheloe, Steinberg & Gresson 1996), the will to know via measurement remains. In Gardner's case, the rhetoric of social efficiency has been replaced with, and at times merges with, that of the human-potential movement. Both seem to value tests and assessments, although the latter with seemingly benign intention, but the will to measurement is still intertwined with the old inequities and injustices, particularly with respect to music and the concept of "talent" as understood in Western civilization. In this context, it is possible to realize that, extrapolating from Small (1980), Gardner is committed to the two major norms of late modernity: rationalist science and classicist music.

Whether one prefers authentic assessment, standardized testing, or any other ways of measuring achievement and talent in use today, they all lose sight of the profoundly human factors that bring the notes of a musical score to life but which are impossible to evaluate objectively. Nevertheless, music conservatories have developed what might be called a "feel" or "intuition" to decide who has talent, as opposed to mere skill, and who has the "right touch" and "emotional disposition" to truly and faithfully render the works of the great masters. What may appear to be an arbitrary process to outsiders is subject to the norms and allegiances of those within the conservatory cultural system, a process which in the end determines who will go on to become concert soloists and who will become accompanists (Kingsbury 1988). Students entering into this cultural system assign meaning to this social construction of talent "to help them in developing strategies to negotiate their way in the community" (Roberts 1990). Paradoxically, as Kingsbury (1984) has noted, "an appraisal of talent is an ex post facto judgment" that is assessed based on performance; therefore in the conservatory cultural system, talent "is a symbol of inequality of potential." This paradox "occasionally leads students into the dilemma where knowledge about a supposed or assumed talent is incongruent with observed knowledge about a performance" (Roberts 1990).

Assessment of talent also relies on "speech about music" (Feld 1984), with the norms of interpretation embodied in the language the experts use to talk about music, talent, and performance. Yet the mystical world of assessing talent demands linguistic vigilance from students entering into the system. Kingsbury (1991) found that, "although 'music' is quite literally a sacred notion within the conservatory, each class is organized in terms of a specific (hence secularized, mundane, practical) topical problem" (203). He concludes that one of the key lessons that conservatory students learn is a "sociocultural skill in the use of verbal imagery" and "how to use and invoke the notion of music" and other socially defined concepts like talent, expression, and feeling (203). At the same time, "the myriad senses of the word 'music' should be understood as at once the social grammar and the social poetic of a rather closely associated community, and that the various uses of the word are in fact learned in the context of interaction in and among such a community" (203). While students subjected to such a regime of assessment learn to work the system, what this suggests is that notions of talent are socially constructed and maintained in a complex ecology of meaning and power. To the extent that influential scholars like Gardner normalize such manifestations of conservatory culture, its assumptions will continue to colonize experience.

Since in the end music is something to be experienced in many different ways, we should be wary of theories that limit possibilities. For example, while he respects and writes about the theory of multiple intelligences with some enthusiasm, Keil also warns that:

> there are alienation effects, misplaced concreteness, misleading objectifications in this literature that, no matter how welcome the news is about the importance of musicking and dancing to full human growth and development, must finally be put aside in favor of a model that stresses one tightly integrated if multifaceted intelligence and one brain inside a whole human being. (1998, 40)

Keil also suggests that debates around multiple versus unitary intelligences are intertwined with broader debates about class versus classless society, and, following Marx, believes the key to good living and good education is for each person to embody the full range of potentials.

So, while the theory of multiple intelligences helps to clarify that there is more to being human than mastering math and language skills, it could also "point toward a world in which the educator's job is to find and bring out the single intelligence that a child is best at, so that society finds niches for and integrates lopsided individuals into an efficient division of labor in which everyone is supposedly happiest doing mostly what they do best" (43). Keil recognizes with others, that, at the end of the day, testing and assessment justify and explain social hierarchies (Lewontin 1991; Hubbard & Wald 1999). No matter how benevolent or broad-minded it might be, any regime of testing and assessment, especially one which relies on unexamined constructs of talent and competition, which has pretensions of universal biologism, and which does not directly address legacies of inequity, will result in success for a few, failure for many, and unjust hierarchy for all, hardly a supportive setting for good musicking.

Adventures in Musical Stupidity

Christopher Small has suggested that everyone "is born capable of musicking" (1987, 52), while John Sloboda has observed that "our society—particularly our system of formal education—is set up to produce a large number of musical 'walking wounded'" (1993, 112). This prompted Allen Farmelo (1997) to ask questions such as, "How is it that people come to be musicians or non-musicians? If born fully capable, why are so many of us walking-wounded?" Part of the answer is that people are sorted by the kind of assessment regimes advocated by many adherents of multiple intelligences methodology. A more sinister function of formal assessment is to give objectivity to failure, providing people with the tools to recognize forms of inferiority and stupidity. American academics have a hard time talking about stupidity with any degree of sensitivity or complexity. This is understandable, since, with a few exceptions, the discourse is either crass and racist, blaming the victims of unjust social systems, or fraught with well-meaning denial and apology. This is due in part to the horrid legacy of the American treatment of stupidity. The connection of Darwin and Galton between intelligence, heredity, and evolution, coupled with the rediscovery of genetics at the turn of the century, resulted in a wide-ranging movement to measure and classify intelligence.

At first, researchers busied themselves by assigning IQs to one another and to Old White Men of the past, but eventually the new science of intelligence was put to work for public policy. Immigration laws barred "idiots, lunatics, and epileptics" and others deemed "feebleminded," with some academics even calling for castration and sterilization to prevent continuity of hereditary stupidity. The eugenics movement gained momentum in the early part of the twentieth century, but when the Nazis put the theories to practice on a larger scale, eugenics became tarnished as a valid science. Though some still cling to its basic tenets, in general, adherence to eugenicist thought remains a barometer for detecting racism and other forms of bias in American culture (Kincheloe, Steinberg & Gresson 1996). This is partly the legacy that Gardner seeks to discredit, too, with his vigilant denunciation of the psychometricians and the cultural literacy movement. But discrediting a particularly virulent form of scientific racism should not be equated with the belief that stupidity does not exist, despite even the most polite academic aversions. I wish to suggest a different way of dealing with stupidity.

Education scholars and activists committed to social justice have developed ways of talking about stupidity without resorting to the barbarisms of the psychometricians and without linking intelligence to dominant Western cultural values. Macedo (1994) uses the term "stupidification" to describe "linguistic games that disfigure reality" (6), which are embedded in educational practices that focus on formal, procedural, and behavioral matters at the expense of larger economic, cultural, and sociopolitical factors that perpetuate race, class, and gender bias. Gatto's (1992) "seven-lesson schoolteacher," who teaches a hidden curriculum of confusion, class position, indifference, emotional dependency, intellectual dependency, provisional self-esteem, and surveillance, has contributed to "dumbing down" children. Shujaa (1994), building on the classic work of Carter Woodson (1933), considers the paradox of "too much schooling, too little education" for black Americans. From Bowers's (1995) conservative ecological perspective, "[u]nintelligent behavior would be seen as any behavior, way of thinking, and moral judgment that degrades the environment" (132). These and other works raise questions about theories of intelligence that do not address stupidity. Fixating on assessment of musical intelligence, coupled with venerating the OWM musical canon, obscures or avoids the more politically and socially significant questions of why many people cannot participate in musicking in their daily lives. For education based on multiple intelligence to be meaningful and just, it needs to take into account what might be called "multiple stupidities."

What I am calling musical stupidity comes in many shapes and forms and has been observed by others. For example, based on decades of teaching Afro-Latin musical praxis to college students, Keil (1990 and 1998) tentatively identified what he calls the "seven incapacities, blocks or obstacles" to participating in musical cultures and developing full musical expression, which include pathological behaviors such as lack of coordination, lack of entrainment, visual dependency, and gender distortion. Building on Keil's work, Allen Farmelo (1997) gave a paper at a popular music conference on the five discourses that block children from learning music and hinder good musicking, which are: inherent talent, musical intelligence, virtuosity obsession, literacy training, and the professional–amateur discourse. Whether we refer to them as incapacities, obstacles, or hindrances, they are worth exploring in some detail within the context of musical intelligence.

For many students lack of coordination is a major obstacle to good musicking. A surprising number of young adults, who may be avid consumers of music, are unable to maintain even a rudimentary steady beat with their hands and feet, much less tap and clap the multiple rhythms necessary for Afro-Latin musics. Keil suggests that this may be because no one ever asked students to keep steady time, that it did not dawn on teachers to ask them. This reflects the OWM bias of music education, teaching students to listen and analyze. Keil found that students who have trouble with drumming are "unentrained," that is, they are unable to synchronize their movements with others. Following the insights of quantum mechanics and cybernetics, as developed in the work of anthropologist Edward T. Hall (1983), entrainment in music means "getting into the groove." Keil noticed that some students can groove alone but not in groups, while others can groove in groups but not alone.

In any case, sustained entrainment seems necessary for good musicking. Being self-conscious overlaps with coordination and entrainment, which points to teaching methods and classroom ecologies as somewhat controllable variables. Keil also noticed that some students got worse when he offered help, while others got worse when he praised them. Since this is a function of classroom ecology, he suggests keeping the focus on the group and working with individuals outside the group setting. Like the other stupidities, being self-conscious is a learned behavior, ingrained by early adulthood, and resulting from insufficient socialization. Visual dependency appears to be a key obstacle to good drumming, especially in students who have learned music notation and feel insecure learning without a notated score. The visual focus on the score as "the music" has incapacitated people who, in another context, may be competent and even brilliant musicians. Keil (1998) suggests that "in a society where 'seeing is believing' in print or on television, there may be a shadow of unreliability to contend with whenever people are interacting with sound and action toward a goal of cohesion" (40).

The fifth obstacle to good musicking is over-specialization. This is especially apparent when people who may have achieved a degree of competence on one instrument try to learn another instrument, or in attempting to learn across styles and in different cultural contexts. As Keil puts it, "things already learned are in the way of new learning." Keil found that gender distortion is a thread running through the first five incapacities, with men and women reacting differently as they encounter and try to deal with the other obstacles to good drumming. As McClusky (1990) suggests, the "politics of vision" may alienate, not only promote, learning in a group setting, especially in the context of the male gaze objectifying women, and notes that teachers can pay attention to the differences and similarities between looking and listening. Keil's seventh incapacity stems from students being "hyper-cultured," referring to the years spent listening to commodified and mediated musics that may have developed an aesthetic, "a definition of good music, that may not let them grasp the subtleties of timing when it comes to drumming with others" (Keil 1998, 40).

Though he urges more research into these areas, I think Keil's incapacities suggest a framework for talking about what I would call "musical stupidity." However, I also agree with Keil that these are "analytically abstractable aspects," that they are not inborn or somehow coded in our being, but that they are intertwined with alienation from our bodies, each other, nature, and musicking, and that, in the end, the "seven stupidities" are socially constructed and therefore socially solvable. Shorn of the proclivity to rank people in social hierarchies, stupidity is actually generative of meaningful questions and serves as a useful heuristic for understanding and action. Along those lines, I would also add an eighth stupidity, which arises in cross-cultural and intercultural situations. For example, when Mozart memorized Allegri's *Miserere,* he basically "removed" the piece from its sanctuary in a chapel, which Gardner hails as a legendary feat (Gardner 1997, 55), but which could also be seen as an act of "stupidity," given the reverence accorded to the work by its protectors.

The same point is more apparent in cross-cultural situations. Anthropologists and ethnomusicologists often proceed from their own cultural stupidity to gain cross-cultural insights that are respectful of indigenous knowledge. While doing research with Yemeni musicians, Schuyler (1990) tried to perform a classical Turkish instrumental piece, which turned out to be a stupid thing to do in a cultural setting that valued vocal music over instrumental music but which led to insights into indigenous performance practice. When Feld was busying himself with categorizing birds in the Bosavi rainforest and trying to get a handle on indigenous taxonomies, his Kaluli interlocutor reminded him that "to you they are birds, to me they are voices in the forest" (Feld 1982, 45), which led Feld to the realization of indigenous natural history as part of a cultural system that integrated birds, weeping, and song into forms of expression. As these examples suggest, research across cultures is about identifying and remediating our own stupidities. The colonial imperative ignores this and instead presses other cultures into service to verify or extend Western understandings of how the world works.

Another aspect of this issue, which is relevant to our discussion, has been addressed by Small (1980, 36). In an attempt to broaden horizons for accepting and exploring musicking outside the West, Small recommends rejecting a number of cultural assumptions. With apologies, I think it fair to term these "stupidities" as well, given the heuristic I am trying to develop here, since without rejecting or rethinking these assumptions (incidentally, there are seven of them), we risk the danger of reproducing Western norms as universals. Here they are:

1. music as a self-contained art, to be contemplated for its own sake;
2. musical compositions as abstract entities, which can be communicated from performer to audience;
3. harmony and counterpoint as the supreme expressions of human musicking;
4. pitch as more important than timbre and texture as structural elements;
5. normalization of an impoverished sense of rhythm;
6. music as linear and teleological;
7. reliance on formalized structure to maintain a sense of time and space.

Normalizing these Western cultural peculiarities excludes "deviations," which in this case includes most other musicking on the planet. To build and implement a theory of musical intelligence that does not take into critical consideration one's own cultural norms (and deviations) borders on white supremacy and cultural imperialism. It is also patently unfair to foist such a narrow and exclusive view of music on students in the name of education and individually centered schooling within a culturally plural and diverse society. Normalizing the narrow modern

Western notion of music is also connected to various performance pathologies, which again returns us to the previous set of "musical stupidities."

While the enumeration and description of musical stupidities might increase ad absurdum, they can open a useful dialogue to uncover the flip side of musical intelligence, which allows us to talk about the powers and processes that get intertwined with learning good musicking, either as a performer or as an observer. The concept of musical stupidity can serve the dual function of complicating and complimenting musical intelligence. In Hall's (1983) work on "out of awareness culture," he identifies three levels of culture, one of which he terms "primary culture." In primary culture, norms are known and obeyed by all but are not stated and occur "out of awareness." His research on out-of-awareness culture includes detailed study of films depicting human interaction, and one theory Hall supports is that meaningful out-of-awareness human interaction is made up of microtimed phenomena, visible only when the films are slowed down. Hall is convinced that these primary-level ways of interacting can be completely different from culture to culture, and he calls this out-of-awareness microtimed human interaction "entrainment."

Viewing his work in terms of positive implications, Hall sees a certain urgency in engaging primary-level culture, suggesting that if human beings don't spend more time figuring out how entrainment works (and doesn't work), there is going to be a lot more intolerance and destruction in the world. If Keil is right about his students' being unentrained and that some form of entrainment is necessary for good musicking, then Hall's work might be suggesting that a lack of entrainment in musicking is indicative of larger cultural problems that extend beyond musicking. This suggests that one way to become entrained, to "get into the groove," whether with Yemenis, or birds, or each other, is to promote ways of musicking that are independent of the elite Western culture-bound proclivities that Gardner seems to favor in his rather ungroovy notion of musical intelligence.

References

Agawu, K. (1997). Analyzing music under the new musicological regime. *Journal of Musicology* 15(3), 297–308.

Bateson, G. (1972). *Steps to an ecology of mind*. New York: Ballantine Books.

Bowen, J. (1998). [Review of Tia DeNora, *Beethoven and the Construction of Genius: Musical Politics in Vienna, 1792–1803*]. *19th Century Music*, 22(1), 91–100.

Bowers, C. (1995). *Educating for an ecologically sustainable culture: Rethinking moral education, creativity, intelligence, and other modern orthodoxies*. Albany: State University of New York Press.

DeNora, T. (1995). *Beethoven and the construction of genius: Musical politics in Vienna, 1792–1803*. Berkeley: University of California Press.

Farmelo, A. (1997). *Producing musicians and non-musicians*. Paper presented at the 42nd Annual Meeting of the Society for Ethnomusicology with the International Association for the Study of Popular Music, U.S. Chapter, October. Pittsburgh, PA.

Faruqi, L. (1984). Unity and variety in the music of Islamic culture. In Y. Haddad et al. (eds.), *The Islamic impact* (pp. 127–143). Syracuse, NY: Syracuse University Press.

Feld, S. (1982). *Sound and sentiment: Birds, weeping, poetics, and song in Kaluli expression.* Philadelphia: University of Pennsylvania Press.

——. (1984). Communication, music, and speech about music. *Yearbook for Traditional Music, 16,* 1–18.

Gardner, H. (1993a). *Frames of mind: The theory of multiple intelligences.* New York: Basic Books.

——. (1993b). *Multiple intelligences: The theory in practice.* New York: Basic Books.

——. (1993c). *Creating minds. An anatomy of creativity seen through the lives of Freud, Einstein, Picasso, Stravinsky, Eliot, Graham, and Gandhi.* New York: Basic Books.

——. (1997). *Extraordinary minds: Portraits of exceptional individuals and an examination of our extraordinariness.* New York: Basic Books.

——. (1999). *The disciplined mind: What all students should understand.* New York: Simon & Schuster.

Gatto, J. (1992). *Dumbing us down: The hidden curriculum of compulsory schooling.* Philadelphia: New Society Publishers.

Gould, S. (1981). *The mismeasure of man.* New York: W. W. Norton.

Hall, E. (1983). *The dance of life: The other dimension of time.* New York: Anchor Books.

Hubbard, R., & Wald, E. (1999). *Exploding the gene myth.* Boston: Beacon Press.

Keil, C. (1990). Blocks to good drumming. *M.U.S.E. Letter 1,* 21–6.

——. (1991). An open letter to the Music Department. *Generation, 12,* 6.

——. (1998). Incorporating the Muses. *Radical Teacher 52,* 37–43.

Keil, C., & Feld, S. (1994). *Music grooves: Essays and dialogues.* Chicago: University of Chicago Press.

Kevles, D. J. (1985). *In the name of eugenics: Genetics & the uses of human heredity.* New York: Alfred A. Knopf.

Kincheloe, J., Steinberg, S., & Gresson, A. (1996). *Measured lies: The bell curve examined.* New York: St. Martin's Press.

Kingsbury, H. (1984). *Music as a cultural system: Structure and process in an American conservatory.* Unpublished Ph.D. dissertation, Indiana University, Bloomington.

——. (1988). *Music, talent, and performance: A conservatory cultural system.* Philadelphia: Temple University Press.

——. (1991). Sociological factors in musicological poetics. *Ethnomusicology, 35*(2), 195–219.

Lewontin, R. (1991). *Biology as ideology: The doctrine of DNA.* New York: HarperCollins.

Macedo, D. (1994). *Literacies of power: What Americans are not allowed to know.* Boulder, CO: Westview Press.

McClary, S. (1991). *Feminine endings: Music, gender, and sexuality.* Minneapolis: University of Minnesota Press.

McClusky, L. (1990). Looking and learning to drum: The paradox of vision in learning participation. *M.U.S.E. Letter, 1,* 27–44.

Rich, A. (1973). *Diving into the wreck.* New York: W. W. Norton.

Roberts, B. A. (1990). Social construction of talent by Canadian university music education majors." *Canadian Journal of Research in Music Education, 32* (2), 62–73.

Said, E. (1991). *Musical elaborations.* New York: Columbia University Press.

Schuyler, P. (1990). Hearts and minds: Three attitudes toward performance practice and music theory in the Yemen Arab Republic. *Ethnomusicology, 34*(1), 1–18.

Schwartz, J. (1995). Feminism and musicology: The reception of Susan McClary's feminine endings. 5 July 1999, *www.gslis.utexas.edu/~jeffs/mcclary.html*

Shujaa, M. (ed.). (1994). *Too much schooling, too little education: A paradox of black life in white societies*. Trenton, NJ: Africa World Press.

Slaboda, J. (1993). Musical ability. *CIBA Foundation Symposium, 178,* 106–18.

Small, C. (1980). *Music, society, education*. London: John Calder Publishers.

———. (1987). *Music of the common tongue*. London: John Calder Publishers.

Steinberg, M. (1990). *The meaning of the Salzburg Festival: Austria as theatre and ideology, 1890–1938*. Ithaca, NY: Cornell University Press.

Woodson, C. (1933). *The mis-education of the Negro*. Washington, DC: Associated Publishers.

Chapter 4

Peter Appelbaum

WHERE IS THE MATHEMATICS?
WHERE ARE THE MATHEMATICIANS?

The multiple intelligences approach encourages teachers to regard intellectual ability more broadly than they might have done otherwise. We are able to see that visual arts, music, and dance can be just as valuable to students' understanding of the world they live in as traditional academic subjects; we are also able to imagine new ways that our students can demonstrate their understanding of concepts. Numerous teachers and administrators have applied aspects of multiple intelligences theory in their classrooms and schools. This chapter focuses on the use of multiple intelligences in the teaching and learning of mathematics. Of particular concern is the role of the theory in codifying commonly held misconceptions regarding the nature of mathematical thought and practice. Because one of the intelligences is named in honor of mathematics, the "logical-mathematical intelligence," I worry about the ways that people are likely to assume that the intelligence is highly correlated with mathematical thinking in general, and therefore how they may be tempted to limit the possibilities for mathematical activity in and out of the classroom.

Multiple Intelligences in Theory

Howard Gardner believes that students will develop a passion for exploring truly profound ideas through the serious and in-depth study of just a few subjects rather than a minimal amount of attention to many subjects. One way to enact this in the mathematics classroom is to spend long periods of time on in-depth investigations rather than to spread the curriculum helter-skelter into isolated tidbits of mathematical ideas and facts. During these investigations, students should be encouraged to demonstrate in as many ways as possible their multiple intelligences, the unique and special ways that they solve problems or fashion products that are valued in one or more cultural settings. We should ask, in what ways do our students solve problems mathematically? In what ways do they fashion mathematical products? In contemporary mathematics education practice, the cultural settings include the classroom, everyday life, applications to other mathematics topics, and students' reflections on their understanding of themselves as problem solvers and posers.

In the ideal classroom, mathematical investigations would incorporate opportunities for students to display all of Gardner's "intelligences." Students should be using language effectively as a vehicle of communication and expression (linguistic intelligence). Students should be thinking logically, using numbers effectively to solve problems scientifically, and they should be discerning relationships and patterns between concepts and things (logical-mathematical intelligence). Students should be thinking visually and orienting themselves spatially; they should also be representing their visual and spatial ideas graphically (spatial intelligence). Students should be using musical patterns and forms as a means of expression, appreciating and discriminating among differences in rhythm, pitch, and melody (musical intelligence). Students should be using their bodies skillfully as a means of expression, and they should be able to create and manipulate objects (bodily-kinesthetic intelligence). Students should be appropriately and effectively responding to others in the classroom, understanding their feelings, perspectives, and ideas (interpersonal intelligence). Students should be able to accurately know themselves, including knowledge of their own strengths, motivations, goals, and feelings in posing and solving mathematical problems, in planning and carrying out mathematical investigations, and in communicating their ideas to others (intrapersonal intelligence). In addition to these intelligences, students should be using mathematical processes to associate themselves with nature, animals, and the environment (environmental intelligence), and to demonstrate the sensitivity and capacity to tackle deep questions about human existence, such as the meaning of life or why we die (existential intelligence).

In my teaching, I can use these multiple intelligences for planning and assessment. As part of both processes, I can think about what my students will be doing or what they are or have been doing and ask how I know that my students are working and thinking in ways that allow them to use their multiple intelligences. Assessment of an individual's multiple intelligences can foster learning and problem-solving styles. By knowing more about each of my students' tendencies to use one or more of the intelligences, I can make it possible both for them to capitalize on these strengths and to develop the other intelligences more fully. I do not use short-answer tests because they do not measure disciplinary mastery or deep understanding; they only measure rote memorization skills and one's ability to do well on such tests. Instead, most of my evaluation techniques value process over the final answer. I structure learning activities around an issue or question, and connect seemingly unrelated subjects, so that my students can demonstrate multiple ways of understanding and value their uniqueness.

However, I am challenged by the conception of mathematics that seems to be constructed through the multiple intelligences theory. First of all, one of the intelligences is named with mathematics as part of its title, suggesting that mathematics is limited to this specific area of intelligence. This does not resonate with my own experiences in mathematics, nor does it appear to do justice to the glorious variety of mathematical ways of being that I want to share with my students. Second, multiple intelligences theory seems to acknowledge diversity in the strengths and interests of my students yet also tends to pigeonhole them as potentially more or less interested in mathematizing than others. This is a problem, since I want to facilitate *all* students' enthusiasm and engagement with mathematics.

Where Has the Mathematics Gone?

One cannot adequately understand mathematics as the focus of the logical-mathematical intelligence. Instead, I would posit that the notion of this intelligence is more a symptom of a poor understanding of the nature of mathematics than an example of a clever understanding of intelligence. Describing mathematical intelligence as having mostly to do with thinking logically, working with numbers and acting scientifically makes it difficult to appreciate the aesthetics of mathematics, the irrationality of much of mathematics, the personal relationship that many people experience with mathematical ideas, and, in general, the humanistic qualities of mathematics as a human endeavor. Lumping mathematical thinking with logic, yet separating it from verbal communication or the kinesthetic experience of space, for example, denies mathematics the very erotic pleasures, emotional interactions, and social politics that lie at the center of its educational potential. If teaching and learning mathematics were proscribed by the logical-mathematical intelligence, then it would be pretty much impossible to ask important or significant questions of mathematics or to expect of mathematics that it contribute much of anything to any of the other intelligences Gardner proposes.

The logical-mathematical intelligence appears to me to be premised on a number of assumptions about mathematics and logic. First of all, it assumes a kind of "givenness" of the mathematical and the logical. One solves problems that are given. One uses systems of logic that are provided by the culture. There is no room for posing one's own problems, questioning what problems are of most worth, challenging the presumptions of a problem, or questioning the legitimacy of a logical system. Indeed, the intelligence seems to imply a sort of simultaneity of mathematics and logic, in turn, suggesting that logic alone rules how we are to make sense of mathematics. There is in this construction no appreciation for the political, aesthetic, and social contexts that influence the evolution of mathematics or that might direct its future development, let alone the ways in which it might be learned. I am left with a wonderless mathematics, a discipline only caricatured by this intelligence, which seems to imagine a mathematics devoid of controversy, paradox, conundrum, or complexity. Only an uninformed educator would conceive of mathematics as if the basic ideas emerged without any pain or controversy or as if all mathematical conclusions were logical deductions, primarily about numbers, predetermined and certain.

By separating the logical-mathematical from related forms of intellectual activity, the theory makes no place for the "self" or "others" in the mathematical experience. Yet for me and my students, mathematics is at once a highly introspective and social encounter. There is no way for mathematics to take place without it leading to a reflection on oneself as a poser and solver of mathematical investigations, or without the communication of one's ideas to others. Nor can mathematics take place without an interest in understanding the approaches, feelings, and meanings of others' mathematical ideas. I understand that scientific descriptions are meant to highlight features of holistic systems and that they are not meant to be more than one partial explanation. Nevertheless, to apply in a classroom the logical-mathematical intelligence distinct from the others is akin to pulling apart the threads of a rope in preparation for mountain climbing. What are we to make of the erased sketches we find on students' papers? Stephen Brown notes that, by hiding what she really thought about mathematics, we are led to believe that her thoughts held very little meaning for her. If these erasures were to be excluded, and if she was embarrassed by her need to resort to their use, we must imagine that it is a weakness to have to engage one's mind in creating images and metaphors that are fundamentally human baggage in all other fields of inquiry (Brown 2001, 20) We are further led to believe that there is something unique about the way in which one thinks in mathematics. Though we might make connections to everyday life for motivational purposes and though we might tolerate or even encourage inductive strategies as part of early stages in mathematical thinking, ultimately, if this intelligence is to make sense, the deductive nature of mathematical thought distinguishes it as a way of knowing from all other world experiences. Yet my students use metaphor, poetry, music, theater, writing, and dance in mathematics class, and they think of mathematics as poetry, music, theater, writing, and dance that they share with each other.

Finally, the logical-mathematical intelligence appears to strip mathematics of awe and wonder. There seems to be little to surprise us, almost nothing to make us disoriented or appropriately perplexed, still less to dream about. If mathematics is to be understood within the logical-mathematical intelligence, then, as a teacher, I cannot locate agency in the subject matter or in the pedagogical practice. Nevertheless, in my classroom, students honor the role of intuition, not only in understanding but also in creating concepts that appear only later, in a highly polished presentation format, to be technical or scientific. They recognize that competition, cooperation, holistic metaphors and representations, and value judgments are important in the growth of any area of inquiry, including mathematics. They understand that logic does not tell them when and where to study what; they challenge each other to account for what is investigated, how it was analyzed, and why this and not something else was the focus of the investigation. Students work within ill-defined situations to map out potential directions for mathematical exploration.

In other words, the logical-mathematical intelligence is not synonymous with mathematics as a discipline but carries with it commonly held misconceptions about mathematics as a field of inquiry. By perpetuating the stereotype of mathematics as logical, given, mostly about numbers, and highly scientific, this intelligence makes it even more difficult than it already is to cultivate mathematics as a humanistic enterprise. As a teacher of mathematics I do not welcome the association of mathematics with this intelligence, even if it is in name only. Because the intelligence sounds so much like the common stereotype of mathematics, I am led to believe that the intelligence really does mean to convey this misunderstood reception of mathematics *as* the intelligence, mischaracterizing both mathematics and intelligence in general.

Where Have the Mathematicians Gone?

My second concern has to do with the ramifications of understanding students as unique in their intelligences. Surely I appreciate the ways that multiple intelligences open up our comprehension of "intelligence" for new possibilities. But I wonder about how my students can act like mathematicians in my classroom if they are strong in only some of the intelligences and not in others. Rather than democratize intelligence to include more potential ways of demonstrating mathematical skills, understanding, and applications, the theory requires that I comprehend my students as potentially weak in some areas as well as particularly strong in others. On the one hand, I can now acknowledge that one of my students might be especially adept at communicating her ideas to another student in my class (interpersonal intelligence) while finding it challenging to reflect on her own approaches to problem-solving (intrapersonal intelligence). I can appreciate that a student may be highly attracted to his mathematics journal (verbal-linguistic intelligence) but uninterested in composing a rap song about his latest investigation (musical intelligence). Yet mathematicians exhibit *all* of these intelligences. Students are sometimes too quick to analyze themselves in ways that justify a self-perception often articulated as "I'm not a math person." Yet students can be fine mathematicians without being particularly oriented toward the brainteasers, numerical patterns, and chains of reasoning emphasized in the logical-mathematical intelligence. I want to comprehend each of my students as individuals who have fully realized and developed their intelligences, including those related to experiencing their world in mathematical ways. But it is almost as if some of my students have been given free license to disdain geometry even as they refine their three-point shots in basketball, while others can be excused from introspective journalizing about problem-solving strategies only to write a poetic memoir during the next period of the school day. Rather than avoiding a connection with the natural world, mathematicians search for representations of mathematical ideas in the natural world. Instead of working alone, mathematicians must be prepared to communicate their insights to others; to be good at this, they must be able to understand others' interests and perspectives. It is a slippery slope from "I am not mathematical" to "I can't do mathematics," and it is challenging to distinguish between these two things. Surely a highly verbal person should be able to verbalize about numbers, shapes, patterns, quantities, information, and possibility. Clearly a highly kinesthetic person should be able to use her body in ways that represent pattern, shape, number, quantity, quality, possibility, and information. A mathematician finds the mathematical in the verbal, kinesthetic, musical, logical, spatial, existential, intrapersonal, interpersonal, and natural worlds.

Thinking mathematically requires that a mathematician suspend logic. A mathematician revels in the absurd, in the incongruous, in the ineffable. Given a clearly logical statement, a mathematician challenges the statement by asking, When is it not true? When can I not know whether it is true or not? What if this did not logically follow? The previous century of mathematics has been a string of such mathematical insights. Gödel's incompleteness theorem helped us understand that we often can never prove something logically within the system that includes what we want to prove. Cantor's continuum hypothesis can be proved neither true nor false. This has been "proven," oddly enough. Statistics is nothing but the study of the unknown, using questionable assumptions about what we do know. Euclidean geometry, once the paradigm of a logical system, is understood as a special case of many possible geometries, none of which make the same irrational assumptions about geometry or our lived world. Chaos theory challenges our notions of the quantifiable and predictable while introducing new models of our known and unknown world. Game theory tells us that the best outcomes of competitive games often result from the least intuitive forms of cooperation rather than competition. To live as a mathematician, one needs to think poetically about ideas not dramatized in quite the same way before, to interact with nature using a new language, to translate one person's mathematical questions into a different set of assumptions using another perspective. In other words, to live as a mathematician is to breathe metaphor, to dance logic, to invent new recipes for unseen occasions.

Logical-Mathematical Intelligences in the Classroom

This is why I find the best use of multiple intelligences to be in supporting students' understanding of their own learning. I can create rubrics in which they must think about each form of intelligence and find examples of how they have used that intelligence. I can ask them to suggest new intelligences of their own that they have been using in their mathematical explorations. Indeed, this can be a problem-solving strategy: Stuck? Don't know what to do next? Try another intelligence; invent your own intelligence and use it. My other favorite use of multiple intelligences is in encouraging students to choose their own format for demonstrating their understanding of the material. They can reflect on each of the intelligences and combine two or three in a project that uses the most important ideas and skills that they have been working with in their mathematical investigations (Appelbaum 1998). In this way, assessment for each student is unique, and the student has a critical role in the design and implementation of the curriculum. If students develop a profile of themselves as learners and then use the profile to understand the ways in which they seem to learn easily, then they can determine how to use their strengths to help themselves be more successful in other endeavors. The profile becomes a way to understand oneself better, to catapult oneself to a better level of understanding or to a higher level of skill (Checkley 1997). Students can also use this profile to identify those areas they wish to work on more. Rather than relying on their strengths, they can focus on improving their weaknesses. A teacher would need to be sensitive to this use of multiple intelligences, as, according to the theory, students who are working with their weaker intelligences will not be the most efficient learners of the material. This has to be not only acceptable but preferable, if students are to develop and grow as learners and mathematicians.

The danger is when teachers start to think that the logical-mathematical intelligence is what mathematics is about.

> Do you often solve arithmetic problems in your head? Do you enjoy playing chess or checkers? Do you find yourself categorizing and classifying objects? Consider how you draw upon your logical-mathematical ability in your work and recreational activities. As you assess your logical-mathematical intelligence, determine where you would place this intelligence area on a graph of your intellectual profile. (ASCD)

Few mathematicians would characterize mathematics as a collection of brainteasers, and while some might enjoy working out an occasional arithmetic problem in their head, most would disdain arithmetic as hardly mathematical. Yet the Association for Supervision and Curriculum Development uses Gardner's theory to encourage lessons that feature brainteasers and require that students do mental calculations; use an interdisciplinary approach that allows students to discover scientific and mathematical connections in history, geography, social studies, and literature; incorporate number games into lessons; employ logical-mathematical centers—math labs and separate areas to conduct scientific experiments—in the classroom; and use strategies such as Socratic questioning and heuristics to give students experience in defending their hypotheses and testing their logic. Such examples perpetuate the stereotyped notion of mathematics as strongly supporting of and describable by the logical-mathematical intelligence.

Preservice teachers are often asked to unearth multiple intelligences in the lessons they observe. In one activity, "multiple intelligences bingo" (Sadker & Sadker 2003, 124–25), future teachers carry bingo cards with a list of multiple intelligences and search for examples of the intelligences exhibited in one of several classrooms, either during instruction or in a display or instructional material. The goal is to fill every slot on the card. The activity asks players to consider whether any observed classrooms were filled with examples of the multiple intelligences approaches to learning, and in how many minutes. Players reflect on which slots remained empty, including what they might do to fill these spaces. Some classrooms might be geared toward only one or two intelligence areas, and some intelligences may appear easier or tougher than others to incorporate. These emerging professionals are being asked to practice the application of a theoretical taxonomy. Yet in my mind essentialism is political; it is based on a strategy of power that deploys appearance in its seduction. "What *appears*," writes, Diane Dubrose Brunner (1998), "is ideological fixity. What is left out of *appearance* are the events that mark historical and derivational contexts." She quotes Foucault about a meaning-event being as neutral as death until it occurs within a particular context. Such a context would be a challenge to appreciate by hopping in and out of a classroom for forty minutes during a bingo game. Yet only when a meaning-event occurs in a particular historical context that is embedded in a particular worldview does the word "death" take on special significance. In other words, it requires the performance of all those contextually related items to become meaningful.

However, even this realization of the importance of context and history is disconcerting. New teachers are armed with a technical form of analysis, "MI theory." They enter classrooms and critique them. Practicing teachers defend their territory with "my own story"—nobody could be as knowledgeable about the meaning-events as the isolated teacher in the classroom, independently slaving away to serve his or her students. There is no new teacher-experienced teacher dialogue about multiple intelligences and what they hide. Nothing disrupts the maintenance of the ebb and flow of professional induction and consolidation, of ideology and social reproduction.

Gardner as Curriculum Frankenstein

Note that Howard Gardner himself would not be pleased with many of the ways that the theory has been adopted by educators. He would never want us to conflate mathematics as a discipline with logical-mathematical intelligence. To do so would be to misunderstand intelligences as "learning styles." No one intelligence is to be theorized as solely responsible for areas of the school curriculum. The name of the intelligence may be a misnomer. Nevertheless, it refers to something Gardner believes could be brought to bear in problem-solving strategies or in fashioning cultural artifacts:

> No intelligence is in and of itself artistic or non-artistic; rather several intelligences can be put to aesthetic ends, if individuals so desire. No direct educational implications follow from this psychological theory; but if individuals differ in their intellectual profiles, it makes sense to take this fact into account in devising an educational system. (Gardner 2003, 5)

Indeed, Gardner has never professed to be qualified to teach mathematics or any other subject. Having given birth to the MI theory, he is no longer responsible for its life once it leaves the nest: "I always maintained that I was a psychologist and not an educator, and did not presume to know how best to teach a class of young persons or run an elementary or secondary school" (Gardner 2003, 6).

The theory may be treated badly, made hideous and unapproachable, much as the creature in Mary Shelley's parable, brought to life by Dr. Frankenstein and abandoned to wander unparented in the outside world. The theory has been misinterpreted ("confounding a human intelligence with a social domain") and wrongly applied ("describing racial or ethnic groups in terms of their characteristic intelligences"). Such monsters are no longer Gardner's baby. As a scientist, he created the theory but is no longer required to nurture it in the outside world. He is surely no longer personally responsible for the life it has on its own. More to the point, MI theory apparently should never be treated as an ethical or moral living theory, but instead as a description of the present moment:

> "Multiple intelligences" should not in and of itself be an educational goal. Educational goals need to reflect one's own values, and these can never come simply or directly from a scientific theory. Once one reflects on one's educational values and states one's educational goals, however, then the putative existence of our multiple intelligences can prove very helpful. And, in particular, if one's educational goals encompass disciplinary understanding, then it is possible to mobilize our several intelligences to help achieve that lofty goal. (Gardner 2003, 9)

That is, MI theory has nothing to add to curriculum design and development beyond a naïve support for Ralph Tyler's "rationale" (Tyler 1949/1969): we can parse activities into categories, but, in the end, according to this worldview, what really should happen in our mathematics classrooms depends on what Tyler called our "philosophical screen." It would presumably be our philosophy of education that determines pretty much everything we do with the ideas of multiple intelligences.

The last fifty years of curriculum theory might have something to add to all of this. Not only must we be held accountable for our theories, we also should not ignore the philosophical screen, where "all of the action is," according to Tyler and Gardner; yet we also need to consider, as the reconceptualization of curriculum studies has taught us, the *lived experience* of the curriculum. Instead of marshalling multiple intelligences toward a disciplinary understanding, I must in my teaching of mathematics enact with my students the multiple possibilities for experiencing the discipline of mathematics. How we live together comes first, before we construct as a community what mathematics "is" through our lived practices. At times I feel like the effect of the logical-mathematical intelligence is to "explain away" the experiencing of mathematics; it is as if I must erase from my classroom something more *basic* than the basic skills of mathematics that would seemingly define the "intelligence."

A Living Inheritance

My question, then, goes something like this: If we can "mobilize the multiple intelligences," as Gardner writes, to (I presume) *attack* the discipline of mathematics, is this what we want to do, or what we should do? Will mobilizing our intelligences bring mathematics as a disciplinary experience alive in our classrooms? Instead of *attacking* mathematics and *breaking it down* to be doled out in ways that can be controlled, predicted, manipulated, and studied as pieces of human artifice, instead of a science of intelligences, we may need to consider the fundamental tasks we strive for—more appropriately in the manner of shared and contested, and living and troubling, *inheritances* (Gadamer 1994; Jardine, Clifford & Friesen 2003). Addition and subtraction, numbers and shapes, patterns and stories, strategies and modes of reflection—each is only a living aspect of what has been handed to us.

> More oddly put, we have been, so to speak, handed to them. We *find ourselves* faced with, surrounded by, in the middle of, and living with these matters. In multiple, contradictory ways, these topics are being lived out. These topics, interpretively understood, *already define us* (through upbringing, language, cultural background, gender, geography, age, interest, decision, imposition, default, or choice) *before* and sometimes *in spite of* the work of formal schooling. (Jardine, Clifford, & Friesen 2003, 53)

Mathematics as a discipline requires things of *us*. For mathematics to be alive, we must bring to it new students who will live with it, experience it, exist with it. There must be people attempting to "get in on" the conversation (Appelbaum 1999). There must be people desiring a relationship with it. Folks must be mulling over new questions and challenging the teacher's authority to control activity. Students must be demanding something *of* the mathematics. Confusion and bewilderment would be, not problems to be fixed by the application of a stronger, more capable intelligence, but, indeed, moments when what seems like a given is "set right anew" by being set back into its living movement as a living question of human inheritance (Jardine, Clifford & Friesen 2003, 54). I search for these living experiences of mathematics in the multiple intelligences but do not find them there. Rather than define a person as more or less mathematical or logical than another, I prefer to understand how each and every person I live and work with is mathematical or logical (Appelbaum 1999 and 1995). My classroom must shift to incorporate *their* ways of being, rather than employing one intelligence or another to make them become more mathematical in a cartoon version of what this might mean.

Ptolemaic Crisis

I realize that I am frustrated not with multiple intelligences as a theory, but with the relationship between the psychological theory and curriculum practice. This may not be particular in any way to mathematics and the logical-mathematical intelligence but may be endemic to this relationship between "scientizing" and "the practical." What complicates the situation is the choice of nomenclature, since the logical-mathematical really does not seem to be mathematical in most reasonable senses of the term. Some theories have longer life-spans than others, and it may be that multiple intelligences, as an explanation, may have run its course. Look at it this way: I am not content with the first seven intelligences, because they do not capture mathematics as a living discipline for my classroom. In fact, I suggest that they leave out significant features of intelligent life. What I describe as missing leads us to a new intelligence. So, for example, we note that a person cannot be a mathematician without being able to relate mathematically to the natural world, to be able to interact ethically and morally, and with respect and understanding, through and in spite of mathematics, with the natural world. A student must be able to recognize meaningful mathematical connections with the natural world but also silly or nonsensical relations as well. What else might be missing? Perhaps an existential way of mathematizing? Well, then, we need to add this to the list.

I am reminded in the history of science of Ptolemy's influential model of the planets and sun revolving around the earth. Each new discovery led to something missing from the theory, and each time, Ptolemy did an eloquent job of incorporating new data and information by adding what he called an "epicycle" to his theory. His theory was based on the simplistic and beautiful truth that all planets traveled in perfect circles. But this did not account for all the observations that people could make about what was going on. Yet he could add a smaller, little circle to his design, maintaining the beauty of the original theory, and account for each new piece of information. While traveling in a larger circle, the planet also made a tiny circular path around a point on the larger circle. In the same way, we never really can find fault with "multiple intelligences." Any new piece of information or description of intellectual life can be accounted for by adding a new epicycle—I mean intelligence—to the theory. Such a totalizing theory can never be disrupted and will always maintain its internal beauty and truth. Mathematicians have a problem with totalizing theories. They reek of a need for contradictions. Any theory that seems to be universal is undoubtedly based on a set of presumptions that are mistakenly being treated as unquestionable. Mathematicians have learned their lesson in the course of history: These presumptions will soon be understood as a special case of an expanded set of assumptions. All numbers are rational—except now we have found irrational numbers; all numbers are rational or irrational—until we need to think about negative numbers, imaginary numbers, transcendental numbers, and so on. Geometry rests on Euclid's postulates—except that we must replace these postulates with others in order to make meaning of a variety of important situations. So, too, I imagine, must we challenge multiple intelligences. As a theory it is pretty; as a long-standing truth, it leaves a lot to be desired: a living discipline of mathematics.

You Are a Mathematician

As Jeannie Oakes and Martin Lipton write:

> [I]t is tempting to accept the categories, explanations, and values that one's culture has constructed as real, true, and "common sense," but clearly they are not. As anthropologists remind us, each culture's meanings and values are simply the particular way a particular group of people has constructed solutions to questions and problems that arise as they create and preserve their society. (1999, 279–80)

There is no simple answer to what makes a person a "good student," even though many cultures treat the categories they construct and the meanings they assign to them as "common sense." Nevertheless, who is a good student in a mathematics classroom? Not necessarily someone who is particularly strong in logical-mathematical intelligence, as our notions of strength are informed by our cultural perspectives. Herein lies the complexity of the multiple intelligences. Let us say we embrace the theory and wish to use it to inform our classroom practices. Who defines what is meant by an ability to discern logical and numerical patterns or to manage long chains of reasoning? To take a now-emblematic example, which constitutes a demonstration of logical-mathematical intelligence more than the other, Munir Fasheh's Palestinian students, trained to parrot Western mathematics, and to do so with the requisite conceptions of identity, rationality, and technology, or Fasheh's mother, creating complex patterns in her weavings at home (Fasheh 1989)? The orientalism that is imbricated in every interpretation of this juxtaposition belies the simplicity of a particular kind of "intelligence."

> Anyone might notice that the last single-digit number is 9, which is a perfect square, $3 \cdot 3$. Is this deeply significant? No, it is more of an accident. However, you might also notice that numbers that are one less than perfect squares are the products of two whole numbers, which differ by 2. For example, $16 - 1 = 15$, and 15 is $3 \cdot 5$. Similarly, $9 - 1 = 8$ and 8 is $2 \cdot 4$, and also, $36 - 1 = 35$ and 35 is $5 \cdot 7$. (Wells 1995, 30)

How does a "good student" respond? Is there a particularly *logical* or *mathematical* way of being that would be demonstrated by specific types of response? Suppose you are a student in this class. You might turn to someone nearby and ask them whether they suppose that this is an *underlying pattern*, or if they believe this property might be generalizable to any conceivable perfect square. You might get out some paper or a calculator and try some more special cases. You might think about organizing this information in a chart according to various schemes. You might write a reflection in your math journal about the sort of question that this implies, whether or not it is interesting, whether or not it shares any rhetorical features with other interesting questions, or about the kinds of potential applications of this investigation you are beginning to imagine. You might start to build some representations of the relationships with little cubes, or with triangular tiles. You might choreograph a set of movements based on the relationships involved. The moment we start to wonder, to use the situation to create an investigation, we are thinking mathematically. In our classroom, we need to try every one of these possible responses. Indeed, there are any number of patterns and relationships in the whole numbers, from simple ones like this one to patterns so complex and subtle that the most famous mathematicians have never been able to prove that the pattern does in fact go on forever or even that it exists at all. Some people panic at the latter prospect: they get a headache, because they need to know the "truth," and the truth is just not something that we can fabricate. Perhaps in this case the most fundamental intelligence exhibited by the successful mathematics student is the existential intelligence—curiously not one of the first to be recognized and only rendered "half status" by Gardner himself until he is certain it is a legitimate intelligence. As Gardner continually repeats, we all have some of each intelligence, including this existential one, dramatizing the profound questions of life and existence. And that is a good thing, because mathematical intelligence is all of them combined.

In what does the enjoyment of mathematics exist? It might start with a feeling of wonder: How extraordinary! Who would have thought that! Or it might begin with a feeling of surprise: Is that really so? Can't be! You would have never. . . . Paradox also gives us a thrill: That's not possible! Don't be absurd! Mystery is yet another commonplace in mathematics—perhaps you search for a mathematical object that you know an awful lot about *if it exists,* only to discover that it can't actually exist! Do we need the paradox resolved, the surprise explained, or the mystery revealed? This is surely delightful but not essential. Perhaps the fundamental element of a reconstructed mathematical intelligence would be an interest in surprise, paradox and wonder and, finally, awe. I can see it now, in a revised description of multiple intelligences:

> Do you get a kick out of a surprise or the feeling of wonder? Do you delight in an unresolved paradox? Do you giggle at a difficult mystery, even if you are frustrated in your initial attempts to solve it? These are signs of the mathematical intelligence.
>
> To make your classroom more open to the expression of mathematical intelligence, encourage students to share surprises, to wonder at new sources of surprise, to discuss and create paradoxes, and to formulate mysteries for each other to try to solve. Make sure that some of these paradoxes cannot be resolved, that some of the mysteries have no solution, and that students get a chance to speak about the new and wonderful things that they have discovered and invented, including new relationships with others.

References

Appelbaum, P. (1995). *Popular culture, educational discourse, and mathematics.* Albany: State University of New York Press.

———. (1998). Teaching/learning mathematics in schools. In S. Steinberg & J. Kincheloe (eds.), *Unauthorized methods: Strategies for critical teaching* (pp. 199–230). New York: Routledge.

———. (1999). Eight critical points for mathematics. In D. Weil & H. Anderson (eds.), *Perspectives in critical thinking: Essays by teachers in theory and practice* (pp. 110–129). New York: Peter Lang.

ASCD (undated). Lesson 4—Learning about logical-mathematical intelligence. June 2003, *http://www.ascd.org/pdi/lesson4.html*

Brown, S. (2001). *Reconstructing school mathematics: Problems with problems and the real world*. New York: Peter Lang.

Brunner, D. (1998). *Between the masks*. Boulder, CO: Rowman and Littlefield.

Checkley, K. (1997). The first seven . . . and the eighth: A conversation with Howard Gardner. *Educational Leadership, 55*(1), 8–13.

Fasheh, M. (1989). Mathematics in a social context: Math within education as praxis versus within education as hegemony. In C. Keitel (ed.), *Mathematics, education and society* (pp. 203–211). Paris: UNESCO Document Series No. 35.

Gadamer, H. (1994). *Heidegger's ways*. Boston: MIT Press.

———. (2003). Multiple intelligences after twenty years. Paper presented at the American Educational Research Association, 21 April, Chicago. *www.pz.harvard.edu/PIs/HG_MI_after_20_years.pdf*

Jardine, D., Clifford, P., & Friesen, S. (2003). *Back to the basics of teaching and learning: Thinking the world together*. Mahwah, NJ: Erlbaum.

Oakes, J., & Lipton, M. (1999). *Teaching to change the world*. Boston: McGraw-Hill.

Sadker, M., & Sadker, D. (2003). *Teachers, schools and society*. Boston: McGraw-Hill.

Tyler, R. (1949/1969). *Basic principles of curriculum and instruction*. Chicago: University of Chicago Press.

Wells, D. (1995). *You are a mathematician: A wise and witty introduction to the joy of numbers*. New York: John Wiley & Sons.

Chapter 5

Richard Cary

HOWARD GARDNER'S THEORY OF VISUAL-SPATIAL INTELLIGENCE: A CRITICAL RETHEORIZING

Introduction

The best thing about Gardner's Theory of Multiple Intelligences is that it moves one step away from the g-theory of intelligence; the worst thing is that it takes only one step. This limited dialectic is the product of Gardner's equivocal strategy of supporting the assumptions of science while foregoing the aggregation of rigorous, detailed evidence sufficient to support his theories as orthodox science requires. Multiple intelligences (MI) theory is at once not scientific enough for one audience and too positivist for another.

A comprehensive critique of MI theory addressing the problems that have prevented a more productive application of Gardner's ideas in contexts such as schooling and the art world is long overdue. This chapter offers an initial approach to that critique with a consideration of one of the multiple intelligences, visual-spatial intelligence. This chapter's retheorizing of visual-spatial intelligence proceeds from the idea that place-making, or conscious formation of a sense of place, is a defining characteristic of visual-spatial intelligence. Further, this retheorizing promotes a critical consciousness of the social and historical contingencies that shape vision. These contingencies involve complex interactions among knowledge, intelligence, power, and the sense of sight. The purpose of this chapter is not to refute Gardner but to critically examine his ideas and enrich them with an infusion of insights from postmodern and critical epistemologies. The outcome will provide more interesting and, I hope, more effective ways to think about visual-spatial intelligence rather than a single, absolutely correct way.

Howard Gardner originally posited seven intelligences: linguistic, logicomathematical, spatial, musical, bodily-kinetic, interpersonal, and intrapersonal. He has recently added an eighth: earth intelligence, or the ability to maintain harmonious, sustainable relationships with the environment. Each multiple intelligence begins as a biological potential that is shaped experientially as the individual develops. High ability in one intelligence does not imply high ability in another. Gardner introduced his theory of multiple intelligences in *Frames of Mind* (1983). *Multiple Intelligences: The Theory in Practice* followed in 1993. Together they have become popular resources for those who contest the monolithic, ubiquitous *g*-theory of intelligence and believe that its consequences are deleterious and unjust.

G-theory defines intelligence as an innate general capacity to learn that varies in amount from person to person but which is relatively stable over the life span. The *g*-theory of intelligence has dominated education, psychology, and the social sciences, business, and the military since intelligence testing began around the turn of the twentieth century. The original purpose of the intelligence test was to predict an individual's abilities to benefit from traditional schooling. Note the implicit bottom line: "Why allocate educational resources to those who cannot use them wisely and in turn benefit society?"

Alfred Binet developed the first credible intelligence test in 1905 in France. Psychologists at Stanford University modified and adopted it for use in the United States. The Stanford-Binet, of course, was neither culture sensitive nor able to detect and control for variations in scores that were associated with individual developmental differences. These limitations meant that society selected and provided an appropriate education for only certain children. Those children who lacked the endowments of cultural capital that are the birthrights of the middle and upper classes or those who were late bloomers were systematically disadvantaged—if not excluded altogether—by these test deficiencies. The standardized intelligence tests focused on education as an investment of limited capital resources, not an individual right. Nonetheless, the intelligence test was such a handy and (for the short term) economically effective tool that it soon became accepted virtually universally as an objective measure of general learning ability. By extension, this measure came to be regarded as proof of the efficacy of society's investment in education. However, despite its popularity and facility, suspicions remained. Alfred Binet himself cautioned against accepting the score as proof of a stable, general ability to learn (Kincheloe & Steinberg 1996, 33).

Its domination is so pervasive that *g*-theory has entered into the public mythos not as mere theory, but as truth—a *commonsense* version of the way things are. More detrimentally, *g*-theory is not perceived as merely a theory in the sense that it provisionally explains observed phenomena. Nor is *g*-theory perceived as merely an innocuous speculation on esoterica by otherwise-idle academics who are safely segregated from everyday reality. G-theory has produced very real negative consequences in many human lives. There is widespread popular awareness of the cultural bias inherent in intelligence tests and related academic achievement tests or similar ability assessment instruments. Such bias has adversely affected groups distinguished by gender, race, class, and geography. Growing numbers of parents and teachers are alarmed—or should be—about the tragic consequences of tests that, being insensitive to the normal developmental variations among individual students, can label so-called late bloomers as lacking ability. Mislabeled children can be assigned to low-ability/low-expectations tracks (for their own good, as common sense tells us) where they too often become acclimated to the culture of low achievement and its inevitable destinies. For those who study the ramifications of *g*-theory and especially for those who experience its negative consequences, the point is clear: standardized intelligence tests are subject to misuse and are not the unquestionable objective means to capture the individual's true ability to learn as uncritical popular opinion believes.

Yet widespread dissatisfaction with IQ testing has failed to produce a widely accepted alternative. No alternative assessment procedure has emerged that solves the cultural bias and developmental mislabeling problems while also demonstrating to the satisfaction of the educational bureaucracy that society's investment in education has paid sufficient returns. But it has become widely recognized that the method by which an individual's abilities are assessed often determines eligibility for educational resources and determines, to a great extent, who a child can become. One-dimensional tests yield one-dimension labels and one-dimensional people. Yet people learn in many modalities through a variety of sensory and intellectual configurations.

British psychologist H. J. Eysenck (1953, 67–72) addressed the uses and abuses of psychology. Questioning the constancy of IQ throughout the individual's life, Eysenck reviewed over thirty longitudinal studies in which researchers administered IQ tests to large samples of children periodically over spans ranging to ten years or more. If IQ is constant, then test-retest reliability would be high. Test-retest reliability is simply the correlation between the subjects' scores on the first test and scores on the next. Eysenck's review indicates that this body of research convincingly demonstrates that the correlation for IQ tests is a function of time between the administration of the two tests. The Stanford-Binet test, for example, has a very high reliability at $r = .95$ when the two tests are administered within a week or so of each other. However, the correlation coefficient drops to $r = .91$ when one year intervenes. This trend continues: after ten years, the reliability coefficient of the Stanford-Binet is only $r = .55$, a low correlation. Eysenck concludes that although IQ tests may be valid measures of intelligence at the time they are administered, such tests are poor indicators of intellectual ability throughout the life of the individual, particularly throughout childhood and adolescence when growth and development accelerate. Eysenck, a major figure in twentieth-century psychology, called the constancy of IQ a "myth," and feared that if IQ was taken literally as a prediction of later intellectual ability, the results would be seriously misleading. His fears have been realized.

The idea that intelligence is composed of multiple subcomponents or subfactors is not new. The multifactor approach was, in fact, a cornerstone of the research in the late nineteenth and early twentieth centuries that produced *g*-theory and IQ tests. L. Thurstone identified seven factors: verbal comprehension, word fluency, number, spatial relations, associative memory, perceptual speed, and general reasoning (Helmstadter 1964, 103). David Wechsler (1944) identified three or four factors, with spatial and visual-motor factors termed the nonverbal factors. Wechsler called *g*-intelligence a "complex constellation of interacting factors" that are best interpreted individually as primary abilities. Weschler goes on to admit that each factor, if measured as part of a *g*-theory, becomes attenuated in the reductionistic workings of the scientific method's demand for parsimony. Jean Piaget, Rudolf Arnheim, and others have also studied discrete forms of intelligence (Gardner 1983).

Visual-Spatial Intelligence: Howard Gardner's Concept

Visual-spatial intelligence is arguably the least understood of the seven multiple intelligences. Gardner describes visual-spatial intelligence as the capacity to construct a mental representation of the spatial realm and to use that representation to perform valued activities in the world. Examples of persons with high degrees of visual-spatial intelligence are artists, architects, engineers, and surgeons (1983, 173). Gardner's version of visual-spatial intelligence incorporates the abilities to perceive the visual world accurately, to evaluate and modify those perceptions according to subsequent experience, and to recreate components of a perception even without the physical presence of the original stimulus. He emphasizes the interdependence of these abilities in visual and spatial tasks, likening their interaction to that of rhythm and pitch in music.

Visual-spatial intelligence is sometimes referred to as "spatial" only. Gardner (1983, 174–75) distinguishes between the two modalities and argues that, while visual activities are central to this capacity, spatial intelligence incorporates other senses and cognitive operations as well. He bases his arguments primarily on neurological and cognitive research on the spatial abilities of blind subjects, in whom spatial intelligence is determined more by auditory than visual sensory experience. Nevertheless, the significance of vision to the workings of spatial intelligence should be underscored, especially in its most familiar application, art. This chapter will use the term "visual-spatial intelligence."

Throughout the modern era and before, vision has been regarded as the primary sensory modality in the organization of knowledge. From the postmodern perspective, we also realize that the role of vision in knowing and knowledge is heavily influenced by the play of power that issues from particular discourses and epistemologies. From a postmodern perspective, we also understand that vision is the sensory modality that is most complicit in and vulnerable to the reproduction of oppressive cultural forms and distorted practices.

The Purpose of MI

MI raised great hopes. Its original purpose was to build a conceptual framework for creating school reform to change what Gardner (1993) called the uniform school. The uniform school, the most prevalent form of educational institution today, is organized and administered on the premise that there is only one set of facts worth knowing, one way to teach them, and one capacity, g, that enables students to learn those facts. General intelligence is presumed to be possessed to different degrees by different students based upon one piece of evidence—their scores on intelligence or IQ tests. Instrumental to these tasks, uniform schools convey the benefits of education to students not only in accordance with the degree to which they are able to demonstrate mastery over the uniform set of facts but also on the basis of students' supposed capacity, g, to gain such mastery. A student's capacity to learn anything and everything is equated with his or her score on an intelligence test. The score, essentially an operational definition of intelligence, is accepted as the student's IQ, the general ability to profit from the educational resources that schools provide (and, to be sure, the economic sector's ability to profit from the student later). In such ways, uniform schools preserve obstacles to our society's attempts to offer an education that meets standards of social justice and democratic ideals.

The uniform school and the lucrative intelligence-testing industry have evolved into a mutually supportive alliance. The intelligence-testing concept, now at the beginning of the new millennium, remains deeply entrenched in the unquestioned practices of the politicized bureaucracies of schooling and in the products and profits of the educational-industrial complex. Forms of testing based on the g-theory of intelligence have become strongly identified in the public mind as a means of discerning incontrovertible and specific truth about individuals' intellectual abilities. Likewise, the equation of the end-of-grade test score with educational achievement has become an unchallenged pillar of common sense associated with the uniform school. Such testing supplies what is popularly but uncritically perceived as a guarantee, certified proof of learning demanded even by those most poorly served by today's schools. Yet the uniform school's reliance on the testing industry (and vice versa) has resulted in the narrowing of the curriculum to a downloadable, fixed subset of facts. This alliance has promoted the popular attitude of grateful acquiescence to the downloadable curriculum on the false pretext that learning documented by quantitative measures is a good return on society's investment in education. The alliance has helped to produce the often dehumanizing, de-skilled instructional practices that enforce the sorting of students into the enduring categories of good student and throwaway kid, thus perpetuating the subtle but frightening attack on diversity in our culture.

Recognizing that individuals have different strengths and weaknesses, Gardner envisions a multifaceted school that provides a curriculum and instruction valuing these primary strengths and weaknesses (he calls them "intelligences") as they are variously configured in individual students. Considering such dark strands in schooling's history as the co-opting of schooling by economic interests (Bowles & Gintis 1976; Spring 1976), Gardner's vision is utopian. But in formulating his theory of multiple intelligences to enact reform, Gardner has tried to avoid the traditional dead ends of utopianism by turning to science to garner enough evidence to support his theory of MI and model schools. However, mainstream science harbors a different set of problems that surreptitiously infect Gardner's theory. Unfortunately, while mainstream science furnishes Gardner a cachet of credibility in some venues, science, by its inherent nature, also becomes an obstacle to the educational reform that Gardner hopes to foster with MI.

Gardner's vision for schooling is decidedly congruent with postpositivist interests. For example, Gardner believes that it is a mistake for teachers and others to seek a quantifiable test for any of the seven multiple intelligences (1993, 244). Yet, ironically, while Gardner's formulation of MI theory as a basis for his vision is too soft for mainstream science, it is too reliant on the assumptions and methods of science. That is, it is too entrenched in the culture of positivism to serve as a unique, rich resource for practice in contemporary classrooms that are characterized by a new openness to multiple sources of knowledge.

MI theory has provoked a multicentered, multilayered debate that has continued since the publication of *Frames of Mind* in 1983. Yet it is apparent today that the diffuse character of this conversation has overshadowed the actual productivity of MI theory, especially in the seats of power, the bureaucracy of education and its political overseers. Moreover, the intransigent power structure of the positivist intellectual culture has contributed to the arrested development of MI as a foundation for contemporary schooling because it is not, according to the strictures of that paradigm, a proper scientific theory. Many teachers and others close to the world of schooling enthusiastically embrace MI. They find themselves pitted against MI's detractors, who argue that it is neither testable nor capable of sufficient explanatory power. Nor does it provide the means to make accurate, reliable predictions. These properties are demanded for application in the real-world contexts of schooling in which political accountability for the economics of education must be demonstrated by quantifiable evidence. These criticisms of MI theory are on target, as Gardner himself admits (1993, 38–39), saying that he prefers to leave details of building such evidence to the "experts."

However, educators, parents, and others concerned with schooling (and for whom theory is not the primary focus) have long been aware of the problems associated with the dominance of g-theory and are anxious for any alternative that appears to offer more humane, equitable practices for schools. Many who see the harsh ramifications of g-theory every day in the real world of schooling welcome MI theory. But perhaps their expectations are too high. Uncritical acceptance of MI theory is often based on its good intentions and on its consistency with contemporary efforts to promote democratic reform of schooling that seeks the best for each individual child. And MI has undoubtedly caused many teachers to think more deeply about their practices. However, despite its intuitive appeal and good intentions, MI's promise goes largely unfulfilled. The reasons are numerous and complex. Among the most important limitations is the resistance, both explicit and implicit, mounted by the testing industry. Testing is a lucrative business. This industry and the dominant model of schooling in the United States are allies in the culture of positivism that has reigned for so long in Western society.

A Critique of MI's Concept of Visual-Spatial Intelligence

Too Subjective for Science, Too Positivist for Postmodernism

The most significant limitation to the promise of MI is MI theory itself. One source of these limitations is the way in which Gardner's commitment to science surreptitiously shapes MI, especially visual-spatial intelligence. MI is at once too soft for mainstream science and too bound up in the culture of positivism for the tastes of contemporary practitioners who work in real-world contexts such as schooling and the art world. Typically, the postmodern practitioner's vision emphasizes the historical, philosophical, or interpretative ways of knowing that have long been marginalized by the scientific paradigm and relegated to inferior status in the broader culture dominated by positivist epistemology.

Gardner supports his concept of visual-spatial intelligence with numerous references to mainstream scientific research on visual-spatial abilities and related topics in psychological and physiological research. The ramification is that MI's concept of visual-spatial intelligence is portrayed primarily as an objective, nomothetic, biological-mechanical skill.

Gardner cites a neuropsychological study conducted in 1981 by Eduardo Bisiach on right-hemisphere–damaged patients (1983, 182). The subjects were persons who were unable to describe the left part of a familiar scene; that is, they exhibited difficulty in seeing the left half of the scenes and places before them in everyday life. In the experiment, the brain-damaged patients were asked to visualize, then to verbally describe, two images from opposite vantage points of a familiar local scene, the Duomo Square in Milan, Italy. The subjects were unable to describe the left side of either image even though they had correctly described the same details from the opposite image. Gardner uses this reference to establish the point that the right hemisphere of the brain is instrumental in the processing of spatial information. But this is hardly a scientific breakthrough. Moreover, it could be cited just as legitimately as evidence for g-theory's visual-spatial subcomponent as for MI's visual-spatial intelligence. In addition, Gardner does not mention the validity problems of Bisiach's study. As for internal validity, Bisiach commingled visual and verbal cognitive processing tasks, making it difficult to ascribe the effects he observed to the visual modality alone. As for external validity, Bisiach's use of brain-damaged patients makes it problematic to generalize to the non–brain-damaged population.

Gardner cites (1983, 174) Roger Shepard's 1971 experiments in which subjects were presented with a series of pairs of complex geometric forms that were rotated in different directions. Subjects were asked to determine whether the forms were identical, and their response times were recorded. Shepard found that judgment time was positively correlated with degree of rotation. The point that Gardner finds most relevant to visual-spatial intelligence is that the subjects apparently formed mental images of the geometric forms and then manipulated the mental images to make their judgments. However, from a critical perspective, Shepard's operational definition of visual-spatial intelligence is too severe and reductionistic. He equates degree of visual-spatial intelligence with the speed with which the mental image is rotated. Reaction time is thus a measure of intelligence, surely a dubious operational definition. For postpositivist epistemologies, this operational definition is absurdly narrow and lacks the compelling explanatory richness that characterizes the concepts of the workings of human intelligence intuited by those who work in applied settings such as the art world or the public schools.

Shepard's mental image experiment illustrates two abilities identified by Gardner as central to visual-spatial intelligence — to perceive and reproduce part of the visual world accurately and to evaluate and modify those perceptions according to subsequent experience. Shepard's investigation demonstrates that these two mental operations do indeed operate in the normal processing of visual-spatial information. Gardner contends that these two core skills in MI's visual-spatial intelligence are indispensable abilities. But they might just as well be identified as salient features of g-theory intelligence.

Citations and allusions to scientific studies dominate the evidence Gardner offers to support MI theory and far outnumber evidence from philosophy, history, art, or anthropology. It is clear that Gardner is intent upon developing a scientific basis for MI theory. But the science cited fails to distinguish MI theory from the g-theory that Gardner hopes to replace. However, citing scientific research and staking claim to it as support for a new theory is an act of ratiocination, not of science. It is interpretation, not controlled observation. One wonders why all the research is cited in Gardner's work. What do the studies actually add to the case for MI theory, which, by its nature, is philosophical, hermeneutic, or, as Thomas Kuhn (1970) would have it, political? Any postmodernist would stipulate that there indeed exists a large body of scientific research on intelligence and its neurological operations. MI does not refute it, nor does it need to be refuted to advance MI as a philosophy. MI and scientific studies of visual-spatial abilities adduced earlier to support g-theory are simply the products of fundamentally different epistemologies. In this instance, Gardner has deployed scientific results for an argument that is propelled by reason alone, not by science.

The evidence and examples Gardner cites to support MI come primarily from traditional grand narrative psychology. This psychology earns the description "grand narrative" because it presumes to be in a position to determine the final, summary truth toward which knowledge, led by science, inexorably marches. But grand narrative psychology treats learning and the intellect as objective totalities independent of the cultural and personal domains of living experience. For example, Gardner (1983) frequently cites clinical studies of brain-damaged patients, idiot savants, and other atypical subjects. Typically, the researchers administered a battery of tests that included assessment of the subjects' abilities to perform both linguistic and visual–spatial tasks. This body of clinical research has produced convincing evidence that damage to the right hemisphere of the brain impairs visual-spatial ability. Also, impairment is exacerbated when right-hemisphere damage is accompanied by even slight damage to the left hemisphere. (The left hemisphere is the site of linguistic functions, such studies show.) Gardner cites Nelson Butters's research with right-hemisphere brain-damaged patients that found that they experienced difficulties in such tasks as reading maps and anticipating how objects or graphic forms would appear from differing vantage points. Elizabeth Warrington, also cited by Gardner, found that right-brain–damaged patients were unable to recognize familiar objects presented from unusual perspectives. Gardner also alludes — but without much detail or critical analysis — to other scientific research, including frequent reference to the work of Piaget.

The question for postmodern practitioners is, what do these studies indicate about the MI theory of visual-spatial intelligence? One answer is that visual-spatial intelligence is a physiological function performed at a specific anatomical location. Another is that the site is probably the right hemisphere of the brain. But it is not clear why Gardner cites this research or what its relationship is to his version of visual-spatial intelligence. These findings say little about how visual-spatial intelligence operates in such cultural settings as schools — even the uniform schools that Gardner has targeted. Gardner reviews scientific research that has established the location of visual-spatial intelligence and that it operates as a biological process. So what? This information contributes little to our understanding of how a visual-spatial intelligence operates in the culture and why we should value it in our daily experience. Science has conceived of visual-spatial intelligence as working in isolation from other mental abilities and from cultural contexts.

Recalling the stipulation in MI's definition of visual-spatial intelligence that the mental representation an individual forms of the spatial realm must be valued in the world, we must look beyond science and the strictures of the culture of positivism to envision a new potential for Gardner's ideas. Gardner's review of the literature succeeds in establishing the fact that a body of scientific research on visual-spatial abilities exists. However, this evidence does not convincingly supply the justification for or the means to parse g-theory into eight discrete intelligences.

Subjective Factor Analysis?

Other problems emerge from MI's entrenched positivist assumptions in the absence of scientific rigor. In April 1989, at the University of South Carolina's Artistic Intelligences Conference, as Gardner described his theory of MI, he called his approach to developing MI theory subjective factor analysis. Of course, Gardner was speaking metaphorically. Factor analysis is not subjective, at least according to the scientists who used it as the primary method of IQ test development throughout the history of intelligence research. But neither is factor analysis a source of incontestable truth.

In fact, statisticians know that factor analysis is a rather gross tool, a conglomeration of quantitative techniques that is used to reduce a broad array of many variables to a few related ones for use in more precise research and testing. One multivariate statistics text (Tabachnick & Fidell 1989, 597) uses the term "first guess" to refer to the purpose of factor analysis. Factor analysis is also known among statistical spin doctors as a tool of last resort for fixing poorly designed research or research with serious construct-validity problems. A more serious caveat against uncritical acceptance of the results of factor analysis is that there are no external criteria against which to compare the results of a factor analysis in order to determine their accuracy. In regression analysis, for example, the accuracy of an equation used to predict, say, college success can be compared later to actual grades earned. Factor analysis is a technique for preliminary analysis only, not, as Gardner suggests, a method for establishing certainty.

Neither statisticians nor scientists using factor analysis consider the factors identified in research to be causes. Factor analysis is basically a reworked version of the statistics of correlation such as the Pearson Product-Moment Correlation (Pearson r), which we know is not conclusive. Correlation does not establish causality. (Causality, moreover, is a philosophical construct that has been under siege for a long time.) That Gardner would place so much confidence in factor analysis is ironic. Factor analysis was formulated and has been used almost exclusively for the development of standardized tests such as the personality and IQ tests that Gardner identifies as so problematic for schooling and against which he has pitted MI theory.

Although Gardner calls his methodology for formulating MI theory subjective factor analysis, he admits (1993, 40) that this is a self-deprecating, semihumorous allusion to his own "primitive" methods. This seemingly innocuous admission is revealing because it underscores the central problem with Gardner's MI work: his inability to step fully free of the constraints imposed by the culture of positivism that has privileged science as the ultimate source of truth. Gardner expends a great deal of effort developing evidence from scientific research for what is essentially his reasoned interpretation—conceiving of intelligence as multiplistic rather than unitary. His obeisance to the powers of science obscures the legitimacy of the phenomenological methodology that seems to have actually played a larger role in producing his theory, but which he either deliberately or unconsciously conceals. Might MI have been a richer resource or a more powerful tool to promote school reform without the superficial trappings of science? Probably not. But, MI has not had significant impact on schooling in terms of mitigating the problems that ensue from the enforcement of standardized testing and procrustean, politically mandated accountability measures. Perhaps the next step for MI theory is to admit that it is a postulate emerging from an interpretative epistemology, not from science.

Two Worlds and Other Issues

MI theory reflects the deep tension in our culture between those who uphold the position that knowledge is and should be objective and those who oppose this view on the grounds that the loss of subjectivity it describes is dehumanizing. Gardner's vision of school reform resonates with such contemporary perspectives as postmodernism, poststructuralism, and the critical pedagogy movement. However, his concept of visual-spatial intelligence is limited by its commitments to positivist premises and reliance upon traditional scientific research on intelligence. Yet ironically, MI, if held to the traditional standards of scientific research, is soft science and devised for popular consumption. Partitioning general intelligence into eight intelligences, each of which retains the same scientific marrow as g-theory, fails to avoid the decontextualization from lived experience that is inherent in positivist epistemologies. Like other positivist constructs, Gardner's concept of visual-spatial intelligence has evolved as a value-free human faculty. Likewise, visual-spatial intelligence is conceived as an amount of some reified entity that is assumed to be stable for the individual over time.

Gardner's reliance on scientific research on visual-spatial abilities may initially appear to establish a degree of credibility in some circles. Although the strategy of aligning MI with science is compromised by Gardner's cursory, uncritical examination and presentation of scientific evidence, MI's theory of visual-spatial intelligence nonetheless remains a legacy of the culture of positivism. In his 1959 Rede Lectures at Cambridge University, Sir Charles Percy Snow described mutually exclusive intellectual paradigms as "two worlds," the literary world and the scientific world. The two different ways of knowing not only shape the world differently for respective subscribers, they also have different rules and procedures for producing their respective kinds of knowledge. If one enlists science's methods and assumptions to repudiate a theory accepted in science's mainstream, one must accept the protocols of the scientific paradigm and carry them out assiduously. This principle applies as well to the world of philosophical, historical, or literary forms of knowledge-making. Visual-spatial intelligence in the scientific world looks different than a concept of spatial intelligence theorized in the literary or phenomenological world. It is not clear that Gardner has consciously decided in which world he intends MI theory's concept of visual-spatial intelligence to reside.

The operational definitions of spatial intelligence in the studies Gardner cites reveal an implicit acceptance of science as the final authority and an orientation that is decidedly positivist. In the Shepard study (cited earlier) visual-spatial intelligence was operationally defined as the speed with which subjects could manipulate the test image. Subjects who performed the mental operations most quickly were deemed the most spatially intelligent. The operationalism of these studies de-skills spatial intelligence, reducing it to a mechanical sequence of meaningless operations independent of context and culture. This purported new visual-spatial intelligence reflects the same Cartesian separation of mind and body that problematizes the g-theory of intelligence. By adducing evidence that presumes the separation of bodily skills from mind, thought, and culture, Gardner implicitly relegates the function of visual-spatial intelligence to that of *techne*.

MI is soft science. Its lack of merit as a product of mainstream science notwithstanding, MI relies on the epistemological assumptions of science to the extent that it decontextualizes visual-spatial intelligence from the subjectivities of real-life experience. These assumptions include the beliefs that empirical verification of observations can produce certainty, that observation can produce value-free facts, that objectivity is attainable, that scientific knowledge is the ultimate authority, that science is proceeding toward final knowledge, and that the world as we observe it will continue. Its inherent decontextualization from lived experience limits the effectiveness of Gardner's conception of visual-spatial intelligence to promote enriched understanding or to support reform in such applied arenas as art and schooling.

Gardner recognizes that his review of the scientific evidence on visual-spatial ability is not consistent with traditional standards of rigor for academic inquiry. In fact, Gardner's comments on this reflect an edge of disingenuousness. He explains that his theory is merely a general one and that he prefers to leave more thorough evaluation of the scientific research to the experts. For one thing, all theories are, by their natures, general. Karl Popper, in *The Logic of Scientific Discovery* (1961), referred to a theory as a net cast to catch the world. Theories are intended to be general explanations that apply more or less universally to observations of phenomena in the world. Also, Gardner has engaged in neurological and cognitive research for decades; his output has been prodigious. He indisputably qualifies as an expert, but perhaps one who apparently believes that addressing an audience of teachers and other academic laity in the workaday world of schooling occasions a relaxation of academic rigor, an omission that relegates MI to the status of pop science.

MI's positivist approach to visual-spatial intelligence avoids such important questions as how visual-spatial experience reconstructs the relations among power, knowledge, and culture. And it avoids the issue of how these forces shape visual experience. Because of traditional psychology's obedience to the myth of objectivity and the separation of value and fact, the theory of visual-spatial intelligence is powerless to address many of the most significant issues of our time. One of the most timely issues related to visual-spatial intelligence is understanding the ways which the environment—both natural and constructed—affects our lives and the ways in which human beings relate to it. These ramifications, which perhaps were not apparent from Gardner's perspective in 1983, compromise MI theory's overall goal of school reform and limit its applications in other areas. The neglect of such issues as the relationships among intelligence, power, and knowledge and how these relationships influence individuals' lives limits the efficacy of the theory of visual-spatial intelligence. What counts as knowledge and knowing from the MI perspective remains virtually identical to the epistemological foundations of positivism. As with each of the other intelligences, Gardner's theory of visual-spatial intelligence appears to assume that the domains that identify and value intelligence are free of power influences.

The positivist roots of Gardner's version of visual-spatial intelligence psychologize human visual experience and lead to a de-skilling of vision by approaching it as a rational, mechanistic, biophysiological process that copies whatever is *out there*. Further, the positivist-bound theory of visual-spatial intelligence reifies the spatial realm as a physically objective, material entity *out there* and implicitly situates the nature of visual-spatial intelligence as independent from actual lived human experience.

From a postmodern perspective, the traditional grand narrative disciplines such as psychology have lost their cachet as final epistemological authorities. Postmodern thought (such perspectives as critical theory, deconstruction, poststructuralism, and hermeneutics) recognizes the roles of culture and contextualized experience in knowledge. These perspectives reject other modernist presumptions implicit in MI's spatial intelligence: that seeing is knowing, that objective seeing involves simultaneous perception of all significant features, and that all individuals experience seeing the same way. MI's visual-spatial intelligence also subscribes to the modernist assumption that greater intelligence means greater reduction, clarity, and more precise representation of the visual-spatial realm.

MI's concept of visual-spatial intelligence presumes that only individuals working in isolation define or act upon space. The individual is the cause; the objectified spatial realm manifests the effect. Yet contemporary thought encourages us to understand how social and cultural institutions play significant roles in the envisioning and shaping of spaces and how spaces shape vision. MI theory is vulnerable to the same criticisms as standardized tests designed to measure g-theory intelligence: that cultural bias confounds scores and discriminates against individuals who are less endowed with the cultural capital favored by the mainstream culture.

Gardner's adherence to scientific premises insures a concept of visual-spatial intelligence that is objective, value-free, and reified. This means that intelligence can be known objectively—that its essential properties are stable and exist independently from human experience as entities that can be identified, quantified, and experienced by all informed observers as essentially the same phenomena. Yet there are two senses in which we speak of intelligence: intelligence as a theoretical construct and intelligence as it exists in living human experience—that is, as an empirical phenomenon in the perceived world where humans actually manifest intelligence, where intelligence is vivified and moves from theoretical abstraction to manifest reality. MI's premise of objectivity is problematic for intelligence because it ignores the many influences that inflect intelligence in the context of lived experience. The relationship between intelligence and knowledge is crucial to a theory of intelligence. In MI, such influences on knowledge include power, which can determine what is regarded as valid or worthwhile knowledge. Other sources of influence include biases based on gender, race, class, progress through psychological or physiological developmental stages, and geography—one's place. Gardner's articulation of MI as a theory developed and supported by scientific evidence renders it unequipped to acknowledge the degree to which knowledge can be determined by particular power interests.

Without consideration of the sources of the construction of reality in lived experience, MI may become another tool that promotes hegemony in our schools, a tool that well-meaning intellectuals have unknowingly supplied to advance covert ideologies and sources of power. Educator and arts integration researcher Barbara Phipps Cary warns that, in the wrong hands, MI theory has the potential to provide *eight* ways, not just one, to discriminate among students and suppress the attainment of diverse potential to learn. The wrong hands belong to teachers, administrators, and others who do not critically examine their own assumptions about knowledge and schooling, especially those assumptions about intelligence and its measurement that are conferred by the culture of positivism.

The contemporary shift from modernism's culture of positivism to the postmodern epistemologies that are skeptical of grand narrative theories of knowledge (Lyotard 1984) provides reformers and intellectuals with new ideas to assess MI and other reform proposals. MI is a text and is subject to challenge and interpretation. The tasks are to retrieve MI's promises and refit its substance to contexts situated in a postmodern landscape that values multiple ways of knowing and is skeptical of teachings that flow from the presumed indisputable authority of science.

Utter Space and Naïve Realism

The potential of MI theory to promote reform in applied fields is also limited by assumptions about the concept of space implicit in visual-spatial intelligence. Gardner's definition of visual-spatial intelligence refers to "the spatial realm," but fails to define or describe its properties. MI's visual-spatial intelligence assumes that space is an unproblematic concept requiring no definition. It is taken for granted that everyone understands what "the spatial realm" means. But the meanings of space are not self-evident. There are many types of space and many approaches to understanding and constructing its meanings. Geometries of space include the personal, interior, exterior, pictorial, positive, negative, public, private, two dimensional, three dimensional, social, and hypergeometric. Art critic Rosalind Krauss (1989) refers to *discursive space* that is created by a discourse or discipline that authorizes ways of knowing and perceiving. The space implicit in MI theory, however, appears to be conceived as a reified, stable entity that is *out there* independent from culture and individual experience. It is an *utter space*.

This concept of space exposes the naïve realism that pervades MI theory's visual-spatial intelligence. Naïve realism, a long-discredited philosophical position, asserts that the world of physical objects exists apart from our perception of it and that we perceive it directly in a value-free and culture-free fashion, unmediated by individual subjectivity. Further, naïve realism upholds the notion that the properties of an object are physically inherent in it and are objectively knowable in the same way by all people. The concept of space implicit in the MI version of visual-spatial intelligence is no different from that underlying *g*-theory intelligence. The body of scientific research Gardner cites to develop a basis for MI's visual-spatial intelligence approaches space as utter space.

The utter space of MI theory is an object, a physical entity upon which visual-spatial intelligence purportedly operates. The spatial realm in which we see this form of intelligence expressed is constituted by utter space. Utter space is a neutrality, a vacuum, a *Ganzfeld* (Haber & Hershenson 1973). In gestalt psychology, a *Ganzfeld* is a featureless void in which no perception is possible because there is no figure-ground relationship, no visual reference points. It is defined by what is absent—features ordinarily perceivable by the sensory processes of vision. No illuminated discontinuities are discernable. There are no differences from which to construct a perception of form. It is no coincidence that the principal philosopher of deconstruction, Jacques Derrida (1986), has identified *différance* as the crucible of meaning. *Différance* is also the crucible of perception. The utter space of MI's visual-spatial intelligence attempts to disguise its own nature as a place by presenting itself as *Ganzfeld*—an abstraction. Utter space is a dehumanized, homogeneous *Ganzfeld* that can be described only operationally by a constellation of Euclidean points projected *out there*. It is an immateriality devoid of distinguishing features. MI advances utter space as independent from lived experience. It is a space that cannot be perceived and, therefore, cannot be known or experienced. Yet utter space is nonetheless a keystone of MI's visual-spatial intelligence.

The autonomy of utter space implicit in MI's theory of visual-spatial intelligence is a modernist concept. It is a fictive strategy that declares MI's visual-spatial intelligence to be free of ideological and cultural influences and remote from lived experience. The postmodern perspective rejects this belief. A critical reconstruction of visual-spatial intelligence should reconnect visual-spatial intelligence to lived experience, with special attention to the subjective experiences produced by the complex relations between vision and knowledge.

Utter space is a legacy from the receding culture of positivism, as much so as the uniform school that Gardner hopes to reform. Reform of these structures is necessary, overdue, and vital to the future; but reform must begin with the recognition that our current social institutions and our daily experiences are products of the epistemologies that we uphold. Our epistemologies are not remote, irrelevant theoretical abstractions; they are manifested in such immediate realities as the content of the school curriculum, the liberty and responsibility we extend to others, political choices, the purchases we make, and the customs we adopt. A re-theorized version of visual-spatial intelligence must address the critical question of how ways of knowing and seeing are shaped and distorted by power interests.

The Gaze

Julian Thomas (1993) observes that a depiction of the landscape is a selection presented from one standpoint. The single standpoint yields an egocentric visualization that is presumed to be universal. The ideal gaze apprehends all the significant features of a landscape, simultaneously "laying bare the land" to form visual truth and knowledge. Landscapes are visual objects, commodities to be looked at by subject-observers who have been granted the privilege of the *Conforming Gaze*.

MI's utter space is an object to be seen from an egocentric standpoint. One particular view is presumed to be universal and objective, the *right* visualization. The objective features are the ones that are worth seeing. Subjective experiences of engaged vision are discounted. Thomas also notes that prehistoric or non-Western indigenous people often describe places as experienced from within. "Impressionistically" is Thomas's word. Such people experience place as a feeling or an intuited meaning. The concept of the Gaze parallels the distorted instructional practices of tradition-bound art educators who teach as *true facts* the professional critics' opinions of the archive of High Art.

The modernist regime implicitly authorized the Gaze as a distinct way of looking (Mugerauer 1995). The Gaze apprehends all features deemed significant. That which is seen by the authorized observer, say, a Renaissance artist or twentieth-century scientist, is assumed to be universally available and objectively perceivable by all to persons with normal perception. Anyone who lacks a conforming Gaze can be labeled delusional, deficient, and permissible to marginalize.

MI's visual-spatial intelligence dresses the Gaze in academic regalia. By definition, visual-spatial intelligence is the ability to impose an individually determined order on utter space. To select from an individual standpoint is tantamount to specifying the important features of place from a priori, or given, space. Since MI theory construes visual-spatial intelligence as more a capacity of the individual than a function of culture, the Gaze is perhaps an appropriate inclusion. But from a critical perspective, MI's theory of visual-spatial intelligence fails to consider how power relations determine knowledge and sight; that is, how specific forms of power-knowledge relations promote the Gaze. MI's individualistic nature and its inherent isolation of visual-spatial intelligence from culture and experience leave the individual's vision vulnerable to particular, unchallenged forms of authority that administer the *correct* ways of seeing and knowing.

The Conforming Gaze produces from utter space (actually from a place, as will be argued below) sites that are spectacles. As French philosopher Guy DeBord (1995) describes, spectacles do not permit engaged participation; they are dehumanized reproductions that contain illusions of life. The Conforming Gaze is regulated vision. The Conforming Gaze commodifies places as spectacles by forming problematic hierarchies. An example is the way in which society distinguishes between wilderness and wasteland. In this binary opposition, some places—those judged to possess scenic beauty—become sacred ground to be appreciated and protected because they contain beauty. Other places become wasteland authorized for commercial exploitation because they are not deemed inherently beautiful. The distinction between the two is obvious to the Conforming Gaze. It becomes obvious, however, not through naturally evolving processes but rather from the power conferred by specific dominant epistemologies. But ultimately, this power proves illusory and transient as privileged ways of seeing displace themselves. Although portrayed as symbols of strength and celebrated for their rugged beauty on calendars and postcards, the spectacle-places deemed scenic wilderness are now understood to be quite fragile in the face of such ecological disasters as acid rain and other depredations that originate as by-products of the commercial exploitation of the wasteland (Cary 1998). The scenic beauty that formed the pretext for privilege proves unstable and becomes the source of its own displacement.

Ludwig Wittgenstein, in *Tractatus Logico-Philosophicus* 3.411 (1963) referred to logical space. In logical space and geometrical space, Wittgenstein wrote, a place is a possibility—something can exist there. Logical space is analogous to a frame for art: it demarcates, sets apart, or encircles something more specific and more important than the space itself. However, like utter space and the *Ganzfeld*, logical space is an entity presumed to exist prior to the specific details—the perceivable features—that reveal its very existence. MI's theory of visual-spatial intelligence assumes that space exists prior to place and therefore prior to the operations of visual-spatial intelligence. The postmodern perspective encourages a view, however, that questions the independence of space and its priority to place and to visual-spatial intelligence. A re-theorized version of visual-spatial intelligence could be called *intelligence of place* or *place-making*.

In 1952, art historian E. H. Gombrich criticized the innocent eye, the assumption that perception is neutral, that seeing is a unmediated form of objective registration of light rays emanating from an object (254). Gombrich argued that there is much cognitive work—thinking—involved in perception and in acts of spatial intelligence. Further, this cognitive work is influenced by cultural factors. We view places through the lenses of experience and culture. MI's version of visual-spatial intelligence seems to give little attention to the roles of culture and experience in visual-spatial intelligence although Gardner would never eliminate the significance of thought.

Gestalt psychologist Rudolf Arnheim referred to perception as "visual thinking" (1969). Arnheim also wrote about the fallacy of regarding visual perception as a matter of simply registering a copy of what is "out there" (1986, 17). He describes the illusion as opening our eyes to find "the world already given." Arnheim then notes that it takes an "intricate process" to form a visual image. His ideas and those of Gombrich became influential in art, psychology, and education as the cognitive revolution overtook the once-dominant modernist school of psychology, behaviorism. Gombrich and other scholars have convincingly prevailed in the view that utter space is not the purview of the innocent eye.

Deconstructing Space/place

Utter space is a kind of *tabula rasa* upon which visual-spatial intelligence purportedly inscribes its products. MI's visual-spatial intelligence thereby presumes utter space to be a transcendental center or vantage point that remains invulnerable to the distorted power relations that are the familiar tools and by-products of positivism. Utter space transcends any particular place. The concept of utter space is analogous to a development in the modernist movement in art in which sculpture literally moved off the pedestal—away from its base, away from a specific place to become independent of place and locatable anywhere. Utter space is describable only in terms of measurements of its physical properties such as direction, topography, latitude and longitude, and elevation. Yet these operational definitions of utter space are markers of the particulars of specific sites, i.e., "places." The experience of place is based upon direct experience—including perception—of the specific features or properties of particular places. The separation of utter space from place construes visual-spatial intelligence as an isolated human faculty independent of cultural influences or personal subjectivity.

A critical reconstruction of visual-spatial intelligence from a postmodern perspective begins with the deconstruction of the concept of utter space implicit in MI's theory. In MI theory, there is only one Space, the privileged term set in opposition to place: Space/place. Space is a transcendental vantage point, an unproblematic neutrality independent of cultural and individual contingencies—not subject to the inflections of power asymmetries. MI's Space is utter space. Space is a stable center to be experienced objectively in MI theory. Space is a spectacle, the remote focus of a panoptical, authorized Gaze. Space is utter space, an abstraction that is independent of the present and inaccessible to direct, conscious experience. MI's Space differs from the space of ordinary language. In ordinary terms, space is often conceived as the accumulation of topological features of terrain, not the accretion of meanings, memories, and myths that humans associate with particular areas through their locally sited experiences. An example is the "wide, open spaces" of the Western frontier celebrated in Hollywood horse operas of the 1950s and 1960s.

Derrida (1986) based deconstruction on the premise that meaning exists through the relationship between the signifier and the signified. The relationship between the two is variable and contingent—i.e., subject to change according to the individual's experience. There is not an absolute relationship between the signifier and the signified. In Derrida's approach to deconstruction, the privilege awarded to Presence is a central problem in Western philosophy and ways of knowing. A speaker's words, for example, are considered superior—more definitive, more trustworthy, less fallible—than a written description or an interpretation of the speaker's words by a member of his or her audience. Presence is a putative criterion for truth, a transcendental center from which to determine veracity.

Like Derrida's Presence, the Space of MI's visual-spatial intelligence is presumed to be a universal omnipresence. Space is presumed to be everywhere and all-at-once and a totality that requires no signification. Space is presumed to be a transcendental construction of which place is only a particular instance. Space is presumed to be prior and superior to place. Place is like the interpretation or memory of the Speaker's words—less trustworthy, less universal, less absolute. Place is a mere instance of Space, an instance which, being particular, embodies less than the totality of Space. But from the postmodern perspective, these presumptions are untrue.

Deconstruction asserts that the privileged term, Space, unravels itself in its opposition to place, the subordinate term. How does Space undermine itself? Being separated from immediate experience, like the object of Gombrich's innocent eye, Space has no perceivable features, no content. It should be cautioned that the deconstruction of Space/place does not deny the existence of space as an abstraction;

rather, it reveals only the fallacy of the privilege of space in its relation to place in the binary opposition. Deconstruction overturns the priority of space. The individual's cognitive or mental representations of space produced by visual-spatial intelligence are constituted by particulars, which remain properties of place, not space. Deconstuctionists often express the binary hierarchy as *space/place*. This expression might be reconfigured as *Nowhere/now here*.

Space is everywhere, an omnipresence experienced by everyone as the same potential frame or vessel to be filled. But place is not universal; it is a particular localized experience, subject to variations and individual differences. Place is therefore not a reliable concept for building scientifically lawful knowledge. Place is supplemental to space because it is (fictively) less stable, less objective, and less true. Yet art, dance, and architecture fracture space, disrupting its fictive strategies for maintaining transcendent continuity and omnipresence. Art creates particularities of place, a set of immediately perceivable features that become invested with value and meaning like all texts. The sense of place displaces space. That which is purported to be self-evident and self-referential in the concept of space is actually self-displacing. Space is prior to place in MI's theory of visual-spatial intelligence and transcends the particular, concrete, immediate experience of human beings. Space is presumed to exist physically as an objectively perceivable entity. But, we do not directly experience utter space; it has no features available to the senses. We experience places instead.

Space is illusionistically generic, an abstraction with no perceivable particulars to constitute the objects of the cognitive visual-spatial processes that comprise intelligence. Space unravels because it is abstracted and isolated from human experience; it is unknowable and unperceivable. We know and perceive the features of place instead. The features of place become the content of the mental representations that, in turn, are the content—reference points—of visual-spatial intelligence.

In MI theory's visual-spatial intelligence, space is prior to place. The coordinates are projected before the construction of place. A postmodern theory of visual-spatial intelligence insists that the priority of Space be overturned. Further, we should understand that when people speak of space, they mean place—a construction that is made in lived experience by investing a site with meaning. Place is more than the sum of its physical features. To the postmodern mind, place is a temporal construction of culture and the experiences of the individual who engages it and invests it with meaning. This understanding must be augured into a postmodern theory of visual-spatial intelligence. A new theory of visual-spatial intelligence must consider the particularity of place and describe how sense of place is constructed. Visual-spatial intelligence involves creating a sense of place.

Toward a Critical Reconstruction of Visual-Spatial Intelligence

Gardner is, of course, under no obligation to abandon his scientific orientation for a postmodern approach. Concepts such as visual-spatial intelligence are not exclusive properties licensed to particular discourses or competing paradigms. Accordingly, practitioners are free to theorize; theorists are free to practice. Distinctions such as theory and practice are dubious to begin with. Those who intuitively sense the potentials of MI and its visual-spatial intelligence are free to refit MI to today's world using today's ways of knowing. This means regrounding visual-spatial intelligence in new ways of understanding. A critical reconstruction of the concept of visual-spatial intelligence has promise for furthering understanding in the domains of art and aesthetics. But its greatest promise is to help attain the original objectives of MI theory—ones shared by postmodern social critics—to reverse the debilitating effects of the g-theory of intelligence and to reform the uniform school. A critical reconstruction of MI's theory of visual-spatial intelligence must incorporate the individual and cultural subjectivities embodied in the concept of place. It must also include the proposition that visual perception is contingent on particular discourses in which power and knowledge interact to exert control over many phenomena such as intelligence.

The approach used here to re-theorize spatial intelligence is "critical reconstruction." This methodology involves reshaping a quantitative variable as a qualitative one employing deconstruction and other postmodern epistemologies including critical theory, semiotics, poststructuralism, narrative psychology, and others. The culture of positivism that legitimated the application of scientific methods to social and cultural questions also precipitated a number of problems, including the uniform school, developmental mislabeling, and the cultural bias of standardized testing. However, the social sciences have identified certain questions and concepts that are relevant to postmodern epistemologies' attempts to understand the human condition. Critical reconstruction reframes these questions, theories, categories, and concepts. Recasting MI's visual-spatial intelligence as the capacity to construct sense of place is an example. It should be noted that not every quantitative variable has a qualitative counterpart. A thorough discussion of the differences between quantitative and qualitative research is beyond the scope of the present discussion. But it should be recalled that the scientific domain considers quantitative measures to be objective, value-free steps toward summary truth. In contrast, qualitative research is interested in the lived experience and personal meanings of particular human beings in the terms they use to express them. Henry Giroux (1992) notes that the postmodern project has often engaged in dialogues of despair. Critical reconstruction provides an opportunity to aim the complex academic dialogues about the nature and meanings of human relations with one another and the world on a more hopeful trajectory.

Sense of Place

The challenge for a critical reconstruction is to develop a concept of spatial intelligence in which sense of place is meaningfully cast. In contrast to Space, a place is experienced directly, immediately, and configured by a geography of individual subjectivity contextualized in living experience. Neither the mere occupation of

Space nor the perception of topological features is sufficient to create a sense of place. Instead, the creation of meaning and the awareness of engagement in the presence of a place initiate sense of place. The critical reconstruction of a new theory of visual-spatial intelligence proceeds literally from the ground up; it incorporates sense of place as a central function.

Sense of place is an idea that emerged from cultural anthropology and cultural geography. Place is the creation of a layer of meanings and myths and sensed realities built from experience at a site. Place is local. The French have a saying about a good local wine. *Un vin qui a gout du terroir* means that a wine tastes of the local soil. A sense of place is comprised of particularities such as the taste of the local soil and expresses the idea that the artifacts of a locale hold its memories; that is, wine, food, and perhaps dialect or accent all are specific qualities associated with particular places. This is a poetic accord, not science.

Individuals who have a high degree of visual-spatial intelligence are those who, through cognitive, affective, and sensory modalities, forge a sense of place from direct experience. This act of making a sense of place is an act of making meaning. The meanings constructed are valued both personally and in cultural contexts and domains described by Gardner. Individuals possess high degrees of visual-spatial intelligence to the degree that their cognitive reconstruction of place includes features and associated meanings valued as relevant to a critical view of the human condition. Value is instrumental in visual-spatial intelligence. Experience of place and the internal, cognitive representation of place are reciprocals that continually reconstruct one another.

As Gardner cites examples of individuals with high degrees of visual-spatial intelligence, we see that meaning and subjective experience play important roles even in MI theory's version of visual-spatial intelligence. In these examples, he departs from his practice of reviewing the results of scientific research and explores more qualitative, interpretative aspects of visual-spatial intelligence. The possibilities for reclaiming lost subjectivity and meaning in a re-theorized visual-spatial intelligence emerge as Gardner takes us through several narratives. He cites (1993) stories of *idiot savants* who, despite their low IQs, can produce aesthetically valued paintings or drawings. He then points to well-known scientists and artists who speak of their abilities to "see" entire finished solutions or results in their imaginations before they actually begin work. But the most interesting examples are the highly developed spatial abilities of indigenous peoples such as the Gikwe bushmen of the Kalihari desert, the Eskimo of the Arctic, and the Puluwat master sailors of the Caroline Islands in the South Pacific. Each group is famous for locating themselves and maneuvering in harsh, dangerous environments that appear virtually featureless to the eyes of the uninitiated. The Puluwat sailors use a system of navigation that relies on the relative position of the sun and stars, the "feel" of the current, the color of the water, the location of reefs, and the effects of weather on all these points of reference. The outcome is that the Puluwat sailors can navigate with a level of skill that awes Western sailors who use the sextant, compass, radar, and other precise navigational technology. The Puluwat sailor, of course, determines location by seeing various signs and interpreting them according to prior knowledge to chart a course to the destination.

The importance of sense of place in the re-theorizing of visual-spatial intelligence is underscored in this example. The sailors use signs that are properties of particular places, not space. The starlight takes on significance to them because it falls on a particular place. The water color is characteristic of a particular place. It is place, not space, in which these signs or reference points reside and are presented for the sailors to perceive and interpret and act upon.

Does the Puluwat sailors' ability meet Gardner's definition of spatial intelligence, i.e., forming and adjusting or manipulating a mental representation of the spatial realm that is valued in a cultural context? In a literal way, yes. A mental representation is formed and changed according to the sailors' progress toward their destination and according to changes in the weather and other phenomena. But it is conceivable that in the Caroline Islands, such sailing ability is admired but not uncommon in everyday life. There, such sailing may not be considered the magic feat that Westerners with the aid of technological instruments consider it to be. This example reminds us that the degree of visual-spatial intelligence deemed high in a particular cultural context may not translate as high in another.

Gardner (1983, 192–94) adduces the example of advanced visual-spatial abilities of chess masters. They must mentally "see" a number of optional moves in advance. In this case, the player visualizes the chess piece at a particular place on the chessboard and considers the consequences of that particular position. This example and that of the Puluwat sailors again suggest that a new theory of visual-spatial intelligence must recognize the importance of sense of place in contrast to space.

Understandings from the art world also inform a new theory of visual-spatial intelligence. Gardner's definition of visual-spatial intelligence calls for the individual to form a mental representation of the spatial realm. This requisite implies that the optical accuracy of the representation of an art work created by an individual can become a criterion for determining that individual's degree of visual-spatial intelligence. This component of the MI definition privileges a single aesthetic strategy for art making, that of *mimesis*. Mimesis is the theory that art should try to render or depict the optical appearance of nature literally (*mime* and *imitate* are its English cognates). Mimesis has been the aesthetic strategy in force and the source for establishing aesthetic criteria since before the Renaissance through the remains of the modernist period of the late twentieth century. Consistent with its modernist foundations, the MI theory of visual-spatial intelligence privileges the aesthetic tradition of mimesis.

Mimesis requires that an artwork include *optically correct* representations that inventory appearances and surfaces of the physical world. Such art creates a special type of space, *pictorial space,* which is the illusion of three-dimensional space in the two-dimensional format. This is accomplished via conventions of linear perspective and other artistic devices such as chiaroscuro, sfumato, and atmospheric perspective employed in art since the Renaissance.

If the awarding of this privilege to mimesis seems a theoretical trifle, it should be noted that it has important implications for school art programs. Mimesis ultimately leads to a form of instruction that essentializes one set of canonical art works and their *correct* interpretations that comprise a safe, highly controlled, but insipid, curricular space for art that is separated from the contemporary art world. Students are also implicitly encouraged to disregard their own personal art worlds in favor of the archive of high art, which is predominantly mimetic and which features optically accurate renderings of the visual world. These representations are typically of such technical virtuosity that most students abandon attempts to make art because they feel that they cannot hope to achieve the standards established by the aesthetic criteria associated with mimetic aesthetic strategies. Many art teachers notice that students typically cease spontaneously making art when they reach adolescence. Other aesthetic strategies, particularly those of contemporary art and those of the diverse forms of ethnic or outsider art, offer school art programs greater opportunities for including art-making in the daily lives of all children. Such strategies include appropriation, bricolage, pastiche, etc. In the Renaissance, the goal of artists was to capture nature's appearance using such artistic practices and conventions as linear perspective and others named above that capture the physical appearance of the world *out there*. As such, this privilege awarded to mimetic aesthetics avoids addressing aspects of art such as its social functions, the ways in which art constructs our experience of the world, and the aesthetic strategies and artistic conventions of non-Western cultures.

Another contribution from art theory to a re-theorized concept of visual-spatial intelligence is the challenge to the legitimacy of the idea of the autonomous art object. MI's concept of space undermines itself by its abstractness or isolation from human experience. The application of the autonomy principle of modernist aesthetics to sculpture brought about the literal movement of the sculpture off-the-pedestal, as noted earlier. Relinquishing the base meant that sculpture could go anywhere and fit into any environment and could be an objective, nomadic art independent from any specific place. But a postmodern challenge ensued. In 1981, sculptor Richard Serra installed his work, *Tilted Arch,* a 12' × 120' piece of Cor-Ten steel. This work was conceived for a specific site, not just any anonymous space a patron happened to prefer. A 1989 attempt to move the enormous piece prompted Serra to protest that to remove it from its original place (to "site-adjust it") would destroy it as a work of art (Kwon 2000, 39). *Tilted Arch* was a site-specific work conceived for the Federal Plaza in Washington, D.C., and nowhere else. It took a measure of its aesthetic value and meaning from the specific site, and it confers certain meaning and value on the place it inhabits. Place is part of the content of a work of art, part of its iconicity, its meaning.

A useful analogy for the creation of sense of place is *palimpsest*. The word evolved from times when paper, parchment, or other material for writing was precious. A palimpsest is a document written on a surface that has been erased, perhaps re-erased and re-used many times. The document currently visible is but one of many layers of meaning that have occupied the surface.

In the MI model, visual-spatial intelligence is temporally independent. That is, an individual's visual-spatial ability is relatively stable, reliable, and consistent over time. Gardner stipulates that visual-spatial intelligence, like all the multiple intelligences, is determined in part according to the value it produces in a recognized domain, say, the art world. However, MI's theory of visual-spatial intelligence cannot account for how cultural change may radically influence the reassessment of an individual's visual-spatial intelligence. Consider Van Gogh. He was definitely not valued during his lifetime — he sold only one painting and that to his brother. Van Gogh therefore would not have been considered to possess a high degree of visual-spatial intelligence. He became posthumously visually-spatially intelligent. A re-theorized visual-spatial intelligence is skeptical of the implicit claim of temporal independence.

In a re-theorized visual-spatial intelligence, the particular supercedes the general. Art historian and theorist E. H. Gombrich (1952) traces the history of the landscape genre in art. He argues that landscape painting developed from the backgrounds in celebratory portraits into a genre in its own right. Gombrich brings to light the work of Richard Norgate. Writing in 1950, Norgate observed that the genre of landscape painting began as incidental background details ("innocent filler") in portrait painting, which were not considered worthy subjects for painterly depiction. Recall that the patronage system that dominated the economics of the art world demanded portraits to memorialize, if not aggrandize, the wealthy or powerful patrons who commissioned them. Landscapes per se, at least the pastoral scenes that we think of today, did not exist as a genre or practice in art until after the Renaissance. Gombrich uses the term "parega" to refer to Norgate's innocent filler. Parega are much like drollery, the whimsical doodling that often appears in the margins of illuminated manuscripts. Gombrich's usage evolved from the word *parer*, a French word that translates as "to embellish or adorn." The painter embellishes the canvas with artistically insignificant gestures as parenthetica to the greater iconic significance of the main subject, the artist's patron. Landscape painting evolved from general features in the backgrounds that were not originally meant to be taken as attempts to depict specific places.

We can also observe from our contemporary perspective that the backgrounds grew to become differentiated, more specific depictions of actual places instead of imagined details, much like portraits of the places themselves. Sense of place is constructed in much the same way that the landscape genre developed. Gombrich cites Norgate's idea to support the theory that the landscape genre developed in response to Renaissance theories of art, including mimesis. For present purposes, Norgate's idea provides an example of the way in which sense of place evolves. Sense of place — a central component of a re-theorized spatial intelligence — evolves in an accretionary, but not necessarily rational, fashion. The development of sense of place is characterized by a differentiation of detail that moves from the general to the specific. Indeed, this differentiation of detail to create a representation of a specific sense of place involves rendering a likeness of the physical properties or topology of a site. But the development of sense of place is not limited to physical structures. The cognitive, affective, and cultural domains are salient as well. The process of making sense of place is a differentiation—a specification of the details of meaning, of myth-making, a differentiation of narrative detail. The place-making that marks postmodern visual-spatial intelligence is more complex than MI theory's visual-spatial intelligence, which required only that a mental representation of the visual realm be formed. Place-making goes beyond imitative, literal visual recording of physical characteristics.

Roland Barthes's use of the term "myth" offers a way to think about how a sense of place evolves. Sites are texts and become places when they are imbued with meaning through the processes generally described as semiosis. In *Mythologies Today* (1972), Barthes argues that myth is a form of signification, a type of speech in which meaning is communicated. The content of the message is not the defining quality of a myth. Instead, a text becomes myth by virtue of being designated as a sign. A signifier—an object, text, or place—becomes invested with meaning by being associated with a signified. The signifier and the signified form the sign or, in Barthes' analogy, a myth. A mythologized place is a palimpsest. It is constituted by the superimposition of lives and culture and history rather than by its content, i.e., physical features. Each layer of myth is constructed by a different individual and should not be considered an objective reality. For example, the ecologist or botanist walking in an old-growth forest experiences it and defines it differently than would a logger. Mythologized places are galleries of multiple subjectivities, sites of particular discursive practices, polysemous signs. The postmodern perspective reminds us that the physical properties of place are incidentals to—not the determinants of—the meanings of a mythologized place. Nor do the physical properties convey the totality of our sense of place. A myth-imbued place is a text that is repeatedly overwritten as individuals mythologize it and give it meaning through their experiences there.

A principle of phenomenology asserts that the world is seen from the individual's vantage point, that is, from the particular place in which the individual is situated. Establishing a role for sense of place in a re-theorized visual-spatial intelligence involves understanding how place operates as a vantage point and how it shapes knowledge and experience of the external world. Further, place-making should not be considered a biological potential like MI's version of visual-spatial intelligence. It is not a capacity waiting to be deployed. Rather, place-making is an interactive activity, a doing, a making, and a praxis in which place and place-maker are both forces that exert influence. It is an engaged construction of meaning. Places and people reciprocally construct one another.

The invention of linear perspective by Brunelleschi (formally described by Alberti in his 1435 *Della Pittura*) was also a factor in the emergence of a landscape art in which specific places were depicted. Linear perspective allowed painters to represent with accuracy. Painters could depict a three-dimensional world on a two-dimensional surface. Objects were organized in a predictable scale and proportion. Linear perspective, however, is merely an artistic convention, a practice by painters, a device used to depict a particular individual's view of reality. It came to be certified as reality itself, the scientifically accurate, true appearance. It is ironic that linear perspective has come to be regarded as a way of revealing truth, because it is actually a system for creating illusion. MI's theory of spatial intelligence implicitly subscribes to this modernist presumption.

Linear perspective has another subtle property that Julian Thomas (1993) brings to light. Linear perspective establishes a relationship between the subject viewer and the object depicted in the picture. The viewer is outside the picture, a nonparticipant, independent, disengaged, out of the story, a voyeur of the spectacle. The implicit feeling is that the viewer is seeing the perfect view, the ideal Gaze, and that the scene is passive, frozen, unchanging, like Keats's lovers on his Grecian urn. This device privileges vision over other senses.

Pictorial space, for example, is a concept familiar to artists and art historians. For philosopher Suzanne K. Langer (1975), pictorial space is the sine qua non of art. However, the presence of pictorial space, an intangible, abstract concept, can only be manifested by the depiction of the features which are the properties of particular places; light that falls on place—not space—illuminates the topological features that the painter paints.

Pictorial space becomes instantiated in particular works of art. Leonardo's *Ecstasy of St. Francis* and Ansel Adams's *Moonlight over Hernandez, NM* are examples of art works notable for their representations of particular places. Each work is characterized by the manifest presence of pictorial space, but pictorial space is not prior in these works to the particular features of the places depicted. Instead, pictorial space emerges from place and does not exist without place. Place itself is prior. Indeed, the entire landscape genre developed out of the emergence of sense of place. Painting particular places instantiates pictorial space.

Critical Sense of Place

Lucy Lippard (1997) writes about the ideas of Marxist art critics who claim that landscape painting often glorifies property rights, buttresses the status quo, and fails to engage viewers in the social dynamics of landscape. MI's version of visual-spatial intelligence is subject to the same criticism.

MI theory stipulates that each intelligence produce outcomes that are valued in the domain of life which each intelligence represents. The art world, for example, is one of the domains that value the products of visual-spatial intelligence. We can transport this requirement from Gardner's MI theory to a new visual-spatial intelligence. The potential outcomes of the new intelligence would include the ability to create place and to discern how place is culturally and politically inflected. Critical sense of place thus leads to agency and the resistance to oppressive practices that occupy and regulate places.

Wendell Berry (1990) has written of a "placed person." A placed person is one who is often identified as "other" because of differences associated with that person's commitment to the culture of a specific place. The mountain accent of a coal miner in the southern Appalachians and the body-piercing of an urban youth are examples. These groups are often marginalized because of these expressions of sense of place. Berry's concept also alludes to the reciprocity among sense of place, sense of self, sense of group identity. Each of the vital components of human life construct and constitute one another. Places inform identities and vice versa. Places, like identity, are developed discursively in processes grounded in social interaction. Accordingly, both may change over time. Kenneth Gergen (1991) questioned the stability and even the future of the concept of the self. As with the self, we need not require that a sense of place manifest stability.

A critical visual-spatial intelligence centered on the ability to construct a sense of place promotes enhanced awareness of sustainable environmental practices. A new conception of visual-spatial intelligence legitimizes such postmodern artistic conventions as pastiche, bricolage, and appropriation, strategies that encourage re-cycling and re-use of images, ideas, and materials. Perhaps the most important outcome of a re-theorized visual-spatial intelligence is the incorporation of a community orientation and connectedness. The conscious placing of self in relation to others and to the physical world is a valuable outcome in any domain.

I. F. Stone (1988) provides a vivid example of the importance of sense of place to a critical visual-spatial intelligence. In contrast to Wendell Berry's concept of a placed person who bears place markers, some enhancing and some diminishing his identity, becoming a displaced person (*apolis*) in the time of Socrates was considered the worst fate that could befall a citizen. *Apolis* means "cityless." Involvement in community and place were principal Athenian values since the times of Herodotus and Sophocles. The Greeks considered being cityless a tragic fate. Stone cites Aristotle's analogy of a cityless man as like a solitary game piece in checkers, which, of course, has no function or meaning when alone. It needs other checkers and placement on a board to have meaning and a purpose. Stone notes that the Athenians believed that a good citizen was educated and continued to improve by participating fully in the affairs of the city. Without involvement in civic affairs, a person was isolated from justice, law, and virtue. Athenians assumed that living in the *polis* was an education in itself. Persons who took no part is civic affairs were considered no-accounts, bad citizens. Solon, the Athenian lawgiver, stipulated that nonparticipation be punished by revocation of citizenship. Stone relates that at the funeral of Socrates, Pericles referred to him as *idiotes,* a disparaging term for a good-for-nothing, apolitical nonparticipant in civic affairs. The term, of course, later came to mean a person with diminished mental capacity. A solitary person is in a place that cannot give his life meaning by association with a community.

I was once a member of an audience on a guided tour of an antebellum plantation outside New Orleans. The plantation manor house was undergoing historic preservation. The tour guide told us of the extensive research about the place. Essentially, this research was limited to the history of the family who owned the plantation and their various business successes and failures. When the guide called for questions, I asked about the rest of the story, i.e., the family histories and biographical details of the slaves who worked on the plantation. These stories were part of the place all along, but they had been suppressed or even erased by a specific way of writing history that postmodern epistemology regards as specious. Critical narratives must be a component of a re-theorized intelligence of place making. A critical visual-spatial intelligence resists attempts to erase the diverse layers of meaning that constitute the palimpsest of place.

The Phenomenology of Sense of Place

In his phenomenological approach to the concept of place, Edward S. Casey (1996) contests the implicit assumption that in human experience, space and time exist prior to place. He also demonstrates the role of personal experience in creating a critical sense of place. He observes that people seem to regard as commonsense the notion that space and time are general universal entities of which place is a mere particular instance, that is, given specific form out of the vast *everythingness* of pre-existing space. He instead argues that human beings experience sense of place directly, immediately, and prior to forming a concept of space. Place, then, is prior to space. Place is the specification of space and time. The addition of temporality to the concept of sense of place gives it a postmodern nuance. Time means that sense of place may not be required to be a stable property of a geographic site; that sense of place can be multiform, an experience of individuals. The sense of the particular in human experience must precede the sense of the universal. Since the Enlightenment and Newtonian physics, the scientism that so permeates our culture has fostered a "natural attitude" that space is absolute and infinite, and that human experience comprehends only appropriated selections of space, much like a sample drawn from a population.

Casey points to an anthropological study of place names that postulates that space is like Locke's tabula rasa, a vast, featureless blank slate upon which place names reflecting human experience are historically inscribed. Placeness is conferred on a particular geographical site as humans interact there. In his study of the Pintupi of the Australian desert, anthropologist F. R. Myers (1991) described the process of place-making as a story becoming attached to a place.

Casey notes that space is prior only for anthropological analysis; place is primary in the lived experience of his human subjects. It is phenomenologically untenable to accept that utter space precedes place in human experience, especially in perception. A person apprehends the particularities of a given place via the senses. Sense of place arises from the sensory modalities and through active knowing situated in the culture. Perception cannot by definition occur where there are no features, such as on a tabula rasa or a completely neutral *Ganzfeld*. People perceive in social, cultural, physical contexts. Sensory operations are inherently involved in place-making.

Casey also notes that place is more like an event than a thing. It occurs within the person, not as a result of the physical properties of topology. Because the dispositions and histories individuals bring to a site, and the experiences they encounter there are so divergent, they may construct very different senses of place at the same site. Also, sense of place is not objectively the same for everyone who encounters it. Place may not evoke the same experiences.

In his 1990 book *The Experience of Place,* Tony Hiss advocates re-evaluating our society's approach to public places based on a new sensitivity to the subjective personal experiences of the individuals who experience them. He believes that we can enrich our lives by creating and sustaining pleasurable, meaningful places that fulfill deep human emotional needs. Hiss calls for us to recognize that damaged places can damage human lives emotionally as well as biologically. Although he avoids articulating an elaborate theoretical structure on which to base his arguments, Hiss offers a concept, *simultaneous perception,* that emerged from his richly detailed personal experiences at various places. Simultaneous perception is one of the psychological processes important to how we experience places and create a sense of place. Simultaneous perception occurs as direct experience of place. It is an awareness of the totality of a place that emerges from the accretionary experience of its details. Simultaneous perception is a consciousness of place in the here and now. It is similar to the concept of synesthesia, the interaction of several senses in an aesthetic experience. Simultaneous perception involves all the senses. In fact, Hiss refers to it as a sixth sense. Simultaneous perception also includes awareness of how the experience of a place operates with the person. It operates continuously, in conjunction with other sensory, intellectual, affective, and cognitive functions. As the terminology denotes, simultaneous perception is an awareness of a variety of things at once: *an all-at-onceness.* The scope of simultaneous perception is seemingly contradictory; it involves focusing on both specific details and the broad, gestalt-like relationships among them. The close-up and the panoramic coexist on the same plane of consciousness.

The types of things circumscribed by simultaneous perception include light, air quality, colors, size of walls, arrangement of rooms, smells, etc. Hiss cites the work of architect Christopher Alexander and Associates (1977), whose research identified over 250 elements or features that influence how people experience places.

Sensing a multisensory pattern is the outcome of simultaneous perception. It is all the ways we are connected to place. Simultaneous perception emerges over time; sense of place or place-knowledge does not happen instantaneously. As Hiss reminds us, achieving knowledge of a place through simultaneous perception requires sufficient time to allow the sense and the mind to act and to form a picture or map from experience.

Simultaneous perception involves making a deliberate judgment about the fitness, promise, or worth of a place. Hiss notes that people are drawn to places that afford rich experiences. Two criteria for making this determination are whether a place seems to promise a richness of sensory information or stimuli and whether there are any signals of danger. Hiss cites the research of Marian Diamond at Berkeley that found that the cortexes of rats placed in enriched environments increased in size while the cortexes of rats placed in impoverished environments were diminished. Since the cortex is the area of the brain associated with thinking and knowledge, these findings support the view that sense of place involves mental activities that are properly considered forms of intelligence.

As an example of the workings of simultaneous perception, Hiss describes and analyzes his own experiences at New York's Prospect Park in the borough of Brooklyn, designed in the nineteenth century by Frederick Law Olmstead and Calvert Vaux. The entrance to Prospect Park is an undistinguished portal into an enriched experience of place forged by simultaneous perception. The entrance is a plaza adjacent to a large and noisy traffic intersection. A large arch honoring the Civil War dead shadows the entrance to Prospect Park. However, after walking for five minutes or so down the pathway from the entrance, Hiss noticed a quietness that seemed to balance bird sounds with the receding traffic din. Beyond the first of several hills, the entrance—and of course—the city—disappears. The visitor sees only the park environment.

The path then leads to the Endale Arch, a vaulted Gothic tunnel one hundred feet long that frames a spectacular vista called Long Meadow. As Hiss emerged from the tunnel, he felt the air cool and noticed subtle gradations of light in the seventy-five-acre meadow beyond. He also heard the sound of his own footsteps and noticed the scents of the park. He realized that this locale was one of the few places—or perhaps the only place—in New York that afforded a mile-long vista containing only grass and trees.

The experience of place in Prospect Park culminated for Hiss in the realization that his way of looking changed while there: his attention was broadly diffused; yet he calmly regarded all the individual things around him. In Hiss's experience of place, vision was realigned to incorporate both the general and the particular. This seemingly contradictory connectedness was the result of simultaneous perception. It is both a prerequisite and an outcome of experiencing place.

Another such prerequisite is the diversion of attention from one's interior monologue, or what Hiss calls "the conversation inside our heads." The consequence is an increased ability to attend to the information available in a place.

Critical Vision

Seeing begins to become critical vision when it incorporates heightened attention to the subtle, often unnoticed details and qualities of places—those features that are not preframed for our visual consumption by a dominant culture. The unnoticed features often occupy the subliminal margins of vision. Consciousness of these details is often the point of departure for the unique personal experiences that become the myths of places. These details are the parega to which Gombrich alluded.

Gombrich, as noted earlier, applied the term to the background filler in early landscape paintings. There is another dimension to the meaning of the word that opens new possibilities for developing a postmodern understanding of the workings of visual-spatial intelligence. Immanuel Kant, in his 1790 *Critique of Judgement,* located aesthetic qualities such as beauty, meaning, and sublimity within the art work. These transcendent qualities were inherent in the art work and were its most significant aspects, since they were essential to its artness. He distinguished between these primary intrinsic properties and parega, those features such as the frame, the materials, a drape on a figure, etc., that were extrinsic to the aesthetic value of the work of art. Parega were the incidentals, mere ornament. But Jacques Derrida, in *The Truth in Painting* (1978), describes how this separation of intrinsic and extrinsic features poses the unanswerable question, what should be included in the work of art and what should be excluded? That is, where does the artness of the art work begin and end? What determines the placement the frame? Derrida argues convincingly that any frame is permeable. Any paregon is an unstable link between the *inside* of the artwork (its aesthetic value) and the outside world. But the limits of inside/outside are not fixed. The aesthetic judgment remains uncertain. With Derrida, a critical theory of visual-spatial intelligence distrusts Kant's binary opposition. The frame of postmodern vision—in personal experience, not just art—is permeable and negotiable.

Our language underscores the primacy of vision in our ways of thinking and knowing. The most common way to express understanding is to say, "I see." Vision equates to knowing in the modernist paradigm. If we assume, in accord with the position of naïve realism, that the world is *out there,* then vision is a simple matter of copying or taking in all the central features of a visual array as they are given. But the critical view (the ubiquitous vision metaphor again) insists that vision is not so simple and certainly not mimetic. The modern mythos regards seeing as a privileged form of knowing the ultimate truth and of experiencing truth firsthand. "Seeing is believing" is a familiar cliché. This proposition brings us to Derrida's (1986) identification of the most perturbing illusion of Western philosophy, the privilege of the present. Most postmodern epistemologies regard vision as a privileged process embedded in virtually all forms of power and knowledge.

While postmodern thinkers and teachers admit that vision is central to knowing and thinking, they decline to characterize it as objective or stable. Vision is historically, politically, and socially contingent. The postmodern understanding of visual perception underscores the constructive nature of vision and knowledge. Certain epistemologies or discourses shape how we see and know. Visual perception pervades what Suren Lalvani (1996, 2) calls the "ocular epistemologies." The ocular epistemology shapes the relations among knowledge, power, and the body. The interactive nature of vision, knowledge, and power is expressed notably by the uses of photographic images. In the contemporary consumer culture, specific images of the body create desire and impel selective actions. Consider images of Schwartzenegger-like superheroes and the tall, slender figures of fashion models. Vision pervades ways of knowing and the discourses and transformations that ensue.

Lalvani notes Michel Foucault's concept of visibility (1996, 25). Foucault argues that things are made visible—authorized to be seen—by the interaction of power and knowledge. Giles Deleuze (1986, 63) refers to this as positive unconscious, or the determination by a specific discourse of what *can* be seen, not what *is* seen. Vision is not only constructed; it is authorized and regulated by historically specific regimes of power and knowledge.

The constructive nature of vision is not an insight exclusive to philosophy. The science of psychology reached a similar conclusion. Gestalt psychologists learned that the mind imposes certain patterns on a stimulus encountered by the eye. In perception, we see a stimulus not in totally objective fashion but rather through the lens of structures already present in the mind. For example, when viewing a line figure of a nearly complete circle, one missing, say, an arc of about ten degrees or so, we tend to see the figure as a closed circle. Our perception tends to be shaped by the pre-existing idea of circleness in our minds. Our perception of the given stimulus conforms to that pre-existing idea.

Conclusion

Kuhn (1970, 92–97) makes a distinction between scientific and political revolutions. In both types, a sense of malfunction or errancy precipitates a crisis of confidence among adherents to a particular paradigm that undermines that paradigm's explanatory adequacy. He differentiates three types of phenomena that, upon observation, may initiate crisis and consequently instigate development of new, more adequate theories. The first type is phenomena which, because they are already well explained by the paradigm, are unproblematic. New theories arising from observations of such phenomena are eventually considered irrelevant. A second type consists of phenomena that fall within the paradigm's definition of an appropriate problem but seem to require extension or modification of existing theories. No new ways of knowing are required. A third category contains observations of phenomena that are anomalous—inexplicable and completely outside the purview of the existing paradigm. Completely new ways of knowing are needed to explain observations of these phenomena.

MI falls into Kuhn's second category because Gardner neither relies upon nor develops new ways of knowing. His evidence is from traditional grand narrative psychology. The ways of knowing in MI remain virtually identical to those that produced g-theory. MI theory is essentially a political revision of g-theory, a scientific theory of intelligence. Although MI theory is more appealing and democratic at first glance, it remains a stepchild of positivism's exclusively quantitative methodologies and of grand narrative psychology.

Further, Kuhn observes that knowledge does not replace ignorance; it replaces a different type of knowledge. In science, crisis sometimes stems from the accumulation of anomalous observations—exceptions that the paradigm cannot explain. In both scientific and political revolutions, the crisis of confidence involves a breakdown of community relations and dialogue about what constitutes an appropriate problem and a solution. Many of MI theory's contemporary adherents are motivated by the crisis of confidence around the old paradigm. However, they are ultimately left without new ways of identifying and solving the problems they identify.

A theory of visual-spatial intelligence reconstructed along postmodern lines can help transform schools, the art world, and environmental practices as well. New ways of interpreting visual intelligence have conceptually challenged some existing schools by opening art education to, among other things, arts integration, the practice of teaching a variety of subjects through art. The Ashley River School in Charleston, South Carolina, The Getty Institute's various integration programs, and the A+ Schools project of North Carolina's Kenon Institute are prime examples. The arts integration concept is that art instruction, when freed from the constraints that impose mimesis-inspired definitions of good art and good art skills, will be freed to accomplish deeper forms of learning. Also, the re-theorized visual intelligence would bring to school art the legitimacy of noncanonical forms and styles of art such as folk, ethnic, and feminist art.

A new theory must also serve such ends as social justice and the enrichment of our lives through learning instead of the production of automatons for the workplace. Psychologist and intelligence researcher James M. Cattell commented in 1926 that psychoanalysis is not so much a question of science as a matter of taste. Cattell's observation aptly describes the choice between MI theory and traditional concepts of intelligence testing. But there are choices other than g-theory and MI theory. The re-theorizing of MI theory will provide a third choice. The future of MI, however, will be determined not in rapprochement between mainstream science and postmodern theory but in its embodiment in critical practice.

References

Alexander, C. (1977). *A pattern of language: Towns, buildings, construction*. New York: Oxford University Press.

Arnheim, R. (1969). *Visual thinking*. Berkeley: University of California Press.

———. (1982). *The power of the center: A study of composition in the visual arts*. Berkeley: University of California Press.

———. (1986). *New essays in the psychology of art*. Berkeley: University of California Press.

Bachelard, G. (1994). *The poetics of space* (M. Jolas, trans.). New York: Orion.

Barthes, R. (1972). *Mythologies* (A. Lavers, trans.). New York: Hill & Wang.

Berry, W. (1990). *What are people for?* San Francisco: North Point.

———. (1987). *Home economics*. San Francisco: North Point.

Bloomer, C. (1976). *Principles of perception*. New York: Van Nostrand Reinhold.

Bowles, S., & Gintis, H. (1976). *Schooling in capitalist America*. New York: Basic Books.

Cary, B. Personal conversation. August 5, 2002.

Cary, R. (1998). *Critical art pedagogy: Foundations for postmodern art education*. New York: Garland.

Casey, E. (1996). *The fate of place: A philosophical history*. Berkeley: University of California Press.

DeBord, G. (1995). *The society of the spectacle* (D. Nicholson-Smith, trans.). New York: Zone.

Deleuze, G. (1986). *Cinema 1: The movement image*. Trans. H. Tomlinson & B. Habberjam. Minneapolis: University of Minnesota Press.

Derrida, J. (1986). Différance. In M. Taylor (ed.), *Deconstruction in context: Literature and philosophy* (pp. 57–79). Chicago: University of Chicago Press.

———. (1978). *The truth in painting.* Trans. G. Bennington and I. McLeod. Chicago: University of Chicago Press.

Elkins, J. (1996). *The object stares back.* New York: Simon & Schuster.

Eysenck, H. (1953). *The uses and abuses of psychology.* Baltimore: Penguin.

Gardner, H. (1983). *Frames of minds: The theory of multiple intelligences.* New York: Basic Books.

———. (1993). *Multiple intelligences: The theory in practice* New York: Basic Books.

Gergen, K. (1991). *The saturated self.* New York: Basic Books.

Gibson, E. (1969). *Principles of perceptual learning and development.* New York: Appleton-Century-Crofts.

Giroux, Henry. (1992). Educational leadership and the crisis of democratic government. *Educational Researcher,* 21(4), 4–11.

Gombrich, E. (1952). *Norm and form: Studies in the art of the Renaissance.* Chicago: University of Chicago Press.

———. (1960). *Art and illusion.* New York: Pantheon.

Haber, R., & Hershenson, M. (1973). *The psychology of visual perception.* New York: Holt Rinehart & Winston.

Helmstadter, G. (1964). *Principles of psychological measurement.* New York: Appleton-Century-Crofts.

Hiss, T. (1990). *The experience of place.* New York: Alfred Knopf.

Kant, I. (1985). *The critique of judgement.* Trans. J. Bernard. New York: Simon & Schuster.

Kincheloe, J., & Steinberg, S. (eds.). (1996). *Measured lies.* New York: St. Martin's Press.

Krauss, R. (1989). Photography's discursive spaces. In R. Bolton, Richard (ed.), *The contest of meaning: Critical histories of photography* (pp. 150–172). Boston: MIT Press.

Kuhn, T. (1970). *The structure of scientific revolutions.* Chicago: University of Chicago Press.

Kwon, M. (2000). One place after another: Notes on site specificity. In E. Suderburg (ed.), *Space, site, intervention: Situating installation art* (pp. 121–137). Minneapolis: University of Minnesota Press.

Lalvani, S. (1996). *Photography, vision, and the production of modern bodies.* Albany: State University of New York Press.

Langer, S. (1975). *The problems of art.* New York: Scribner.

Lippard, L. (1997). *The lure of the local: Senses of place in a multicentered society.* New York: New Press.

Lyotard, J. (1984). *The postmodern condition.* Minneapolis: University of Minnesota Press.

Merkin, D. (1998). Freud rising. *New Yorker,* 9 November, pp. 50–57.

Mugerauer, R. (1995). *Interpreting environments: Tradition, deconstruction, hermeneutics.* Austin: University of Texas Press.

Myers, F. (1991). *Pintupi country, Pintupi self: Sentiment, place, and politics among western desert Aborigines.* Berkeley: University of California Press.

Popper, K. (1961). *The logic of scientific discovery.* New York: Science Editions.

Snow, C. P. (1964). *The two cultures and the scientific revolution: A second look.* Cambridge: Cambridge University Press.

Spring, J. (1976). *The sorting machine.* New York: Longman.

Stone, I. (1988). *The trial of Socrates.* New York: Doubleday.

Tabachnick, B., & Fidell, L. (1989). *Using multivariate statistics* (2nd ed.). New York: Harper & Row.

Thomas, J. (1993). The politics of vision and the archeologies of landscape. In B. Bender (ed.), *Landscape: Politics and perspectives* (pp. 207–216). New York: Oxford University Press.

Wechsler, D. (1944). *The measurement of adult intelligence* (3rd ed.). Baltimore: Williams & Wilkins.

Wittgenstein, L. (1963). *Tractatus logico-philosophicus* (D. Pears & B. McGuinness, trans.). London: Routledge & Kegan Paul.

Chapter 6

Donald S. Blumenthal-Jones

BODILY-KINESTHETIC INTELLIGENCE AND THE DEMOCRATIC IDEAL

When Howard Gardner broached the idea of multiple intelligences in 1983, many educators, myself included, embraced his thoughts. We believed that, after many years, a major thinker in education had, at last, acknowledged what many of us understood tacitly or quietly: there is more to a human being than his or her ability to compute or read or write.

Gardner was presenting countervailing ideas to the conventional curricula favored by school leaders and policy-makers. Such curricula are informed by three underlying ideological positions: faculty psychology (the mind as a set of muscles needing particular exercise) (Kliebard 1995); Western thinking that the best kind of knowledge can be found in mathematics (Giddens 1976), and thus certain muscles need more exercise than others; and a perceived need for a certain kind of literacy that moves civilization forward (Eagleton 1983), thus a focus on the literary canon. This approach fulfills not only the mandate laid out by Charles Eliot in the mid-nineteenth century (Kliebard 1995) but also the expectations of the business community that relies upon schools to tacitly license people through the legitimating process of gaining a high school diploma and a college degree (Spring 1997; Perkinson 1995). The business community clearly accepts the credentialing process of students although most people's lives will not be taken up with advanced mathematics or close literary analysis. Nevertheless, the adage "to get a good job get a good education" holds cultural center stage, and it is apparently believed that "a good education," as presently constituted, will lead to a good worker.

Some of us who accepted Gardner's notions often took great exception to the idea that "educated person" and "good worker" are synonymous. Our interests focused upon an holistic understanding of human beings and a concomitant education that would enable a flourishing of the many capacities which cultures, the world over and throughout history, have shown to be part of the human condition. If a person became a "good worker" that was fine, and if a person found a different adult destiny, that was all the better. This different destiny did not necessarily have to be focused through an exclusive emphasis upon mathematics and literacy. The world needs a multiplicity of human beings able to find fulfillment within their lives; this can only contribute to the evolution of society.

Even now, as I write this response to Gardner's notion of bodily-kinesthetic intelligence, I do so with the understanding that, on the whole, I am appreciative of his ideas. I do, as you will soon see, have issues with how he has gone about developing the notion of bodily-kinesthetic intelligence. But I have no doubt that he is correct in asserting its existence. My experience as a professional dancer and dance educator tells me that a certain capacity named "bodily-kinesthetic intelligence" exists as I recall those dancers and dance students for whom the learning of dance was never difficult. I remember, for instance, one of my students at Duke University who, when I would suggest an alteration in how she was performing a particular phrase of movement, would immediately be able to take that suggestion and enact it. I found it extraordinary. In another example, Robert Small, who danced with Murray Louis for many years, always danced with a kind of facility available to few of us. So I would not deny that these two individuals possessed a high level of "bodily-kinesthetic intelligence."

Despite my fundamental appreciation of Gardner's work, I still have difficulties with his mode of discussing bodily-kinesthetic intelligence. Specifically, I am disturbed by the ways in which he uses exemplars for bodily-kinesthetic intelligence in general and the specific exemplars he employs. I want to examine what, in shorthand form, I will call his "genius" approach. In so doing I hope to demonstrate why it presents problems for education. I will also link these issues with what I will call the democratic ideal. Prior to this, however, I want to accomplish two tasks in order to contextualize my discussion. First, I will explain how I understand "bodily-kinesthetic intelligence" and, second, I will explain how I view "dance."

Bodily-kinesthetic intelligence is comprised of many interrelated abilities. First, it is the ability to be aware of one's motion: kinesis (Greek for "motion") and aesthesis (Greek for "sensory")—thus, the sensing of one's motion. Viewed from this perspective we can understand bodily-kinesthetic intelligence as "a personal knowing of one's own motion," which does not require that knowing to be visible to another. Given that Gardner draws exclusively upon public knowing in all his examples, we can see that, to begin with, he has artificially narrowed the scope of the intelligence. Although admittedly, in order to adequately discuss this intelligence, we must have a public record to examine and discuss, it does not obviate the possibility that nonpublic display is an equally valid part of the "record" of its existence. We must not think that because we have not identified it in a particular individual, that person does not possess it.

For most people "a personal knowing of one's own motion" is not easily achieved: to be aware in a full way of one's own motion requires a level of attention not accomplished simply in a matter of days or weeks. It requires years of trial and error to develop it. There are, however, those few individuals who possess the gift of such awareness as a seemingly native capacity. This awareness becomes apparent to the rest of us when, for example, we notice the speed with which such a gifted person learns new motions. With such people there appears to be a direct line between their seeing another's motion and reproducing that motion. In such people this immediacy of response bypasses the kind of work which most of us have to do in order to produce the same reproduction. Even more, such gifted people seem to have a direct access to the relation between spoken words and rudimentary motional illustration (such as might be offered by a dance teacher in a classroom when making corrections during a dance class) as he or she makes rapid and accurate desired changes in his or her motion. I have personally witnessed such ability and it is nothing short of amazing. It is interesting to note, I think, that such people often do not make for good teachers of dance. They have a bodily understanding at such an immediate level that it is difficult for them to analyze what they do, explain it or show it in its particulars to another, and help that person do as they do. They have not acquired it through the process of learning in our ordinary sense (didactic coupled with experience).

Gardner, as I have written, offers as part of his illustration of this intelligence the "greats" of dance, and he uses these people to forward his ideas. Let us better understand what it is that makes such dancers "great." They are so designated for multiple reasons. I have already stated that such people have a phenomenal personal knowing of their own motion. They possess a depth of awareness and intensity of attention to their motion coupled with an ability to display that attention. Second, they are able to couple that attention with the intentions with which they perform their movement such that their intention is also visible. I will illustrate this point with two examples.

Many years ago I was attending an American Ballet Theatre performance in the New York State Theater at Lincoln Center. This is a huge theater seating several thousand people. One of the dance offerings was a duet for Mikhail Baryshnikov and Natalia Makarova. Baryshnikov had been doing some spectacular work holding onto Makarova's hand as they proceeded upstage side by side. He would jump to the side while holding her hand, with his legs held together and becoming horizontal. He would hover for a moment and then come down. He did this three times. The hovering was the extraordinary thing, for he was up so long it seemed almost as if he would remain suspended in the air. I didn't believe I'd seen it the first time, and then he did it twice again, as if to say, "Just in case you didn't believe it the first time" or "You thought I couldn't do that again." This part of the anecdote illustrates one accepted aspect of bodily-kinesthetic intelligence: the ability to perform extraordinary motion.

The above anecdote does not, however, illustrate what I consider to be the important part of the performance. Later on in the same dance Baryshnikov offered his hand to Makarova. It was a small gesture, a seemingly inconsequential gesture. Yet in that vast theater (and I was sitting in the top balcony, far away from the stage) there was an incredible hush, a riveting of attention as every eye in that theater became focused upon that hand, was swept to it by Baryshnikov's wholehearted attention to the moment. His ability to pour himself into that nonspectacular moment fixated us, not through the bravado of his elevations but through his total devotion to his motion.

One more anecdote completes the notion. A few years prior to this, I was attending a performance of Martha Graham's full-evening dance *Clytemnestra*. The role of Clytemnestra was being danced by Pearl Lang, one of Graham's most respected dancers, who was long past her spectacular movement prime. At one moment during the dance, Lang seated herself upon the sculpture stage right. There was much else going on onstage at that moment. But all I could see was Lang sitting down. She commanded my attention by the thoroughness of her attention. And not just my attention. You could feel every eye move to her. Lang was revealing the regality of Clytemnestra, her stubborn pride, her overwhelming desire, and Lang, via Graham's choreography, achieved this by sitting down!

In both examples it is not just complete attention that is at work but also a precision of attention. It is clear that each dancer *knew* exactly what he or she was doing with every fiber of his or her body. This quality of precision is a transcultural value, as we know that ritual dance, for instance, relies upon precision for its efficacy. Those dancers who are acknowledged as great within their traditions are recognized due to their ability to fulfill the dance in nuanced complete absorption and precision so that they take what might be merely movements and transform them into dance. They are entirely the dance. This constitutes, I would argue, the virtuoso performance.

There is, beyond these qualities, the ability to perform particularly difficult movement or motional sequences, such as Baryshnikov did with Makarova. Such performance requires an internal balance and harmony (even when in an unbalanced state). Bodily-kinesthetic intelligence is, I think, most often associated with this ability to be spectacular, but this, I have been trying to show, is neither the whole nor even the most important aspect. If it were, then exemplars of Northern Indian dance, for instance, would not be considered as displaying a high degree of bodily-kinesthetic intelligence, for theirs is not a spectacular practice in this sense but a more subtle rendering of bodily skill.

Please notice what I have *not* mentioned in discussing this intelligence: choreography and art. I have used examples of conventionally identified great dance artists, but I have written nothing about the choreography they performed, only of the performances themselves. Just as it is said that there are no small parts, only small actors, so, I would say there are no small movements, only small performers of those movements. The important part of bodily-kinesthetic intelligence is not the ability to rise to difficult movement but to know, in a thorough way, what you are doing with your body.

So far I have enumerated a number of characteristics which I believe delineate bodily-kinesthetic intelligence: internal knowing of one's motion, facility at reproducing motion, ability to display one's attention linked to intention, a knowing precision of motion, and the ability to perform particularly difficult motion with relative ease. A careful reading of Gardner shows that he, too, sees these qualities as components of bodily-kinesthetic intelligence. However, in my discussion I have also been attempting to undermine what I think of as culturally normative visions of this intelligence. That is, the intelligence is usually associated with the spectacular, whether it be embodied, as Gardner avows, in Marcel Marceau, Mikhail Baryshnikov, or Michael Jordan (Gardner 1993). Although I have used Baryshnikov, I have not focused upon the spectacular in his dancing but, instead, other, more fundamental attributes of his abilities. As I will explain later, thinking of the intelligence in these ways leads to a specific approach to educating for the intelligence. But first, since Gardner develops most of his thinking through discussions of dance, I need to explore dance movement and the act of dancing in more detail.

First, what is dance movement? Although normally thought of as codified movement, we should understand the origin of that movement. All dance movement is based on ordinary, everyday movement. No matter how strange the dance movement may appear, it can never exceed either the natural capacities of the human body nor escape its ordinary origins. The battement of ballet, the twisted fourth position of Graham technique, the stylization of arms in Balinese dance, are all, in this sense, no different from a casual stroll down the street. This suggests that even the casual stroll is, or potentially can be, dance.

What transforms the stroll into dance? It is nothing else than the primary component of bodily-kinesthetic intelligence: attending to one's movement. But, in fact, more than simply attending to one's movement (casually strolling down the street, swinging one's arms), it is paying attention to all the connections between indentifiable movements (steps and arm swing). Alwin Nikolais (Siegel 1971) always made a distinction between movement and motion. Movement is moving from point A to point B. Motion is paying attention to the itinerary of that movement. There are many ways to get from point A to point B. When you can pay close attention to the itinerary of your motional journey, you may be said to be dancing.

How different this is from attending to the brilliant, sometimes nearly supernatural iconic performance (thinking here of Nijinsky's legendary single leap through an open window from upstage to fully downstage in *La Spectre de la Rose* [Buckle 1979]). Now dance becomes something graspable by many people, and the associated intelligence becomes more possible as well as more relevant. Rather than an us/them condition, the intelligence can be viewed as a continuum of possibility.

Gardner also employs the criterion of "evolution" to include an intelligence in his list. He wants to discover whether or not a particular intelligence is foundational to the development of humankind. Given the above discussion about the dimensions of bodily-kinesthetic intelligence, I want to focus now on how developing attention and intentionality of attention can be linked to the intelligence's evolutionary contribution.

In discussing this intelligence, Gardner focuses much of his efforts on tool manipulation in lower primates. I find this a curious choice given that, in my analysis, tool manipulation does not count as an example of the intelligence. This is because tool manipulation is not directly an expression of bodily-kinesthetic intelligence (thinking here of inner attention rather than the outer ability to handle objects). Of more immediate importance are the bodily capacities of a person to attend to personal motion itself, with or without tools, for such an ability can contribute to the ability of the species to survive. Human beings are weak in the usual hunting senses of sight and smell. Additionally, they are much less swift than their prey, as well as physically weaker. They needed other means for securing food. Development of the bodily-kinesthetic intelligence led to an increased ability, on the part of hunters, to focus upon their bodily motion so that they would not be seen by their prey, could physically understand their prey, could get closer to their prey, and, consequently, could kill their prey for food.

Further into the history of human beings, bodily art became equally important evolutionarily. Ellen Dissanayake (1995), an anthropologist, has argued this point rather directly as she assigns the production of art a biologically evolutionary role in the development of humankind. She writes that the arts have been around a long time, "[a]nd so have ideas of beauty, sublimity, and transcendence, along with the verities of the human condition: love, death, memory, suffering, power, fear, loss, desire, hope, and so forth" (41). In the place of a view of art as the making of nonuseful objects for contemplation (a rather recent development along with the notion of "aesthetics"; Eagleton 1990) she proposes a "species-centric view of art" which "recognizes and proclaims as valid and intrinsic the association between what humans have always found important and certain ways—called 'the arts'—that they have found to grasp, manifest, and reinforce this importance" (41). What human beings have always found important are those major questions about love, death, and so forth. Dissanayake views art as a natural or "core behavioral tendency upon which natural selection could act" (41). For instance, physical adornment in the form of a highly decorated body, which in the West is often viewed as "superficial . . . nonessential . . . frivolous" (102), is thought, in the view of the Wahgi people of Papua New Guinea, to reveal, not conceal. "[A]n adorned person is more important and 'real' than an unadorned 'natural' person" (102). The Wahgi distinguish between an everyday and a special realm. In this way they use the arts to make sense of their experiences.

> Beautification, such as the use of cosmetics or hair styling, can be regarded as a means to instill culture, to cultivate, to civilize. Some Temne hairstyles require several days to fashion and complete; such plaiting of the hair suggests the order of civilization just as the cultivation of the land in fine rows indicates the refinement of the natural earth. (105)

She names this kind of production "making special." The enhancement of our world contributes to our understanding of that world.

As one variant on that theme, the ability to know one's own bodily motion aids the potter and the woodworker, who use clay or wood, in making things special and meaningful for her or his culture. Tool-making becomes important not only for how it extends our bodies (Gardner's focus) but for how it is also an extension of inner knowing (when the tool is both made and handled well). This enhancement, or "making things special," might be understood in two ways: as making things of use and beauty (see Barone 2000) and as focusing of attention which makes even the smallest, most trivial motion become special because of our loving attention to it. Both kinds of "making special" contribute to our development, and show a gradation of the ability to make special which is amenable to the educational project. We can teach people this way of thinking (bodily-kinesthetic intelligence must encompass a way of thinking or what would be the point of declaring it discrete?) with the hope that they will develop a deep understanding of themselves as bodily-kinesthetically intelligent beings. When Gardner focuses upon great artists and when the culture will, generally, understand bodily-kinesthetic intelligence as an ability to perform spectacularly, it becomes far more difficult to educate for that intelligence, as it makes a distinction between those who are gifted (can produce spectacular movement) and the rest of us.

In the light of all the above I want now to re-examine the "genius" criterion used to include this intelligence. Two considerations come to mind. First, if Gardner is seeking fundamental, biological bases (brain aphasias and evolution) for declaring an intelligence to belong to the list, by implication, these cultural exemplars are natively endowed with the intelligence. He seems to be saying that the acknowledged artists who gain a wide audience achieved their status through a sheer genius both with which they were born and which was environmentally nurtured, and that this genius is bodily-kinesthetic intelligence.

Second, when we examine Gardner's main choices for the mature form of the intelligence, we find a review of various great twentieth-century choreographers who have shown the ability to compose motion in new and inventive ways. This implies that the ability to compose such motion is part of bodily-kinesthetic intelligence. We may, however, legitimately ask whether or not Balanchine's recasting of classical ballet vocabulary (prominently displayed, for instance, in *Agon* and *The Four Temperaments*), Graham's invention of a contraction-release dance vocabulary, or some Thai dancer's offering of new possibilities for traditional Thai dance qualify any of them as geniuses of bodily-kinesthetic intelligence.

I would argue no. Balanchine's work, offered in another era, would not have been lauded and declared to be "genius" but might have been ignored as merely ugly. Graham was not the only person to work in the contraction-release area. Her one-time husband and dance partner, Erick Hawkins, also developed a contraction-release approach and yet was never declared a genius. Nor have the modern dance forms of German expressionistic dance (Mary Wigman and Hanya Holm) or fall-recovery (Doris Humphrey) been given the same kind of star treatment. All these people displayed beautiful manifestations of dance (possessed, according to Gardner's criteria, the biological gift of bodily-kinesthetic intelligence), but for all that, they did not garner the kind of fame and accolades accorded Graham and Balanchine. This suggests that "genius" is not necessarily a biological endowment (although it might have some biological component). If it is not purely biological, then how can we account for its designation?

Let me begin by posing a hypothetical situation for the inclusion of another intelligence. If the culture overwhelmingly valued the practice of "car mechanic" such that particular car mechanics were known throughout the culture as exemplars of car mechanic intelligence, then there would have to be something special about that practice. If there were car mechanics who had achieved, for instance, mythic proportions in the cultural psyche (such as dancers, actors, and athletes have), then that might suggest that "car mechanic" was an example of a discrete intelligence. Since Gardner and others have not undertaken the research on car mechanics to know whether or not there is an aphasia for them, nor have they developed an evolutionary argument around car mechanic practice, then we will have to take it as a given that car mechanic might be a possible candidate for inclusion in his list of discrete intelligences. It is not that Gardner has not proposed that other intelligences may exist (of late he has deemed to include a naturalist intelligence, an existential intelligence, and spiritual intelligence as a possible half-intelligence) but, rather, that even these additions speak to a certain social status reflected in the list. Indeed I have known car mechanics who had such a feel for car engines and their bodies in the process that I could only say that they possessed a discrete car mechanic intelligence. I am not being facetious with this example. We must seriously examine Gardner's selection of "geniuses" and note that, in this case, he has privileged certain kinds of physical behavior and ignored others. Highly skilled car mechanics do not make the list of special-abilities people. Why is this? It is not disingenuous to note that Gardner's list of intelligences and his lists of exemplars within intelligences are replete with high-culture icons. This makes the genius criteria automatically suspect, since he does not create these lists from a broad spectrum of cultural possibilities but, rather, echoes the prejudices of the culture.

Gardner appears, then, to be using the concept in the form of a cultural affirmation. This becomes more clear in another of his books (Gardner 1993), where he elucidates his intelligences and points out, in each chapter, exemplars of the intelligence. These exemplars represent the genius criterion. In the chapter on bodily-kinesthetic intelligence he chooses Martha Graham for his exemplar. A discussion of Graham will reveal more of the problematics of this attribution. (For historical-biographical information, see DeMille 1991; Garfunkel 1995; McDonagh 1973; and Terry 1975).

Graham began her major dance career as a dancer with Denishawn, the modern dance company and choreographic/movement invention approach developed by Ruth St. Denis and Ted Shawn. She became one of Denishawn's stars, along with Doris Humphrey and Charles Weidman. All three dancers eventually left Denishawn in order to pursue visions of the dance art that differed markedly from Ruth St. Denis and Ted Shawn. All three became well-known and well-respected practitioners of the emerging "modern dance." However, only Graham earned a worldwide reputation and the cultural imprimatur "genius." Was this because she possessed a special bodily-kinesthetic genius which eclipsed her contemporaries? The historical evidence reveals, I think, not so much that she possessed a special bodily-kinesthetic genius but, rather, a genius for finding financial support (wealthy and powerful patrons) and a genius for choreography. That is, if the bodily-kinesthetic intelligence is one of bodily motion skillfully performed, then these two forms of genius have no place in designating her as an exemplar of bodily-kinesthetic genius. She possessed great social and political acumen and a strong choreographic sense. This choreographic sense meant, in many ways, that Graham perhaps displayed more of the "spatial intelligence" in Gardner's list than bodily-kinesthetic intelligence. Choreography is clearly a motional art, but the great choreographers were as much about arranging motion *in space* as they were *inventors of motion*. That is, while choreography begins in motion, it moves toward motional *design,* which is a visual art as well as a bodily-kinesthetic art. Spatial motion that is badly organized will make the choreography muddy and unintelligible. Indeed, thinking of the concert work of Graham, one is immediately struck by the look of the space. The use of the sculptures of Yamaguchi delineates that space in amazing ways. Again, the power of Graham's work often lies in the sculptural qualities of the dancing. This is also an example of spatial brilliance.

I am arguing that Graham's genius may have much less to do with bodily-kinesthetic intelligence than with other forms of intelligence that either do not make Gardner's list (political intelligence is never mentioned, yet her abilities to garner support are legendary) or come from other areas of the list. Her renown is not based solely on her bodily technique (as important as it may be) but on her aforementioned business skills and her artistic eye (a form of spatial intelligence according to Gardner). Further, her ability to join her choreography to cultural currents is not mentioned by Gardner, and yet this is the aspect of her work which seems so culturally important. I am thinking of her "American" work, which forged a vision of the emerging new American self-awareness, and her "Greek" work, in which she attempted to make visible Freudian insights through the classic Greek tragedies and, thus, reveal depths of psychology in an exciting and new way. Make no mistake: I am not denying her brilliance. Rather I am asking why Graham is designated as a bodily-kinesthetic genius, and saying that I find using her for an exemplar of bodily-kinesthetic intelligence seems beside the point in terms of why she is designated a genius. Perhaps Gardner needs a different kind of intelligence to account for art which gains great social recognition. Perhaps there is a discrete intelligence for being able to read one's time and translate it into a legible art that moves the art forward. Further, Graham was not, at first, lauded for her originality. She drew upon her reputation to gain provisional acceptance for her new work. She used her fame to forward her project. We may also ask whether or not this is a form of genius.

I have moved the issue from a biological one to a sociological one. This enables us to connect the preceding discussion logically with educational thinking. Education is, like the genius designation, a sociological process, proceeding through human social interactions and intended, in one way or another, to affect the development of society. Development of any intelligence, including bodily-kinesthetic intelligence, is not for the mere purpose of its self-development. There are social outcomes and responses to consider. It is, then, to educational issues that I turn, and I will focus my discussion on dance education because I certainly agree that dance education (with its focus most directly on the body) holds the greatest potential for developing bodily-kinesthetic intelligence.

To begin with, coupling genius-thinking with education creates, as I have already suggested, a difficulty in identifying a person who exemplifies it. Taking Dewey's notion (Dewey 1988) of finding out what dance is to the child and then teaching dance to the child in the light of that suggests that the child has dance-related questions and dancelike positionings which hold the potential for the mature form but are not yet the mature form. Dewey argues against beginning with the iconic mature form because this is not where the child exists. The mature form becomes only an inert, dead object lying there to be slavishly imitated, but nothing of value is found out about the child's capacity for dance.

If dance is the art of paying attention to one's motion, then dance education ought to begin with paying attention and not with already-created forms which one must learn and against which one's genius is measured. In Russia one is measured in terms of thigh size, femur length, build, etc., to determine whether or not one will be allowed to dance. In England there is the Royal Ballet syllabus by which the adequacy of ballet students is determined and individuals are or are not offered subsequent dance opportunities. In the United States there was, for many years, the Graham technique, which was built on Graham's idiosyncratic body, the strange structure of her hips, knee, and ankles. Very few could actually emulate her. The concept of contraction and release was instantiated in a particular way by her, but it was and is not the only way to dance out of that concept. Graham rigidly defined one way and only one way for contraction release to be realized.

If dance is defined, as I have suggested, as paying attention to one's motion, then no matter what motion is being performed, by paying attention to it one is dancing. There are, of course, differing capacities for attention. Merce Cunningham has talked about an appetite for movement (Cunningham 1977). This appetite is felt especially sharply by dancers or at least some dancers. It does not mean the need to display oneself, but rather, the need to be moving and to feel and think movement. It does not mean that one always has to be moving, but rather, that one feels another's motion almost as if one were also moving. We call this the bodily-kinesthetic response, and some people may possess this responsiveness more than others. It might also be developed in people as the significant part of the dance education process. This kind of "genius" is different than being a great artist. By using such great icons *as icons* Gardner may be cutting off access to many who might have potential talent but may never find it because they do not initially appear to measure well against the icons. Further, to call something "genius" is to already set up a barrier between the thing desired and the possible doers of the thing. It suggests that only some will have this capacity and others ought not to pursue it. The sorts of criteria described above will sort out people before they ever begin.

But, of course, we won't know it ahead of time. We don't know what contributions a person might make to that domain of knowing. An after-the-fact designation such as genius ("Ah, I see she is a genius") makes it difficult to know ahead of time who will have that genius. It is easier, however, to see into an appetite for motion that a person cannot seem to help.

Remembering that dance vocabulary comes out of the everyday and is only an exaggeration of the everyday creates a continuum along which to proceed as one begins to develop oneself as a dancer. This development can come through the encouraging eye of the teacher of movement who is not looking for genius but only for attention and desire. Awkwardness, not usually associated with dance, might become a sort of beauty because the dancer is very aware of his or her awkwardness and attends to it in a strong way. In some contexts, such awkwardness is presented as an aesthetic form.

I am arguing that learning to dance, learning to develop a bodily-kinesthetic intelligence, is a *process*, not a product, of self-actualization. Genius-talk only communicates that not everyone can become self-actualized, so why begin? One is immediately overwhelmed with inadequacy. If we take it that culture is a set of social agreements for living and thinking in particular ways, then Gardner is saying that there is a high degree of social agreement about this domain. But when we see what or who has been left out of this agreement, we can see that we have denied the culture a plurality of possibilities.

This brings me to my final point. I entitled this chapter "Bodily-Kinesthetic Intelligence and the Democratic Ideal." For myself, the democratic ideal involves an inclusion of multiple voices and possibilities, not exclusionary practices. I do not mean to state that Gardner desires such exclusion. However, as I have been trying to show, the ways in which he writes about this intelligence can lead in that direction. Jurgen Habermas (Young 1990) has written in the area of communication theory about the ways in which communications among people are filled with distortions, due, in large part, to power differentials. He has proposed the notion of the Ideal Speech Situation, in which multiple voices be heard and would not be distorted. He recognizes this as a utopian aspiration but one toward which he is attempting to guide us (as a destination which we might not attain but which gives direction to our efforts). I am arguing, in a similar fashion, for an approach to educating for the bodily-kinesthetic intelligence that eschews exclusion and finds a way for participation which is legitimate and legitimated.

This participation, based on the ability to pay attention, no longer discriminates between professional knowers of the intelligence and nonprofessional knowers. In my experience as a choreographer (and in my observation of other choreographers), my greatest successes have come with people who would not be deemed to possess this intelligence (in the normative way I have described it) and yet were fully professional. I mean by this that these people took the notion of "professional" to mean "to profess, or express, one's belief with great conviction." When they performed their movement, no matter how simple, in their dedication to that movement, in their intense focus, they could be perceived as beautiful. They were beautiful and exemplary not in any conventional sense but rather, in the way of being so immersed that the viewer could not but help be immersed also. Did they display spectacular bodily-kinesthetic gifts in the usual way? No. Did they display something powerful? Yes. If I had practiced a form of dance education that paid more attention to codified mature forms of the dance art and less attention to the ways in which I have described the bodily-kinesthetic intelligence and the act of dancing, these individuals would never have found for themselves a level of personal knowledge and growth rarely achieved. If I had undemocratically discriminated among them on the basis of those conventional categories, they would never have danced, never would have explored their intelligence.

I am stating that education for bodily-kinesthetic intelligence requires departing from taken-for-granted paths to its fruition. The taken-for-granted response to educating for intelligence could, I think, apply in the area of dance education. A school or district might seek a dance person (educator or professional) to enable its students to develop this intelligence, with little consideration for exactly what would be taught. There would be an assumption that since Gardner has focused upon great dance art as the prime exemplar of the mature form, all they need is a fine dancer to help develop the intelligence. Indeed, that is the implication one receives from Gardner's work. His notion is that students who show some nascent ability in this area ought to "apprentice" with someone who has already developed that intelligence. Given the conventional view of this intelligence, as I have discussed it in this writing, it would be logical to employ a fine dancer.

However, as I have described the intelligence and the practice of dance, education for this intelligence requires an approach quite different from merely studying with a fine dancer. It requires, rather, a focus upon the components I have described. It requires an educator who will seek the potential in each person in the ways of paying attention and will aid the learner in refining attention-giving. It requires a labor bent toward each person engaged in finding him- or herself "inside motional activity." Given that we can never be sure who will blossom, who will make that "significant" contribution to what we label "genius," we may deny our community of even this possibility by not teaching in this way.

Yet more serious than the possible loss of "genius" is the problem of denial of access. Much of the history of the United States has been about the struggle for greater and greater access for more and more individuals and groups. To teach this bodily-kinesthetic intelligence in the conventional ways only perpetuates another area for exclusion and denial. In so doing we will be denying the very potential of democratic expansion. I am not arguing that the kind of teaching I have been describing will solve the ills of our society or that democracy will be healed. Rather, through a series of small interventions such as this, we have an opportunity to work toward democracy and build it from the ground up. Efforts are needed in many venues and through many activities, and the democratic education for bodily-kinesthetic intelligence ought to be a site for the expansion of the democratic ideal.

References

Barone, T. (2000). Things of use and things of beauty: the Swain County arts program. In T. Barone, *Aesthetics, politics, and educational inquiry: Essays and examples*. New York: Peter Lang.

Bornstein, M. (1986). [Review of Howard Gardner's *Frames of Mind*.] *Journal of Aesthetic Education, 20,*(2), 120–122.

Buckle, R. (1979). *Diaghilev*. New York: Atheneum.

Cunningham, M. (1977). Event for television in the TV series *Dance in America*. www.merce. org:80/filmvideo_danceforcamera.html.

DeMille, A. (1991). *Martha: The life and work of Martha Graham*. New York: Random House.

Dewey, J. (1988). The psychological aspect of the school curriculum. In J. Gress with D. Purpel (eds.), *Curriculum: An introduction to the field* (2nd ed.) (pp. 129–39). Berkeley, CA: McCutchan.

Dissanayake, E. (1995). *Homo aestheticus: Where art comes from and why*. Seattle: University of Washington Press.

Eagleton, T. (1983). *Literary theory: An introduction*. Minneapolis: University of Minnesota Press.

———. (1990). *The ideology of the aesthetic*. London: Basil Blackwell.

Gardner, H. (1983). *Frames of mind*. New York: Basic Books.

———. (1993). *Creating minds: An anatomy of creativity seen through the lives of Freud, Einstein, Picasso, Stravinsky, Eliot, and Gandhi*. New York: Basic Books.

Garfunkel, T. (1995). *Letter to the world: The life and dances of Martha Graham*. Boston: Little & Brown.

Giddins, A. (1976). *New rules of sociological method*. London: Hutchinson.

Kliebard, H. (1995). *The struggle for the American curriculum, 1893–1958*. 2nd ed. New York: Routledge.

McDonagh, D. (1973). *Martha Graham: A biography*. New York: Praeger.

Perkinson, H. (1995). *The imperfect panacea*. 2nd ed. Boston: McGraw-Hill.

Siegel, M. (ed.). (1971). *Nik: A documentary*. New York: Dance Perspectives.

Spring, J. (1997). *Deculturation and the struggle for equality*. Boston: McGraw-Hill.

Terry, W. (1975). *Frontiers of dance: The life of Martha Graham*. New York: Crowell.

Young, R. (1990). *A critical theory of education: Habermas and our children's future*. New York: Teachers College Press.

Chapter 7

Joe L. Kincheloe

GETTING PERSONAL: RETHINKING GARDNER'S PERSONAL INTELLIGENCES

In the same way that the idea of multiple intelligences is not new, the concept of personal intelligence has been discussed and debated for a long time. Scholars sometimes used diverse names to designate what Gardner labels the personal intelligences, also known as interpersonal and intrapersonal intelligences. Gardner's delineation of these intelligences in 1983 certainly contributed to the conversation, but was only one of numerous voices involved in the discourse. The contemporary conversation involves everyone from Daniel Goleman (1994) and his "emotional intelligence" to Kevin Kelly and Sidney Moon (1998) and their "personal and social talents." In the 1930s, for example, Edward L. Thorndike argued that there were three intelligences: abstract, mechanical, and social. Thorndike defined social intelligence as the "ability to understand others and act wisely in human relations" ("If You're So Rich" 2000).

Gardner's definition of interpersonal and intrapersonal intelligence is typically more narrow than that of many of the scholars studying social or emotional intelligence/talent, as he maintains that his notion is scientifically produced, is separate from the moral realm, and that he is interested in modes of thinking about feelings instead of the role of emotion in shaping intelligence. Specifically, Gardner defines interpersonal intelligence as the capacity to discern distinctions in the moods and feelings of other people. Making sense of interpersonal cues, an interpersonally intelligent individual possesses the ability to respond to such cues in a way that influences other individuals to pursue a particular mode of action. Gardner defines intrapersonal intelligence as a form of self-knowledge that involves the ability to act by making use of such knowledge. Self-knowledge as employed by Gardner involves developing a realistic view of oneself as well as an understanding of one's moods, motivations, and desires. Such insight, Gardner concludes, produces self-discipline and self-esteem (Gardner 1983).

This analysis of Gardner's concept of personal intelligences will focus on several of his assumptions that tacitly shape his perspectives in this domain. His notion of the self and the relationship between self and society and self and other is central in this context. Gardner's understanding of the self as a relational entity is fuzzy at best and needs to be understood so as to clarify the limitations of his delineation of interpersonal and intrapersonal abilities. I argue in this chapter that to achieve more textured and complex insight into the personal domain we need to develop a far more historicized view of the self. In this context, Gardner's lack of social grounding thwarts his ability to escape the most mundane Cartesian perspectives on the topic. Moving beyond Gardner's blinders, we will examine socially and historically contextualized modes of personal insight that learn from interaction with cultural difference and move the individual to what might be described as a "critical ontology"—the development of interpersonal and intrapersonal insights that conceptualize new ways of being human.

The Concept of Self and the Personal Intelligences

One of the most important aspects of human experience involves the phenomenon of self. No psychological theory, no articulation of educational psychology, no pedagogy can escape having to deal with the concept. Diverse cultures and historical eras deal with selfhood differently, as some groups focus on autonomy while others emphasize affiliation. Some argue that agency, the ability to shape one's own behavior, is a central dimension of selfhood. Others maintain that the development of a conceptual system that produces a chronicle of interactions with the world—an agentive memory of past encounters and a projection of possible ones in the future—is a key aspect of selfhood. Many analysts argue that these dimensions of the self are profoundly affected by the evaluations of the process by others. Thus, no way exists, they maintain, to place boundaries between the self and other. This position, of course, complicates our view of the self as well as our ability to posit what knowledge of the self—of one's self and of the self's relation to others—involves.

Gardner picks up on these themes, arguing that "the roots of a sense of self lie in the individual's exploration of his own feelings and in his emerging ability to view his own feelings and experiences in terms of the interpretive schemes and symbol systems provided by the culture" (1983, 294). As so many other authors in this collection have argued, on first glance Gardner seems to be making a case for a progressive awareness of different cultural influences on diverse individuals. The implication here to the progressive interpreter is that such cultural insight should help break the oppressive hold that a decontextualized psychometrics and cognitivism have on the field of educational psychology. But subsequent readings of Gardner make us less sure of such intentions.

In *Frames of Mind* Gardner debates with himself over what to do with this culturally informed sense of self. He asks if he should declare it:

- a separate domain of intelligence—the eighth one before the naturalist category was created;
- a mature form of intrapersonal intelligence;
- a new construct, a privileged function of mind, a central processor that reflects upon the other domains of intelligence; or
- an emergent capacity coming out of the personal intelligences that provides a special kind of explanation involving everything the individual is and does (this is the model Gardner favored in 1983).

Basic criticisms of Gardner's notion of self have come from feminist, postmodern, and psychoanalytic theory. Charging that such a perspective merely gives lip-service to cultural influence, critics in these domains charge that concepts of the self such as Gardner's dismiss the complications of desire and irrationality, the entanglements of the unconscious, the unpredictability of individual interpretation of experience, and the instability of selfhood. This is especially the case in an information-saturated, image-bombarded contemporary electronic reality—hyperreality.

Cultural context to Gardner is viewed as an indispensable dimension of understanding the self, but a careful reading of *Frames of Mind* and Gardner's subsequent work reveals that self and context are two discrete realms. The individual makes her way through the contextual terrain but always remains separate from it. Feminist, psychoanalytical, and postmodern analysts understand that context is a web of countless cultural dynamics that are constantly shaping and reshaping the individual/learner. This web is always implicated in the nature of experience, the way it is engaged, and the manner in which individuals deal with it. To Gardner knowledge is a thing-in-itself created by the individual and stored in her brain. Indeed Gardner vociferously objects to any notion that power inscribes language and everyday life and thus cannot be separated from what is called knowledge and self. Where does one of these entities end and the others begin? Gardner is quite comfortable with imposing visible and impermeable boundaries between them (Gergen 1991; Shotter 1993; Kincheloe, Steinberg, & Hinchey 1999; Fenwick 2000).

With the growing acceptance of more process-oriented views of the self that stress its interrelatedness with the world (Pickering 1999), scholars will come to view a notion of intelligence constructed on a Cartesian "bounded" self increasingly archaic. Engaged in its own production and ever concerned with self-perpetuation, the self as process not only demands a reconceptualization of intelligence but new methods to study its complexity. Postmodern studies of self reflect these same processual concerns, focusing on a post-Cartesian notion of "self-in-relationship" (Bodeau 1999) and the complex system such a term implies. Even self-in-relationship is reductionistic as it fails to signify all that is involved with the complexities of selfhood. With the growing popularity of Humberto Maturana and Francisco Varela's enactivist psychology and its rejection of a centralized unitary self, Gardner's Cartesian conception will increasingly be viewed more critically (Varela 1999; Sumara & Davis 1997).

Because of these notions of process and relationship involving the emerging view of self, a more sophisticated understanding of the social domain is necessary. From Vygotsky's notion of the zone of proximal development (ZPD) on, the history of psychology has been moving toward a more socially constructed conception of self. With this in mind, this book in general and this chapter in particular address the nature of this influential social domain. Put bluntly, psychologists such as Gardner in the twenty-first century have to become sociologists and students of cultural studies. We will all gain from such a move, as we become better acquainted with how the world is implicated within us. Such insights will provide a new appreciation of where and how we stand in the web of reality and how we might move to a new consciousness of our roles in the larger scheme of things. In the process, a different conception of the interpersonal and intrapersonal domains will emerge.

Specifying the Personal Intelligences

Before I return to the critique of the sociopolitical, cultural, and philosophical assumptions on which Gardner's personal intelligences rest, it is important to specify what exactly he is describing when he uses the term. Gardner has argued for years that the personal intelligences were the most controversial aspects of multiple intelligences (MI) theory. Such intelligences, Gardner maintained, involve complex concepts such as "the existence of one's own person, the existence of other persons, the culture's presentations and interpretations of selves" (1983, 276). In such domains Gardner posited that there will develop inevitable controversies and disagreements. In this complicated context Gardner contended that intrapersonal intelligence involved the following:

- access to one's feelings;
- the capacity to set goals and track progress toward them;
- awareness of one's existing emotional state;
- self-reflection;
- the ability to express a broad range of feelings;
- the scholarly ability to pursue self-directed and independent learning.

At the same time he maintained that interpersonal intelligence involved these features:

- capacity to make distinctions among other individuals;
- ability to detect affective changes in others;
- proficiency at reading motives and desires of diverse individuals;
- talent to use these insights to influence people to act in certain ways;
- ability as a student to engage successfully in peer tutoring (Gardner 1983, 1999a; Shephard, Fasko, & Osborne 1999; Cantu 1999).

With these notions clarified I will continue with the critique and rethinking of Gardner's constructs. As an introductory note, in the same manner as in the introduction I am particularly interested in analyzing the personal intelligences in light of the macro-sociohistorical effort to deal with our own social construction as humans. In this context we are referring—contrary to Gardner's perspective—to the necessary effort of Western societies to pause and reflect on not only modes of self-production but modes of knowledge and values-construction employed by Western societies over the past 350 years. As we learn more about how power shapes the ways we see the world and the self, we come to understand where specifically Gardner is coming from in his psychological labors. We gain a clearer insight into how particular discourses of power—for example, the scientific conventions of mainstream psychology—have shaped his delineation of personal intelligences. Such analyses are not merely some arcane form of academic quibbling but ways of exposing modes of thinking, teaching, and conceptualizing that harm specific individuals in particular ways. It is the avoidance of this type of lived-world regulation that motivates our work.

Understanding the Self as a Relational Entity

A survey of Gardner's work on the personal intelligences over the last twenty years reveals that he has little sense of the self as a relational dynamic. He makes brief references to the importance of culture in understanding the individual but leaves the nature of this importance unspecified. The nature of the individual's relation to the culture of the group is central to understanding personal intelligence and cannot be conveniently swept under the psychological rug (O'Sullivan 1999; Shoham 1999). Is personal intelligence bound up in the head, an isolated capacity of the abstract individual? Or is there more to it? Is there a cultural, political, economic, social, religious, philosophical, mythopoetic set of relationships set of relationships that must be worked out in order to understand the nature of intelligence, self, and inter/intrapersonal modes of existence in general (Haggerson 2000)? Obviously, the personal intelligences are socially constructed phenomena and can only be understood within the context of that social construction. This is why the authors of *Multiple Intelligences Reconsidered* are so intent on bringing multiple theoretical lenses to their analyses: critical social theories, feminist theories, postcolonial analyses, poststructural theories, postformal theories, processual analysis, systems theories, complexity theories, the Santiago theory, Batesonian theory all show up in the various chapters. The purpose of such eclecticism is to gain as many perspectives as possible on the complex processes of self-production, to provide as rigorous an analysis as possible of the relationship between self and society.

Gardner studiously avoids these lenses but affirms the importance of the cultural domain in which the individual operates in shaping the cognitive process. Questions of the role of power and ideology in shaping the nature of personal intelligence and what is considered personal intelligence are off limits in the world according to Gardner. He would be well served in his delineation of the personal intelligences to attend to Michel Foucault's concerns with who we are and how we got this way. These questions lay the foundation for Foucault's critique of psychology in general and the construction of identity or subjectivity in particular. Asking these questions would have brought Gardner to an appreciation of not only the ways mind is constructed by dominant forms of power but the ways knowledge itself bears power's fingerprints. Such knowledge would serve as an antidote to his naivete concerning the political impact of both how he defines intelligence and how he advocates a curriculum of traditional European disciplinary truths for elementary and secondary students (Gardner 1999a; May 1993; Kincheloe & Steinberg 1997).

Understanding that the line demarcating mental processes and social processes is more indistinct than originally conceived, psychologists in the tradition of Lev Vygotsky, Jean Lave, James Wertsch, and Kenneth Gergen have reconceptualized thinking as a relational activity. Shirley Steinberg's and my work (Kincheloe & Steinberg 1993; Kincheloe, Steinberg, & Villaverde 1999; Kincheloe, Steinberg, & Hinchey 1999) and Ray Horn's (2000) research on postformalism have also emphasized this relational dimension. Philip Wexler (1997 and 2000) has promoted a "postindustrial psychology" that attempts to undo the Cartesian psychology of the industrial era. Such an "undoing" involves the re-absorption of the abstracted, decontextualized self into multiple contexts and environments. Such separation of the self from context reduces our ability to answer Foucault's questions of who we are and how we got this way.

In the reductionism of modernist psychology the mind is equated with the physicality of the brain. The materialism—the belief that consciousness and selfhood are nothing more than the operation of measurable material agents—successfully precluded study of the nonmaterialist notion of relationship between mind and world. Such ontological (the branch of philosophy that studies what it means to be or exist, for example, or what it means to be human) reductionism assumes that psychology can reduce all aspects of humanness to their smallest parts so they can be analyzed, categorized, and measured mathematically. An ontological question such as "where is the 'me' in me," a central question of the intrapersonal realm, is also one of the most important queries in psychology in general. Where is the place of humans in the natural order? The social order? The political order? The dominant psychological paradigms of the twentieth century suppressed these questions. As we have observed various dimensions of how humans affect and are affected by these orders, late-twentieth- and early-twenty-first-century cultural psychology has attempted to raise these questions again. Gardner drags mainstream psychology's resistance to such inquiries into the twenty-first century (Gergen 1996; Cannella 1997; Griffin 1997; Pickering 1999).

Gardner's protestation that personal intelligences are objective, value-free descriptions of the nature of the mind reflects the seventeenth-century Cartesian delineation of knowledge as disinterested reflections of reality—i.e., verified truth. In this context of tacit philosophical realism a folk psychology develops, insisting that individual behavior and modes of interaction are shaped by personally formed and individually bounded beliefs, desires, and values. Cultural, linguistic, historical context has little to do with this process. The notion of the self operating here is a creation of modernist psychology—as Foucault labels it, psychology constructs the modern soul. As Danny Weil writes in this volume, Gardner doesn't understand that psychology is a technology of power emerging at a particular time and place. He doesn't see the personal intelligences as a construction of Eurocentric power that values and devalues particular modes of human behavior. Gardner dismisses the racial, gender, and class dimensions of what is designated sophisticated modes of thinking and behaving. Broad generalizations about universal modes of human cognition endure across time and place, Gardner asserts. Thus, expressions of personal intelligence in the United States in the twenty-first century are the same as in African tribal villages in the eighth century (Allen 2000; Bereiter 2002; May 1993; Gardner 1999a).

What we are observing here is the same form of psychological colonialism that Yusef Progler referenced in his chapter on Gardner's concept of musical intelligence. European ways of being are normalized as the modes of thinking/behaving for which everyone should strive. Gardner's consistency in this mode of operating is disturbing to all concerned with cultural respect and intercultural relationships. To overcome such modes of psychological colonialism, postformalists argue that Gardner's personal intelligences must be investigated in sociohistorical context. Such investigations could help to undermine particular ways of being personally intelligent and open up a wider range of such talents. Again, as Foucault maintained, we study the included and the excluded. Who doesn't possess personal intelligence according to Gardner? Why? Where do we begin in our analysis of the personal intelligences? What ideologies are embedded within them? What rhetorical and linguistic dynamics have shaped them? What modes of cultural power are at work (Gergen 1997)?

Relational Ontologies: Pushing the Limits of the Self

The concept of relatedness or relationship is central to the understanding of self that is implicated in the personal intelligences. Gardner studiously avoids this dynamic throughout his work, falling back on the comfortable Cartesian notion of the independent self. Relatedness, however, seems to have properties and influences that are just beginning to be understood. In the twenty-first century no cognitive understanding, no conception of self can overlook it. Relatedness overwhelms Gardner's cognitive essentialism—the notion of a knowable, measurable, and objectively describable domain of the personal interior. In cognitive essentialism the "I" is the center of being, and no relationship can be more important than this bounded self. The more information technologies we develop, the more individuals encounter the presence of other people, and in this context the harder it becomes to protect the idea of an essential self. The development of poststructuralist social theories has contributed to the de-essentialization process as well, as scholars such as Derrida, Foucault, Baudrillard, Donna Haraway, Francisco Varela, Valerie Walkerdine, and many others all engage in the decentering of the self from the dominant position it once occupied in Western culture.

In the contemporary electronically produced hyperreality of information saturation and technological change, we observe living people being replaced with digital icons and other modes of representation in virtual reality, computer chat rooms, and phone sex. In all of these domains the essentialized self gives way to an expanded and malleable identity complete with different names and personal characteristics. Thus, the de-essentialization of self takes many forms, in the process indicating not only that the self is not as stable as we thought but that its relationship to culture is different than previously assumed. Culture is not simply the context in which mind operates, but is "in the mind"—an inseparable portion of what we call the self. Thus, those cultural producers that have the most power to engage us also have the most power to shape us. As I have written in other places (Kincheloe 1993 and 2001), power plays an exaggerated role in shaping our consciousness, our subjectivity. Power is not only connected to the distribution of political and economic capital, but to the very production of lived experiences and ways of being (Gergen 1996; Bruner 1996; Giroux 1997). Power's role in constructing self and, in turn, shaping the personal intelligences is not a part of Gardner's MI theory.

Those who have diverse relationships to power will be shaped in divergent ways—empowering or disempowering, for example. This relationship would exert a dramatic impact on Gardner's concept of the characteristics of interpersonal intelligences, in particular the ability to use interpersonal insights to influence people to act in certain ways. An individual in a disempowered situation, enculturated in a lower socioeconomic class-relation to power, would find this task much more difficult because of his or her social location. Middle- or upper-middle-class people would be less prone to be influenced by an individual from the lower middle class than by an individual from a higher status group. This would be the case regardless of how "interpersonally intelligent" the lower-socioeconomic-class individual might be. Thus, power does not involve simply by applying its force to the sociocognitive dimensions of interpersonal intelligence; it creates these dynamics. Power produces the self, power creates interpersonal interactions—neither process is simply affected by power. Relatedness is the central dynamic at work here—who we are depends on the nature of this relatedness. Hence, the term "relational ontologies."

In the context of power and self-production, psychologists and students of cognition such as Gardner also would be informed by an understanding of the diverse forms of power (ideological, hegemonic, disciplinary, regulatory, discursive, etc.) along diverse axes (race, class, gender, sexuality, religion, language, geographical place, age, etc.). Social theorists are far past the point where they assume a monolithic dominant ideology that determines the lives of passive and homogeneous dupes (Hinchey 1998; Fenwick 2000; Steinberg 2001). These diverse and complex modes of power and the nature of their roles in the self-production process create cultural, linguistic, and semiotic dynamics that precede the individual's coming into the world. To make meaning, to be, to engage in interpersonal and intrapersonal behavior, is to participate in this matrix of preshaped and ever-emerging relationships. This brings us back to the original concept: relatedness sets the stage and even writes some of the dialogue for what psychologists call the self (Gergen 1996).

As we explore these relational ontologies, in the process pushing the limits of the self, we have moved into a new domain of complexity. Complex-systems theory posits that the various parts of living systems are continuously changing. Diverse matter from a system's environment is always moving through a living entity. Even tissues and organs are constantly engaged in a process to replace their cells, thus perpetually rebuilding themselves. To live, proponents of complexity argue, is to grow, develop, evolve, and, of course, change. Our notion of self as a relational ontology fits the model of complexity theory's process of life. In this context the self is never finished, never fixed, always changing as a result of its interaction with the various dimensions of its environment. Gardner would be well served to consider the personal domain within this conceptual context. In Gardner's theory of personal intelligences, the self operates at the center of the universe. Such a conceptualization often operates to reaffirm the tendency in Western modernism toward personal isolation and alienation. Selfhood in this framework comes first; relationship is a relatively insignificant dimension of the abstract individual.

It is important to note that none of Gardner's characteristics of intrapersonal intelligence have anything to do with relationship or understanding the self-production process. In his delineation of interpersonal intelligence, relationship with others operates only to serve the ego needs of the isolated self: the talent to use interpersonal insights to influence people to act in certain ways. The "certain ways" of acting involve serving the best interests of the interpersonally intelligent individual. Gardner argues that his is not a moral theory. But the notion of the isolated self employed in the theory holds particular moral inscriptions: one being that interpersonal intelligence is not employed for mutual benefit but for the needs of the isolated self. A notion of interpersonal facility employing the concept of a relational self, constructed by reference to the various theoretical traditions authors have referenced in *Multiple Intelligences Reconsidered,* would involve careful attention to the power-related productive qualities of language, information production and reception, ritual behaviors, cultural dynamics, ideology, discursive practice, the cultural pedagogy of hyperreality, and diverse sign and symbol systems (Capra 1996; Zuss 1999).

Allow me to be very specific about the notion of the relational self or relational ontology being deployed here. Environmental/cultural context, for example, is referenced in even the most positivistic psychological theories. In behaviorism environment is seen as a stimulator or an informant of the internal dimensions of the self. In cognitivism environment serves as an unfiltered resource for cognitive use. In these psychological schools the environment or context, however, plays no role in producing the self. This is the point where Gardner's personal intelligences falter, as his interpersonally intelligent individual may have no understanding of this process. There is no need for his personally intelligent people in general to understand their historicity, their social construction, the reasons why they see themselves and their relationship with others, the culture, diverse cultures, and the cosmos in particular ways. There is no purpose for such individuals to explore the ways these dynamics shape their feelings, impulses to action, interests, and self-concepts (Gergen 1997). Here their alienation extends to new levels, as they are isolated from the history, culture, and cosmos embedded within them. When one studies the social amnesia and decline of historical and political literacy in the late twentieth and early twenty-first centuries in U.S. society, these dynamics can be traced in personal and socially pathological ways (Kincheloe 2001).

Self-Production, Personal Intelligence, and Cognitive/Scholarly Ability

There is great possibility for extending the progressive impulses within MI theory, rethinking its limitations, and extending the possibilities of cognition and mind in general that are embedded in the notion of relational ontologies. In such a context we can be more sensitive to the limitations that cultural power enforces via discourse and symbol systems. Such dynamics validate particular experiences while invalidating others, especially around issues of race, class, and gender. Particular students from differing racial backgrounds, for example, are represented in particular ways in these systems—ways that dramatically shape their relationships with schools, social institutions, workplaces, and other individuals. Put another way, such dynamics contain or expand the potential of one's subjectivity and cognitive ability. So many relational dynamics emerge here that involve issues relevant for teaching reading and writing, problem detection and problem solving, curriculum development, teaching strategies, social skills in collaborative research, and rigorous scholarly work in general.

Critical theoretical analysis assumes great importance in this study of the connections between relational ontology, self-production, personal intelligence, and cognitive/scholarly ability. A traditional feature of critical analysis in education has involved teachers and students exploring the power-related limitations of learning contexts (McLaren 1995 and 2000; Giroux 1997; Aronowitz & Giroux 1991;

Hinchey 1998; Macedo 1994; Kincheloe & Steinberg 1997). Paulo Freire (1978) described critical consciousness as an understanding of these restraints, and I have described a similar process in my notion of "critical" critical thinking (Kincheloe 2000; Weil & Anderson 2000; Weil 2001). Gardner is dismissive of this scholarship and the insights it provides in the area of the personal intelligences. Tara Fenwick (2000) conceptualizes these critical dynamics astutely, arguing that criticality involves an awareness of how development is "measured," who gets to judge whom and why, and the interests that are served by resistant or development initiatives. Educators help themselves and others become more aware of their own constituted natures, their own continuous role in power relations and the production of meaning, how representations act to represent and construct reality, and how difference is perceived and enacted. People learn how what they may experience as personal yearnings, despair, and conflict and identity struggles are shaped partly by historical cultural dynamics and ideologies of particular communities.

Self-production, personal intelligence, and cognitive/scholarly ability and the multiple relationships connecting them are inherently political—implicated in power relations. For Gardner (1999a) to make disparaging comments about postmodern social theory's concern with the role of power in the construction of knowledge is unwise, for it blinds him to the political universe in which multiple intelligences and the personal intelligences operate. There is a dramatic difference between what Gardner refers to as pure postmodernism's abandonment of standards in the "claim that knowledge is essentially about power" (55) and our critical understanding of the influence of power in shaping what psychology labels the self, intelligence, and cognitive/scholarly ability. I am baffled by Gardner's reluctance to study the ways that power helps construct the capacities of diverse individuals to operate successfully in the activities of particular social systems. Since such dynamics play a significant role in how individuals live their lives and operate in institutions such as school, one would think this might be a central concern of one attempting to change psychology in a progressive and inclusive manner.

But detailed analysis reveals Gardner seems to be both uninterested and clueless about such dynamics of power, selfhood, and ability. As Danny Weil argues in his chapter, Gardner "has not considered how assessment and standardized testing are constructed by race, gender, and class and how assessment typically serves as a technology of power." A cursory reading of the history of psychology available in multiple sources in the twenty-first century tracks the ways the discipline has been used to oppress and control those deemed abnormal and deficient. Many scholars, of course, have worked to reveal that the oppressed and controlled individuals in question were not really abnormal or deficient at all—just deemed that way by particular power-wielders operating in that time and place. If learning according to enactivist theories emerging from Maturana and Varela's Santiago School cannot be separated from one's history in their socioeconomic and cultural environments, then how can the effect of power be dismissed in the personal intelligences?

When I observe students in contemporary New York who come from poor neighborhoods where hope is in short supply, I understand the effect of power on, say, their disposition toward schooling. Many of the students in question have never known anyone whose efforts in school resulted in some concrete benefit. And in this and thousands of other contexts, scholars of cognition have no reason to study the role of power in shaping the self, personal intelligences, or cognitive/ scholarly ability? In paradigmatic frames the study of power moves beyond particular empirical confines of mainstream psychology. One can rarely measure mathematically how much power shapes the intrapersonal domain. Mainstream psychological research has often viewed intelligence and similar types of knowledge as categories removed from the social, cultural, and historical forces that shaped them. In this epistemological framework, intelligence and its measurability were seen as transcultural and transhistorical givens. The fact that these constructions legitimated or delegitimated particular groups and individuals was of no consequence to many psychologists. That these psychological constructs served the logics of class and race domination was of no consequence (Gresson 1995 and 2004; Courts 1997; Giroux 1997; Hanrahan 1998; Edwards 2000).

Gardner's claim of the progressive mantle is troubling in light of his lack of concern with these sociopolitical processes and the oppressive and hurtful circumstances they produce. Throughout his work Gardner assumes that schools are instruments of democracy and that democracy itself has been achieved in the United States. Such tacit assumptions exert a profound influence on how Gardner sees the world, himself, the discipline of psychology, and the nature and uses of the personal intelligences. Gardner is a curious progressive in his sidestepping of questions of power, justice, and threats to democracy. He tiptoes around the antidemocratic tendencies of corporations and their role in education, never referring to the corporate power in contemporary societies to shape the nature of the information we obtain and how this affects our view of self and other (Gardner 1999a and 1999b).

Consistently, Gardner fails to see any threat from right-wing power brokers who want to create Eurocentric schools that celebrate whiteness and patriarchy as the highest forms of civilization or want to use schools to adjust students to exploitative workplaces. Gardner takes for granted the neutrality of these processes. He assumes that curricular knowledge and scientific knowledge about education are ideologically pure and disinterested. Careful analysis of the production and validation processes of such knowledge is to Gardner a waste of time, if not a misguided attack of nihilism. Indeed, Gardner has insulated himself from some of the most important intellectual currents of his era; ironically, many of these currents are directly related to the construction and nature of selfhood and his conception of personal intelligence.

Cognitive Complexity:
Personal Intelligences, Reason, and Emotion

Gardner tells us that he was moved to include the personal intelligences in his theory because such emotional and affective concerns had been typically left out of educational psychology and education. Ray Horn (2000) describes the situation Gardner sought to address:

> [M]odernistically oriented educators invariably maintain the archaic separation of the intellect and emotion through the continuation of dry, unnatural pedagogical strategies of worksheets, lectures, movies, and rigidly controlled group work. Affect never left the classroom; it was merely repressed. Recognition of student and teacher emotion is usually relegated to classroom management and teacher control contexts. But for educational change to be successful on any level, affect must be recognized and nurtured in all educational contexts. (102)

Progressive educators were excited by MI's promise to reconnect cognition and emotion—a fusion that would grant insight into the ways that an individual's reasoning could not be separated from issues of psychic health, disposition, affect, and the subconscious. In the promising context delineated by Gardner in the early 1980s, progressive educators believed that professionals could begin to understand the nature of consciousness construction in new ways. As the multiple nature of intelligence with its connection of logic and emotion was outlined, psychologists, students of cognition, and educators dissatisfied with mainstream cognitive science would begin to gain insight into the complexity of the process. Such complexity would provide a deeper understanding of the ability of individuals to act when situations were not well defined. Sensing that intelligent behavior in such circumstances was based on a complex interplay between emotional intuition and reason, progressives concerned with the learning process believed that MI theory could help them operate more successfully.

The complexity of the human mind and the cognitive processes in all of their rational, emotional, and subconscious dimensions has been evaded by mainstream educational psychology and Gardner's work. This complexity is so profound that we still understand relatively little about the working of the mind and the possibilities enfolded within it. Rational action is simply not as clear-cut and categorical as Gardner thinks it is. Those aspects that lend themselves to particular types of measurability are the domains and properties that psychologists tend to see. Gardner's personal intelligences are reduced in this conceptual context to a circumscribed number of operations, objects, and components that are familiar to and valued by a particular historical era and a specific cultural locale. Gardner deals with neither historical/cultural situatedness nor the inseparability of cognition and emotion. How, for example, do we separate linguistic intelligence from the personal intelligences? The myriad of cultural assumptions and values tacitly embedded in language concerning the nature of who we are and the characteristics of "normality" don't have to be delineated here. At least, in the early twenty-first century we can generally agree that the relationship connecting language, self-knowledge, and knowledge of others is a complicated maze of mutual influences.

Digging deeper into the complexity of this interconnectedness of the personal realm, we recognize that what is deemed cognitive ability cannot be separated from the construction of identity with its motivational and dispositional elements.

These features always emerge from an intricate interplay of cultural, economic, political, economic, and psychological forces. If this social construction is the case, then psychologists cannot summarily dismiss such forces when it comes to making judgments about an individual's facilities in these areas (Gardner 1983 and 1999b; Capra 1996; Shephard, Fasko, & Osborne 1999). Unfortunately, this is what Gardner tends to do. Does personal intelligence involve one's ability to adapt to her environment? What if that environment is unjust? Class-biased? Sexist? Racist? Homophobic? In such cases, is a refusal to adapt accompanied by a decision to resist a manifestation of a lack of interpersonal intelligence?

For example, does a child from a low socioeconomic background in the rural southern Appalachians who gains a sense of the class bias she is facing in school and reacts forcefully and with anger to it deserve to be described as possessing "low personal intelligence?" How might such dynamics affect her disposition to succeed in school? And is it possible that Gardner might perceive (or misdiagnose) a cynical disposition in this area as low cognitive ability—especially in linguistic and mathematical intelligence? In delineating the personal intelligences, how does Gardner account for individuals from marginalized backgrounds who understandably harbor less hope about their futures than those who come from more privileged backgrounds? Does this affect what he calls personal intelligence? How does a young man who holds little hope for his future "get motivated?" How does he gain Gardner's "scholarly ability to pursue self-directed and independent learning?" Gardner is uncomfortable with these important questions and their implications for an essentialized notion of intrapersonal and interpersonal intelligence.

The more sociologists and psychologists learn from the Santiago School's enactivism, the more expanded and complex their notions of cognition, mind, and self become. A complex notion of cognition involves the total life process, an inseparable embodiment of perception, emotion, reason, and behavior. According to Maturana and Varela the cognitive domain for any living system—including even bacteria, for example—involves the range of connections it can make with its environment. The analysis of such connections, of course, is central to any critical analysis of multiple intelligences. Indeed, in the domain of Gardner's personal intelligences emotions and their relationship to selfhood are of paramount importance, as they "color" every aspect of the cognitive act (Maturana & Varela 1987; Sumara & Davis 1997). Thus, rationality is always a convoluted interaction of all these contextual, emotional, and even bodily dynamics. The nervous system is not constructed in some hierarchical manner with the brain ruling the body. Aspects of the body are parts of the mind; such aspects are part of a chemical matrix that interconnects various human dimensions that used to be considered separate entities with discrete functions. We all have sensed this connection as we experience various degrees of pleasure when we devise a solution to a problem plaguing us or grasping a complex concept that had eluded us.

Such knowledge moves scholars to question Gardner's assumptions about cognition. In Steinberg's and my postformal analyses of cognition, Kenneth Gergen's relational self, and Santiago enactivism, a set of understandings are created that questions the reductionism of Gardner's

- essential self;
- disinterested, objective articulation of the personal intelligences;
- belief in the scientific "purity" of rationality and its unqualified benefits to "mankind"; and
- celebration of psychology's contribution to human progress.

Drawing upon the work of sociocognitivists such as Jean Lave (Lave & Wenger 1991) and Valerie Walkerdine (1984), I am suspicious of what Gardner refers to as the universal personal intelligences because of the plethora of subjective forces that shape such a definition. In the context of Gardner's descriptions of certain characteristics of the personal intelligences, the following queries emerge:

- Does engagement in accessing one's personal feelings bring joy?
- Does everyone have similar access to the cultural tools that help us value and express a wide range of feelings?
- Does a student's inability (or refusal) to set goals and track progress toward them in school mean that she will exhibit this deficiency in other activities?
- Might different observers with divergent interests and value structures reach different conclusions about an individual's ability to read the motives and desires of other people and use them to influence people to act in certain ways?

The Complexity of the Personal Intelligences: Connecting the Theory to the Contemporary Social Terrain

As the concept of complexity and complex systems theory has entered the lexicon of various academic disciplines over the last few decades, Gardner has retreated more and more into the reductionistic cocoon of the traditional disciplines. Operating in closed systems where variables are controlled, positivist psychologists have often promoted an orderly and predictable view of change. When the variables are controlled and protected from outside (sociocultural) contamination, equations could be formulated and exact predictions devised about the mind. But such psychologists have not realized that even ostensibly "minor variables" could have dramatic effects, sometimes not exhibiting themselves immediately to the researcher. When they did manifest themselves, their effect seemed to the positivist psychologist to be an aberration, probably a mistake in the construction of an equation. The socioeconomic context in which a student taking an IQ test was raised, for example, has been viewed as irrelevant in examining the forces that shape performance on such tests. A complex view of intelligence maintains that it is absurd to discount the importance of context in such testing. It makes a dramatic difference whether a child is raised in an upper-middle-class home where both parents have Master's degrees as opposed to a lower socioeconomic home where both parents dropped out of junior high school.

In the context of such complexity, Marla Morris asks in her chapter in this volume: "What is it like to experience?" Her point is to illustrate the psychoanalytic complexity of subjectivity, of the conscious and the unconscious mind. Gardner dismisses both Morris's concerns and social analysts' interests in the social context of self-production and academic performance. Both the social and psychoanalytical domains push cognitive psychologists to dig deeper into the interconnections that shape the complexities of the personal talents. All features of the cosmos— biology, physics, chemistry, sociology, politics, economics, and culture—are part of the braid we label "the self." And how we engage in the activities Gardner places in the realm of the personal intelligences cannot be understood and certainly not ranked and evaluated without insight into the complexity of these interconnections. In the language of complexity theory the intersections of these multiple domains create unities of a higher order.

Living-systems theory contends in its analysis of life processes that as a certain level of complexity is reached, a life form couples structurally not only with its environmental context but with itself. Such a coupling elicits, amazingly, both an external and an internal world. In *Homo sapiens* this so-called internal world is the domain of self. This self cannot be separated from language; cultural values; socioeconomic influences; ideological, discursive, and other modes of power; the thought processes; and the nature of consciousness. One of the central reasons that the authors of *Multiple Intelligences Reconsidered* are uncomfortable with modernist ways of seeing and with Gardner's psychological heritage involves their lack of interest in this relational dimension of both the cosmos in general and selfhood in particular. In Gardner's description of the personal domain this relationality as expressed by the structural coupling of living organisms has gone AWOL. The complex nature of relationship that produces a sense of belongingness and security in an individual's world is not relevant here (Capra 1996; Jardine 1998; Kincheloe, Steinberg, & Hinchey 1999; O'Sullivan 1999; Horn 2000).

Sociocognitivists—whom Gardner salutes but does not integrate in his recent work (1999b, 24)—use the zone of proximal development (ZPD) in a neo-Vygotskian articulation to illustrate some the concepts delineated in the previous paragraphs. Individuals, the argument goes, make use of the cognitive accomplishments of others and the know-how embedded in social and technological tools and organizational cultures to develop their own cognitive functions. Thus, power-related access, especially to such academic and dominant cultural personal dynamics and to mentorship in their use, becomes extremely important to the success of the learner (Gee, Hull, & Lankshear 1996; Samaras 2002). Understanding these neo-Vygotskian concepts, a reconceptualized notion of interpersonal and intrapersonal facilities would have to delve into the specifics of the structural coupling taking place in the ZPD. A theory of personal intelligence that does not examine the genesis of such personal facilities is reminiscent of the theory of spontaneous generation in which maggots were thought to spontaneously emerge from rotting meat.

A key aspect of the context that helps us understand the production of the personal facilities involves the alienation of both modernity and the contemporary postmodern condition. Some degree of depression and emotional discomfort is not an unreasonable response to contemporary social conditions. Anxiety about one's place in the cosmos or in the culture is quite understandable in an electronic hyperreality that shoots exploding images of selfhood and manipulative knowledges at every individual on the planet who is reachable. Gardner is oblivious to such despair. His is a comfortable academic world where hegemony doesn't exist, environmental destruction is irrelevant, racism is a relic of a distant past, and the globalized economy is bringing U.S.-style peace, prosperity, and democracy to earthlings. At the end of the twentieth century he wrote:

> [D]emocratic forms of government are on the rise: and with readier communication among individuals and nations, certain patterns of human interaction (such as free press and ready migration) become more attractive, while others (such as censorship or violations of human rights) less easy to advocate. (Gardner 1999a, 46)

No wonder Gardner is comfortable in his home in Celebration, Florida—the total community built by the Disney Corporation to emulate an early-twentieth-century lifestyle.

Gardner's sanguine worldview belies the poverty, economic exploitation, racism, sexism, homophobia, violence, religious hatred, displacement, and depression of globalized hyperreality. Especially in the domain of the personal, the human quest for belongingness, participation, and affection is being thwarted by contemporary social conditions. Gardner simply cannot understand the vicissitudes of the interpersonal and intrapersonal terrain in light of his disregard of the condition of the world and its people. "The privatization of everyday life," as Danny Weil phrases it in his chapter, and its accompanying privatization—e.g., the corporate takeover—of government and education is destroying the socially protective features of the public space. All of this is taking place so that the wealthy few may enjoy even bigger profits. In this hostile environment the truncated, increasingly disconnected self struggles to find meaning, to gain a sense of purpose. For Gardner to remove the personal domain from the contemporary crisis of meaning reveals a profound interpersonal insensitivity. The physician might be well served to heal himself.

Studies point to the statistical rise in depression, anxiety, and psychosis in Western societies over the last several decades (O'Sullivan 1999). Because of the breakdown of social supports and community, shared meanings have often been lost. In this context individuals experience a loss of self-worth, a decline in self-esteem. Such a crisis of selfhood triggers compulsive consumption, sexual obsessions, fundamentalist religious zealotry, and narcissistic self-absorption. Even though there has been an avalanche of literature on psychoanalysis in relation to these dynamics and their relationship to the world of education and schooling, Gardner ignores the topic in his delineation of personal intelligences. The relationship individuals develop in the interplay between the social alienation of the world-at-large and the inner world of libido and desire cannot be separated from concerns with school performance and psychological health. A theory describing the ability to know oneself and to discern the motives and drives of individuals around one demands engagement with such psychoanalytical questions (Britzman & Pitt 1996; Britzman 1998; Fenwick 2000).

Issues of personal intelligence and the corresponding notion of self-esteem are psychologized in Gardner's theory. As the properties of abstract individuals, such concerns are relegated to the psychological domain with little concern for the insights of other analytical traditions. Any time in the first decade of the twenty-first century concerns with the personal domain or self-esteem are brought into an educational discussion, the conservative tenor of the public conversation relegates such concerns to the trash heap of pedagogical trivialization. Gardner's work is often unfairly located by such conservative critics simply because he raises such issues (Traub 1998). Concern with the personal domain and self-esteem is not a trivial educational topic. And I would argue, as one who seeks a rigorous and just reform of American education (see my work on "standards of complexity" in Horn & Kincheloe 2001 and Kincheloe & Weil 2001), such concerns can synergize complex and challenging conceptions of what pedagogy could be.

Thus, an awareness of the way the dominant cultural messages of school are internalized by students—especially marginalized students—via the mundane practices of everyday life in the classroom is important. In this sociocultural microcontext, analysts of the personal domain come to see the specific ways personal abilities are shaped if not sometimes crushed. In such a microcontext, informed analysts may observe empowering experiences for students that allow them to develop and utilize interpersonal and intrapersonal talents. Unfortunately, the exploitation and alienation of contemporary society are often reproduced in classroom in race-, class-, and gender-specific ways. Because of socially decontextualized ways of seeing self-production such as Gardner's MI theory, these dramatically important aspects of personal development are invisible to most observers. Professionals who work with young people need to be aware of the effects of these oppressive social relations and their impact on the personal facilities and, in turn, academic performance. Gardner has to gain a better grasp of the complexity of these issues.

Social Fragmentation and the Personal Domain: Questioning Cartesianism and the Move Beyond

Social fragmentation pushes individuals to the personal extremes of radical individuation or the destruction of selfhood. From socially induced egocentrism to autism, we live in a perilous age for the well-being of the self, an era where relationship to a vast variety of important domains is subverted. This closing off of the relational self leaves us without a sense of place or belonging (Kincheloe & Pinar 1991)—a condition that demands the attention of psychologists and educators. This problem has not arisen in a historical vacuum. Saint Augustine, for example, was writing at the end of the fourth century about the incomprehensible way mind is related to body and the difficulty of studying the formation of self. It could be argued that the birth of modernist science and the concurrent rise of Cartesianism in the seventeenth century has not merely failed to help us understand these issues but, because of particular epistemological assumptions, has made their analysis more difficult. The production of self and the nature of the relational self do not lend themselves to Cartesian empirical analysis (Madison 1988; Kincheloe 1993; Kincheloe, Steinberg, & Villaverde 1999; O'Sullivan 1999).

Cartesianism has been marked by a tendency for dualism resulting in alienation. In this context we find the fragmentation and alienation of:

- the knower from the known;
- the subject (self) from object (context);
- the mind from the body;
- the individual from the natural world;
- the self from history.

Subjectivity from consciousness—here the individual is alienated from aspects of her own selfhood

As I have pointed out so often in this chapter, Gardner operates outside of this important contemporary (and in this case historical) conversation. As he maintains in *The Disciplined Mind:* "if you want to understand what it means to be alive, study biology" (218). He further reveals his social insensitivity a couple of lines later, adding: "if you want to understand your own background, study national history and immigration patterns and experiences." The reduction of the human life processes, of the ontological realm of being to biology, is disturbing. The racial insensitivity illustrated in the above quotation is overt; national histories and immigration patterns do not chronicle African American experience and the construction of black people's selfhood. Far more study of diverse and often counter-canonical sources is necessary if we are to understand the complex processes involved with Gardner's own delineation of the realm of the personal.

Tying the understanding of living to biology, one's personal background to canonical history, and the personal domain in general to mainstream psychology supports a Cartesian view of individuals as free standing and self-sufficient. My critique of Gardner, obviously, is grounded on the premise that Cartesianism tends to separate various dimensions of self and world into discrete parts in the process, losing the interdependent dimensions that contemporary systems theory and postformalism value so much. Since the world operates in an integrated mode, we distort it when we isolate its parts for scientific study (Kincheloe, Steinberg, & Tippins 1999). This is one of the reasons that interdisciplinary work is so important—another tenet that Gardner rejects. A close reading of Gardner's work reveals no concern with these fragmentary dynamics, no discomfort with the limits of Cartesian modernism in psychology or anywhere else, and no problem with the colonial nature of Cartesian science's degradation of other ways of seeing the world.

Gardner mentions contemporary "dis-ease" in *The Disciplined Mind* but fails to historicize it or conceptually develop it. His solution to the problem involves applying the multiple intelligences and recognizing different individual talents. There is no larger historical problem at work here, nothing wrong with the ways of seeing tacitly embedded within Western cultural history. Gardner provides us no sense that he understands that it was this cultural dis-ease that contributed to the success of multiple intelligences in the first place. As individuals concerned with the fragmentation and alienation of Cartesianism come to recognize that Gardner fails to question the epistemological structures on which it is based, I maintain that MI theory will lose its unquestioned status as an alternative to such frames of reference. Gardner's rejection as nihilistic of the questioning of Cartesianism evidences itself in his disdain of postmodern analysis: "the pursuit of disciplines and disciplinary thinking is not controversial, except in certain postmodern educational circles" (1999a, 218). Here Gardner is in denial. He does not want to acknowledge that from a macrohistorical perspective the West is still in the middle of a worldwide anticolonial revolution in which individuals from diverse backgrounds are questioning what they consider the epistemological imperialism of Cartesianism.

The Personal Domain and the Power of Cultural Difference

In his conceptual encapsulation in the Cartesian box, Gardner succumbs to the naive realist view that the personal intelligences are objectively real and exist "out there." He argues that interpersonal and intrapersonal intelligences operate independently of his imaginative construction of them in a particular historical time and cultural place. Cultural knowledges that have been developed outside the Cartesian box have nothing to teach Gardner. African, Native American, and other indigenous cultures (Lepani 1998; Weil 1998) who refuse to split the materiality of the lived world with their spiritual and moral traditions are irrelevant to Gardner's multiple intelligences theory. This is one reason why Aostre Johnson's (1999) work in spirituality is so important—she always brings these cultural knowledges to psychological and educational conversations. In the process she helps create new ways of seeing and thinking about Western knowledge production in these areas.

Without this confrontation with the cognitive power of cultural difference, Gardner and many other Western scholars determine there is only one correct way to study the personal domain. Just as Gardner's revered Western scholarly disciplines provide students with the correct interpretations of the world around and within us, his view of the personal intelligences limits the "horizons" or contexts within which we can raise questions about these dynamics. Richard Cary provides an excellent example of this tendency in his discussion of Western canonical art and its mimetic aesthetics in his chapter on visual-spatial intelligence. Ghana-born Canadian scholar George Dei (1995), in his studies of indigenous knowledge, devises alternatives to the Cartesian view of self and world. As he explores diverse ontologies grounded on a sophisticated sense of the relationships connecting self to both society and the natural world, new ways of defining personal talent emerge.

As different cultures interact and astute scholars compare and contrast their assumptions, everyone benefits. Drawing on the power of cultural difference, such scholars expose previously invisible philosophical and scientific assumptions. In the domain of personal intelligences we begin to see Gardner's assumptions about the abstract individual, the relative unimportance of relationship, and the dismissal of the historicization and cultural embeddedness of self-production. Such insights change our orientation to the personal intelligences and any pedagogical assumptions about how we might develop students' abilities in this area. Cultivating the personal talents is a part of a rigorous general education that utilizes the power of cultural difference to help students explore the dominant assumptions that invisibly surround them and the way these forces insidiously shape them, their values, and their ways of perceiving. Such an education rigorously studies Western ways of seeing but always within the critical framework of what Theodor Adorno and Max Horkheimer (1979) termed the concept of "immanence." As Western Cartesianism is studied in light of other cultural constructs, an immanent critique develops that considers "what is" in relation to "what could be."

Such scholarship produces a well-informed, rigorous mode of self-analysis. After studying one's sociohistorical construction and an immanent analysis of "how I could be," individuals are empowered to play a conscious, active role in shaping who they want to become. Better aware of why and how they are oriented to the world, they are better equipped to change socially constructed aspects of themselves that they find to be racist, sexist, homophobic, culturally narrow, or previously unquestioned. From a critical and postformal perspective, this is a cardinal feature of becoming an educated person, a democratic moral agent. In my own life, I have pursued such a critical consciousness of self and world via the use of knowledges from cultures different than my own—especially those African American and Native American epistemologies and ontologies that Gardner avoids throughout his work.

The "double consciousness," for example, of African Americans so profoundly described by W. E. B. Du Bois is a profound American historical example of interpersonal genius. If African Americans were to survive throughout the American experience, they needed to gain a profound understanding not only of themselves but also of the individuals who held power over them. Du Bois labeled this interpersonal understanding a form of "second sight"—the ability to see oneself through the perception of others. Drawing upon Du Bois, a postformal rethinking of the personal talents is grounded on the understanding that a critically educated person knows more than merely the validated knowledges and epistemological frames of the dominant culture (see Kincheloe & Steinberg 1997 for an extension of these ideas). Such an individual would understand Western knowledges, subjugated knowledges, and the ways he or she was positioned in relation to them.

In my own life such understandings were extremely important, for in order to navigate the domain of academia I had to understand the way the dominant culture positioned me. Especially in the dominant culture's imprint on psychometrics and vocational aptitude testing, I was a lower-class hillbilly with little academic ability and low-status cultural capital. Once I gained awareness of this perception, I was empowered to deal more effectively with both the interpersonal and the intrapersonal realms. I realized that to understand these domains in my life, I needed a wide body of social, cultural, ideological, discursive, economic, and political understandings. There was no way to separate such insights from my knowledge of self and my awareness of how others would perceive me. I consider myself privileged to have had such experiences. Gardner's truncated view of the effects of such sociocultural dimensions on the personal domain may in part be the result of his always being considered an intelligent child, a good student, and a gifted researcher. Positioned in this way, it may be more difficult for Gardner to empathize with the personal struggles of and the particular interpersonal and intrapersonal abilities needed by those who come from the other end of the "perceived ability" continuum.

Exploring the Ontological Frontier: Constucting New Modes of Selfhood

Employing our understanding of complexity, Santiago cognitivism as the process of life, our critical theoretical foundations, the critique of Cartesianism, and post-structuralist/postmodernist analysis, we can lay the conceptual foundations for a new mode of selfhood. Such a configuration cannot be comprehensively delineated here, but we can begin to build theoretical pathways to get around the Cartesian limitations of Gardner's personal intelligences. With Maturana and Valera's concept that living things constantly remake themselves in interaction with their environments, our postformal notion of a "new self" or a "critical ontology" is grounded on the human ability to use new social contexts and experiences to reformulate the self and interpersonal/ interpersonal facilities. In this context the postformal concept of personal ability becomes a de-essentialized cognition of possibility. No essentialized bounded self can access the cognitive potential offered by epiphanies of difference or triggered by an "insignificant" insight.

As we begin to identify previously unperceived patterns in which the self is implicated, the possibility of cognitive change and personal growth is enhanced. As the barriers between mind and multiple contexts are erased, the chance is increased that more expanded forms of "cognitive autopoiesis"—self-constructed modes of higher-order thinking—will emerge. A more textured, thicker sense of self-production and the nature of self and other is constructed in this process. As we examine the self and its relationship to others in cosmological, epistemological, linguistic, social, cultural, and political contexts, we gain a clearer sense of our purpose in the world, especially in relation to justice, interconnectedness, and even love. In these activities we move closer to the macroprocesses of life and their microexpressions in everyday life.

A key aspect of the life processes is the understanding of difference that comes from recognition of patterns of interconnectedness. Knowing that an individual from an upper-middle-class European background living in a Virginia suburb will be considered culturally bizarre by a group of tribespeople from the Amazon rain forest is a potentially profound learning experience in the domain of the personal. How is the suburbanite viewed as bizarre? What cultural practices are seen as so unusual? What mannerisms are humorous to the tribespeople? What worldviews are baffling to them? The answers to such questions may shock the suburbanite into reorienting her view of her own "normality." The interaction may induce her to ask questions of the way she is perceived by and the way she perceives others. Such a bracketing of the personal may be quite liberating. This interaction with difference could be another example of Maturana and Valera's structural coupling that creates a new relationship with other and with self. In Maturana and Varela's conceptualization a new inner world is created as a result of such coupling. In the context of *Multiple Intelligences Reconsidered* we might contend that a new mode of personal awareness is evoked.

Such explorations on the ontological frontier hold profound educational implications. As students pursue rigorous study of diverse global knowledges, they come to understand that the identities of their peer groups and families constitute only a few of countless historical and cultural ways to be human. As they study their self-production in wider biological, sociological, cultural-studies, historical, theological, psychological and countercanonical contexts, they gain insights into their ways of being. As they engage the conflicts that induce diverse knowledge producers to operate in conflicting ways, students become more attuned to the ideological, discursive, and regulatory forces operating in all knowledges. This is not nihilism, as Gardner claims; this is the exciting process of exploring the world and the self and their relationship in all of the complexity such study requires.

In this context of pursuing insight into selfhood and the personal domain, Gardner is not comfortable with our call for the embrace of diverse cultural traditions and divergent traditions of knowledge production. His battle with E. D. Hirsch's "cultural literacy"—which many progressives argued left out global knowledges, information about U.S. sub-cultures, and women in general—was on pedagogical grounds, not cultural ones. In no way am I trying to dismiss the importance of pedagogy, but Gardner was concerned only about the way—the drill and memorization techniques—Hirsch chose to get his information across to students. There are better ways to accumulate a lot of information, Gardner (1999a) argued. In the debate with Hirsch we discern Gardner's cultural and ideological insensitivity as well as his failure to perceive the relationship between cognition, knowledge, and ontology. The way we make such curricular decisions reflects not only how and what we learn but who we perceive ourselves to be. Gardner sees students as bounded selves with discrete intelligences in diverse domains whose relationship to their culture and other cultures is not very significant. After all, such cultural dynamics fall outside the traditional concerns of psychology and are difficult to frame in the scientific language of Cartesianism.

Thus, returning to a central theme of this chapter, Gardner's concept of self subverts efforts to move to a new domain of interpersonal and intrapersonal cognition. The processual and relational notions of self advocated here structurally couple with the sociocultural context and can only be understood by studying them with these dynamics in mind. These characteristics of self hold profound implications politically, psychologically, and pedagogically. If our notion of the self emerges in its relationship with multiple dimensions of the world, it is by its nature a participatory entity. Such an interactive dynamic is always in process, and thus demands a reconceptualization of the concept of individualism and self-interest (Pickering 1999). The needs of self and others in this context begin to merge as the concept of self-reliance takes on new meanings. Notions of educational purpose, evaluation, curriculum development, and other pedagogical concerns are transformed when these new conceptions of the personal domain come into the picture. In the first decade of the twenty-first century we stand merely on the threshold of the possibilities this notion of selfhood harbors. We hope that Gardner will join us in this exciting journey along the ontological frontier.

References

Adorno, T., & Horkheimer, M. (1979). *Dialectic of enlightenment*. London: Verso.

Allen, M. (2000). Voice of reason. *www.curtin.edu.au/learn/unit/10846/arrow/vorall.htm*

"An inclusive paradigm for education." (1998). *Initiatives, 58*(3).

Aronowitz, S., & Giroux, H. (1991). *Post-modern education: Politics, culture, and social criticism*. Minneapolis: University of Minnesota Press.

Bereiter, C. (2002). *Education and the mind in the knowledge age*. Mahwah, NJ: Lawrence Erlbaum.

Bodeau, D. (1999). Metabeings and individuals: Aids and obstacles to growth. *www.gurus.com/dougdeb/essays/metabeings.html*

Britzman, D. (1998). *Lost subjects, contested objects: Toward a psychoanalytic inquiry of learning*. Albany: State University of New York Press.

Britzman, D., & Pitt, A. (1996). On refusing one's place: The ditchdigger's dream. In J. Kincheloe, S. Steinberg, & A. Gresson (eds.), *Measured lies: "The Bell Curve" examined*. New York, St. Martin's Press.

Bruner, J. (1996). *The culture of education*. Cambridge, MA: Harvard University Press.

Cannella, G. (1997). *Deconstructing early childhood education: Social justice and revolution*. New York: Peter Lang.

Cantu, D. (1999). An Internet-based multiple intelligences model for teaching high school history. *www.mcel.pacifica.edu/jahc/jahc113/k12113.cantuindex.html*

Capra, F. (1996). *The web of life: A new scientific understanding of living systems*. New York: Anchor Books.

Courts, P. (1997). *Multicultural literacies: Dialect, discourse, and diversity.* New York: Peter Lang.

Dei, G. (1995). Indigenous knowledge as an empowerment tool. In N. Singh & V. Titi (eds.), *Empowerment: Toward sustainable development.* Toronto: Fernwood.

Edwards, A. (2000). Researching pedagogy: A sociocultural agenda. Inaugural lecture, University of Birmingham. *www.edu.bham.ac.uk/sat/edwards1.html*

Fenwick, T. (2000). Experiential learning in adult education: A comparative framework. *www.ualberta.ca/~tfenwick/ext/aeq.htm*

Freire, P. (1978). *Education for critical consciousness.* NewYork: Seabury.

Gardner, H. (1983). *Frames of mind: The theory of multiple intelligences.* New York: Basic Books.

——. (1999a). *The disciplined mind: Beyond facts and standardized tests, the K–12 education that every child deserves.* New York: Penguin.

——. (1999b). *Intelligence reframed: Multiple intelligences.* New York: Basic Books.

Gee, J., Hull, G., & Lankshear, C. (1996). *The new work order: Behind the language of the new capitalism.* Boulder, CO: Westview.

Gergen, K. (1991). *The saturated self: Dilemmas of identity in contemporary life.* New York: Basic Books.

——. (1996). Technology and the self: From the essential to the sublime. In D. Grodin and T. Lindlof (eds.), *Constructing the self in a mediated world* (pp. 127–140). Thousand Oaks, CA: Sage.

——. (1997). The place of the psyche in a constructed world. *Theory and Psychology, 7*(6), 723–746.

Giroux, H. (1997). *Pedagogy and the politics of hope: Theory, culture, and schooling.* Boulder, CO: Westview.

Goleman, D. (1994). *Emotional intelligence.* New York: Bantam.

Gresson, A. (1995). *The recovery of race in America.* Minneapolis: University of Minnesota Press.

——. (2004). *America's atonement.* New York: Peter Lang.

Griffin, D. (1997). *Parapsychology, philosophy, and spirituality: A postmodern exploration.* Albany: State University of New York Press.

Haggerson, N. (2000). *Expanding curriculum research and understanding: A mytho-poetic perspective.* New York: Peter Lang.

Hanrahan, M. (1998). A legitimate place for intuition and other a-logical processes in research and hence in reports of research. Paper presented at the Australian Association of Research in Education, November–December. Adelaide. *www.aare.edu.au/98pap/han98331.htm*

Hinchey, P. (1998). *Finding freedom in the classroom: A practical introduction to critical theory.* New York: Peter Lang.

Horn, R. (2000). *Teacher talk: A postformal inquiry into educational change.* New York: Peter Lang.

Horn, R., & Kincheloe, J. (eds.). (2001). *American standards: Quality education in a complex world—the Texas case.* New York: Peter Lang.

Howley, A., Pendarvis, E., & Howley, C. (1993). Anti-intellectualism in U.S. schools. *Education Policy Analysis Archives, 1*(6).

If you're so rich, why aren't you wise? (2000). www.sd.znet.com/~normanl/socint1a.htm

Jardine, D. (1998). *To dwell with a boundless heart: Essays in curriculum theory, hermeneutics, and the ecological imagination.* New York: Peter Lang.

Johnson, A. (1999). Teaching as sacrament. In Kincheloe, J., Steinberg, S., & Villaverde, L.

(eds.) *Rethinking intelligence: Confronting psychological assumptions about teaching and learning* (pp. 105–116). New York: Routledge.

Kelly, K., & Moon, S. (1998). Personal and social talents. *Phi Delta Kappan, 79*(10), 743–746.

Kincheloe, J. (1993). *Toward a critical politics of teacher thinking: Mapping the postmodern.* Westport, CT: Bergin & Garvey.

———. (2000). Making critical thinking critical. In D. Weil & H. Anderson (eds.), *Perspectives in critical thinking: Essays by teachers in theory and practice* (pp. 37–55). New York: Peter Lang.

———. (2001). *Getting beyond the facts: Teaching social studies/social science in the twenty-first century* (2nd ed.). New York: Peter Lang.

Kincheloe, J., & Pinar, W. (1991). *Curriculum as social psychoanalysis: Essays on the significance of place.* Albany: State University of New York Press.

Kincheloe, J., & Steinberg, S. (1997). *Changing multiculturalism.* London: Open University Press.

Kincheloe, J., & Steinberg, S. (1993). A tentative description of post-formal thinking: The critical confrontation with cognitive theory. *Harvard Educational Review, 63*(3), 296–320.

Kincheloe, J., Steinberg, S., & Hinchey, P. (eds.). (1999). *The post-formal reader: Cognition and education.* New York: Falmer.

Kincheloe, J., Steinberg, S., & Tippins, D. (1999). *The stigma of genius: Einstein, consciousness, and education.* New York: Peter Lang.

Kincheloe, J., Steinberg, S., & Villaverde, L. (eds.). (1999). *Rethinking intelligence: Confronting psychological assumptions about teaching and learning.* New York: Routledge.

Kincheloe, J., & Weil, D. (eds.). (2001). *Standards and schooling in the United States: An encyclopedia.* 3 vols. Santa Barbara, CA: ABC-CLIO.

Knijnik, G. (2001). Ethnomathematics and postmodern thinking: Conver/divergences. *www.nottingham.ac.uk/csme/meas/papers/knijnik.html*

Lave, J., & Wenger, E. (1991). *Situated learning: Legitimate peripheral participation.* New York: Cambridge University Press.

Lepani, B. (1998). Information literacy: The challenge of the digital age. *www.acal.edu.au/lepani.htm*

Macedo, D. (1994). *Literacies of power: What Americans are not allowed to know.* Boulder, CO: Westview.

Madison, G. (1988). *The hermeneutics of postmodernity: Figures and themes.* Bloomington: Indiana University Press.

Maturana, H., & Varela, F. (1987). *The tree of knowledge.* Boston: Shambhala.

May, T. (1993). *Between genealogy and epistemology: Psychology, politics, and knowledge in the thought of Michel Foucault.* University Park: Pennsylvania State University Press.

McLaren, P. (1995). *Critical pedagogy and predatory culture: Oppositional politics in a postmodern era.* New York: Routledge.

———. (2000). *Che Guevara, Paulo Freire, and the pedagogy of revolution.* Lanham, MD: Rowman & Littlefield.

O'Sullivan, E. (1999). *Transformative learning: Educational vision for the 21st century.* London: Zed.

Pickering, J. (1999). The self is a semiotic process. *Journal of Consciousness Studies, 6*(4), 31–47.

Reason, P., & Bradbury, H. (2000). Introduction: Inquiry and participation in search of a world worthy of human aspiration. In P. Reason & H. Bradbury (eds.), *Handbook of action research: Participative inquiry and practice* (pp. 1–14). Thousand Oaks, CA: Sage.

Samaras, A. (2002). *Self-study for teacher educators: Crafting a pedagogy for educational change.* New York: Peter Lang.

Shephard, R., Fasko, D., & Osborne, F. (1999). Intrapersonal intelligence: Affective factors in thinking. *Education, 119*(4), 525–541.

Shoham, S. (1999). *God as the shadow of man.* New York: Peter Lang.

Shotter, J. (1993). *Cultural politics of everyday life.* Toronto: University of Toronto Press.

Steinberg, S. (2001). *Multi/intercultural conversations: A reader.* New York: Peter Lang.

Sumara, D. & Davis, B., (1997). Cognition, complexity, and teacher education. *Harvard Educational Review, 67*(1), 75–104.

Traub, J. (1998). Howard Gardner's campaign against logic. *New Republic,* 26 October.

Varela, F. (1999). *Ethical know-how: Action, wisdom, and cognition.* Stanford: Stanford University Press.

Walkerdine, V. (1984). Developmental psychology and the child-centered pedagogy: The insertion of Piaget into early education. In J. Henriques, W. Hollway, C. Urwin, C. Venn, and V. Walkerdine (eds.), *Changing the subject* (pp. 153–202). New York: Methuen.

Weil, D. (1998). *Towards a critical multi-cultural literacy: Theory and practice for education for liberation.* New York: Peter Lang.

———. (2001) Florida state standards—Florida's advanced academic standards for the assessment of critical and creative thinking. In Kincheloe & Weil (2001), 429–480.

Weil, D., & Anderson, H. (eds.). (2000). *Perspectives in critical thinking: Essays by teachers in theory and practice.* New York: Peter Lang.

Wexler, P. (1997). Social research in education: Ethnography of being. Paper presented at the International Conference on the Culture of Schooling, March, Halle, Germany.

———. (2000). *The mystical society: Revitalization in culture, theory, and education.* Boulder, CO: Westview.

Zuss, M. (1999). Subject present: Life-writings and strategies of representation. New York: Peter Lang.

Chapter 8

Marla Morris

THE EIGHTH ONE:
NATURALISTIC INTELLIGENCE

Who is intelligent? What counts as intelligence"? Who decides? For the benefit of whom? Who is stupid? Why is it that the notion of intelligence is too often associated with its opposite, stupidity? What monster hides under the notion "intelligence"? These questions depend on who defines intelligence and why. There is a social and political agenda attached to this term that historically has served to "otherize." White supremacists have historically labeled minority groups "stupid." White supremacists are not just quacks; many are scientists, educators, doctors, and policy-makers. Stephen Jay Gould (1996) remarks that in 1913 H. H. Goddard, the American popularizer of the Binet Intelligence Test, "[s]ent two women to Ellis Island for two and a half months. They were instructed to pick out the feeble-minded by sight" (195). The so-called "feeble-minded" were mostly European Jewish immigrants whom Goddard determined ranked "below the age of twelve on the Binet scale" (196). It is no accident that intelligence tests and immigration restrictions went hand and hand. "Immigration policy" in the United States historically has been a code for racism.

Policy is a result of measurement. Measuring skulls in Nazi Germany "proved" Jews' inferiority. Crainiometry is not that different from psychometry. Numbers prove "facts" about innate inferiority: genetic fault lines. Numbers were the well-proven method of Nazism. But psychometricians do not make this connection. They often claim that numbers and measurement prove the innate inferiority of minority groups, blacks, Hispanics, women, the working class, Jews, queers, anybody who is Other. Psychometricians set out to prove their own prejudices, to prove their projected hatreds. Psychometricians often deny that the subjectivity of the researcher, the prejudices of the researcher, are built into the test. Testing is not innocent. In fact, it is insidious. However, psychometricians claim that intelligence has nothing whatsoever to do with culture, environment, or the idiosyncratic nature of knowledge. Psychometrics is, as Donna Haraway (1991) might say, the culture of no culture. Joe Kincheloe and Shirley Steinberg criticize the implicit and perhaps explicit agenda of psychometrics. "Proclaiming that race and culture are irrelevant in psychometrics, the authors [of *The Bell Curve*] produce data that (they argue) justifies a range of policies—especially those that undermine the efforts of non-whites and poor to gain financial and social stability" (1997, 8). The Bell Curve, SATs, GREs, and Intelligence Testing generally serve to Other by offering up a politics of oppression, a politics that is insidiously racist, sexist, and classist. From measuring skulls to measuring intelligence, from immigrant restriction to concentration camp, from restrictions on education to prison, the myth of a genetic, innate, heritable "intelligence" lives on into the twenty-first century.

But there is a counternarrative that attempts to dismantle and dislodge the idea that intelligence can be measured as a single entity or single thing. Stephen Jay Gould explains that "phrenologists celebrated the theory of richly multiple and independent intelligence. Their view led to Thurstone and Guilford earlier in our century, and to Howard Gardner . . ." (1996, 22). The gist of multiple intelligences theory, or MI, is that human beings are "intelligent" in many ways, not just one. Further, MI suggests, according to Gardner, that intelligence may be both inherited and affected by the environment. Intelligence, then, is malleable. What is the point of education if minds are not malleable? Why bother teaching kids who are born stupid? Why bother at all with smart kids if they are already smart? Being smart, then, is not just an innate trait; it is possible to get smart. And that is where education becomes valuable. Whereas a single intelligence theory produces a caste system whereby individuals are born into stupidity and therefore must remain stupid for the duration of a lifetime, MI theory suggests that, like a class system which allows individuals social mobility, an individual born with fewer advantages might be able to get smart or might be recognized as smart in a way that differs from logicomathematical or linguistic skills.

Generally speaking, I find the notion of multiple intelligences superficial, reductionistic, and naive. Gardner suffers from a culture of no culture (Haraway 1991). He does not take into account the ways in which the notion of "intelligence" might be shaped from one's own situatedness. Race/class/gender play a huge role in the way people think about what is and is not intelligent. His theory is ahistorical. Gardner seems to operate out of a vacuum. He writes as if modernity has not been challenged and questioned by the advent of the postmodern. He is a modernist through and through. He writes through the lens of white male privilege. He is popular because he is simple; he reduces complexities to the simple. He is a Cartesian at heart.

Gardner reduces intelligence to eight things. I deliberately use the word "things" because that is what Gardner wants us to believe. There are eight things or regions in the brain—brain-things—that correspond (read outmoded correspondence theory) to eight attributes of intelligence. To suggest that there are eight, nine, or a thousand things which can be located in the brain and correspond to kinds of intelligence is problematic. Gardner suggests that these eight intelligences are expressed as "core competencies" (1999b, 99; and 1983/1993, x). This claim makes little sense in a postmodern era. Even in a premodern era, in the wake of Buddhism that dates from 580 BCE, the notion of "core" was seen as a mistake. Surely, the human psyche is more complex than this. A core, whether it is an intelligence core or, say, a gender core, serves as a "regulatory fiction" (Haraway 1991, 135). A core, or eight cores, if you will, keeps us from thinking the unthinkable. Cores regulate and normalize the ways in which thought can be thought or feeling can be felt. Cores regulate the complexities of lived experience into neat and tidy places. Cores squash out the mystery of being and becoming, the Otherness within and without. The chaos, instability, and ambiguity of lived experience are nicely tucked away behind the cores of certainty, the core intelligences. Lakoff and Johnson (1999) tell us that cognitive science teaches that 95 percent of the mind's activities, or what it is that might create "intelligence, is unknowable and inaccessible." Although cognitive scientists may not make the claim that repression is the cause of unconscious processes, some cognitive scientists are in agreement with psychoanalysts who have been claiming since Freud that most of our lives are guided by the unconscious. The upshot of these claims is that, at the end of the day, we know little about what makes us tick.

Post-Freudian psychoanalysts such as Jean Laplanche (1999) suggest that the unconscious is not a core. It is an Other place within; it is the stranger that we cannot understand. Thus, to posit eight or nine or a million intelligences that are located in specific regions in the brain becomes problematic. Even if broad regions in the brain correspond to activities that can be observed, the question still remains: why? Phenomenological questions remain. What is it like to experience? My experience is mine. Radical alterity shapes the experience of phenomena. Experience, after all, is personal. And yet object-relations theorists teach that experience is not solipsistic, either. The ghosts of internal others haunt subjectivity. My experience is haunted by my primary others, my mother, my father. But these early memories of primary others, which perhaps have been forgotten and repressed in that place that is other and strange, haunt in uncanny ways. As soon as I try to grasp these ghosts, transferences of these ghosts which get re-presented slip through my fingers. So it becomes unclear who is self and who is other. It does not seem that firm boundaries exist between self and other. Subjectivity is slippery.

More psychological questions remain. I feel depressed over my father's recent death. Does sadness correspond to a region in the brain? A psychiatrist might think so. A drug might trigger that region called depression. Take some Prozac and feel better. But scientists do not really understand the ways in which these psychotropic drugs affect people in the long term. Why that easy faith in psychotropic drugs? Because it is easier to take a pill than to think or feel. Covering over pain is America's talent. Unlike psychiatrists who prescribe pills in order to "cure" the soul, some psychoanalysts might not think the cure for depression so simple. The cure is not found in the pill either. Perhaps the trope of cure is inadequate. How about the trope of strangeness? Laplanche (1999) argues that whatever the unconscious is, it is strange. The trope of The Other within the self? A stranger. The other within might be a ghost who causes pain. These trope-ghosts may be unraveled through free association. Dream work is supposed to demonstrate the strangeness of the human psyche. Of course, there is more to it than that. What makes human beings tick is a mystery. Thus, in light of this digression, I think Gardner is too certain, too sure of his theory. I think many people like his work because it makes them feel at ease. Conversely, suggesting the unknowable and otherness within is threatening because it undermines stability. And there is nothing easy about uncertainty. My narrative questions theories that are too easy and comfortable.

We have to remember that theories of intelligence are just that—theories. And theories are narratives. Donna Haraway (1989/1991), Gregory Bateson (1979), and Bruno Latour (cited in Haraway 1991) claim that science is not dissimilar from storytelling. Haraway (1989) tells us that "Bruno Latour, radically rejects all forms of epistemological realism and analyzes scientific practices as thoroughly social and constructionist [as] 'inscription devices,' i.e. devices for transcribing the immense complexity—chaos of competing interpretations" (6). But Gardner's MI theory reads as a correspondence theory, a realist theory. Not a re-presentation, but a representation of the real. And here is the lie. Haraway suggests that science is fiction. And we have to be careful not to be fooled by numbers, language, charts, and patrilineal heritages. The patrilineal heritage demands investigation.

So let us do a little inquiry here. If there are eight intelligences which are located in the brain, who runs them? Are there eight little homunculi running them? Or even if intelligence is "distributed" (Gardner 1999a, 98), how is it distributed if, as Gardner suggests, these intelligences are independent and separate? It is as if these eight intelligences neatly line up one against the other. But it is hard to believe that the mind is so simple. Gardner tells us that:

> Intelligence tests typically tap linguistic and logical-mathematical intelligence. . . . But as a species we are also possessors of musical intelligence, bodily-kinesthetic intelligence, naturalistic intelligence, intelligence about ourselves (intrapersonal intelligence) and intelligence about other persons (interpersonal intelligence). And it is possible that human beings also exhibit a ninth existential intelligence. . . . (1999a, 72)

These seats of intelligence, Gardner argues, are universal (72). Further, their function is to solve "problems or create products that have value in some cultures" (1983/1993, x). But who determines what is valuable? What is valuable to one culture is not always intelligent. The Nazis valued solving the "Jewish problem" and created products (gas chambers) to do the job. Not only was this method of problem-solving valued in Germany, it was also valued in many collaborating countries. Thus, to counter Gardner, what is considered "intelligent" is highly contingent, political, situated, and contested. There is nothing universal about intelligence or value.

Gardner's Naturalistic Intelligence

My task now is to take a look at Gardner's eighth intelligence, which he terms naturalistic intelligence. Gardner comes up short epistemologically and ontologically. Drawing on Gardner, I hope to develop a holistic model for what I call an ecological sensibility. I argue that an ecological sensibility might be grounded in an epistemology and ontology that are compatible with social justice. How humankind situates itself in the ecosphere is highly political. Ethically sound and politically moral debates on the ecosphere are discourses that embrace antiracist, antisexist, and anticlassist sensibilities. An ecological sensibility, thus, cannot be compatible with any discourse that perpetuates racisim, sexism, classism or any other oppressive narrative. Bateson and Buddhism offer an epistemology and ontology, respectively, that satisfy my criteria for an ethically sound ecological sensibility. Educators need to understand that humankind is extinction bound at the current rate of ecological devastation. So Gardner's call for a naturalistic intelligence is troublesome.

Who is the "naturalist"? What kinds of intelligence does he or she exhibit? Gardner says "[a] naturalist demonstrates expertise in the recognition and classification of the numerous species—the flora and fauna . . ." (1999b, 48). Naturalists are biologists, ornithologists, hunters, farmers, and even "cooks" (49–50). A naturalist expresses "core capacities to recognize instances as members of a group (more formally, a species; to recognize the existence of other, neighboring species. . ." (49). But are naturalists always intelligent? If intelligence is related to ethicality, as I think it should be, I suggest that naturalists might not always exhibit intelligence just because they can categorize species. Although a farmer might be a prophet (here I am thinking of the example of Amos, the Hebrew prophet, who was just a "herdsman, and a dresser of sycamore trees" but called to fight for social justice), agrarian movements in the 1930s and 1940s in the United States have been noted for their anti-Semitic attitudes (Gerber 1986). A naturalist such as Carl Akeley, whose dead elephants were stuffed for exhibition in the Museum of Natural History in New York, was racist, sexist, and classist. His exhibitions and hunts were built on the backs of blacks, women, and the poor (Haraway 1989). Moreover, naturalistic movements such as conservation and preservation, especially before World War II, went hand in hand with eugenics. The halls of the Museum of Natural History are stained with such a past:

> Three public activities of the museum were dedicated to preserving a threatened manhood: exhibition, eugenics, and conservation. Exhibition was a practice to produce permanence, to arrest decay [of "civilization," read white supremacy]. Eugenics was a movement to preserve hereditary stock, to assure racial purity, to prevent race suicide. Conservation was a policy to preserve resources, not only for industry, but for moral formation [read family values], for the achievement of manhood [read sexism, colonialism, homophobia]. (Haraway 1989, 55)

A naturalist is intelligent if and only if he or she is engaged in nature (whatever that means) in a way that does not perpetuate oppression. Otherwise, the naturalist is stupid. Furthermore, what kind of hunter is intelligent? Since when is killing animals ethical? Read Donna Haraway's (1989) accounts of taxidermy, killing for so-called preservation, and her accounts of experimentation on nonhuman primates. What kind of a scientist injects an innocent animal with toxins? Is this intelligent? Not if intelligence has anything to do with ethics. If we are to talk about a naturalistic intelligence, we need to understand that intelligence does not mean anything goes, just because a scientist works with or in nature. I argue that an ecological sensibility springs from a sensitive, ethical, and holistic understanding of the complexities of human situatedness in the ecosphere.

In order to develop an ecological sensibility, a Copernican revolution of sorts needs to take place once again. Nature does not stand outside or over against creatures. Nature is, of course, a social construction. The definition of nature is cultural. Creatures are inside nature and nature is inside creatures. There is no inside/outside dichotomy. Gardner seems to presuppose that naturalistic intelligence is gotten at through an individual who perceives nature out there. But there is nothing out there to perceive because the out there is in here. Further, anthropocentric models like Gardner's need to change. The world does not revolve around human beings. Human beings and other creatures are interconnected within a complex ecosphere. As C. A. Bowers explains, "We need to adopt a view of the individual as an interactive member of the larger and more complex mental ecology that characterizes the culture/environment relationship" (Bowers 1993, 15). Further, Bowers argues that when intelligence is seen as an individual attribute (13), intelligence itself contributes to the ongoing ecological problem, because it posits individuals against nature. This mindset thus contributes to an "inadequate basis for education, [it is] even reactionary in the light of the ecological crisis" (15). Although Gardner calls for ecological "awareness" (1999a, 48), naturalistic intelligence (as long as it is posited in the head of the individual, and as long as the MI theory is about intellect only) and a truly ecological sensibility can never result. Gardner tells us that "MI theory makes no claims to deal with issues beyond the intellect" (1999b, 88). Here is the root of Gardner's problem. If creatures are embodied and interconnected to a biosphere, ecosphere, hemisphere, and cosmos, clearly ecological sensibilities must move out of the intellect or out of the head only and into the world. An ecological sensibility is one that confronts false dichotomies between head/world, mind/body. From a psychoanalytic perspective, these dichotomies are formed by the ego. The ego posits boundaries so that distinctions between things can be made. In one sense, of course, we need to make distinctions so that we can function in reality. Thus, the reality principle.

However, a more primal way of understanding our interconnectedness with the universe is through primary process-thinking, the stuff of dreams, the stuff of the unconscious, the place where time and space do not exist in real time. Inside/outside is a lie. Dichotomies come tumbling down in the space of primary process-thinking. Schizophrenics "lapse" into these troubling waters and so do dreamers every night. Western modernistic modes of thought tend to split the dream and the real into two, relegating dreams and primary process-thinking to a lower form of thought. Freud understands that the road to the unconscious is the dream. Dreams teach us that dichotomies are masks, defense mechanisms that keep us from thinking the unthinkable. Breaking those false dichotomies is necessary if we are to understand just how interconnected we are with the world and with "nature." Dualisms are not just posited by the ego. They are posited by Western culture. The Judeo-Christian "script" states that God created human beings: man first, woman second, animals third. Man conquers woman; man conquers beasts; man conquers nature. This is the script we have inherited. And this script is the root of ecological devastation and oppression of the Other. Conquer the beast. Gardner says one of the tasks of the naturalist is to "tame" (1999b, 19) animals— just as Carl Akeley tamed his wild elephants by murdering them. Taxidermy tames. Let us not tame.

Bateson's Epistemology: Ecology of Mind

Part of the problem for Gardner is that he lacks a coherent and ethical epistemology to undergird his notion of natualistic intelligence. Let us turn then to Gregory Bateson's ecology of mind, for his theory might offer clues as to how we might build an epistemology that fosters an ecological sensibility. Bateson avoids some of the problems inherent in Gardner's theory because he situates mind in the larger ecosphere and connects all living things in a "sacred unity" (Bateson 1979, 19). Unlike Gardner's realist narrative, Bateson suggests that his epistemology is a story. Stories are modes of interpretation. Further, Bateson says that stories are, by their very nature, vehicles of interconnection:

> Thinking in terms of stories does not isolate human beings as something separate from the starfish and the sea anemones, the coconut palms and the primroses. Rather, if the world be connected . . . then thinking in terms of stories must be shared by all minds, whether ours or those of redwood forests and sea anemones. (13)

Thus, for Bateson, mind "obviously does not stop with the skin" (1991, 165). Living creatures are interlocked in a network that resembles a mandala (265). The symbol of the mandala re-presents recursivity, circularity, nonlinearity, complexity, and interconnection. Ecology of mind is not just about mind per se, but it is about mind's nesting in networks of webs of worlds of creatures and the universe at large. Bateson comments:

> [P]eople have asked me, "what do you mean, ecology of mind?" Approximately what I mean is the various kinds of stuff that goes one in one's head and in one's behavior and in dealing with other people, and walking up and down mountains, and getting sick, and getting well. All that stuff interlocks, and, in fact, constitutes a network. . . . (265)

Bateson's epistemological network is grounded in cybernetics. Although I find cybernetics problematic because of its machinelike imagery of information-processing and computer-based models of mind, Bateson's position overall is a complex narrative that helps us understand that mind is a vast network that does not stop at the skin. I find his epistemology useful because it demonstrates the complexity of our interconnections with creatures and the world.

The ways in which information is recognized, transmitted, coded, and represented are some of Bateson's primary concerns. Bateson says: "After all, the subject matter of cybernetics is not events and objects but information 'carried' by events and objects" (Bateson 1987, 407). Bateson is interested in the motion of mind, the process by which we perceive. The process is highly complex, nested within complex systems. Three interlocking cybernetic systems are coupled by consciousness. The individual, her society, and the "larger ecosystem" are nested together in complex pathways of information that express homeostatic patterns as well as patterns of entropy (446).

Information is perceived and recognized through the notion of difference. In order to recognize something it must be different from some other thing. It also has to be *significantly* different to make a difference. Bateson claims that:

> [I]t takes at least two somethings to create a difference. To create a difference, to produce news of difference, i.e., information, there must be two entities (real or imagined) such that the differences between them can be immanent in their mutual relationship; and the whole affair must be such that news of their difference can be represented inside some information-processing entity. . . . (Bateson 1979, 68)

Difference "triggers" activity in the mind. When difference is significant, it transforms "neural impulse[s]" in complex "pathways" (Bateson 1991, 164–65). But Bateson points out that what it is that creates a significant difference, which in turn allows us to *perceive* something, remains a mystery. He compares this mystery to a Zen koan. What is the sound of one hand clapping? Well, we do not really understand this question. Perhaps it is that unknowable otherness that permeates our existence. Bateson does not fear the unknowable, whereas I think Gardner, because of his realist position, fears this. Or perhaps he thinks it unscientific to admit that at bottom we do not know why we think at all, or why we even exist.

Bateson suggests that differences in order to make a difference must be "coded" (Bateson 1979, 70). These codes become representations. And it is the representations of the object that allows us to perceive them as different from some other object. Representations are patterns, and patterns emerge in hierarchies, or what Bateson calls logical types (which he borrows from Bertrand Russell and A. N. Whitehead). Patterns also form "metapatterns" (91), which are the highest logical type. The mind acts as a web of patterns of difference. Ultimately the mind works as interacting "aggregrates" (91), which form patterns and metapatterns. These metapatterns, according to Rodney E. Donaldson, "eliminate the supposed dichotomy between mind and nature" (Donaldson 1991, xi). Bateson remarks that what is in here is out there and what is out there is in here. I suggest that what Bateson is describing is a state of egolessness. In an egoless state, the "mind is empty; it is a no-thing. It exists in its ideas, and these again are no-things" (Bateson 1979, 11).

> It is surely the case that the brain contains no material objects other than its own channels and switchings and its own metabolic supplies and that all the material hardware never enters the narrative of the mind. Thought can be about pigs or coconuts, but there are no pigs or coconuts in the brain (190).

Representations fill the empty state of mind through complex pathways and channels of interlocking information-processing webs. Moreover, these pathways are not stuck in the head. "Messages" (476) reside outside the mind in the "larger mind" and the "total interconnected social system and planetary ecology" (1987, 467). Thus, Bateson's ecology of mind complexifies notions of interconnectivity between creatures and cosmos. Again, I stress that cybernetics is limited because we know that the mind does not work like a computer and computer analogies, although popular, are problematic because minds do not compute and do not follow logical rules to operate. Minds are vastly more complex than language. In a sense they are beyond re-presentation. Still, we need some kind of narrative to capture what we think minds are and how they are situated in bodies and ecosphere at large. Interestingly enough, Fritjof Capra suggests that Bateson's ecology of mind is similar to Maturana and Varela's Santiago theory. Here, it is thought that a "living organism brings forth a world by making distinctions. Cognition results from a pattern of distinctions and distinctions are perceptions of difference" (Capra 1996, 305). Perhaps the cybernetic discourse is limiting, but the overall point of Bateson's theory is compatible with newer science and the newer discourse of Santiago theory.

A limitation of Bateson's theory is that as Capra comments, "As social scientist Paul Dell puts it in his extensive paper 'Understanding Bateson and Maturana,' Bateson concentrates exclusively on epistemology . . . at the expense of dealing with an ontology" (273). I think Dell is onto something here. Epistemology is not enough. An ecological sensibility must be grounded in some kind of ontology as well. We should have some understanding of how we know what we know (epistemology) as well as understanding who we are in connection with being/becoming and existence generally (ontology).

Of course, there are many kinds of ontological narratives. In order to build on Bateson, in order to build on a compatible ontological framework for developing an ecological sensibility, I turn to Buddhism. More specifically I turn to two connecting notions within the Buddhist tradition, interdependent co-arising or *pratityasamutpada* and emptiness or *sunyata*.

Building a Buddhist Ontology

The paradox about a Buddhist ontology built on the notion of interdependent co-arising is that all being is becoming, and underneath all becoming is nothing or emptiness. All being which is becoming co-arises together in a nonlinear, complex, interconnectivity. This ancient doctrine (dated perhaps formally to five hundred years after the death of the Buddha) complements Bateson's epistemology, especially in the sense that Bateson suggests the interconnectiviy of living creatures and the emptiness of mind.

Before discussing the doctrine of interdependent co-arising and emptiness, though, it is important to understand that there are, of course, many different kinds of Buddhism. After the Buddha (which means enlightened one) died in approximately 483 BCE, rival schools of thought emerged over what it was that he taught. The two main schools of Buddhism are the Theravada school, the conservative branch, which cultivated the notion of *arhat* or saint, and the Mahayana school, the liberal branch. For Theravadans, the arhat's mission was to meditate in order to find release into nirvana (which means "to extinguish"). Women were not thought capable of release and so had to be reborn. Only men could reach the highest state of salvation. Mahayana Buddhism developed the notion of the *bodhisattva* (which translates loosely as close to the enlightened one). The bodhisattva's mission was to go out into the world and help others find release or nirvana. The bodhisattva postponed the attainment of nirvana in order to help others first. Women could reach nirvana and become monks as well. Gomez (1989) explains that Mahayana initially split into three main schools: Madhyamika, Yogacara, and Saramati. Madhyamika is associated with Nagarjuna (a logician who fleshed out the doctrine of interdependent co-arising in what are called sutras—but his sutras are, at least for the twentieth-century nonlogician, difficult to understand and nearly unreadable).

Both Madhyamika and Yogacara "dominated the intellectual life of Mahayana in India" (Gomez 1989, 74). Buddhism, born in India, was a reaction against the caste system of Hinduism. Many forms of Buddhism left behind the polytheistic nature of Hinduism. Some consider Buddhism atheistic because there is no belief in God. In fact, the Buddha teaches us to believe nothing (Batchelor 1997). Siddhartha Gautama went in search of a teacher when he first left his affluent home. All he found were lies. So he turned inward and meditated under the bodhi tree. It was here that he uncovered the Four Noble Truths and the Eightfold Path. The basic message is that life is filled with suffering. This suffering is caused by ignorance. Ignorance happens because of attachment to things. Nonattachment will begin the process of release. Following the middle path (no excess) toward an ethical and good life will lead to the path out of samara or the cycle of rebirth toward nirvana, which is release into emptiness and nothingness. To believe nothing means that one should not get caught up in the dogma of religious systems, because dogma is nothing more than lies and is couched in fields of ignorance that foster caste mentalities and oppression. Unfortunately, once Buddhism became institutionalized, it also became dogmatic and oppressive, especially for women (Boucher 1993; Brock 1989).

Mahayana's branch of Yogacara Buddhism broadly explores interlocking notions of cognition, evolutionary processes, and existence. Cognition as an evolutionary process, which is not separate from the world or any other life process, is termed *vijnanaparinama* (Nagao 1991). Cognition is in perpetual process and motion. This evolution of cognition is tied into the notion of *karma*. Karma simply refers to deeds. If you do good deeds, chances are you might be able to reach nirvana and go out into the nothingness that is. If you do not do good deeds, you will probably be reborn and have to do this thing called life over again. Nietzsche called this the eternal return. Legend has it that Nietzsche found the eternal return such an awful idea that it drove him mad, though perhaps it was syphilis that drove him mad. At any rate, the point of Buddhism is not to come back but to blend back into the emptiness and nothingness that is.

Cognition, accordingly, is not something that is stuck in the head. It arises codependently with the universe. It is a "cause" among many causes that co-arise together. According to Joanna Macy (1991), for Buddhists there are twelve causes or *nidanas* which co-arise in nonlinear fashion in an ever-evolving world. That which underlies our existence, nothingness, is co-fashioned with cognition and other causes. Ontology is not separable from cognition. Who we are is not separate from what we are. Macy contends that:

> In *paticca samuppadda* he [the Buddha] presented causality not as a function of power inherent in an agent, but as a function of relationship—of the interactions of multiple factors. . . . No effect arises without cause, yet no effect is predetermined, for its causes are multiple and mutually affected. Hence there can be novelty as well as order. (1991, 19)

Process thought, systems theory (Macy does a brilliant job of fleshing out this connection in particular), chaos and complexity theory, Santiago theory, and Bateson's epistemology are all compatible with the Buddhist notion of *paticca samuppadda,* which is the Pali translation of the term interdependent co-arising, an ever-evolving ontology. Being is becoming and underneath becoming is nothing. One of the most interesting aspects of this Buddhist ontology is that interdependent co-arising is shaped by the way in which we think about things. Macy comments that:

> Integral to the concept of dependent co-arising is the belief that the preconceptions and predispositions of the mind itself shape the reality it sees. This runs counter to commonsensical notions of the world "out there" distinct from and independent of the perceiving self. (1991, 19)

For Gardner, it seems that the individual sees the world from a God's-eye perspective, discovering the world as it resides independently from the gaze of the viewer. The viewer has only eight ways, or eight combinations of ways, in which to view the world. Thus it seems that for Gardner, the mind is, in a sense, predetermined at the outset to view the world through eight lenses. But for Buddhism, this predeterminedness is absurd. Interdependent co-arising unfolds in zillions of ways, which are not predetermined. Interdependent co-arising complicates lived experience because cause and effect are endlessly cylical: consciousness and cognition, ignorance and volition, name and form, the six senses, contact, feeling, craving, grasping, becoming, birth, and death unfold spontaneously in this life and possibly the next (Macy 1991).

Unlike most Western versions of cognition, Buddhism posits no ego. There is nothing standing under the "I." Buddhists call this concept *anatman*. No self. Not that literally there is no self but that there is no core to the self. This premodern concept of anatman is actually quite postmodern. The concept of anatman is compatible with Bateson's notion of the empty mind but conversely is incompatible with Gardner's notion of core intelligences. I find the notion of egolessness compelling and helpful in understanding that what connects and what is underneath forms is empty. Emptiness, like the Freudian notion of the unconscious or primary process-thinking, is a notion that knocks down the walls, tears down boundaries that we posit, since boundaries are illusory and often oppressive. At a primal level we are situated in a sea of nothingness. Animals, plants, human beings are but a small nothing in the space of the universe. Consequently, the universe is in us and we in it. The Buddhist idea of "know thyself" is different from the Judeo-Christian one.

Here, to know thyself is to know no self. It is to get rid of the oppressive boundaries between the self and world, the self and the other. And perhaps this knowing embraces the otherness of emptiness that is within/without, both here and there, now and then, ever evolving in uncanny mysterious ways. Buddhism can be interpreted to say that the many reduces to the one sea of nothingness. This, I think, would be a liberal, humanistic interpretation. But this is not my take on Buddhism. I think that when Buddhists talk about emptiness, this notion strikes in me a chord that is other, strange. Emptiness is the stranger within and without. There is no getting hold of emptiness: When we try to grasp it, it moves away, like an alien from outerspace. It is, as psychoanalyst Jean Laplanche (1999) might say, the alienness within. This alterity keeps us from collapsing the many into the one. In fact, it helps us to understand that alterity is a radical notion of difference.

Emptiness as difference is the mystery that connects, that helps us dissolve the ego, for it is the ego which creates oppressions, lies, and illusions. In psychoanalytic terms no-thingness would be the unconscious, the other within and without. Here there is no sense of time and space. The barrier between inside and outside disappears. Interestingly, scientist Rupert Sheldrake associates the unconscious with dark matter. He says that in the world of physics there is something that cannot be explained, that there is something the matter with matter. There is something really strange about the universe that scientists cannot put their microscopes on. This strange dark matter is everywhere, and yet it remains a mystery:

> Recent estimates of the amount of dark matter in the universe vary from around 90 to 99 percent. Some of this dark matter may be dark remnants of stars, including black holes; most of it probably consists of exotic kinds of particles, unlike any actually detected by nuclear physicists. (Sheldrake 1994, 94)

Sheldrake declares that "[i]t is as if physics has discovered the unconscious" (95). Recall, Bateson claimed that what is inside is outside. Unconscious stuff is inside and outside, and we just don't have a clue as to what it is.

One thing physicists do know, however, is that it is dark matter that, if there is too much of it, will eventually cause the Big Crunch. Our stupidity and continuation of ecological devastation may hasten the arrival of the Big Crunch. We are indeed speeding up the process of extinction; of that ecologists are certain. At any rate, this is a stranger planet than we think. But it is the ego which keeps this strangeness at bay. It is the ego which fosters unequal power arrangements that mark the other as inferior or stupid. It is the ego that positions the genetic fault line, that puts up the barbed wire and tames the wild. It is the ego that kills. Tearing down the boundaries is a first step to building an ontology that fosters an ecology. As Stephanie Kaza points out, "Respected Buddhist teachers such as His Holiness the Dalai Lama and Vietnamese Zen Master Thich Nhat Hanh frequently point to the interdependence of human life and the environment" (Kaza 1997, 219).

An ecological sensibility might embrace the idea that the cosmos has a mind of its own, one that human beings are situated in and one that humankind simply cannot grasp. What drives the ecosphere, biosphere, and cosmos is instability and chaos, stability and homeostasis. But mostly what drives the cosmos is chaos and instability (Sheldrake 1994; Prigogine & Stengers 1997). What drives the chaos remains a mystery. Jay Lemke remarks that Peirce "tried to say what was madness in his day, and still heresy in ours: that semiosis, meaning-making, is not solely the province of human minds. We do it a bit differently, but all matter is capable of semiosis, of intelligence if you wish" (Lemke 1997, 42). Who is intelligent? What is intelligence? Intelligence is certainly not stuck in the head. But who decides who or what is intelligent? What counts as intelligence? What is naturalistic intelligence? Perhaps it is for the cosmos to decide. Yet we need to think again. Ecological destruction is everywhere, and we are running out of time. An ecological sensibility rethinks and reconceptualizes our enmeshment in a largely strange planet. As long as we continue to think that we are alone and certain about our place in the world, as long as we continue to think that we are lone individuals viewing the world from afar, ecological devastation will continue. Then, surely, we are doomed.

David Jardine reminds us that "one of the claims of an ecological understanding is that life on earth involves a multitude of different interweaving and interconnecting voices, of which the human voice is but one of many" (Jardine 1998, 77). One of many. Not alone, not superior, not here to conquer, not here to kill. We live in a complex world interdependently co-arising with stars, birds, other planets, the moon, dogs, cats, ants, worms, and parasites. Mother Earth is very angry with us. Global warming is killing our planet. The arrogance of modern mindsets, the stupidity of religious dogma, the greed of politicians and corporate capitalism, the models of cognition that are Cartesian nightmares all perpetuate oppressions, including the oppression of Mother Earth. Racism, classism, sexism, anthropocentrism, hubris, and arrogance are incompatible with an ecological sensibility. Educators should embrace an ecological sensibility that welcomes otherness, strangeness, instability, and mystery. This strange world in which we are connected is dying because of our stupidity. What we know and who we are can either build the bomb of destruction or build a world that is intellectually sensitive to our tenuous gift, this tenuous lifeworld.

References

Batchelor, S. (1997). *Buddhism without beliefs: A contemporary guide to awakening.* New York: Riverhead Books.

Bateson, G. (1979). *Mind and nature: A necessary unity.* New York: E. P. Dutton.

———. (1987). *Steps of an ecology of mind: Collected essays in anthropology, psychiatry, evolution, and epistemology.* Northvale, NJ: Jason Aaronson.

———. (1991). Ecology of mind: The sacred. In R. Donaldson (ed.), *A Sacred unity: Further steps to an ecology of mind* (pp. 265–70). New York: HarperCollins.

———. (1991). Intelligence, experience, and evolution. In R. Donaldson (ed.), *A Sacred unity: Further steps to an ecology of mind* (pp. 271–81). New York: HarperCollins.

———. (1991). Mind/environment. In R. Donaldson (ed.), *A sacred unity: Further steps to an ecology of mind* (pp. 161–73). New York: HarperCollins.

Boucher, S. (1993). *Turning the wheel: American women creating the new Buddhism.* Boston: Beacon Press.

Bowers, C. (1993). *Educating for an ecologically sustainable community: Rethinking moral education, creativity, intelligence, and other modern orthodoxies.* Albany: State University of New York Press.

Brock, R. (1989). On mirrors, mists, and murmurs: Toward an Asian American theology. In J. Plaskow & C. Christ (eds.), *Weaving the visions: New patterns in feminist spirituality* (pp. 235–43). San Francisco: Harper.

Capra, F. (1996). *A new scientific understanding of living systems: The web of life.* New York: Anchor Books.

Donaldson, R. (1991). Introduction. In R. Donaldson (ed.), *A sacred unity: Further steps to an ecology of mind* (pp. ix–xix). New York: HarperCollins.

Gardner, H. (1983/1993). *Frames of mind: The theory of multiple intelligences.* New York: Basic Books.

———. (1999a). *The disciplined mind: What all students should understand.* New York: Simon & Schuster.

———. (1999b). *Intelligence reframed: Multiple intelligences for the 21st century.* New York: Basic Books.

Gerber, D. (1986). Anti-semitism and Jewish-Gentile relations in American historiography and the American past. In D. Gerber (ed.), *Anti-semitism in American history* (pp. 3–54). Chicago: University of Illinois Press.

Gomez, L. (1989). Buddhism in India. In J. Kitagawa (ed.), *The religious traditions of Asia* (pp. 41–95). New York: Macmillan.

Gould, S. (1996). *The mismeasure of man.* New York: W. W. Norton.

Haraway, D. (1989). *Primate visions: Gender, race, and nature in the world of modern science.* New York: Routledge.

———. (1991). *Simians, cyborgs, and women: The reinvention of nature.* New York: Routledge.

Holy Bible. (1989). New revised standard version. Iowa Falls, IA: World Bible Publishers.

Jardine, D. (1998). *To dwell with a boundless heart: Essays in curriculum theory, hermeneutics, and the ecological imagination.* New York: Peter Lang.

Kaza, S. (1997). American Buddhist response to the land: Ecological practice at two West Coast retreat centers. In M. Tucker & D. Williams (eds.), *Buddhism and ecology* (pp. 219–45). Cambridge, MA: Harvard University Press.

Kincheloe, J., & Steinberg, S. (1997). It can't happen here? In J. Kincheloe, S. Steinberg, & A. Gresson (eds.), *Measured lies: The Bell Curve examined* (pp. 3–47). New York: St. Martin's Press.

Lakoff, G., & Johnson, M. (1999). *Philosophy in the flesh: The embodied mind and its challenge to western thought.* New York: Basic Books.

Laplanche, J. (1999). *Essays on otherness.* New York: Routledge.

Lemke, J. (1997). Cognition, context and learning: A social semiotic perspective. In D. Kirshner, & J. Whitson (eds.), *Situated cognition: Social, semiotic, and psychological perspectives* (pp. 37–56). Mahwah, NJ: Lawrence Erlbaum Associates.

Macy, J. (1991). *Mutual causality in Buddhism and general systems theory: The dharma of natural systems.* Albany: State University of New York Press.

Nagao, G. (1991). *Madhyamika and yogacara: A study of Mahayana philosophies: Collected Papers of G. M Nagao* (L. Kawamura & G. Nagao, trans.). Albany: State University of New York Press.

Prigogine, I., & Stengers, I. (1997). *The end of certainty: Time, chaos, and the new laws of nature.* New York: Free Press.

Sheldrake, R. (1994). *The greening of the rebirth of nature, science and god.* Rochester, VT: Park Street Press.

PART III

THEMES AND ISSUES

Chapter 9

Jay L. Lemke

MULTIPLYING INTELLIGENCES:
HYPERMEDIA AND SOCIAL SEMIOTICS

In his influential work *Frames of Mind,* Howard Gardner (1983/1993) has offered us the useful view of human sense-making capacities as multiple distinct intelligences. Already in that early work Gardner recognized that, however distinct they might be biologically, and however useful it might be to separate them analytically, multiple intelligences are intimately integrated with one another in practice (1983, 313–16). What is the significance of this integration? How can we conceptualize what happens when, say, verbal inference, abstract visualization, and mathematical symbolic representation are combined in scientific reasoning? What are the implications for education of attending to the explicit teaching of skills and strategies for codeploying our multiple intelligences? And for doing so in socially collaborative media?

In this chapter I want to present a social semiotic approach to these questions. Social semiotics suggests that each intelligence is mediated by an analytically distinct semiotic resource system, such as language, visual depiction, or mathematical symbolics, and that when we combine these resources their meaning-making potentials quite literally multiply one another, making possible distinct kinds of meaning that cannot be made in each one separately. The advent of computer-based multimedia and hypermedia offers us new opportunities to fashion multimedia genres and new associated forms of individual and collaborative reasoning.

Building on prior research on multimedia semiotics in science classrooms and scientific print publications, and new work on multimedia Web sites and the semantics of hypertext, I will analyze the semiotics of hypermedia as both requiring and facilitating a multiplication of verbal, visual, mathematical, motor, and social intelligences in new ways. From this analysis I will draw out a number of important implications for educational research and practice in teaching students how to multiply their intelligences.

From Lumping and Splitting to Multiplying and Dividing

Gardner explicitly situates his arguments for multiple intelligences within the historical debate between the "lumpers"—those following Spearman's *g*-factor model of a single general intelligence realized in different ways in different settings—and the "splitters," who, like Thurstone and Gardner himself, emphasize the differences among verbal, mathematical, or spatial abilities. For a long time this debate was a technical one, turning on the issue of how to mathematically model the larger or smaller correlations among various quantitative measures of each different "intelligence" or aspect of the one single "intelligence." Gardner brought two major additional lines of argument to this debate, one biological and the other semiotic. He pointed out that various kinds of biological evidence, such as aphasias resulting from brain damage that impaired one kind of intelligence but not another, pointed toward separate biological bases for distinct intelligences. He also followed the lead of his mentor, Nelson Goodman (1976), and saw that different intelligences specialized in different kinds of meaning-making, or meaningful action (speaking words, composing music, calculating quantities, imagining spatial relationships) had evolved correspondingly distinct notational or symbolic systems (writing, musical notation, mathematical symbolism, architectural drawings).

Beneath these arguments lie deeper questions. Is intelligence, whether single or multiple, an inherent property of each human organism, or is it an aspect of human-situated behavior, dependent not just on the organism, but on the setting and tools available (Lave 1988)? Is intelligence definable in purely biological terms (e.g., as speed or energy-efficiency of neuron functioning), or do we call behavior intelligent depending mainly on how closely it conforms to what is valued in our culture? Finally, is intelligence in fact solely a "cognitive" phenomenon, a matter of individual psychology alone, or does it represent the individual's use of semiotic tools and resources, such as language, systems of pictorial conventions, mathematics, and musical genres, that cannot be found within individuals but only between them? I will not attempt answers to these questions here, but they underlie many of the issues I do wish to discuss.

In one sense the core issue between lumpers and splitters that motivates Gardner's work is this: What is more important, the similarities or the differences in the ways we speak well, paint or sculpt brilliantly, dance with inspiration, juggle logical abstractions insightfully, lead nations effectively, or know ourselves deeply? The answer to such a question must depend on the uses to which we will put our model of intelligent behavior.

By narrowing the range of behaviors considered to those that define upper-middle-class cultural capital (Bourdieu 1984 and 1990) in a technological society (e. g., verbal skill, logic, mathematics, spatial reasoning), the lumpers demonstrate that up to a point all of these are of a piece. Facility in this kind of behavior is highly useful for making money and developing profitable technologies, as it is for designing modern weapons and planning modern battles. It has been argued (e.g., Walkerdine 1988) that it is, moreover, largely a masculinized kind of behavior, encouraged in males and dismissed as unfeminine or inappropriately employed by females. The unitary notion of intelligence justifies meritocratic rule and embodies the values of the twentieth century's dominant subculture: instrumental rationality, quantitative evidentiality, technological growth, economic and military dominance. With a single measurable "intelligence" as a fixed property of each individual that predicts "success" by these values, society becomes naturally and biologically ordered in a strict hierarchy. It is a short political step to advocating the right or the necessity of having the most intelligent make decisions for all.

By expanding the range of behaviors considered intelligent to also include musical composition and performance, dancing and athletics, painting, sculpting, and architectural design, as well as social insight and leadership, self-understanding, and insight into nature, Gardner reduces the possibility of establishing quantitative correlations among measures of these abilities. Without correlations there is no one-dimensional hierarchy anymore. Instead we find ourselves in a multidimensional space of human abilities; those who excel in some respects may be mediocre or disastrous in others. Politically, it is not now so easy to say who should rule, but how much change has there been in the underlying value assumptions about what forms of behavior matter most? Gardner's "naturalist" intelligence gives some political support to the values of environmentalists. "Social" or interpersonal intelligence recognizes communitarian values and perhaps is an area in which males do not excel, as our society is presently gendered. The value of the arts is an easy sell to upper-middle-class people who count "high culture" among their valued cultural capital. It would be interesting to know if there are quantitative measures of bodily-kinesthetic intelligence in which working-class athletes and upper-middle-class ballerinas fare equally well, of musical intelligence in which rock and classical composers are also equal, or measures which treat on equal terms the social intelligence of gossip mavens and corporate-ladder–climbers. We can fashion discursive technologies to treat differently valued practices as "the same," but we cannot escape from the role that values play in determining what shall count as intelligent behavior.

The original logic that gave birth to the modern concept of intelligence was that there was a common factor across highly correlated quantitative measures of how well people did somewhat different things: remember words, images, and numbers; solve verbal, visual, and mathematical puzzles. Gardner's proposal that there is not one common factor among a few kinds of behavior that should be called intelligence, but rather several factors, each common to a different behavioral domain and "intelligence" and each mostly uncorrelated with the others, relies on the same common-factor logic but multiplied. And yet, *how* are we to reduce the vast diversity of human behavior to a small number of domains and factors (six to eight in various versions of Gardner's model)? Again Gardner's strategy was to combine biological criteria and semiotic criteria: Was there a dominant sensory mode or motor repertory? Was there a distinctive form of representation which mediated the behavior? For the record, and for candor's sake, let me say that I agree that the analysis of human behavior is mainly the project of figuring out how our biological and ecological behavioral possibilities (what our bodies can do in interaction with object- and agent-filled settings) get enhanced and restricted by using semiotic resources (language, depiction, mathematics, music, dance, cuisine, dress—routine systems of culturally meaningful procedures of many kinds). But I do doubt that we can usefully reduce the domains of intelligent human behavior to a small number, and I mainly fear that every attempt to do so that claims the universal validity of objective science may in time become part of political projects to unjustly advance the values and interests of some social and cultural groups in the world at the expense of others.

Suppose, however, that we acknowledge that everything we say on this subject reflects our particular cultural and historical position and our social and political viewpoints and interests. What are the uses of splitting, as opposing to lumping, our view of intelligence? One advantage, clearly, is that we can better resist efforts to evaluate individual human beings along a single scale; instead, we place them somewhere in a large space of multiple dimensions. We become less likely to assume that someone who does one thing well will also do other things well. We begin to suspect that, to the extent that many people who do some valued things well also do many other valued things well, the correlation may lie primarily among the *values;* that all these things may be valued by some particular social group because such values accord with their interests. This, to me, is useful intellectual progress.

Suppose we also acknowledge that what seems to some to be the same task, in an abstract way, when it is presented in different settings, or for different examples, or with different available tools, partners, and contextual cues, is *not* the same task functionally for the same individual (Lave 1988; Cole 1996, chs. 5 and 8), much less across different individuals with different interests, desires, and experiences (quite apart from any differences in brain function or sensorimotor physiology). This means that how intelligently we behave, as judged by the criteria of some observer, may depend on whether we happen to enjoy the particular example chosen for the task, whether it has positive cultural associations with our sense of personal identity, or whether it is presented in a setting in which our preferred tools are available or where the other persons present are to our liking (Walkerdine 1988 and 1997). With this view, we are less likely to assume that just because someone cannot perform what seems to us the same task in one case or one setting, they could not perform it exceptionally well under other circumstances. We begin to see success and failure not in terms of inherent and constant abilities but in terms of matches and mismatches among persons, tasks, contents, and settings. We begin to doubt that it is so easy to separate cognitive from affective from sensorimotor processes in practice and outside laboratories specifically built to try to do so (Latour 1987 and 1993). We may even begin to think of reasoning and rationality as one particular affective mode, always mixed with others, and to see affect, desire, and identity as more central to behavior than ability. How can we even *define* the "level of ability" to do something if the quality of performance varies tremendously across different instantiations of the "task"? What makes these occasions instances of the same "task" except our own desire to see them as such and to ignore their differences?

What then is left of the notion of an "intelligence"? Perhaps a consistency in peak performance, under optimal conditions for the individual, across a range of behaviors that are valued in some community, widely regarded in the community as similar or of the same kind, and for which the community recognizes substantial individual variation in consistent levels of peak performance of a kind that matters. Without inquiring here as to why these variations exist, from occasion to occasion for one individual, or across occasions from one individual to the next, we can still ask what it might be about a community that could lead it to name and pay attention to a small number of distinct kinds of intelligence. For one thing, clearly, its values. And for another, its systems of semiotic resources. Both are primarily characteristics of the community, but as we say, they are "internalized" in individuals as well. This metaphor may be an unfortunate one. We are speaking here of aspects of interactional processes; they are not replicated inside individuals. Rather, individuals learn to play their parts in these social processes, and by virtue of being able to do so, and by the miracle of (perhaps) re-entrant connectivity in our brains (Edelman 1992), we can enact both sides of a social interaction in imagination and integrate imagined action with real action. We learn to talk with others, to talk to ourselves, and to talk our way through tasks even when alone. We learn to interact (and so act) consistently with the social values of those with whom we interact most, and with whom we care most about our interactions. We learn to use language, make gestures, draw pictures, play music and games in the same way. We learn, in effect, to make situated sense to and of others, and so to act meaningfully and make meanings for ourselves as well.

I am trying here to build a bridge of words from the culturally aware but still basically psychological perspective of Gardner's book to my own way of seeing these matters. What matters for Gardner are different mental intelligences—biologically rooted, semiotically mediated, and functionally integrated in specific culturally meaningful activities. What matters for me are situated social practices, deploying various semiotic resources in ways that are permitted but not required by the interaction of organism and object- and agent-filled settings. In my own social semiotic perspective, what lends commonality to these practices are the lifeways of particular subcommunities, including their beliefs, values, habitual styles of action, and distinct "dialects" of language and other semiotic resources. If we consider aggregate larger-scale communities, then across their internal diversity there is less and less in the way of shared beliefs, values, and actional styles, but there is still quite a bit in common among their semiotic resources. One reason for this is that the primary function of semiotic resources is communicating meaning. Or perhaps it is better to simply say that all meaning is at least implicitly communicative: "addressed" (Bakhtin [1953/1982] on dialogism in language, or Halliday [1978 and 1994] on its pervasive interactional meanings) and "positioned" (Bakhtin's [1935/82] heteroglossia or my [Lemke 1989 and 1995] generalization of Halliday's attitudinal function to orientational meaning) within a diverse community. Semiotic resources function to link communities together across their differences, as well as to create and maintain distinctive practices within each community. Thus it happens that the semiotic resource systems, the "meaning potentials" (Halliday 1978) of different communities which are regularly in contact, and particularly of different subcommunities of the same larger community, can provide a common denominator at the wider social scale.

The multiplicity which Gardner discerns among intelligences corresponds very largely, from the social semiotic viewpoint, to the multiplicity of the semiotic resource systems themselves: to the different kinds of meanings people can make, and to the different ways in which these meanings can be made. From the social semiotic viewpoint, there is no question that semiotic systems for making meaning are multiple, but there is a mystery as to why. Would not a single unitary semiotic resource be ideal for communication, articulation across diversity, and the production of intelligible meaning within communities? If there were such a single semiotic, those who mastered it, or who were physiologically pre-adapted to use it more effectively, might indeed be counted "most intelligent" across a wide range of tasks and settings. But it is not so. There is no single semiotic common denominator across all meaningful human behavior. Why not? What is there about the uses to which semiotic resources are put that has led biological-cum-cultural evolution to a different strategy? That strategy, I will argue, is "divide and multiply." Understanding it perhaps gives some insights into not only why there is a multiplicity of broad modes of intelligent behavior but why real social practices always necessarily combine distinct semiotic modalities together.

Divide and Multiply:
Semiotic Differentiation and Functional Integration

A semiotic strategy of "divide and multiply" means that:

1. phylogenetically and ontogenetically there were fewer, perhaps just one, semiotic modalities, and that with evolutionary and developmental time an initial semiotic becomes progressively differentiated into diverse practices, which, under the functional pressures of use, become separately organized into distinct semiotic systems ("divide"); and

2. historically in each culture, and biographically as each individual learns to participate in cultural practices, the newly separate and distinct semiotic systems come to be co-deployed simultaneously in integrated ways that permit more

complex and precise meanings to be made through their combinations than could be made with any one separately, or with the protosemiotics from which they descend ("multiply").

In less formal parlance, when you combine two semiotic modalities, such as writing and drawing, the set of possible combinations is multiplicatively greater because each possible text (N) can in principle combine with each possible drawing (N x M), and so in any actual case, the meaning value of the combination is greater and the meaning made potentially more precise because it is one combination out of (N x M) and not simply one text out of N possible ones plus one drawing out of M possible ones (N + M). To get the multiplicative advantage (100 + 100 = 200; 100 x 100 = 10,000) two conditions are necessary. First, the two modalities cannot be redundant with one another; that is, they cannot simply present the same meaning in two different forms. Second, some system of conventions must exist (multimodal genres) whereby it makes sense to combine text and drawing, i.e., the meaning of the text must potentially change when accompanied by a different drawing, and the meaning of the drawing be potentially different when accompanied by a different text.

The first condition is met if you accept, as I do, the principle of the incommensurability of different semiotic presentations. In general, there is no possible one-to-one correspondence between the meanings of texts and those of pictures. Even if we artificially create a correspondence between their forms (i.e., reckon their formal information content, not their cultural meanings, as a computer would do, reducing both to strings of numbers), this does not create a correspondence between their meanings because their meanings depend on how we interpret that particular medium. We read a text in relation to many other texts in very different ways than we read a picture in relation to other pictures. A picture always has pictorial meaning that is qualitatively different from textual meaning. No number of words can ever have the same meaning as a picture, and no picture or pictures can ever have the same meaning as some text.

But the more we see the incommensurability of meanings made verbally and pictorially, the more mysterious it becomes how they could in fact combine with one another. How do we make pictorial-textual meanings? These must themselves be incommensurable, as meanings, with either the pictorial or the textual meanings of their components taken alone. What is the nature of all that extra meaning that we get, beyond the sum of the parts (N + M), up to a maximum of the multiplicative product (N x M)?

Our theories of meaning are still quite primitive. We can reasonably say something about how a single sentence of a few clauses means what it does for people, at least in terms of the semiotics of language (lexis, grammar, and semantics; e.g., Halliday 1978), but much less about how that sentence contributes to the meaning of a whole novel, or how its meaning for us is changed by the preceding and following sentences, paragraphs, sections, or chapters. The task of saying how its meaning becomes different when accompanied by a picture or when said in the context of some particular social activity, is one that has just begun to be undertaken. Likewise we can say something reasonable and informative about how we read pictures (e.g., Arnheim 1956; Kress & van Leeuwen 1996; O'Toole 1990) in isolation, one at a time, and even how we integrate one part of a picture with another. It is much more difficult to explain how we intepret pictures in relation to other pictures or to architectural settings or social activities in which the pictures play some role.

Nevertheless, it has been possible to find common denominators in our accounts of how at least texts and pictures (including diagrams) mean, and these common principles seem extensible to sculpture and architecture (O'Toole 1994), music and bodily action (van Leeuwen 1991, Martinec in press), and mathematics (Lemke 1998a, O'Halloran in press). We can take these shared principles among different semiotic systems as evidence of their common ancestry (differentiation from proto-semiotics), and/or as helping to explain how it is possible for us to make combined or joint hybridized meanings with them despite their semiotic incommensurability.

In generalizing Michael Halliday's original insights into the semantic functions of language and of every text as a unit of meaning (as an utterance rather than as a formal unit such as a sentence), I have proposed that across all semiotic systems, every meaningful unit means simultaneously in three parallel ways (generalizing Halliday's metafunctions for language): presentational (creating or describing a world, a state of affairs, a content, however abstract), orientational (taking a stance toward the presentational meaning and its audiences; addressed dialogically and positioned heteroglossically), and organizational (linking parts into wholes, and the whole to its exterior contexts; Lemke 1989 and 1995). For instance, representational imagery in painting presents the world, but figure perspective orients the viewer to it, and the composition of masses and vectors of edges and lines organize its parts into a coherent whole. In text, we present with propositional content ("John is coming"), orient with mood (command versus question: "Is John coming?") and modality (may versus must: "John may be coming"), and organize with genre structure (introduction, body, conclusion) and cohesion ("John is coming. He wants to"; *he* links to *John*), among other resources.

Thus the possibility arises that the overall presentational meaning of a combination of text and picture can be produced because both are contributing functionally to this aspect of meaning and likewise for combining their orientational and organizational meanings. Of course it is not so simple. Within a single semiotic modality, the three functional aspects of meaning interact with another. A smile on a pictured face both presents a smile and orients to the viewer by engaging us; similarly the eyes are shown either looking directly at the viewer or not. In a text, a consistent orientational stance of skepticism toward what is being said also helps contribute to the cohesion of the text, and a change in that stance can contribute to marking the boundary between two textual units of organizational structure. Similarly, the three functional aspects of meaning can also interact across semiotic modalities: the presentational content of verbal labels in two diagrams or two parts of one diagram can create organizational ties between the visual elements to which they are attached.

To the extent that the three generalized semiotic functions (presentational, orientational, organizational) are applicable to all semiotics, they provide a basis for analyzing and explicating how joint meanings are made in multimodal combinations of elements from different semiotic resource systems (Lemke 1998a).

It is not so surprising that there is an underlying commonality among the meaning functions in different semiotics if we imagine that they have all descended from a common ancestor. On the principle that each new developing organism must recapitulate the steps by which historically, and perhaps phylogenetically, the process of differentiation occurred, we might imagine that meaningful motor activity, especially social interactivity, was itself the original protosemiotic. Coordinated gross motor activity precedes the coordinated fine motor activity of speech, and initially vocalizations are not necessarily differentiated as signs from the rest of the stream of communicative (or at least functionally interactive) motor communication. Speech develops, and probably evolved, as part of interactional synchrony—the bodily and material integration of individual organisms with one another and the rest of their ecosocial environments. The intonational patterns of speech and the musical patterns of song descend from common ancestral modes of behavior. The rhythms of synchronization are the likely precursors of drumming and dancing. The synchrony, not just in individuals but across dyads and groups, of verbal action with other body movements and rhythms signals the participation of gesture and movement in the unitary communication system from which we abstract the semiotic systems we call language and gesture (Kendon 1990; Scheflen 1975). Our perception as well as our production of semiotic interaction makes use of visual and kinesthetic information and responsiveness as much as it does of the auditory channel.

Ontogeny also shows that writing and drawing also share a common ancestry, that each generation must be taught anew to make the separation between them. Writing is not merely the annotation of speech, as drawing is not simply the inking of images. Drawing begins as the extension to paper of gesture, as the product of lasting visual traces of our gestures in acts which are indiscriminately gesturings and drawings (Arnheim 1956, cited in Kress & van Leeuwen 1996, 25). And these are accompanied, you can be sure, by vocalizations which are not as distinct from other motor gestures as the abstractions of linguistics and the ideology of intellectual verbalism dispose us to believe. It is not surprising that children do as one act what adults have been taught to separate into two: drawing and writing (Dyson 1991; Hicks & Kanevsky 1992). Like our first drawing, our first writing is not a *representation* of speech but an *extension* of it that produces a lasting visual trace.

If we compare this semiotic phylogeny with Gardner's multiple intelligences we find striking parallels and some key differences. In following modern linguistics by separating the semantics of verbal language from the motor vocalizations of speech, there is a danger that "linguistic intelligence" may be defined in a way that does not take account of the ways in which rhetorical brilliance and poetic achievement depend on the sound effect of language, on a kind of "singing" and even breathing and swaying that entrains an audience in an almost magical communion of speech. The African American preacher, the Jamaican storyteller, and the enacted and performed Shakespeare may represent the heights of linguistic intelligence, not the fluent writer of winning legal briefs or the successful print novelist. Perhaps it is even the case, contrary to our logocentric ideology, that not verbal semantics but the sound-spell of speech is what gives it its greatest social power. That is what the Hindu linguists believed when they wrote the first treatises on language; it is what Afrocentrists affirm when they ground Ebonics in the music and affect of African American speech, recalling that of Africa, and not in the standard linguistic features by which European linguists define it as merely another dialect of English.

Gardner also associates language with music physiologically but as aural forms, not oral ones. He does not appear to be thinking of the motor dimensions of speech and song but only of the auditory sensory modality. For too many people today, music is something heard, not something made. How does a drummer's supreme effort differ from the kinesthetic-bodily intelligence of a dancer or an athlete? Should we take tone to be more fundamental to music-making than rhythm? Were the motor areas of the deaf Beethoven's brain less active than the auditory ones when he was in a fit of composition? Do we imagine Mozart just sat still and listened to inner music as he composed or that he danced about and pounded his instrument? How long in phylogenetic terms can it have been since "pure music" was culturally distinguished from singing-and-dancing and singing-and-drumming? Long enough for a separate biological basis to arise? Or is "pure music" in the modern European sense a hybrid intelligence, with a mathematical-logical parent as well as a kinesthetic-bodily one? Motor-logic, with auditory feedback?

The area of mathematical-logical intelligence also raises interesting questions from a semiotic point of view. Both mathematics and logic quite clearly descend, at least on one side of their parentage, from language. That side is their algebraic-symbolic side. Mathematics, one can argue (e.g., Lemke 1998a), functions historically as the bridge between conceptual, categorial language and other semiotics with which we cope with matters of continuous quantitative variation. The latter are mainly spatial-motor and visual. You can describe an irregular shape accurately with a gesture or a drawing but not very well in words. You can calculate a nonsimple ratio with numbers, or visualize it in a triangle, or experience it moving on a slope, but the linguistic name for it is intuitively meaningless ("nine twenty-thirds"). Our scientific theories are built from relations among concepts, which are language's forte, but they can be applied to phenomena that depend on continuous quantitative covariation only through translation into numbers, graphs, and motor actions. It is the job of mathematics to achieve this translation, to provide a common semiotic with language, which gives rise to algebra, and with visual-spatial-motor semiotics, which give rise to geometry. It may be only a conceit of modern European mathematics that logic is its heart and that it concerns itself with relations of pure form. For most of its history, and in most cultures, mathematics has been about quantity and ratio, and its operations were often performed as much manually and bodily-kinesthetically (the abacus or Oksapmin body mathematics; Saxe 1982) or visually (geometric diagrams and modern graphs), as symbolically and logically.

Gardner distinguishes a spatial intelligence from the bodily kinesthetic one, presumably on the grounds that it is entirely a matter of visualization. But this again, as in the case of music, seems to separate the sensory too radically from the motor elements of how we know the brain works. Pure spatial visualization, as in the three-dimensional rotation tasks beloved of laboratory psychologists, does not seem to me a good candidate for an evolutionary intelligence apart from its integration with motor-coordination in three dimensions (e.g., arborial monkeys and our brachiating primate cousins). Perhaps the brain does three-dimensional processing differently than it does two- and one- dimensional spatial-visual tasks, but I would not think 3D visualization would evolve apart from 3D motor proficiency. Certainly there is some fundamental semiotic differentiation between the spatial-motor-visual cluster and the language-logic mode. Musical intelligence perhaps specializes the rhythmic aspects of the former and hybridizes with the intonational qualities of speech. Mathematics functions in much more recent cultural history to bridge across the divide of the two main clusters. But semiotically it is hard for me to see all these intelligences as independent and equal peers, each with its own separate phylogenetic roots.

Finally, Gardner proposes separate status for the "personal intelligences," i.e., interpersonal or social intelligence and intrapersonal or introspective-reflexive intelligence. I would certainly agree that these two are linked to each other and that they touch on something fundamental. If we assume that meaning begins in sensorimotor interaction of the organism with objects and other persons, then the meaningfulness of relationship to others, even mediated by things, tools, and signs, is fundamental indeed. But I am a little warier of the eighth, "naturalist" intelligence, not because I doubt that interaction with nature is as fundamental as interaction with other humans, but because the very nature/society dichotomy is so obviously cultural and historically recent (Latour 1993). It seems to me that we relate to nonhumans in exactly the same ways we relate to humans, except where this is taboo in our culture, and our individual proclivities lead us to develop our intuitions about people, other animals, plants, and the rest of the arbitrarily distinguished "natural" and "artifactual" settings to vastly different degrees. Intrapersonal intelligence is interpersonal intelligence turned inward, and naturalist intelligence is interpersonal intelligence turned outward, and developed less species-centrically. Of course it is difficult in all these cases to identify in what modes of behavior and perception these intelligences consist apart from their mediation by language. Introspective intelligence has the least to go on other than language; we rarely see ourselves, and we hardly know what to make of how we feel, physiologically and emotionally, apart from the names and discourses we can put to these feelings, or at best how these inner sensations correlate with our assessments of outer circumstances or our outward imaginings. Perhaps it is no accident that Freud proposed a "talking cure" for our inner disturbances. Nonetheless, even if the intrapersonal is a latecomer, reflecting interpersonal intelligence back on itself with the help of language, there is still very likely some early core semiotic, which we might call interpersonal-ecological or perhaps "ecosocial" intelligence, which may be the progenitor of a third main cluster, and itself may have arisen from the one original protosemiotic of sensorimotor interaction.

But are these all there are? In terms of social semiotics, there are of course many more organized resource systems for making meaning, derived from various kinds of social activity which have become ritualized and systematically differentiated in meaning and value, one form of action from another, by kind or by degree. Some of these are clearly hybrids; for example, writing, with its visual typography, combines language and depiction (with late parallels in musical notation and dance notation). Some are further specializations, such as the use of typical cultural narratives to make meaning by allusion and expectation. But what of acting or cooking or fashion? Or if we are looking back as far as possible along the family tree, what about sexual intelligence? Is it an early hybrid of bodily-kinesthetic and interpersonal intelligences? Or is that just our modern sex-shy analysis trying to deny it a more fundamental role? Certainly if we define it as broadly as Freud did, it could well be a forerunner of interpersonal intelligence, or kindred to and coeval with it. Since our definitions of intelligence are clearly bound up with what we value culturally, it is not surprising there might be strong ambivalences about sexual intelligence. This case in turn suggests we ought to at least consider whether some forms of human behavior that are negatively valued by us but positively valued elsewhere might also be candidates for either primary intelligences or important semiotics.

What about warrior intelligence, killer instinct, or torturer's intelligence? What about religious or spiritual intelligence? Or the ability to totally suspend rationality or ego-dominance in states of trance or possession, or when "berserk"? What of shamanistic intelligence or mystic intelligence? What about the ability to become totally incorporated into herd behavior, resulting in mass hysteria or mob riots? What about submissive intelligence or the ability to deceive with total sincerity and effectiveness? Such examples, I think, again point to the need for a very careful analysis of the role of local cultural and subcultural values in defining any number of intelligences.

From the perspective of a theory of multiple intelligences it becomes very important to decide what are the few substantially distinct core intelligences, because the claim of the theory is twofold: first, that there is more than one such mode of intelligence, and second, that each of the core intelligences is rooted in physiology and phylogeny. Social semiotics, on the other hand, can be perfectly content with multiplying the number of recognized semiotic resource systems indefinitely. Every specialized mode of human interactivity in the ecosocial setting for which a community construes systematic relations of meaningful differences of kind or degree in the participating actions, events, objects, and persons can define a distinct semiotic resource system. It is a useful task within the theory to examine the kinds of relationships among these semiotics, whether by classifying them (e.g., by their typological and/or topological strategies), adducing probable genealogical relations (differentiation from precursors), or formulating the principles underlying their potential integration or co-deployment with one another.

From the viewpoint of social semiotics, what matters most is not how we decide to divide up the systematic semiotic resources of the human behavioral repertoire but how well we can explicate how those resources are co-deployed to create complex multimodal meanings. For in this model, *all* actually produced meaning is multisemiotic in nature. We cannot mean with just one analytically separable semiotic system. There are no pure instances of linguistic meaning, no material signifiers that mean in terms of the linguistic (or depictional, or gestural, or mathematical, or any specialized actional) semiotic system alone—at least not past any imaginary point early in human development, preceding differentiation of distinguishable semiotic systems. (By the way, you distinguish such systems by their different systems of relationships among signs, even for the same signifiers.) Every spoken utterance means not just linguistically but also vocally; we interpret it as a sign of the speaker's social status, geographical origins, state of health and state of mind; we appreciate its musicality and timbre, its intonational colorings, and the "grain of the voice" (Barthes 1977) along with the verbal semantic meaning of the words. Every written sentence means something not just linguistically but also by its choice of typeface and font or its calligraphy and orthographic features by which some experts and many amateurs read all kinds of meaning about personality, etc. (whether usefully or not). Speech in person cannot fail to be accompanied by body movements and gestures, the grounds of interactional synchrony, facial cues, eye blinks, breath rhythms, etc., all of which are physiologically coordinated in a single (two- or many-person) dance, with many meanings other than the verbal ones exchanged. Language, moreover, often conjures for us or inspires in us visual images and kinesthetic tensions and many inner sensations which have their own kinds of meaning for us. And once we have caught the language disease, are we ever again entirely free, except for fleeting moments, of the filtering grids of linguistic semantics when we examine a painting or choose our wardrobe?

How could it be otherwise? Every act of meaning-making is a material process, and by its very materiality it cannot be totally comprehended by any single system of representation. So also every material signifier. You cannot speak a pure phoneme; every actual sound has acoustic properties in excess of the minimal distinctive features, we can only speak "phones." All interpretation is experiential, and as phenomenology has long maintained, experience always overflows in meaning and specificity and uniqueness any formal categorization that can speak only of generals and not of particulars. Semioticians at an event are like the blind men feeling the elephant: each knows only those aspects which matter semiotically in some one system; none knows the whole elephant. Even collectively, they do not comprehend the whole elephant, real, unique, and present, though they can perhaps say as much as can be said of elephants.

In some ways this argument underestimates semiotics because it usually assumes that all semiotic systems are fundamentally like language in being based on distinctions of kind or type among signs. But this "typological" semiotics is not the only way in which meanings are made. We also make meaningful distinctions between signs by degree as well as by type. In speech there are an infinite number of sounds between "take" and "took," but there are no intermediate linguistic-semantic meanings corresponding to those sounds. The sound must be interpreted as one word or the other, the verb as in one tense or another, categorially, to be linguistically meaningful. Not so for the visual and spatial-motor semiotics, where degrees of color and shading, rate of movement, or difference in shape or position can be meaningful at any level of detail that can be perceived or implied. These semiotics of degree, of continuous quantitative variation, which (after the topology of the continuum or the real numbers) I have sometimes called "topological semiotics," are often functionally complementary to the typological or categorial semiotics. As I suggested before, much of mathematics historically has been an effort to create a hybrid semiotics that allows us to bridge between conceptual-categorial language and these topological semiotics (see also Lemke 1999). If we include both the topological and the typological resources of semiosis, there is much less of the unique experience of a particular elephant that escapes the semiotic sieve though still something does.

The rest of this chapter will describe several examples of how we actually do multiply our meaning resources by combining different semiotics, thus multiplying our intelligences. I want to concentrate on the human activities I have studied most: the use of language, gesture, visual representation, and social interaction in professional scientific communication and in science education. I will try to argue that we do not do enough to teach students how to combine and integrate their different intelligences or to integrate their individual intelligences in different domains with one another in collaborative work. I will draw my examples briefly from my previous research on the multimedia semiotic demands of the science classroom and studies of multimodal integration of different semiotics in scientific print publications and, more extensively, from work in progress on professional and educational multimedia in science as presented in Web sites on the Internet.

Multiplying Intelligences for Learning and Communication

Academic perspectives analytically exaggerate the autonomy of the different semiotic resource systems and the intelligences we can recognize in how well people make use of them. One can find academic treatises in which there is only text; typography and page layout contribute only minimally to relevant meanings. But any newspaper or glossy magazine will show the complex integration of text, typography, layout, visual imagery, and use of color effects that we take for granted in everyday life. Japanese newspapers make very heavy use of quantitative graphs (Tufte 1983, 83), reflecting cultural preferences and the education of readers. Hobbyist magazines about cars, computers, stereos, boats, and even golf are filled with specialized diagrams of many kinds. The business pages of daily papers everywhere contain extensive numerical tables and some amount of accompanying explanatory or commenting text. Japanese popular reading consists less of the inexpensively printed text-only paperback novels of the West and far more of the image-centric *manga,* often mistaken for their nearest Western relative, the comic book (a closer comparison would be to the postmodern graphic novel). From illuminated manuscripts to profusely illustrated classics, the Western tradition also favored the combination of image and text in the humanities until economics and logocentrism ruled images dispensable, if not intellectually suspect. Gardner would remind us that few great writers were also great artists (one thinks of Blake); social semiotics suspects the impoverishment of European humanistic culture since it abandoned the multiplication of meanings that the text-image combination affords. If it is true that we do not often find the peaks of achievement in these two media in the same individual, there is still no reason not to favor collaborative production, other than a fetishism of the individual author.

Film, television, and video are also multimodal media, at least since the advent of the talkies. Take away the sound, and how much of the total meaning remains? Take away the image, and how much do we miss? Construe both together, and how much more, qualitatively, does the experience engender? The great Sergei Eisenstein, an innovator of the film genre, wrote brilliantly (Eisenstein 1943) about the art of coordinating image composition, cinematic action, shot montage, music, dialogue, and narration. The music-and-light shows of the psychedelic 1960s prepared the way for the creative fusion of music, singing, and dynamic images in the modern music video genre. Dance as art today fuses musical and visual-motor semiotics in new ways. The tradition of grand opera was always that of the *Gesamtkunstwerk,* varying only in the mode and degree of integration among music, dance, singing, lighting, costume, stage setting, and action. Popular musical theater and many films and television productions continue this tradition for large audiences.

Life itself is a multimodal experience, not just in terms of multisensory input, but perhaps more significantly in terms of action and activity. We talk, gesture, mime, act, write, sketch, calculate, and perform meaningful social actions of infinite variety every day; there are systematic actional semiotics of driving, cooking, cleaning, shopping, and certainly of teaching or office work. Classroom activity is a particularly well-documented domain of action in which the meanings and typical actional patterns (activity genres) have been thoroughly studied, not just with regard to language and discourse, but for the use of gesture, mime, writing, diagrams, maps, charts, video, computer media, and science demonstration apparatus. Science classrooms are perhaps particularly rich multisemiotic sites because of both the scientific tradition of combining language, mathematics, and visual representations with experimental activity that I argued above is necessary if we are to study natural and experimental phenomena of continuous covariation and complex quantitative ratios.

Multiplying Intelligences in the Classroom

In a recent analysis of videotape data following one student through a day of advanced chemistry and physics classes (Lemke 2000; see also Cumming & Wyatt-Smith 1997), I observed that in his chemistry lesson this student had to interpret a stream of rapid verbal English from his teacher; the writing and layout information on an overhead transparency; writing, layout, diagrams, chemical symbols and mathematical formulas in the open textbook in front of him; the display on his handheld calculator; more writing, layout, diagrams, symbolic notations, and mathematics in his personal notebook; observations of gestures and blackboard diagrams and writing by the teacher; observations of the actions and speech of other students, including their manipulation of demonstration apparatus; and the running by-play commentary of his next-seat neighbor. In fact, he had quite often to integrate and coordinate most of these either simultaneously or within a span of a few minutes. There is no way he could have kept up with the content development and conceptual flow of these lessons without integrating at least a few of these different literacy modes almost constantly.

In one episode in the student's physics lesson that same day, there was no role for the notebook, and not even a diagram, but a pure interaction of language and gestural pantomime, including whole-body motion. The teacher is standing just in front of the first (empty) row of student desks, at the opposite end of the room from where the student is sitting. The student sees his teacher's hands cupped together to form a sphere, then the hands move a foot to the left and cup together to make another sphere. Then back to the first, and one hand and the teacher's gaze make a sweeping gesture from one to the other; then he begins to walk to the left, repeating these gestures and walking down toward the student's end of the room. Fortunately, the teacher now is also talking; by integrating the teacher's precise and conventionalized mime with his accompanying technical speech, this student can interpret that the cupped hands are atoms, the sweeping hand a photon, emitted by the first, traveling to the second, absorbed there, re-emitted after a while, passing on down through a ruby crystal, producing a "snowball effect" of more and more photons of exactly the same energy. In other words, the crystal is a laser, and we are experiencing a multisemiotic performance explaining how it works.

The teacher says he's going to add more complexity to the picture now. An atom "might shoot out a photon in this direction"—gesture away from the axis of the room-sized imaginary ruby crystal toward the students—"or in this one"—gesture back toward the blackboard—"or . . ."—oblique gesture. How do we get a laser beam then? He walks back and forth between the ends of his now-lasing, imaginary ruby crystal, describing the mirrors he gestures into being at each end, but saying they differ in reflectivity and transmissivity, to build up and maintain the avalanche of photons, while letting some out in the form of the laser beam. The student has seen mimes like this before; he has seen diagrams of atoms and crystals, of photons being absorbed and emitted by atoms. By making connections to these other visual-verbal-actional "texts," he can use his visual intelligence and experience of these past diagrams, together with his bodily-kinesthetic intelligence in pantomime, and his linguistic intelligence in interpreting the discourse of atomic physics to make sense of how a laser works. But he cannot deploy these intelligences separately; they must be complexly and effectively integrated with one another. The meanings he makes must be multisemiotic meanings in which far more is meant by the combinations of word, image, gesture, and mime than each can mean or does mean separately or even in simple addition (e.g., if experienced separately and without interconnection).

In his classroom learning activity our student must constantly translate information from one semiotic modality to another: numerical to algebraic, algebraic to graphical, graphical to verbal, verbal to motor, pantomime to diagrammatic, diagrammatic to discursive. But simple translation is not enough; he must be able to integrate these multiple semiotics simultaneously to reinterpret and recontextualize information in one medium in relation to that in the other media all in order to infer the correct or canonical meaning on which he will be tested. In most cases, the complete meaning is not expressed in any one channel, but only in two or more, or even only in all of them taken together (see detailed examples in Lemke 2000; Roth, Bowen & McGinn, 1999).

Multiplying Intelligences in Technical Writing

In another recent study (Lemke 1998a), I examined the semiotic forms found in the standard genres of research articles and advanced treatises of professional scientific publications. In a diverse corpus across disciplines, venues, and formats of publication, the clear finding was that there is typically at least one and often more than one graphical display and one mathematical expression per page of running text in typical scientific print genres. There can easily be three to four each of graphics displays and mathematical expressions separated from verbal text per page.

In one prestigious journal of the physical sciences, each typical three-page article integrated four graphical displays and eight set-off mathematical expressions. Some had as many as three graphical displays per page of double-column text or as many as seven equations per page. In another journal, in the biological sciences, each typical page had two nontabular visual-graphical representations integrated with the verbal text, and each short article (average length 2.4 pages) typically had six graphics, including at least one table and one quantitative graph.

To appreciate the absolutely central role of these nonverbal textual elements in the genres being characterized, it may help to ponder a few extreme (but hardly unique) cases:

- In one advanced textbook chapter, a diagram was included in a footnote printed at the bottom of the page.
- In one seven-page research report, 90 percent of a page (all but five lines of main text at the top) was taken up by a complex diagram and its extensive figure caption.

- The main experimental results of a 2.5-page report were presented in a set of graphs occupying one-half of a page and a table occupying three-fourths of another. The main verbal text did not repeat this information but only referred to it and commented on it.
- In most of the theoretical physics articles, the running verbal text would make no sense without the integrated mathematical equations, which could not in most cases be effectively paraphrased in natural language, even though they can be, and are normally meant to be, read out as if part of the verbal text (in terms of semantics, cohesion, and frequently grammar).

A more detailed analysis in this study showed how absolutely normal and necessary it is to interpret the verbal text in relation to these other semiotic formations, and vice versa. It is not the case that they are redundant, each presenting the complete relevant information in a different medium; rather, the nature of the genre presupposes close and constant integration and cross-contextualization among semiotic modalities. (For a confirming study of the frequency of nonverbal elements in professional scientific writing and in school science textbooks in one field, see Roth, Bowen, & McGinn 1999.)

Multiplying Intelligences in the New Hypermedia

Finally, I want to take an example that look toward the future. The future of communication, and of education, lies fairly clearly in the use of the new genres of the global Internet. Of these the most prominent today, and the likely forerunner for many future developments, are the Web page and the Web site. The moment of revelation for me, after several years of using the Internet for e-mail and file transfers, came when I first launched Mosaic, the original graphical Web browser, on a Sun workstation. After several lines of text appeared on the screen, a small full-color photograph of Vice President (and Internet booster) Albert Gore downloaded into view in the middle of the first home page (at the government-sponsored supercomputing center in Illinois). Multisemiotic expression had arrived on the Internet, where formerly even font and page layout were not usually transmitted faithfully, and where images could be sent as files but not in a way that permitted them to be integrated into text documents. This Web page had far more meaning than just a page of text and a picture file of Gore would have had separately. The implications were staggering, because for science multisemiotic media are a necessity, not a luxury. (There were, before the Web, large complex postscript-file formats that could be downloaded and printed; the result was not too different from using a fax machine.) And for many other social activities, what humans can do with communication that engages multiple intelligences simultaneously, whether in advertising or education, is far greater than what can be done with words alone or isolated picture images.

What has been done so far is well known. Every domain of human activity is represented today on the World Wide Web, from science to sex, commerce to cookery. Limited only by speed of transmission, text and images are now joined by elaborate page layout, animation, audio, video, and manipulable virtual three-dimensional objects and navigable virtual 3D spaces, unique to the computer medium. Also unique to the computer medium, though not unprecedented in other genres, is the principle of hypertext: segments of text can operate as links to other segments of text, with no intermediate reading or searching. And on the Web, this becomes hypermedia: images can link to other images, and also to text, and indeed all combinations can link to all combinations, elements of one Web page to another complete Web page. I will not discuss here the enormous implications for education of this new medium (see Lemke 1998b), which is not simply a medium for access to multisemiotic information but also a new medium of communication and collaboration between individuals and among groups, and perhaps most importantly a new medium of creative and intellectual expression, with implications for modes of thinking and ways of learning.

In a research project in progress, I am examining two sets of Web pages within the large metasite of the National Aeronautics and Space Administration's government domain, *nasa.gov*. NASA's more than 435,000 Web pages are distributed among hundreds of servers in the many laboratories and project sites of this large government agency. From among them I am currently examining just two small subsets: parallel presentations of satellite data about the earth intended for, in one case, the educated public, and in the other, professional scientists and researchers. I have described my initial analysis of these Web sites elsewhere (Lemke, in press). Here I mainly want to comment on some of the multisemiotic features of these sites and the ways that they engage our multiple intelligences and encourage us to multiply meanings made with each. I also want to consider some of the implications of the collaborative, as opposed to the individual, multiplication of intelligences.

At the NASA Earth Observatory (*http://earthobservatory.nasa.gov*) Web site, data on conditions of the atmosphere, oceans, land, and biosphere of the earth as observed from space are presented for science teachers, students, and interested members of the educated public.

The level of multisemiotic proficiency required at the Earth Observatory (EO) site is hardly minimal. Users of these Web pages confront the complexities not just of simplified scientific text but of an interactive glossary function, links to background information in documents accessed from a Library page, links to closely related Web sites documenting research projects on related scientific topics (the Study), and most notably the option of linking to an interactive system for scientific visualization of relevant satellite data (the Observation Deck). By selecting a "parameter" (i.e., type of data derived from satellite sensors, such as Vegetation) and a time range, users can display, in the form of color-coded maps, an animated display that shows changes in the values of this parameter worldwide over the chosen time range, and even display side by side for comparison maps coded for two different parameters. Users have the choice of three display modes: Mercatorlike projection maps in an animated strip (rather like cartoon frames that can be flashed by quickly to show a single dynamically changing image); a grid or matrix table of maps, each for a different fixed time within the range; and a globe which shows only a single time frame but can be rotated to show the color-coded values of the parameter(s) at all points on the earth or as seen from any direction in space above the earth.

Moreover, the color-coding in the maps and globes is quantitatively based, providing a good example of a topological semiotic, and a key is provided that shows a continuously variable color spectrum and the corresponding numerical values. Along with this is an explanatory paragraph discussing what the color-coded image maps show that is of scientific importance, and in some cases what the technical nature of the parameter is and from what satellite instrument it is derived.

In making use of the Observation Deck's scientific visualization facility, visitors must integrate scientific language, specialized visual display genres, quantitative values, and time-dependent animation. The latter is also interactive; the user employs a motor routine to control the animations by dragging the mouse over the images while a counter changes to show the month and year of each frame. What are the intelligences at stake in proficient use of these pages? In learning by interacting with this new multisemiotic medium?

Surfing the Web, or just linking among the Web pages within a particular integrated Web site such as the Earth Observatory, is an interactive experience with a much more prominent component of bodily-kinesthetic or motor intelligence than reading print or viewing a video. It involves also some transposition of the resources of spatial intelligence, since the primary metaphor of Web site design and use is "navigation" as if in a virtual space where we must remember, if not three-dimensional spatial relationships, then at least pathways and sites of intersection, rather as in learning a maze (or in the aboriginal Australian view of territory spatialized by sacred paths joining landmark sites). The semantics of hypertext introduce a new element to the organization of textual or hypermedia meaning: trajectories across scales in these virtual topological spaces (Lemke 1998c). Meanings are made by users of the Web as they create a trajectory or pathway from page to page: some kinds of meanings are typically made in related, consecutively traversed pages; others are made on the longer pathscale of pages across different subsites, different sites, and different content domains. A whole session of surfing brings new contexts to any visit to the *nasa.gov* domain, and within that domain, at the scale of the Earth Observatory site, there are meaning-relations to be made among pages in its different divisions (the Library, the Study, etc.). Then at a finer scale there are the meaning-relations within its Observation Deck subsite.

In this example, passing the cursor over each menu item on the right (Atmosphere, Oceans, etc.) causes a different frame to appear to the immediate left. Within the frame for Life on Earth is an image of the earth globe colored according to the patterns of a (land and sea) measurement of vegetation, and a link menu to the page for scientific visualization of datasets relevant to each topic in the menu. Just within this one page, linguistic, visual, and motor intelligences are at work making meaning. At the next hypertextual scale, the pages actually linked have particular complex meaning relationships to the Observation Deck page and to each other. To identify, for example, the basis of the color-coding of the Life on

Earth globe on the Observation Deck page, one has to use visual memory and discrimination of a fairly fine order to make the identification with the globe shown on the Biosphere page, rather than, say, that on the Vegetation or the Chlorophyll page. On such a page, we must use page-layout savvy and linguistic intelligence to see how the color-code key toward the bottom of the page corresponds to the coloration of the strip map and globe at the top of the page. We need to combine visual with mathematical intelligence, and an understanding of a standardized technical genre (in the key), to relate color values to numerical values of the NDVI vegetation index, which then, with further use of visual intelligence, can help us interpret quantitative variation in the strip map.

At another fine scale of hypertext linking, each Dataset View page links to a set of possible new pages which are dynamically generated by our interacting with the View page. In the View page we use motor and visual and linguistic and numerical intelligence to interpret and operate the dropdown boxes in which we select the range of dates and possible comparison datasets for generating our animation. Clicking the Build Animation button leads to a page, which has linguistic-cum-visual-cum-quantitative meaning relations to the page. We now see the strip map enlarged and keyed to our range of dates, with the color code and numerical value key below. Visual-motor intelligence is needed now to operate the animation, by dragging the mouse and observing the changing date-counter as well as the changing colorations of the map. At this coarse timescale, there is not true continuous variation (the animation actually jumps from month to month), but our visual intelligence interpolates the continuous intermediate changes. In a more complex view, we would have a second map at the right, color-coded for a different kind of data and for the same or a different time range; we would now motor- and visually coordinate animated changes in time for both of these, while reading the date-counters with a combination of visual-linguistic-and-numerical intelligence, all the while interpreting the color changes in terms of two different keys (one below each map if we have chosen datasets for different parameters), and, again, both visually and numerically. This is a high order of amateur multisemiotic meaning-making!

I have also compared other NASA Web pages which begin in multisemiotic complexity where these leave off (Lemke, in press) and are meant for science professionals. No one should wonder, after a visit to this NASA site for the educated public, at the emphasis in the new U.S. science education standards on achieving higher levels of visual scientific literacy. But it is not the isolated visual literacy that matters in practice; it is the integrated use of language, visual representations, mathematical-quantitative reasoning, and motor and spatial intelligence. If the level of motor intelligence seems quite modest in these examples, that is not true in the various 3D immersive data worlds that are today mainly accessible only with more powerful computers but are coming to a screen near you very soon as presaged by the extreme popularity of 3D computer games, where the levels of bodily-kinesthetic intelligence required for success often exceed my own limits. They are also very clearly tightly integrated with high levels of visual and spatial intelligence. Once the linguistic and mathematical-quantitative semiotics are added to this mix, the multiplied power of semiotic possibilities will certainly challenge even the multiplied intelligences any one of us can bring to bear.

But what of our collective multisemiotic intelligence? Neither 3D videogames, nor the NASA Web pages in the Earth Observatory or other similar sites, are produced by single individuals. On the EO Masthead page, we find a team leader, system administrator and Webmaster, an art and design specialist, and a programmer as well as an editorial staff of eleven more people, including an Observation Deck editor and a science writer. Finally there is a scientific advisory board of twelve specialists and acknowledgments of the contributions of seven other individuals. Many of the Web pages in the Study and Library also originated with outside contributors as did the basic data and scientific visualization methods in the Observation Deck (for the origin of one, see Lemke, in press). The combined talents of ultimately thousands of people went into creating what we see (many thousands if we count those who helped build and launch and monitor the satellites). But even at the most immediate level, this multisemiotic site is the product of multiplying the specialized intelligences of a writer (linguistic), an art designer (visual), a programmer (logical), and a team leader (social). At the least, the semiotic resource systems of language, page design and color graphics, computer programming (another offshoot of language, but back-hybridized with finitary mathematics), scientific visualization (the topological semiotic relevant here), and Web site design (based in a specialized hypertextual-spatial intelligence) are involved in production.

This fact, too, has important implications for education and not just for education in science. One of the goals of collaborative learning ought to be not just learning to work with others in the sense of developing interpersonal or social intelligence but specifically learning how to integrate the semiotic forms of meaning-making that I prefer and excel at with those that you can contribute to our joint project. We can teach students effectively how to integrate their own work with that of others as well as how to integrate their own multiple intelligences and semiotic skills, only if we better understand just how, in our own community and others, in this period of history and in the human past, people have found ways to multiply our resources for making meaning by multiplying one intelligence by another in multisemiotic projects. It may even be, if we look to find it, that the interaction and integration of different semiotic skills and intelligences will help students to leverage their strengths in some domains to build up better skills in others. Multiplication, in all these senses, may yet be education's best strategy for the future.

References

Arnheim, R. (1956). *Art and visual perception*. London: Faber.

Bakhtin, M. (1953/1982). Discourse in the novel. In M. Holquist (ed.), *The dialogic imagination: Four Essays* pp. 259–422. Austin: University of Texas Press.

———. (1953/1986). *Speech genres and other late essays*. Austin: University of Texas Press.

Barthes, R. (1977). The grain of the voice. In R. Barthes (ed.), *Image—Music—Text*. New York: Hill & Wang.

Bourdieu, P. (1984). *Distinction: A social critique of the judgment of taste*. Cambridge, MA: Harvard University Press.

———. (1990). *The Logic of practice*. Stanford, CA: Stanford University Press.

Cole, M. (1996). *Cultural psychology*. Cambridge, MA: Harvard University Press.

Cumming, J., & Wyatt-Smith, C. (eds.). (1997). *Examining the literacy-curriculum relationship in post-compulsory schooling*. Brisbane, Australia: Griffith University.

Dyson, A. (1991). Toward a reconceptualization of written language development. *Linguistics and education, 3*, 139–62.

Edelman, G. (1992). *Bright air, brilliant fire*. New York: Basic Books.

Eisenstein, S. (1943). *The film sense*. London: Faber.

Gardner, H. (1983). *Frames of mind*. New York: Basic Books.

———. (1993). *Frames of mind* (2nd ed.). New York: Basic Books.

Goodman, N. (1976). *Languages of art*. Indianapolis, IN: Hackett.

Halliday, M. (1978). *Language as social semiotic*. London: Edward Arnold.

———. (1994). *An introduction to functional grammar* (2nd ed.). London: Edward Arnold.

Hicks, D., & Kanevsky, R. (1992). Ninja Turtles and other superheroes: A case study of one literacy learner. *Linguistics and Education, 4*(1), 59–106.

Kendon, A. (1990). *Conducting interaction*. London: Cambridge University Press.

Kress, G., & van Leeuwen, T. (1996). *Reading images*. London: Routledge.

Latour, B. (1987). *Science in action*. Cambridge, MA: Harvard University Press.

———. (1993). *We have never been modern*. Cambridge, MA: Harvard University Press.

Lave, J. (1988). *Cognition in practice*. Cambridge, UK: Cambridge University Press.

Lemke, J. L. (1989). Semantics and social values. *WORD 40* (1–2), 37–50.

———. (1995). *Textual politics: Discourse and social dynamics*. London: Taylor & Francis.

———. (1998a). Multiplying meaning: Visual and verbal semiotics in scientific text. In J. Martin and R. Veel (eds.), *Reading science* (pp. 87–113). London: Routledge.

———. (1998b). Metamedia literacy: Transforming meanings and media. In D. Reinking, L. Labbo, M. McKenna, & R. Kiefer (eds.), *Handbook of literacy and technology* (pp. 283–301). Hillsdale, NJ: Erlbaum.

———. (1998c). *Hypertext semantics*. Paper presented at the International Congress of Systemic Functional Linguistics, July, Cardiff, Wales. *academic.brooklyn.cuny.edu/education/jlemke/webs/hypertext/tsld001.htm*

———. (1999). Typological and topological meaning in diagnostic discourse. *Discourse Processes, 27*(2), 173–85.

———. (2000). Multimedia demands of the scientific curriculum. *Linguistics and Education, 10*(3), 1–25.

———. In press. Mathematics in the middle: Measure, picture, gesture, sign, and word. In M. Anderson, V. Cifarelli, A. Saenz-Ludlow, & A. Vile (eds.), *Semiotic perspectives on mathematics education*.

Martinec, R. (1998). Cohesion in action. *Semiotica*, vol. 120 no. 1/2, 161–180.

O'Halloran, K. In press. Towards a systemic functional analysis of multisemiotic mathematics texts. *Semiotica*.

O'Toole, L. (1990). A systemic-functional semiotics of art. *Semiotica, 82*, 185–209.

———. (1994). *The language of displayed art*. London: Leicester University Press.

Roth, W., Bowen, G., & McGinn, M. (1999). Differences in graph-related practices between high school biology textbooks and scientific ecology journals. *Journal of Research in Science Teaching, 36*(9), 977–1019.

Saxe, G. (1982). Developing forms of arithmetic operations among the Oksapmin of Papua New Guinea. *Developmental Psychology, 18*(4), 583–94.

Scheflen, A. (1975). Models and epistemologies in the study of interaction. In A. Kendon, R. Harris, & M. Key (eds.), *Organization of behavior in face-to-face interaction* (pp. 159–173). The Hague: Mouton.

Tufte, E. (1983). *The visual display of quantitative information.* Cheshire, CT: Graphics Press.

van Leeuwen, T. (1991). The sociosemiotics of easy listening music. *Social Semiotics, 1*(1), 67–80.

Walkerdine, V. (1988). *The mastery of reason.* London: Routledge.

———. (1997). Redefining the subject in situated cognition theory. In D. Kirshner & J. Whitson (eds.), *Situated cognition* (pp. 57–70). Mahwah, NJ: Erlbaum.

Chapter 10

Gaile S. Cannella

MULTIPLE INTELLIGENCES IN EARLY CHILDHOOD EDUCATION: A POSTSTRUCTURAL/FEMINIST ANALYSIS

In the early 1980s I, like many other early childhood educators, was concerned about the influence of psychometric theory on beliefs about human beings and education in general, and on views of young children specifically. I believed that drill-and worksheet-oriented approaches to learning treated all human beings as if they were passive, mindless creatures. Developmental psychology, and especially the work of Piaget, on the other hand, fostered a perspective through which human beings, including young children, were viewed as active, autonomous agents in their own learning and decision-making. Further, as the work of Vygotsky gained attention in the United States (having been translated to English), an avenue was created for attending to the social and cultural aspects of cognition. During this time period (or at least in my own experience as a worker in the field of education), I also read three books that profoundly affected my thinking and that seemed to complement the scholarship of Piaget and Vygotsky: Stephen Gould's *The Mismeasure of Man* (1981), David Feldman's *Beyond Universals in Cognitive Development* (1980), and Howard Gardner's *Frames of Mind: The Theory of Multiple Intelligences* (1983). I began to integrate the readings and ideas of these authors regularly in both my teaching and research.

Agreeing with many other educators (Reiff 1997; Lazear 1991 and 1994; Armstrong 1994), I found that the work of Howard Gardner broadened my notions about knowledge and the variety of ways that it could be approached and developed by human beings. The data used to explain the theory are well researched, logical, interconnected, and interdisciplinary. Further, the theory addresses diversity and culture by tying values, beliefs, strengths, and skills to cultural context. It both supports the work of Piaget by reifying his developmental focus on logical-mathematical thought and expands notions of intellect by introducing a Vygotsk-ian belief in cultural values and construction. The notion of multiple intelligences is compelling, especially in a society dominated by calls for diversity and tolerance within expectations of progress, scientific truth, and accountability.

As a scholar, and perhaps more importantly as a human being, I was drawn even more profoundly to such Gardner statements as "we use it (intelligence) so often that we have come to believe in its existence . . . rather than as a convenient way of labeling some phenomena that may (but may well not) exist" (Gardner 1983, 69). "The intelligences are fictions—at most, useful fictions . . ." (70). Additionally, as a female I began to be aware that the voices that had influenced my thinking were predominantly male and white and represented the culture of psychology. I began to believe that if I wanted to be open to possibilities for social and cultural construction of values, I must explore diverse philosophical perspectives, cultural experiences, and overall views of the world, that I must listen to diversely gendered voices, people of color, and human beings who view the world from a variety of cultural and professional lenses.

More importantly, those who are younger, or those who for various reasons have been identified as the "other" (e.g., children, women, the poor, people from the Third World, those who are labeled as linguistically diverse because one standard language form dominates, groups identified as "at risk," African Americans), have not often benefited from our psychological conceptualizations of human nature, intellect, or intelligence, however broadly we define our construction. Although I appreciate the contributions that Howard Gardner's work makes to broadening views of human intellect and learning, I have come to believe that the views themselves remain grounded within one cultural construction of human life. Even beliefs that would appear to broaden our interpretations of the world, that would appear to increase openness and tolerance, should be critiqued. As Foucault (1983) explained, no discourse is entirely good or bad, but all discourses are dangerous and require continual critique.

Therefore, from within my own context and recognizing (if not always mentioning) the biases within my own time, politics, history, and reflections, I will discuss the work of Howard Gardner as related to early childhood education from a postmodern feminist/poststructural perspective. This postmodern interpretation places the work into three interrelated categories: (1) the creation of the theory of multiple intelligences and its embeddedness within developmental psychology; (2) the construction of Project Spectrum, a program designed to broaden the conceptualization of intellectual potential and techniques for assessing/educating young children; and (3) recent interpretations of the early childhood education of Reggio Emilia, an Italian program for young children.

Enlightenment/Modernist Discourses and Developmental Psychology: Constructing Multiple Intelligences/Education

Recognizing that many chapters in this book address in detail the overall concept of Multiple Intelligences, I will simply summarize the basic ideas as a background for a more feminist/poststructural discussion that is related to early childhood education. The theory proposes that all human beings possess, to varying degrees, at least eight separate types of intelligence that function fairly separately. The forms of intelligence are: linguistic, logical-mathematical, spatial, musical, bodily-kinesthetic, naturalistic, intrapersonal (knowledge about ourselves), and interpersonal (knowledge about other people), with each type demonstrated and illuminated through particular forms of representation. Further, each intelligence "reflects the potential to solve problems or to fashion products that are valued in one or more cultural settings" (Gardner 1999, 71–72). The criteria used to qualify an ability as an intelligence are the possibility of isolation and breakdown of skills through brain damage, the existence of individuals with exceptional ability, psychological support through psychometric and training studies, a set of advanced adult end-states with a distinct developmental history, potential ties to evolutionary processes, core operations that can be clearly defined, and the potential for representation through a symbol system (see also Gardner 1983; Feldman 1998).

Following an examination of seven of the originally proposed intelligences in *Frames of Mind* (naturalistic intelligence was added in 1998a), Gardner provided educational implications that have been interpreted in a variety of ways by various scholars, including those in early childhood education. Most recently, he has proposed a sequence for educational activity (Gardner 1999). MI is seen as useful for providing guidance as educators who (1) plan entry points for the introduction of topics (2) provide analogies related to topics, and (3) plan multiple representations of core ideas. As teaching illustrations of the educational model, he uses the theory of evolution, the music of Mozart, and the historical events that surrounded the Holocaust. "By now, my educational model should be clear. Deep understanding should be our central goal, we should strive to inculcate understanding of what, within a cultural context, is considered true or false, beneficial or unpalatable, good or evil" (186).

Explaining that some have reacted to the multiple intelligences construct by maligning his beliefs with individuals who profess that "anything goes" and recognizing that "progressives" believe that his focus on truth and standards is excessive, Howard Gardner says that he is a "demon for high standards and demanding expectations" (25). He believes that it is very important to plan curriculum for kindergarten through secondary school that includes the search for truth, beauty, and goodness; he even states: "allow me to fashion curriculum" (56), proposing that current cultural conceptions be included in the search for positive and negative examples.

Although I believe that many postmodern educators appreciate that Gardner's arguments are created with the intent to foster cultural diversity and an appreciation for a broad range of human experience and skill, the underlying Enlightenment/ Modernist assumptions of the theory cannot be denied. Gardner supports this perspective himself in stating: "I reveal my Enlightenment allegiance in my conviction that, over time, humanity has made some progress in the three realms I cherish" (1999, 57). However, the work of a variety of philosophers, poststructuralist early childhood educators, and feminist developmental psychologists challenges the very truth-oriented developmental foundation upon which the theory of MI is grounded.

The work of such philosophers as Michel Foucault and Julia Kristeva challenges the nature and origins of systems like those so eloquently proposed by Gardner. Foucault (1965 and 1972) has demonstrated how knowledge and reality—and, I would add, the concept of intelligence(s)—are potentially created through language practices. Further, in *The Archeology of Knowledge,* he examines the embeddedness of so-called universal human "constructs and truths," and even the need to believe in those truths, from within a particular historical, political, situational place. Kristeva (1986) reveals breaks and contradictions even in the notion of sexual differentiation (a "truth" that some have believed to be both naturally and scientifically defined). From these historical, critical, and feminist perspectives, constructs that are very important to Gardner's theories such as intelligence (in however many forms), development, progress, truth, beauty, and dichotomies such as good/evil, adult/child, male/female, mature/immature, must be considered at least as potentially monocultural psychological constructions that are biased toward belief in predetermined scientific truth. While giving the appearance of addressing ontological and epistemological concerns (Guba & Lincoln 1994; Lincoln & Guba 1985), by focusing on the importance of cultural diversity and values in the development of knowledge, Gardner's proposals themselves are embedded within an acceptance of intelligence, truth, beauty, and goodness, and, perhaps more importantly, one group's right to decide for the other (i.e., the rights of those who are older to decide for those who are younger).

The scholarly writings of Erica Burman and Valerie Walkerdine provide examples of feminist research in developmental psychology that questions intelligence as a human truth and specifically addresses the problems with grounding such a construct in psychometric, developmental, isolated criteria that would lead to adult competence (however culturally based that competence might be characterized). In *Deconstructing Developmental Psychology,* Burman (1994) demonstrates the ways in which our psychological construction of development reflects an underlying interest in the maintenance of social control. In an indepth analysis of the field, she reveals the ways that women, children, and so-called primitives have been linked together as without logic, objectivity, or maturity, and therefore without power or agency. Further, she demonstrates how the language (and behavior) of the middle class is used to construct notions of the "good mother," the "good child," or the "good teacher."

Walkerdine (1984, 1987, 1988, and 1990) shows how the ideal, quintessential child progressing developmentally is a male. The child is positioned as a pioneer, an explorer, an independent constructor. The developing child falls into the stereotypic masculine image. She further demonstrates how Piagetian theory is used to legitimate masculinized constructions of the individual as separate from the world.

Poststructural work in early childhood education has demonstrated the power created by "experts," usually in psychology, over children, parents, and the field of early childhood in general. This work challenges the existence of structures (however culturally defined) over which human beings (i.e., young children) have no control. First, scholars like Marianne Bloch (1987; Beyer & Bloch 1996) have demonstrated the historical ways in which the profound belief in the power of science to reveal human structural truths has lead to the unchallenged assumption that younger humans are a distinct group of beings (designated "children") who are not as advanced as those who are older (designated "adults"). These children must be guided by those who are "grown-ups" toward self-competence, logical reasoning, and positive self-image. Examples tied to even more specifically defined structures include the research of Daniel Walsh (1991), contradicting the universalization of Piagetian stages; Elizabeth Graue's (1992) work that challenges the dominant notion of readiness as a developmental construct within the individual; and Jonathan Silin's (1987) work calling for reconsideration of the knowledge base that grounds our interpretations of experiences with those who are younger. In my own recent book, I historically examine the ways in which developmental psychology and discourses of predeterminism, need, and innocence create power for adults over those who are younger and actually limit and devalue the multiple ways that we as human beings may learn to hear and connect with each other (Cannella 1997). The work of a growing number of early childhood educators expands, contradicts, challenges and even calls for reconceptualization of the underlying views of human beings and science that ground the theory of MI and the ways in which we educate young children (Cannella & Bailey 1999; Baker 1996 and 1999; Boldt 1997; Silin 1995; Swadener & Lubeck 1995; O'Loughlin 1992; Kessler 1991).

In his book *The Disciplined Mind: What All Students Should Understand* (1999), Howard Gardner provides some insight as to his view of "relativism . . . , poststructuralism, deconstruction" or those views that, although recognized as varied, "collectively challenge the certainties assumed during earlier epochs" (55–57). He states that postmodern views are mentioned (in his book) for one reason: "Taken at face value, the postmodern stance invalidates my enterprise of creating an education that focuses on the true, the beautiful, and the good" (56). "I admit that I have little or no tolerance for the 'pure' version of postmodernist thought" (55). He further explains: "I am willing to cede a lot of running room to the postmodernists at the college and university level (particularly in elective courses!), as long as they will allow me to fashion curricula for kindergarten through secondary school" (56), a perspective that sounds somewhat egotistical to a former early childhood and elementary teacher. This interpretation of postmodernism appears to represent the dichotomous thinking that has become so common to modernist methods that would discredit the postmodernist exposure of binarisms (e.g. pure/ impure, modern/postmodern, valid/invalid, right/wrong, good/evil, human truth/ relativism). Gardner's interpretation of postmodernism does not appear to include either the "unthought of" or possibility.

However, as Patti Lather (1991) points out, postmodernism is not some form of dichotomous opposition to modernity. Postmodernism is the intersection of multiple and diverse perspectives, the creation of potentially new positions from which human beings can function. Rather than attempting to define "postmodern," to label it as relativistic and its scholars as purists (Gardner 1999, 55), or to replace a new dominant knowledge for the old, a variety of postmodern scholars and interpretations challenge us to replace our modernist necessity to understand with an openness to the hidden, to the unexplained, to the unpresentable (Lather 1991; Lyotard 1984). I would suggest that the variety of postmodernist philosophies, whether more moderate or radical, and even Gardner's modernist theories themselves, are all complex, contradictory constructions of the world that provide perspectives that should be heard and from which to take action in our everyday lives with younger human beings. Rather than challenging the validity of anyone's ideas, everything is important; nothing is disqualified. However, perhaps all perspectives, and especially those that have dominated throughout disciplines and fields like psychology (including multiple intelligences), are viewed as tentative, constructed, limited, and requiring continual critique.

Ultimately, critical questions could serve to expand, reinvent, and ground the reconceptualization of the theory of multiple intelligences and related educational implications. Examples include the following:

- What is implied when we believe that we can actually know how others think and learn, whether the "others" are humanity as a whole as the object of psychology or children as the object of our "good" educational intention?
- What are ways that various groups of human beings have been privileged or damaged by our psychological constructions of them? Would individuals and groups of people from various backgrounds agree with these judgments?
- How could questioning the creation of such constructs as intelligence, thinking, learning, teaching, and education add to the broader, more politically and historically cognizant understanding of the struggle to live with each other as human beings?
- Do the theories that we create (in this case MI theory) actually generate new, unthought-of connections between those who are younger and those who are older, especially for children who have not historically been privileged by our "understanding" of them?
- Does MI theory open up and expand communication between a greater variety of people, or must participants in the theory possess privileged knowledge?
- How does MI theory as applied to educational philosophy, goals, and practice recognize the political, historical, and socially complex and power-oriented

world in which young children (and other human beings such as parents and teachers) live?

- How is the thinking of historically colonized peoples represented in the construction of beliefs about intelligence that ground MI theory?
- Are there underlying assumptions within the theory that privilege particular views of the world (e.g. individualism, exploration, social construction, hierarchical relationships, patriarchy)?
- Are views of younger human beings expanded through the theory, or are children placed under greater adult restraints through the expectation of adult end states? Or is the issue too complex to engage in such deterministic notions?

The Construction of Project Spectrum: Assessing and Educating Young Children

Challenged (or awakened) by the public response to their work, Howard Gardner and David Feldman launched Project Spectrum with a grant from the Spencer Foundation in 1984. The project was tied to attempts to identify particular intellectual strengths in young children. Beginning with preschool-age children, the researchers hoped to assess how early intellectual strengths could be discovered and to determine the types of educational experiences that would not only foster intellectual strengths but keep those with nontraditional abilities from "falling through the cracks" of the system (Feldman 1998, 2). The emergence of Project Spectrum coincided with a variety of events and philosophies that were influencing the education of young children.

First, Feldman and Gardner believed that although essential goals for schooling included reading and mathematics, there are multiple pathways toward productive citizenship. They believed that much could be gained from facilitating each individual child's potentially unique contribution. They found problematic the notion that everyone should be expected to learn the same things. Additionally, the increased use of standardized testing, they believed, placed young children at special risk. Recognizing that educational decisions may be made on the basis of one test and that tests used with young children are of questionable validity (Meisels 1989), they were determined to find ways to identify the broad range of distinctive individual strengths of young children and to determine ways to educationally support those strengths.

Theoretically, the Project Spectrum team accepted the work of Jean Piaget (1983) that proposes the intellectual construction of increasingly more advanced structures. Educationally, this perspective was seen as consistent with the dominant psychological view that young children need an environment that could be termed "child-centered," free of pressure or competition. The rubric of "developmentally appropriate practice" (DAP), marketed by the National Association for the Education of Young Children (NAEYC), was accepted as the applicable view of learning. The theory of MI and nonuniversal theory were used in conceptualizing areas for alternative, and, when possible, naturalistic assessment (Feldman 1998).

As the project progressed, the team began to believe that the most successful assessment experiences involved hands-on activities, appealing materials, and an easy fit into the classroom context. The focus became authentic assessment located within the context of children's classroom work and linked to adult competence in particular domains. The goal was to "create the kind of classroom culture in which children could show their strengths" (Chen, Krechevsky, & Viens 1998, 22). The result was a set of classroom assessment activities in seven domains (defined as cultural bodies of knowledge) that influence the entire early childhood learning environment (Krechevsky 1998). The team now views the activities as tapping into a broader range of cognitive and sylistic strengths than traditional assessments without requiring young children to use the written word (Chen, Isberg, & Krechevsky 1998).

In recent years, Project Spectrum has been implemented in preschools, primary grades, and children's museums, with the involvement of musicians, poets, park rangers, and even urban planners (Chen, Isberg, & Krechevsky 1998). "Spectrum classes are richly stocked with materials designed to stimulate the several intelligences, as if a children's museum . . . has been transported into a nursery or kindergarten class" (Gardner 1999, 104). Working in a variety of communities did, however, reveal to the team that different institutions and settings have different goals and orientations (Gardner 1998b). Rather than a discrete program, Spectrum is described as "a theory-based approach that emphasizes the importance of recognizing and nurturing children's diverse cognitive abilities" (Chen, Isberg, & Krechevsky 1998).

The members of the Spectrum team have compared their work with other programs in early childhood education, specifically the Montessori method and project-oriented approaches. Montessori and Spectrum are considered similar in focusing on active involvement, individualization, and the need for a learning environment that is prepared by teachers for children. Spectrum is interpreted as less regulatory and less prescriptive, fostering a more open-ended use of materials. Project-based models and Spectrum are considered similar in following a Piagetian constructivist tradition, yet Spectrum children are not as intimately involved in planning, implementing, and evaluating the curriculum. Spectrum highlights the disciplines and is much more focused on adult end-states (Chen, Krechevsky, & Viens 1998).

Feminist poststructural issues surrounding Project Spectrum can be characterized in much the same way as in postmodern critiques of the theory of multiple intelliegences. However, critique of Project Spectrum can more specifically be tied to (1) the acceptance of assessment as a legitimate activity, and (2) the "child-centered" pedagogy that is assumed in the construction of the assessment/learning environment.

Although writing with the recognition that assessment is a constant struggle to broaden conceptions and to reveal strengths, the appropriateness of observation and judging others is accepted. Some form of assessment becomes the grand narrative; for Spectrum, assessment (however authentic or contextual) appears to be the truth that guides action. Those of us who have dedicated our professional lives to work with those who are younger share the Project Spectrum concern that "very young children will find themselves subjected to high-stakes testing" (Feldman 1998, 5). However, from a postmodern perspective the construction of new forms of surveillance to replace the old must be challenged and the following questions asked:

- What values are embedded in the acceptance of any notion of assessment?
- Is assessment an activity that will ever be fair?
- Does one group of human beings have the right to continuously observe and judge another?
- Would adults accept being continuously observed, judged, and written about in profiles?

In Project Spectrum classrooms, children use much the same materials and engage in many of the same activities and experiences as in most child-centered, discovery-oriented, DAP classrooms. Project Spectrum authors set out to "develop a kind of alternative assessment compatible with this view of learning in early childhood" (Feldman 1998, 6). Poststructural researchers have already critiqued the notion of "child-centeredness" as related to a variety of early childhood programs. These critiques are applicable to Project Spectrum.

Valerie Walkerdine provides an excellent example in her explanation of child-centeredness as actually a "reproduction of ourselves" (1984, 194). Many people genuinely believe that child-centeredness liberates children, often because the perspective is consistent with their own experiences (e.g., middle class, sometimes liberal, sometimes feminist). It appears to provide a wonderful alternative to overt oppression. However, critique from a variety of perspectives reveals major issues that must at least be considered:

- Child-centeredness may actually reproduce the cultural capital of the dominant group while using the language of democracy and human nature (Cannella 1997; Burman 1994; Delpit 1992; Walkerdine 1984; Foucault 1978).
- "Child-centeredness constructs the illusion that children in educational environments have choice when actually the 'will' is imprisoned through the pretense of freedom. Self-regulation is used as more effective than overt control, which may actually be more easily resisted" (Cannella 1997, 135; see also Burman 1994; Singer 1992; Woodhead 1990; Kelly-Byrne 1989).
- Child-centeredness is used to further legitimate adult power of surveillance and judgment over children; since adults must learn to know and understand children, their rights to privacy are denied (Foucault 1984; Walkerdine 1984).

- Child-centeredness perpetuates stereotypically masculine images of independence, individualization, exploration, and discovery (Walkerdine 1984, 1987, 1988, and 1990).
- Child-centeredness is often associated with a variety of resources and materials (a notion that is very consistent with the Project Spectrum approach). This dependence on materials constructs a view of education that is capitalist, Western, and dependent on the equitable availability of money and resources (Freire & Macedo 1987).

Early childhood educators and developmental psychologists whose scholarship represents the various postmodern perspectives that would challenge regimes of truth do not critique broad-based assessment or child-centeredness to build a case for worksheets, drill, or various other forms of didactic learning for young children, or any other group of human beings. Critique requires that assumptions must be revealed and hidden messages uncovered to create new and previously unthought-of perspectives from which to take action. Project Spectrum reflects much of the dominant discourse in developmental psychology and education, as do most currently practiced programs in early childhood education.

Multiple Interpretations of Educational Practice: Examining Reggio Emilia

In his 1999 book *The Disciplined Mind: What All Students Should Understand,* Howard Gardner discusses at length one particular early childhood education program, the Reggio Emilia schools of northern Italy, and labels them "the best preschools in the world." The Reggio Emilia schools are located in the region of Emilia-Romagna, just west of Bologna. They are a network of schools serving children from birth to six years of age that was begun at the end of the Second World War as a collective activity of parents, children, educational practitioners, and politicians. The schools have been recognized and admired worldwide but have gained special attention in the United States as models of "quality" early childhood education.

The interpretation of Reggio Emilia education provides an excellent illustration of the perspective from which Howard Gardner's work draws, a view that is psychological, developmental, and tied to expectations that would result in some form of culturally determined high standards (Gardner 1999) or adult end-states (Gardner, Torff, & Hatch 1996). This interpretation of Reggio can be compared to the neocolonial interpretations of such scholars as Richard Johnson or the postmodern/poststructuralist analysis of Reggio by Gunilla Dahlberg, Peter Moss, and Alan Pence that will follow. I must admit that I have never visited the Reggio schools; however, perhaps that is an advantage for this work because I do not write to present my interpretation of Reggio (which would obviously be influenced by visitation) or the interpretations of the people involved in Reggio. The following are comparative summaries of the written interpretations of Howard Gardner by those who are more neocolonial and postmodern in perspective.

"The Best Preschools in the World"

Incorporating throughout a belief in multiple intelligences and a belief in the "truth" that "from the moment of conception, people are enveloped in the assumptions, biases, and visions of particular cultures" (Gardner 1999, 97), Howard Gardner's interpretation of Reggio Emilia focuses on three elements: (1) descriptions of the environment, from the way it looks to the interactions among children, teachers, and parents; (2) cautions for other educators in believing that Reggio can be modeled or transported; and (3) discussion of the ways that Reggio illustrates current work in developmental psychology.

First, Reggio Emilia is described as a "prosperous region" with arts that "are admired all over Italy" (86). The community exhibits high political participation with orientations toward socialistic democracy.

The physical environment of the school is described as beautiful, spacious, healthy, and filled with love (Gardner 1993a), as "like the hundreds of affluent preschool programs around the world" (Gardner 1999, 87). Groups of children may spend months exploring areas that interest them, ranging from sunlight, rainbows, or shadows to building an amusement park for birds. These unlimited project themes are represented in multiple ways through the very substantive displays created for parents. "Particular reactions of particular children to particular experiences become the bedrock . . . of the curriculum" (88). The environment is described as one in which teachers are continuously developing "techniques for taking the ideas and actions of young children seriously" (88). "Their goal is to capture and make public the hundreds of languages . . . that children naturally use, produce, and share with one another" (91). "Each child's intellectual, emotional, social, and moral potentials are carefully cultivated and guided" (Gardner 1993b). As an early childhood educator reading Howard Gardner's description of Reggio Emilia, I think of such child-centered methodologies as whole language, webbing, project approaches, learning centers, and emergent curriculum.

The instructional staff engages in an elaborate system of documentation, recording in detail the words, drawings, actions, and representations of the children. Gardner compares this documentation to the activity of a photographer who must continually shoot pictures so that nothing will be missed. Exhaustive detail is necessary because anyone who is interested must be able to read and understand the record later. Even more importantly, clear details are needed on all activities because any moment could prove to be the one that reveals information about a child or a "puzzling phenomenon" (Gardner 1999, 89).

Illustrating Vygotskian perspectives and described in the language of scaffolding and co-construction, children are seen "aping" (89) the activity of teachers, especially the scribbling of teachers involved in documentation. Further, children who work in groups are described as meeting levels of understanding that are advanced, even by standards that would be expected for individual adults. "Reggio . . . students undergo a sustained apprenticeship in humanity, one which may last a lifetime" (Gardner 1993b, xiii). "What better demonstration of the potency of the apprenticeship?" (Gardner 1999, 90).

Reggio Emilia methodology is presented as cultivating multiple forms of representation and, therefore, fostering the multiple intelligences in individual children. Young children are invited to explore a wide range of challenging materials and are exposed to human beings who model respectful relations with others. These experiences are viewed as "a powerful set of entry points to the community's cherished truths, sense of beauty, and ethical standards" (91).

Howard Gardner addresses the notion of transporting the Reggio Emilia program to other settings. Invoking his belief in cultural embeddedness, he states that what he has "described is closely tied to the specifics of the part of the world where it initially developed, and to the particular people who have been involved for decades" (92). He reminds the reader that the Reggio team does not claim that the program can be used by others. Further, they are not concerned with American research-oriented questions, standardization of assessment, or follow-up assessments of children after they leave Reggio Emilia. Gardner states he does "not want to suggest that Reggio cannot be re-created elsewhere, at least in part" (92), but reminds the reader that educational institutions are grounded in the culture from which they arise.

The ways in which psychologists frame their work are demonstrated through the construction of ties to Reggio Emilia. First, learning is understood as situated, as contextual and not always transferring to unfamiliar environments. Children are described as questioning and recording within the Reggio school context; yet, the point is made that this way of functioning may be confined within the walls of the school and within interaction with teachers and classmates. The behavior may not be exhibited at home. Second, knowledge is viewed as distributed, as emerging from both the technical and social context. The high levels of understanding that appear in Reggio schools may not be in the "mind-brain" (98) of an individual child; these understandings may be the result of adult probing and group production. Third, Gardner introduces the social science phrase "legitimate peripheral participation" to describe the ways that children begin to learn by observing skilled adults using the observation, guided participation, apprenticeship sequence. Time spent in the environment is important, as illustrated by the notion that the Reggio experience is "in the air" (98). "Adults set the tone; children are drawn into its spirit . . ." (99).

Gardner seems to feel that Reggio Emilia schools are the way that one particular culture addressed "universal needs." Although history and context affect the ways these universal needs are addressed, children are expected to master the knowledges that fit the culture and to learn in the educating body designed by the culture, an approach that includes cultural diversity with a universalist psychological world view.

Neocolonial Views and the Cargo Cult

As a scholar who has worked with native Hawaiians for many years and become aware of the various forms of intellectual and economic colonization that are growing in today's world, Richard Johnson (1999) examines the reaction to Reggio Emilia exhibited by Western educators, especially those from the United States. He reveals the discourses that have surrounded Reggio and the mechanisms of power that have been generated through the discourses. Johnson begins with descriptions of the narratives that have surrounded Reggio Emilia and concludes by positioning the program, and especially Western reactions to the program, within cargo cult theory.

A variety of resources illustrate how scholars in the field of early childhood education have been "so 'impressed' that we seemingly unequivocally trust Reggio Emilia" (Johnson 1999, 68). The desire to "import and support" is obvious in the construction of workshops and preconference sessions at the NAEYC conference, the development of proposals for "Reggio-inspired" schools in the United States (62), and workshops and training sessions for which individuals spend hundreds of dollars, even thousands when pilgrimages are taken to the sites in Italy. Johnson further illustrates "the power with which Reggio attracts our collective psyche" (67) with quotes from teachers, textbook authors, and those considered leaders in the field. "The educational experiences these preschools provide are truly remarkable" (quoted by Johnson from Henniger 1999, 69). "Stunned by the exquisitely intricate art of children in Reggio Emilia, Italy, educators throughout the world stand in awe and wonder" (quoted by Johnson from Seefeldt 1995, 39). "Reggio Emilia proves that preschool education . . . can be the single most crucial element in the intellectual development of children" (quoted by Johnson from Palestis 1994, 32). Johnson uses multiple data sources to illustrate how the field of early childhood education (especially in the United States) has assumed a type of cargo cult mentality regarding Reggio Emilia.

The concept of "cargo cult" (70) is described as the expectations that develop when so-called primitive groups are, for a short period of time, exposed to the unfamiliar materialism and material wealth of affluent industrialized societies. Various groups have experienced an influx of material goods during recent periods of war; however, this influx was only temporary. When the materials were no longer brought in, the rituals surrounding the exposure to overpowering wealth continued. Not understanding how and where the supplies were generated, people believed that they were sent from the spirit world and thus continued the rituals (Lindstrom 1993). In this same manner and without any form of intellectual debate (Delpit 1992; Walkerdine 1984), Reggio Emilia has been taken up as the new wealth, the Western answer to the best education for all children (Rose 1994). If those in the field just understand the philosophy, the practice, and appropriate teaching behaviors, the ritual is complete; the wealth will be attained. Further, this wealth can be distributed all over the world.

Richard Johnson describes how Reggio Emilia has been legitimized as a new and improved practice from a local situation and used to reinscribe (however unconsciously for some) American developmental imperialist reality. He reminds the reader that "Reggio does not necessarily bring any new or reconceptualized theory to the table. Much of what Reggio offers . . . are the cornerstone features (New 1994) upon which early childhood education programs here have been built . . ." (71). Educators who are concerned with young children, especially in the United States, have created the cult of Reggio Emilia because it reinforces long-held beliefs, reinstates materialist rituals, and appears to be consistent with the theoretical and practical discourses that have dominated the field (and been taught each semester within schools and colleges of education/child and family studies for years). An example is the concept of documentation, an activity that legitimizes further surveillance (Foucault 1984) of children within "the powerful fiction" that it is for their own good (Walkerdine 1984, 187). Further, a Reggio cult creates new sites of power by placing it in the hands of those with access to the new knowledge, in many cases those with money to travel to Italy.

Finally, Johnson suggests that the characteristics of Reggio that are most admired are impossible to import simplistically to other settings; these include materials and resources, fifty years of building community, and two thousand years of Italian culture. These points are similar to those made by Howard Gardner when he states that the program is culturally grounded and that the team does not claim that it can be used by others. However, by claiming that the schools are the "best in the world," the recognition of cultural context is actually denied—or there is an assumption that one culture is better than others.

From a neocolonial perspective, Johnson proposes that scholarly engagement involves a continual critical disposition and that, therefore, broader questions must be asked. First, using the work of Tsing (1995) and Spivak (1995), he insists that we must learn to "de-colonize, unlearn historically determined habits of privilege and privation, of ruling and dependency" (Johnson 1999, 72). As a white male professor, he believes that he may not be able to go beyond a paternalistic desire (Mohanty 1995) to interpret (and colonize) the interests of others. Additionally, "all intellectual positions involve complicity with power" (Tsing 1995, 304). "Persistent unlearning of privilege" (Spivak 1995, 251) is continually necessary in a neocolonial world, whether that privilege is intellectual complicity regarding developmental psychology and educational discourse, cultural values tied to judgments of beauty and truth as observed in Reggio, or economic privilege that facilitates travel and exploration. Rather than engage in interpretations of Reggio that further colonize others and reproduce the status quo, Richard Johnson introduces broader questions for educational concern. Examples include:

- What does Reggio Emilia have to do with poverty, the homeless, and children living in refugee camps?
- When we believe in programs like Reggio Emilia as the "best," how are those who do not accept the programs treated?

• What in our individual and collective identities (especially in the United States) causes us to embrace Reggio Emilia?
• Who speaks for the majority of people who share their lives with young children (whether parents, grandparents, teachers, friends) who cannot afford three-hundred-dollar Reggio seminars, much less visits to Italy?
• Who has the right to tell the "marginalized masses of women making slightly better than minimum wage" (Johnson 1999, 73) in child care centers how they should do their job?
• In what ways does the "cult" of Reggio perpetuate capitalist, materialist, consumer cultures, or other ways of being in the world (e.g. Western, Enlightenment thought) that have been oppressive to particular groups?

Poststructural Interpretations

From within a European context, Gunilla Dahlberg, Peter Moss, and Alan Pence (1999) interpret Reggio Emilia education from a postmodern perspective that problematizes notions of quality and standards while denying the modernist assertion that postmodern perspectives mean that anything goes (also implied by Gardner 1999, 55–57). Dahlberg (1995) compares the pedagogues of Reggio Emilia to postmodernist and poststructuralist thinkers who attempt "to move away from the legacy of modernity with its universalism and binary oppositions . . . to disrupt processes of normalization, standardization, and make way for and celebrate diversity, difference, and pluralism" (8, 16).

Dahlberg, Moss, and Pence (1999) experience Reggio Emilia not as an educational model or truth, but as a moment in their own human experience. From this moment, new spaces and possibilities for conversations about early childhood education are generated. Three example themes of Reggio Emilia are constructed through this interpretation: (1) the creation of a language of possibility, community, and relationships (rather than the acceptance of dominant educational or psychological discourses); (2) a focus on working together to offer possibilities to children without concern for outcomes or standard criteria; and (3) the recognition that organizational and structural supports are necessities, even though human agency may be functioning throughout.

The Reggio Emilia community is interpreted as engaging in a language that focuses on the "richness" of the child and the existence of human beings through relationships. The idea of the "rich child" is not an individualistic "child-centered" focus but an emphasis on the richness of the community of human beings. Children, as people, are all considered intelligent, diverse, and rich in potential, strengths, power, and competence. "If you have a rich child in front of you, you become a rich pedagogue and you have rich parents, but if instead you have a poor child, you become a poor pedagogue and have poor parents (Dahlberg, Moss, & Pence 1999, 50). Further, all possibilities, if important to children and community, are understood as rich and meaningful (even to the extent of studying modern fairy tale figures such as He-Man and My Little Pony).

Relationships among children, parents, teachers, and society are considered the center of the environment, with early childhood institutions viewed as places in which adults and children share their lives and relationships. Human encounters are considered the foundation for pedagogy; therefore, multiple forms of communication that encourage belonging, participation, diverse perspectives, and argument are considered necessary. The authors quote Loris Malaguzzi's (the first head of the Early Childhood Service) discussion of communication: "Actually, in communication the child's whole life is contained, man's whole life. . . . To learn how one can speak and listen are some of the big questions of life" (1993, 57). The focus on relationships and communication produces a "pedagogy of listening," being with other human beings, and striving to hear rather than to speak. This engages everyone in the struggle to avoid predetermined ideas of what is valid or correct. A language of hearing, possibility, and relationships dominates rather than discourses of development, readiness, intervention, risk, school performance, outcomes, models, accountability, regulation, standards, and quality.

For Dahlberg, Moss, and Pence (1999), the focus on working together in addition to human agency in Reggio Emilia illustrates how early childhood institutions can be conceptualized as forums in a civil society. Viewing civil society as spaces in which human beings engage in uncoerced activities of common interest, these forums are presented as public places "in which children and adults participate together in projects of social, cultural, political and economic significance" (73). Studies of Italian regional government reveal a variety of democratic civic associations, for example, neighborhood groups, sports clubs, choral societies, and cooperatives. Further, regions with the largest number of civic associations appear to have successful economies and regional governments (Putnam 1993). In their postmodern interpretation, Dahlberg, Moss and Pence focus on Reggio Emilia as a context in which this "social capital" (Putnam 1993, 173) is illustrated through community trust, respect, reciprocity, solidarity, and public-spiritedness. The institutions are viewed as forums in civil society in which the only generalization is that a space of opportunity and possibility is provided in which children "live their childhoods" (Dahlberg, Moss, & Pence 1999, 75). The institution is interpreted as similar to "cultural centers" as discussed by Paulo Freire, as public spaces for dialogue and the construction of new hypotheses "for reading the world" (Freire 1996). Projects for the early childhood institution, or forum in a civil society, are thus considered to be (1) dialogue with the world (2) construction of a critical democracy locally that is informed and participatory (3) creation and strengthening of social relational networks, and (4) reconstruction of the welfare state in ways that provide for and include all children and their families in the practice of freedom.

The reader might contend that these three interpretations focus on different aspects of Reggio Emilia, on different philosophical or contextual issues; that is exactly the point. These multiple interpretations provide a kind of postmodern view of a specific educational environment, revealing possibilities and challenging orientations toward particular truths. More directly, tied to the work of Howard

Gardner, multiple interpretations reveal the forms of knowledge that are disqualified by the psychological lens, that are excluded from the interpretation.

Final Thoughts

As an educator and a person who has been profoundly influenced by the work of Howard Gardner, I believe that his theories and the educational programs for young children that he has chosen to tie to that work represent an honest, tolerant, and well-intended intellectual search for ways to broaden and extend possibilities for other human beings. I do, however, believe that in the modernist context from which we have emerged, none of our work is separate from who we are as human beings. No idea represents truth for all other humans. For example, I recognize that my work is oriented toward issues of power, probably grounded in my own feelings of oppression as a child and as a woman. Further, I am constantly reminded of the unfair, inequitable, unjust ways that particular individuals and groups of people are treated in the United States and around the world. These issues are part of who I am, part of the lens(es) with which I interpret the world, just as Howard Gardner's work reveals his passion for tolerance, exploration, standards, beauty, and forms of enlightened progress. Neither of the two perspectives are bad, nor are they totally inconsistent with each other. However, both views of the world (and all others) require continual examination and critique, analysis from positions of flexibility, from ambiguous positions of complexity and openness, and from unthought-of positions that would reveal multiple human possibilities.

References

Armstrong, T. (1994). *Multiple intelligences in the classroom.* Reston, VA: Association of Supervision and Curriculum Development.

Baker, B. (1996). Rethinking the child: Childhood-as-rescue and child-centeredness. Paper presented at Reconceptualizing Early Childhood Education: Research, Theory, and Practice, Sixth Interdisciplinary Conference, October, Madison, WI.

———. (1999). "Childhood" in the emergence and spread of U.S. public schools. In T. Popkewitz & M. Brennan (eds.), *Foucault's challenge: Discourse, knowledge, and power in education* (pp. 117–43). New York: Teachers College Press.

Beyer, L., & Bloch, M. (1996). Theory: An analysis (part II). In S. Reifel & J. Chafel (eds.), *Advances in education and day care: Vol. 8. Theory and practice in early childhood teaching* (pp. 3–39). Greenwich, CT: JAI Press.

Bloch, M. (1987). Becoming scientific and professional: An historical perspective on the aims and effects of early education. In T. Popkewitz (ed.), *The formation of school subjects* (pp. 25–62). Basingstoke, England: Falmer.

Boldt, G. (1997). Sexist and heterosexist responses to gender bending. In J. Tobin (ed.),

Making a place for pleasure in early childhood education (pp. 188–213). New Haven, CT: Yale University Press.

Burman, E. (1994). *Deconstructing developmental psychology*. New York: Routledge.

Cannella, G. (1997). *Deconstructing early childhood education: Social justice and revolution*. New York: Peter Lang.

Cannella, G., & Bailey, C. (1999). Postmodern research in early childhood education. In S. Reifel (ed.). *Advances in early education and day care*, 3–39. Greenwich, CT: JAI Press.

Chen, J., Isberg, E., & Krechevsky, M. (1998). *Project Spectrum: Early learning activities*. New York: Teachers College Press.

Chen, J., Krechevsky, M., & Viens, J. (1998). *Building on children's strengths: The experience of Project Spectrum*. New York: Teachers College Press.

Dahlberg, G. (1995). Everything is a beginning and everything is dangerous: Some reflections on the Reggio Emilia experience. Paper presented at an international seminar Nostalgio del Futuro in honour of Loris Malaguzzi, October, Milan, Italy.

Dahlberg, G., Moss, P., & Pence, A. (1999). *Beyond quality in early childhood education and care: Postmodern perspectives*. Philadelphia: Falmer.

Delpit, L. (1992). The silenced dialogue: Power and pedagogy in educating other people's children. *Harvard Educational Review, 58*(3), 280–98.

Feldman, D. (1980). *Beyond universals in cognitive development*. Norwood, NJ: Ablex.

——. (1998). How Spectrum began. *Building on children's strengths: The experience of Project Spectrum*. New York: Teachers College Press.

Foucault, M. (1965). *Madness and civilization: A history of insanity in the age of reason*. New York: Pantheon.

——. (1972). *The archeology of knowledge* (A. Smith, trans.). New York: Pantheon.

——. (1978). *The history of sexuality: Vols. I–III*. New York: Pantheon.

——. (1983). The subject and power: In H. Dryfus and P. Rabinou, *Michel Foucault: Beyond structuralism and hermeneutics* (pp. 208–64). Chicago: University of Chicago Press.

——. (1984). *Nietzsche, genealogy, and history*. In Paul Rabinow (ed.), *The Foucault reader* (pp. 76–100). New York: Pantheon Books.

Freire, P. (1996). *Letters to Christina: Reflections on my life and work*. London: Routledge.

Freire, P., & Macedo, D. (1987). *Literacy: Reading the word and the world*. Westport, CT: Bergin & Garvey.

Gardner, H. (1983). *Frames of mind: The theory of multiple intelligences*. New York: Basic Books.

——. (1993a). Foreword: Complementary perspectives on Reggio Emilia. In C. Edwards, L. Gandini, & G. Forman (eds.), *The hundred languages of children*. Norwood, NJ: Ablex.

——. (1993b). *Multiple intelligences: The theory in practice*. New York: Basic Books.

——. (1998a). Are there additional intelligences? The case for naturalistic, spiritual, and existential intelligences. In J. Kane (ed.), *Education, information, and transformation* (pp. 111–31). Englewood Cliffs, NJ: Prentice Hall.

——. (1998b). The bridges of Spectrum. *Building on children's strengths: The experience of Project Spectrum*. New York: Teachers College Press.

——. (1999). *The disciplined mind: What all students should understand*. New York: Simon & Schuster.

Gardner, H., Torff, B., & Hatch, T. (1996). The age of innocence reconsidered: Preserving the best of the progressive traditions in psychology and education. In D. Olson & N.

Torrance (eds.), *The handbook of education and development: New models of learning, teaching, and schooling* (pp. 28–55). Oxford: Blackwell Publishers.

Gould, S. (1981). *The mismeasure of man.* New York: W. W. Norton.

Graue, M. (1992). *Ready for what? Constructing meanings of readiness for kindergarten.* Albany: State University of New York Press.

Guba, E., & Lincoln, Y. (1994). Competing paradigms in qualitative research. In N. Denzin & Y. Lincoln (eds.), *Handbook of qualitative research* (pp. 105–17). Thousand Oaks, CA: Sage.

Henniger, M. (1999). *Teaching young children: An introduction.* Columbus, OH: Merrill.

Johnson, R. (1999). Colonialism and cargo cults in early childhood education: Does Reggio Emilia really exist? *Contemporary Issues in Early Childhood,* 1(1), 61–78.

Kelly-Byrne, D. (1989). *A child's play life: An ethnographic study.* New York: Teachers College Press.

Kessler, S. (1991). Alternative perspectives on early childhood education. *Early Childhood Research Quarterly,* 6(2), 183–97.

Krechevsky, M. (1998). *Project Spectrum: Preschool assessment handbook.* New York: Teachers College Press.

Krechevsky, M., Feldman, D., Chen, J., Gardner, H., Harvard Project Zero Staff. (1998). *Building on children's strengths: The experience of Project Spectrum.* New York: Teachers College Press.

Kristeva, J. (1986). *The Kristeva reader.* New York: Columbia University Press.

Lather, P. (1991). *Getting smart: Feminist research and pedagogy with/in the postmodern.* New York: Routledge.

Lazear, D. (1994). *Multiple intelligences approaches to assessment: Solving the assessment conundrum.* Tucson, AZ: Zephyr Press.

———. (1991). *Seven ways of knowing: Teaching for multiple intelligences.* Palentine, IL: Skylight Publishing.

Lincoln, Y., & Guba, E. (1985). *Naturalistic inquiry.* Beverly Hills, CA: Sage.

Lindstrom, L. (1993). *Cargo cult: Strange stories of desire from Melanesia and beyond.* Washington, DC: Smithsonian Institution Press.

Lyotard, J. (1984). *The postmodern condition: A report on knowledge* (G. Bennington and B. Massumi, trans.). Minneapolis: University of Minnesota Press.

Malaguzzi, L. (1993). History, ideas, and basic philosophy. In C. Edwards, L. Gandini, & G. Forman (eds.), *The hundred languages of children* (pp. 49–97). Norwood, NJ: Ablex.

Meisels, S. (1989). High-stakes testing in kindergarten. *Educational Leadership,* 46(7), 16–22.

Mohanty, C. S. (1995). Colonial legacies, multicultural futures: Relativism, objectivity, and the challenge of otherness. *PMLA,* 111(1), 108–18.

New, R. (1994). Reggio Emilia: Its vision and its challenges for educators in the United States. In L. Katz & B. Cesarone (eds.), *Reflections on the Reggio Emilia approach* Reggio Emilia, Italy: Edizioni Junior. (pp. 33–40).

O'Loughlin, M. (1992). Appropriate for whom? A critique of the culture and class bias underlying developmentally appropriate practice in early childhood education. Paper presented at the Conference on Reconceptualizing Early Childhood Education: Research, Theory, and practice, September, Chicago.

Palestis, E. (1994). The Reggio way. *American School Board Journal,* 181 (8), 32–35.

Piaget, J. (1983). Piaget's theory. In P. Mussen (ed.), *Manual of child psychology* (pp. 103–28). New York: John Wiley.

Putnam, R. (1993). *Making democracy work: Civic traditions in modern Italy*. Princeton, NJ: Princeton University Press.

Reiff, J. C. (1997). Multiple intelligences, culture and equitable learning. In L. Orozco (ed.), *Perspectives: Educating diverse populations* (pp. 63–65). Boulder, CO: Coursewise Publishing.

Rose, D. (1994). Ned Kelly died for our sins (Aboriginal histories, Aboriginal myths). *Oceania, 65*(2), 175–87.

Seefeldt, C. (1995). Art—a serious work. *Young Children, 50*(3), 39–45.

Silin, J. (1987). The early childhood educator's knowledge base: A reconsideration. In L.G. Katz (ed.), *Current topics in early childhood education* (pp. 17–31). Norwood, NJ: Ablex.

——. (1995). *Sex, death and the education of children: Our passion for ignorance in the age of AIDS*. New York: Teachers College Press.

Singer, E. (1992). *Child care and the psychology of development*. New York: Routledge.

Spivak, G. (1995). Teaching for the times. In J. Pieterse & B. Parekh (eds.), *The decolonization of imagination: Culture, knowledge, and power* (pp. 177–202). Atlantic Highlands, NJ: Zed Books.

Swadener, B., & Lubeck, S. (eds.). (1995). *Children and families at promise: Deconstructing the discourse of risk*. Albany: State University of New York Press.

Tsing, A. (1995). *In the realm of the diamond queen*. Princeton, NJ: Princeton University Press.

Walkerdine, V. (1984). Developmental psychology and the child-centered pedagogy: The insertion of Piaget into early education. In J. Henriques, W. Hollway, C. Urwin, C. Venn, & V. Walkerdine (eds.), *Changing the subject: Psychology, social regulation, and subjectivity* (pp. 153–201). London: Methuen.

——. (1987). Sex, power, and pedagogy. In M. Arnot and G. Weiner (eds.), *Gender and the politics of schooling* (pp. 166–74). London: Hutchinson.

——. (1988). *The mastery of reason: Cognitive development and the production of rationality*. London: Routledge.

——. (1990). *Schoolgirl fictions*. London: Verso.

Walsh, D. (1991). Extending the discourse on developmental appropriateness: A developmental perspective. *Early Education and Development, 2*(2), 111–19.

Woodhead, M. (1990). Psychology and the cultural construction of children's needs. In A. James & A. Prout (eds.), *Constructing and reconstructing childhood* (pp. 60–78). New York: Falmer.

Chapter 11

Danny Weil

HOWARD GARDNER'S THIRD WAY: TOWARD A POSTFORMAL REDEFINITION OF EDUCATIONAL PSYCHOLOGY

Human history becomes more and more a race between education and catastrophe.
— H.G.WELLS

In this chapter, I examine the theories of Howard Gardner as they relate to a postformal educational psychology. Such an attempt must always be based on an appreciation of the context of inequality in which the globalized world exists at this historical moment. No psychology can ignore this context with its misery, social injustice, and inequality that pervade both schools and society at large. In the current social climate it is our responsibility as educational workers to dream a new intellectual template into being; one that promises to democratize intelligence so that all of our students can be given powerful opportunities to develop their critical and creative thinking.

Current notions of intelligence based on formal psychology are technicist dinosaurs from another time and place, and serve to marginalize and hamper the quest for human liberation. Their continuation as operative theories stands as an encumbrance to authentic reform in education precisely because they rest on calcified theories of formal educational psychology that pose a hindrance to democratizing intelligence and multiple ways of knowing. Formal educational psychological theories serve as gatekeepers for the dominant social and economic order and the power relations inherent in it. As theories, they produce inauthentic and often inhumane educational practices that can never prepare students for democratic living or cope with the grim reality of American life.

The purpose of this chapter is to examine and appropriate the positive insights of Howard Gardner's contributions. Through constructive critique, I hope to go beyond these contributions and contribute to the development of an emerging postformal psychological theory (Kincheloe, Steinberg, & Hinchey 1999) motivated by emancipatory and participatory visions of human liberation and freedom.

Frisking Ideas for Truth:
Reconceptualizing Educational Psychological Theory

Ours is an age that is proud of machines that think and suspicious of men who try.
— H. MUMFORD JONES

When Howard Gardner's theory of multiple intelligences exploded on the educational scene in 1983, it marked a major theoretical advance in the field. In his first book, *Frames of Mind* (1983), Gardner challenged formal psychological pronouncements of intellectual universalism as well as Piaget's stages of linear cognitive development. Gardner appeared to be keenly aware that intelligences are situated within the complex web of the social, psychological, and cultural lives of human beings and that formal psychological definitions of intelligence have served to suffocate and strangle the development of critical and creative thought. He also seemed to comprehend that an understanding of intelligence needs to be situated and fathomed within the context of what is valued within a specific community of peoples, and that not all intelligence is valued by all peoples within the same communities (Gardner 1993). His work also displayed an understanding of the pernicious implications of centering an educational practice on formal psychological principles allied solely to Cartesian-Newtonian ways of knowing. Like Dewey, he argued that educational practices tended to be irrelevant, boring, repetitive and uninspiring (Gardner 1995; Dewey 1933). And by defining intelligence as problem-solving and creativity, Gardner gives credence to postformal psychological exhortations that learning needs to be problematized (Giroux 1989; Gardner 1993).

Gardner also furnished theoretical support for an awareness of the need to link human reason to human emotions and feelings. His notions of intrapersonal and interpersonal intelligences help us see that Cartesian-Newtonian ways of knowing have blistered reason from emotion and provided us with an incomplete picture of what it means to be intelligent. Adding affective and emotional dimensions to intelligence helps us reconnect cognition to emotion and assists us in seeing just how subjectivity is implicated in the intricate and complex processes of desire, motivation, and psychic well-being. Furthermore, by focusing on an intrapersonal intelligence that helps us situate our own cognition (Kincheloe, Steinberg, & Hinchey 1999) in the context of personal and social constructs and transformation, Gardner affords us a convincing argument for wedding a postformal psychology to Freire's conception of conscientization, Pinar's Currere, and what I have termed elsewhere as transformative metacognition (Freire 1970; Pinar 1999; Weil 1998).

Intrapersonal Intelligence as Transformative Metacognition

Intrapersonal intelligence conceived of as transformative metacognition allows us to see thoughts underlying emotions and feelings and emotions and feelings underlying thoughts. Transformative metacognition helps us isolate and define these thoughts and feelings relative to historical constructs and sensibilities. Developing this notion of an interpersonal intelligence entails a rethinking of our thinking and individual experience as public creatures in the interest of personal and social change (Weil 1998). It specifically asks that we understand our life and consciousness as history *made* and history-*making*. By meshing our history, the present and the future, into a journey of self-analysis, transformative metacognition asks that we learn to take a critical self-inventory with an interest in ferreting out what is oppressive and nonliberatory in our psychological assemblage. This amounts to an endeavor to uncover and analyze our feelings, the sources for our epistemology, and subsequently relate this understanding to contemporary reality and especially to oppression and resistance. We learn to situate our consciousness within history, to develop a sense of intellectual humility that beseeches us to replace self-righteousness with self-questioning in the quest to develop a new humanness, a new way of being. We discover the development of a curious sense of self-confidence in our reasoning abilities as we ascertain how to locate our individuality amidst, between, and within our socioeconomic and cultural awareness.

Intrapersonal intelligence as transformative metacognition encourages us to situate, interpret, and shape our behavior toward liberatory ends. And it allows us to grapple with a sense of psychological purpose, devote attention to our own estrangement, wrestle with issues of power and authority, grasp a deeper awareness of oppression, and squarely engage issues of freedom, dignity, and personal and social responsibility.

Interpersonal Intelligence, Emotional Development, and Values and Dispositions of Fair-minded Reasoning

Gardner's notion of an interpersonal intelligence connotes an external awareness of others, their feelings, emotions, and thought processes. It is significant, for it allows us to resituate emotional development within the realm of intelligence. It exhorts us to develop a more sensitive and tentative approach to emotional life. Interpersonal intelligence is important, for it allows us to make sense out of the feelings and thoughts of other human beings and helps us critically map our relationships with others.

Interpersonal intelligence is also affectively concerned with developing values and dispositions of reasoning and fair-minded thinking, essential to collaborative living and learning—dispositions such as intellectual empathy, placing our judgment on probation until we have accurately considered another point of view, and intellectual humility and courage. An interpersonal intelligence is discursive, and effectively sanctions us to work collaboratively to overcome obstacles and problems we might face as human beings by helping us reconceptualize and sort through the relationship of power, thinking, and emotions.

The necessity for values and dispositions of reasoning to inform transformative metacognition accentuates the need for both interpersonal and intrapersonal intelligence. Both intelligences promote an acceptance of the fact that feelings, emotions, and sensation have their own special merits and limitations. And it permits us to understand how our one-sided emphasis on either rational thought or emotional thought is a result of particular historical forces underlying our personal and social development.

The absence of inter/intrapersonal intelligences may account for the heightened levels of incivility prominent in today's society. Certainly the development or cessation of these intelligences has implications for discursive experiences and how we conceptualize difference. Thus, these intelligences hold consequences for how we learn to perceive new ideas, discuss new points of view, question ourselves and others, and monitor our own thinking in the interest of good judgment. And because they are uniquely human, they are inextricably entwined and dialectically interrelated.

Gardner's theory of multiple intelligences adds important contributions to the development of a postformal psychology. Accepting that we have multiple intelligences democratizes intelligence in the interests of inclusivity; it allows us to redefine and appreciate difference in intelligence as an asset rather than a deficit and encourages and permits a radical pedagogy to explore and examine the interplay and complexity of situated intelligence. His theories add credence to postformal claims that intelligence is learned activity, not a genetic ability that is handed down from generation to generation. And because intelligence is learned, critical pedagogues know that they must provide opportunities for their students to develop multiple intelligences as holistically and interdisciplinarily as possible. Gardner's arguments squarely support the contention that intelligence is teachable and not something bequeathed to the select few.

By arguing for intellectual accessibility, Gardner helps us conceive of how we might cultivate and harvest multiple forms of intelligence in our students. Gardner's theory of multiple intelligences not only affords a powerful argument for democratized, teachable intelligences, but it also represents a powerful shift in the critical lens we use to examine educational theory and practice. This has practical implications for how we organize learning and teaching. Gardner has furnished solid support to the task of challenging androcentric and Eurocentric Newtonian-Cartesian ways of knowing; his work in this area provides an important contribution that will help us redefine a postformal educational psychology in the interests of emancipation and liberation.

Theories of Intelligence as Social Constructs: The Limitations of Gardner's Theories

We see the unhistorical character of bourgeois thought most strikingly when we consider the problem of the present as a historical problem.
— GEORGE LUKACS, *History and Class Consciousness*

In *The Disciplined Mind,* Gardner reveals the severe limitations of his theoretical constructs in his introduction:

> Frankly, I am tired of writings by educators that focus on the instrumental or the momentary: Should we distribute vouchers so that youngsters can attend schools? What are the advantages of charter schools? Are teacher unions the problem? . . . Should we have local control, national standards?. . . And I am equally weary of debates that array one educational philosophy against another—traditionalists versus progressives, proponents of phonics versus advocates of "whole language." (Gardner 1999, 16)

He goes on to implore us to leave these issues behind and focus on the purposes of education—the reason why as a society we allocate resources to educate our citizens. However, by evading objective reality and dialogue, Gardner avoids critical scrutiny of his ideas; he refuses to recognize his historically privileged position. As Freire wisely noted, without dialogue there is no communication, and without communication there is no learning (Freire 1970). I want to discuss some of the limitations of Gardner's thinking in the interest of dialogue and learning.

To begin with, discussions of educational purposes as they relate to how education might prepare citizens to combat repression, stand up for social justice, and conceive of and participate in emancipatory democratic life and the construction of their own identities are conspicuously absent from Gardner's writing. While John Dewey vehemently argued that educational purpose and design should not be contrived to prepare students for a life of conformity and control, Gardner fails to espouse or expand Deweyian themes of progressivism. He is unwilling, or ill-prepared, to link educational purpose with human liberation, self-authorship, social justice, resistance to oppression, and the struggle for sovereignty and freedom. Gardner's work simply refuses to understand the current role of schooling as a sorting machine for the new corporate order. He seems unaware of androcentric and Eurocentric educational practices, questions of socioeconomic class, patriarchy, homophobia, and racism, and specifically how the inhumane practices of primitive postmodern capitalism function to construct and restrain liberatory pedagogical practices. As a result, his theories offer only partial contributions in dire need of a postformal overhaul.

Ethics without Values

In his introduction to *The Disciplined Mind,* Gardner asks us to focus on truth, beauty, and morality as three important concerns he feels should animate and fuel our understanding of educational purpose. He apprises us that we can't understand the world in which we live unless we embrace the truth of evolution and understand our ecological niche. He declares that within the realm of beauty, we as human beings constantly seek to develop and inspire new and beautiful creations as artists so that as a society we might decide what is art and how it should be taught. In his treatment of morality, he asks us to consider the lessons of the Holocaust to discover how human beings are capable of inflicting unspeakable horrors on each other (Gardner 1999, 16–17).

A postformal psychology understands that the abstract truth of which Gardner speaks is part of a larger social and political system of power and control. Embracing the insights of Foucault, postformal psychology understands that truth does not exist outside of the power relations that construct it. On the contrary, it is always conditioned and sanctioned by administrations of power that align themselves to specific historical and sociopolitical formations and contexts. Foucault's famous words on this subject remain insightful:

> Truth is a thing of this world: it is produced only by virtue of multiple forms of constraint. And it induces regular effects of power. Each society has a regime of truth, its "general politics" of truth: that is, the types of discourse which it accepts and makes function as true; the mechanisms and instance which enable one to distinguish true and false statements, the means by which each one is sanctioned; the techniques and procedures accorded value in the acquisition of truth; the status of those who are charged with saying what counts as true (Foucault 1980, 132).

Foucault's notion of *regimes of truth* and how these regimes function to legitimize select voices while smothering difference and dissent, doesn't inform Gardner's work (Foucault 1980). He fails to see how sociohistorical contexts of relations operate to generate epistemological truths that serve to legitimate and structure particular forms of personal experience and social, cultural, and psychic life. His work doesn't address the sociopolitical problem of the suffering of the oppressed, and he seems unconsciously unaware of how class, race, and gender are implicated in an axiomatic and fundamental configuration of social reality. His concern with truth seems merely biological, not social—subject to a debilitating essentialism. His myopic, apolitical view of social constructs coupled with his ahistorical posturing fuels an insidious individualism already perniciously rampant in formal educational psychology. The limitations of his theory are conspicuous, for they prevent educators from developing and birthing theoretical understandings to examine their social and political formations as teachers as well as the sociopolitical formations that help shape the lives of their students. Take for example, his discussion of assessment:

In the uniform school, there is a core curriculum, a set of facts that everybody should know, and very few electives. The better students, perhaps those with higher IQ's, are allowed to take courses that call upon critical reading, calculation and thinking skills. In the "uniform school," there are regular assessments using paper and pencil instruments, of the IQ or SAT variety. They yield reliable rankings of people; the best and the brightest get into the better colleges, and perhaps—but only perhaps—they will also get better rankings in life. (Gardner 1980, 6)

It is clear from this statement that Gardner has not considered how assessment and standardized testing are constructed by race, gender, and class and how assessment typically serves as a technology of power (Foucault 1980): sorting, classifying, ranking, tracking, and otherwise controlling who gets the "wink and nod" to enter the corridors of power—who becomes thought of as and labeled normal.

A postformal psychology concerns itself with beauty and morality as well (Freire 1999). However, a postformal preoccupation with these concepts is fueled by an attempt to understand how these abstractions are ensconced and made specific within certain political, social, and cultural formations of a given society at a particular juncture in history. By historicizing and politicizing our understanding of beauty, ethics, and morality, postformal psychology recognizes the power of discourse and the responsibility teachers have in providing empathic, discursive reasoning opportunities for students to entertain difference in dialogical encounters with others.

Postformal psychology would argue that morality is not a universal individual construct, understood as existing outside of and disconnected from cultural and economic structures of control and authority. On the contrary, postformal psychology recognizes morality and ethical posturing as intertwined and shaped through hegemonic configurations of control and power amidst historically situated struggles against oppression and for freedom. Any examination of moral and ethical behavior must of necessity argue for an understanding of situated subjectivity—what Kincheloe refers to as situated cognition (Kincheloe 1999); a consciousness and cognition of ethics and moral behavior couched within specific historical, social, cultural, and economic realities. Thus, from a postformal point of view, ethics and morality can only be understood and examined in relationship to subjugation and resistance to regimes of power and truth.

Authoritative knowledge and an ethics of power (Wexler 1996) operate to define control and authority and serve to label what is recognizable beauty and functional ethics. Developmental psychology is itself an ethic and a morality, a technology of power that surfaced under and within distinct historically constructed conditions, and it performs distinct operations, entertains special functions, and produces tangible and visible consequences within particular historical and psychological realities. Gardner wants us to separate beauty, ethics, and morality from historical interplay and conceive of them outside of the conditions that create and sustain them. He eschews the interdisciplinary and dialectical nature and interlacing of sociology, history, culture, and economics when theorizing about educational psychology. His theories neglect to address the manner that subjectivity, interiority, sensitivity, creativity, and ethical and moral behavior are subjugated by techno-capitalist interests through discrete forms of social and cultural domination. As a result, he fails to consider what McLaren refers to as moral technologies and how these moral technologies function under our system of primitive postmodern capitalism to instill specific geneses of values, ethics, and behavior in individuals (McLaren 1995, 72).

Further, in order to be ethical itself, a critical postformal psychology must take an ethical position regarding oppression, struggles for freedom, personal sovereignty, emancipation, and the struggle for human dignity. Gardner conveniently avoids these issues. And because postformal psychology is not interested in puritanical preaching or benign didactic moralizing, it is compelled to inquire as to how teachers might promote the establishment of ethics *without* indoctrination. This suggests an obligation to provide students with discursive, fair-minded reasoning opportunities so they might arrive at ethical and moral positions forged through dialectical reasoning processes that engage difference. Postformalism understands that positions of morality and ethics surface through discursive journeys with others—through contact with difference—where inquiry is heralded through questioning in an environment of civility. Realistically and practically, this means furnishing students with opportunities to reason through multiple points of view on issues of relevant ethical and moral concern such as social justice, racism, sexism, homophobia, and social class. As Freire noted:

> As men and women inserted in and formed by a socio-historical context of relations, we become capable of comparing, evaluating, intervening, deciding, taking new directions, and thereby constituting ourselves as ethical beings. . . . It [critical pedagogy] presupposes an openness that allows for revisions of conclusions; it recognizes not only the possibility making a new choice or evaluation but also the *right* to do so. (Freire 1999, 38–39)

Gardner's analysis of cultural values suffers from similar debilitating dialectical deficits. For example, he invites us to embrace the notion of cultural transmission as a universal educational constant (Gardner 1983, 28). The epistemic foundations of Gardner's universality and metanarrative approach to cultural values not only reinforce formal educational psychology's rigid and insipid individualism, they avoid the indispensability for cultures to continually engage in cultural self-critique. For Gardner, every society "must ensure that its most central values—valor or peacefulness; kindness or toughness; pluralism or uniformity—are passed on successfully to those who will themselves one day transmit them" (28). Yet postformalism would argue that all cultures have an obligation to discover and disarm their own biases, to unseat their own sociocentricity, to ferret out their oppressive assemblages, and to engage in constant and vigilant self-critique in the interests of human freedom (Weil 1998). To simply conceive of cultural values as permanent, universal, and immutable, as Gardner seems to do, is once again a failure to situate theoretical discernment psychologically, historically, economically, socially, and culturally.

Gardner's Third Way: Reinforcing the Politics of Neoliberalism

At the same time, really effective oppositional struggles can't be directed at solving the contradictions of capitalism, but must be aimed at detaching social life from the logic of capitalism altogether.
—ELLEN MEIKSINS WOOD, *Monthly Review*

For Gardner, the transmission of values, the modeling of roles, the mastery of notions and disciplines—all of this entails the purposes of education (Gardner 1991, 40). In developing his theories, Gardner gives us a theory with a ghostly similarity to the Clintonian Third Way. By carving out a Third Way, Gardner would like to transform what his book calls "the tired debate between traditionalists and progressives" (Gardner 1999, 77). Yet I want to argue that this politics of the Third Way actually serves as an architect for a new ideological, neoliberal politics of restraint. Gardner's positions obfuscate more than they illuminate and thus serve as a reactionary apology for a new psychology of containment.

Postformal teaching and educational psychology recognize that the debate is not a false binarism between progressive approaches and traditional approaches to education. Without going into great detail, the debate among educational theorists crosses variegated chasms. Cultural conservatives argue for a notion of education based on inculcating specific Eurocentric and androcentric virtues and ethics (Bennet 1995). Economic conservatives conceive of schooling as a preparatory site for rational capitalist production. Progressive educators, such as Dewey, perceived of schooling as a site for liberation from undemocratic practices and as a journey into relevance and meaning (Dewey 1933). Early Marxist critiques of educational sites and the role of schooling argued that schooling served to produce workers who were malleable and unquestioning in their acceptance of capitalism and their role as producers and consumers within the capitalist system (Bowles & Gintis 1976).

Later, radical pedagogy or critical theory, informed by the Frankfurt School and specifically recognized in the writing of Paulo Freire and his contemporaries, attempted to go beyond the constraints of rigid Marxist economism and argued that educational locations be conceived of as political sites of resistance and struggle. They called attention to issues of identity and human agency and pointed to what they termed the hidden curriculum (Giroux 1989), elucidating how this curriculum served to shape behavior and impose power and control on students and teachers. Progressive postmodernism, in this case postformal psychology, in agreement with radical pedagogical concerns, is informed by voices of people of color and feminists and is embued with an adamant critique of essentialism. Postformalism's concern is to expose oppressive exploitative features of social practices in the classroom used to marginalize and otherwise exclude the voices of females, minorities, and members of disenfranchised groups (Benhabib 1987; Harding 1986).

Foucauldian, Freirean, Marxist, feminist, and racial awareness seek to open epistemological considerations to accommodate multiple voices of difference in the pursuit of knowledge (Foucault 1980; Harding 1986; hooks 1994). Their concern is the notion of power and control and the subtle interplay between these concepts and actual educational practices. Postformal psychology is specifically interested in how subjectivity is entangled in the intricate web of history, hegemony, and authority, and postformal approaches to educational theory assert that education should be a quest for liberation—an emancipatory attempt to cast off the shackles of oppression and repressive practices in all aspects of life.

By falsely bifurcating and reducing the debate over educational purpose and function to the fatigued categories of traditional and progressive, Gardner's reductionism dismisses these insights. Gardner seems unable or unwilling to come to terms with the epistemological and pedagogical implications of his own individualistic portrait of educational psychology and practice. Gardner simply cannot accommodate his own ideological position in the social order that defines his work. His Third Way positioning obfuscates the true nature of the educational debate by not inquiring into postformal psychological concerns. For example, how schooling, and its technologies of power—developmentalism, educational psychology, standardized testing, assessment, and classroom management—restricts and controls educational opportunities, marginalizes and disenfranchises students' voices and experiences, and classifies and sorts students into cruel cognitive categories that are based on linear and hierarchical notions of intelligence. Gardner's theory suffers from an insidious individualism that seeks to reconcile itself as uniquely distinct and separate within its own discourse. His neoliberal Third Way is a distressing hoax perpetrated on an educational community at an inopportune time—a time when paradigms need to be shifted, when claims to truth need to be frisked and rethought, and when rigorous critique urgently needs to be undertaken. His positive contributions should be appropriated and wedded to a postformal notion of educational psychology that would theoretically entertain and practically confront postformal concerns.

The implications of Gardner's Third Way are clear: the educational practices born from his theories are, and have been, relegated to helping privileged students attain higher levels of individual achievement within elite venues, as opposed to becoming powerful public activities that engage all of our nation's teachers and students. Gardner poses no threat to primitive postmodern capitalism precisely because he does not level a challenge to the structural corridors of its power. By ignoring how educational psychology and educational practices are embedded in a situated sociohistorical framework that serves the elite, Gardner's theories are, at best, imperfect. And his failure to consider how technologies of power implicate themselves in the regulation, management, monitoring, and surveillance of students and teachers renders Gardner's Third Way domesticating, untenable, and impractical.

Dissent or Descent: Confronting a New Psychology of Containment and Constraint through Radical Inquiry

The spirit of the age is filled with a disdain for thinking.
—ALBERT SCHWEITZER

A new hierarchy of authority and control is wedging itself into our psyche and inserting itself into what were once our public spheres. A subtle yet distinct ideological reformation is taking place as the realm of consumption and production is being re-engineered and restructured by neoteric, cybernetic robber barons; identity is bequeathed while rationality is beguiled.

The neoscientism of the new psychology of containment endeavors to partner with subjectivity in the colonization and domination of identity—to work harmoniously with the media and popular culture to rationalize hegemony and inequality under the rubric of authoritarian entertainment and a new inequality. The instrumentality of scientific rationality now operates as a totalizing experience whereby the imposition of systemic immutability announces itself to us as ahistorical truth. The actual mercurial and transitory relations that compose the primitive postmodern condition are presented to us as static, ahistorical, invariable, and permanent. The message is loud and clear: there is no way out—our social structures and our authored ideological formations are immutable, impenetrable and nontransitory. Resistance is both dangerous and useless. We must accept, for we are at the end of history and this is progress.

Here, in the throes of primitive postmodern capitalism, we can see and describe the madness. Eric Fromm's notion of a necrophilious society is no longer simply a prognosis—it has become our current reality (Fromm 1966). According to Fromm:

> While life is characterized by growth in a structured, functional manner, the necrophilious person loves all that does not grow, all that is mechanical. The necrophilious person is driven by the desire to transform the organic into the inorganic. . . . Memory, rather than experience; having, rather than being, is what counts. The necrophilious person can relate to an object—a flower or a person—only if he possesses it; hence a threat to his possession is a threat to himself; if he loses possession he loses contact with the world. . . . He loves control, and in the act of controlling he kills life. (41)

In this artificially generated and engineered world in which we live, many citizen-consumers wander wide-eyed and beleaguered through a dystopic landscape of moral decay and economic uncertainty. Too often they are deracinated and destructive, beguiled and betrayed.

Under primitive postmodern capitalism, the new emerging relations of production demand unquestioning consumer citizens who accept the power and authority of their cyborg masters without dissent, without doubting, questioning, or inquiry. In such a system, inquiry must recede into passivity as the mythic, permanent image of manufactured change totalizes and immobilizes reality. The nontransitory falsehood and the end-of-history myth must be accepted by unquestioning consumer-citizens precisely because the stakes are so high. In the new Gilded Age of cybernetic robber barons, there is simply too much profit to be made for a privileged few.

Under the new psychology of containment, dissent is valued in rhetoric but harshly disciplined and condemned in reality. Difference collapses into a debilitating sameness; a difference *without* distinction. For example, music loses its resistant character as commodified synthesized noise attached to TV commercials. This is the reified new-world order, neoliberalism's compassionate Third Way, Fukuyama's end of history (Fukuyama 1993).

The dilemma deepens when we consider the deficit of dissent and the treatment of difference in the country's media. With the investment of billions of dollars over the past quarter of a century, Washington's conservative media-political apparatus increasingly dictates the terms of political and social discourse. For the past two decades, conservative fund-raisers have been investing hundreds of millions of dollars into building a huge echo chamber consisting of newspapers, magazines, websites, think tanks, radio stations, television networks, and publishing houses. Think tanks, pressure groups, and public relations firms have joined ranks in an attempt to marginalize difference and manage citizen perceptions by purchasing public discourse and reducing it to the tyranny of privatized monologue. A foundation-supported right-wing constituency has been engrossed for the past quarter of a century building a huge media-infrastructure. In the new political climate of containment, fear of offending conservative masters now becomes a self-imposed form of censorship as working journalists realize that being "branded" as a liberal or dissenter can end their careers. Too many questions, too much critical scrutiny, and too much inquiry can result in career suicide. The result is the imprisonment of voice, the subjugation of dissent, and the containment of difference. The media now conceals more than it reveals. Thinking is not simply discouraged; it has become subversive.

Pepi Leistyna illuminates the subtle and covert workings of the new psychology of containment in a recent essay about his experiences in Harvard's Graduate School of Education. When he challenged traditional theories regarding cognitive performance in his teacher training class, he was completely ignored by both his teacher and other class members. As he continued questioning, he noticed: "I was getting the feeling that, in the eyes of the group, my questions were being perceived as disruptive rather than as potentially edifying" (Leistyna 1999, 56). The new psychology of containment is a subtle normalizing process that works to subtly discourage questioning, marginalize dissent, and create criteria for what is acceptable behavior.

Educator and author Kris Gutierrez shares a similar experience her biracial twelve-year-old son had in his honors history class. The class was studying Mecca, and in an attempt to provide students with a visual portrait of Mecca, the teacher played a segment of the movie *Malcolm X*. The segment depicted Malcolm arriving in Mecca. After viewing the scene, the teacher asked the students to identify what they thought was important. Her son's hand shot up and he offered the teacher his response: "Well, I think that the fact that Malcolm is being followed by two white CIA agents as he goes to worship in Mecca is very interesting" (Gutierrez 1995, 147). He was publicly chastised for being off topic and unfocused.

Civil society is losing its use-value in a hyper–exchange-value society and, for many people, the ability to form trusting relationships, to find affiliations with others around public issues in public spheres. All of this is becoming unattainable by a civilization devoted to private property, profit maximization, commodity gratification, and visual manipulation. A longing and desire for materiality seem to slowly be replacing human dreams of hope. When private life replaces public life, private relationships replace public relationships; individuals scramble to determine how to compete in the new market configurations of the market civilization, and relationships often turn antagonistic and adversarial. We are witnessing the emergence of a new privatized individualism: one that corresponds to the privatization of primitive postmodern capitalism and the corresponding changes in the forces and relations of production. The new psychological order expects to provoke within us a refusal to challenge perceived truths or accepted conventions, an adamant refusal to question anything. We are at a dangerous crossroads.

We need a public politics of dissent to confront the ruthless agenda of primitive postmodern capitalism. A public politics of dissent is a politics of utopia precisely because dissent is engaged in for purposes of resistance for, not simply resistance against. It couples realistic assessment with a utopian quest for social and individual liberation. It is at once imagination against and at the same time imagination for. As educators, we should apprehend that the new primitive postmodern capitalism cannot effectively realize its mission or accomplish or achieve its goals without creating a new psychological order of containment. This realization should allow us to advance our mission as human beings—to seek to smuggle truth out of a system that makes mendacity the norm.

Conclusion

This is the new psychology of containment, what Wilhelm Reich years ago termed the mass psychology of fascism (Reich 1948). It is the Foucauldian use of discrete technologies of power to surreptitiously colonize, regulate, and appropriate behavior for normalizing purposes (Foucault 1980), to force us to accept an unquestioning social and individual landscape, where questions are perceived as incendiary intimidations. This is the shrewd and sophisticated way the state maintains its concentrated mechanisms for actively constricting and sabotaging individual and group behavior. We are implicated in a new world order in which inquiry is disparaged and questioning is discouraged, challenges to authority are considered insurgent and subversive, conformity is rewarded by commodification, and the management of individuals and groups is assured through surveillance and monitoring—specialized and hidden within the fabric of daily life. The development of new technologies and their appropriation by those in power only promise to add to this regulation and colonization.

Our need as citizens to penetrate social appearance and pierce the veil of imagery and mendacity has presented itself to us as a social assignment and personal responsibility like as in no other time in history. Moacir Gadotti, the Brazilian educator, has keenly noted:

> [W]e can say that the twentieth century has represented . . . the century of the discovery of the plot behind power, the century of attention to power and domination. This [twentieth century] is the century of awareness of rights, exactly when they were most disrespected. As the last [nineteenth] century was the century of natural science, this has been the century of the human and social sciences. It is not yet the century of the creation of rights, just of awareness and of the defense of human rights. (Gadotti 1996, 6–7)

To go beyond the new psychology of containment and into the century of the creation and sustenance of human rights, we need a postformal educational psychology that helps us and our students radically comprehend how our subjectivity and identities are constructed, implicated, and represented in the interplay of sociohistorical economic and cultural relations. We must seek to engage both ourselves and our students in discursive and social practices that embrace diversity as something to be appreciated, not simply something to be tolerated. As educators we must imbue in students the beauty of the quest—the process and journey of continuous internal and external questioning that afford us authenticity and self-governance. We must seek to excavate counternarratives of dissent and disenfranchised narratives of difference as we challenge the market manufacture of social and personal identity. For this we need an educational theory of psychology that attends to the specificity of issues like educational purpose, race, gender, class, and sexual orientation, while at the same time linking our critical awareness and appreciation of these specificities of difference to the universal struggle for human dignity and freedom.

References

Benhabib, S. (1987). *Feminism as critique: On the politics of gender.* Minneapolis: University of Minnesota Press.

Bennett, W. (1995). *The children's book of virtues.* New York: Simon & Schuster.

Bowles, H., & Gintis, S. (1976). *Schooling in capitalist America.* New York: Basic Books.

Dewey, J. (1933). *How we think.* Lexington, MA.: Heath.

Foucault, M. (1973). *The birth of the clinic: An archeology of medical perception* (A. Smith, trans.). New York: Pantheon.

———. (1980). *Power knowledge: Selected interviews and other writings.* New York: Pantheon.

Freire, P. (1970). *Pedagogy of the oppressed.* New York: Seabury Press.

———. (1999). *Pedagogy of freedom.* Rowman and Littlefield Publishers: New York.

Fromm, E. (1966). *The heart of man.* New York: Harper and Row.

Fukuyama, F. (1993). *The end of history.* New York: Avon.

Gadotti, M. (1996). *Pedagogy of praxis.* Albany: State University of New York Press.

Gardner, H. (1980). *Artful Scribbles.* New York: Basic Books.

——. (1983). *Frames of mind: The theory of multiple intelligences.* New York: Basic Books.

——. (1991). *The unschooled mind: How children think and how schools should teach.* Basic Books: HarperCollins.

——. (1993). *Multiple intelligences: The theory in practice.* Basic Books: HarperCollins.

——. (1995). Reflections on multiple intelligences: Myths and messages. *Phi Delta Kappan, 75* (3), 200–209.

——. (1998). *Building on children's strengths: The experience of Project Spectrum.* New York: Teachers College.

——. (1999). *The disciplined mind.* New York: Simon & Schuster.

Giroux, H. (1988). *Teachers as intellectuals.* New York: Bergin & Garvey.

——. (1989). *Critical pedagogy, the state and cultural struggle.* Albany: State University of New York Press.

Gutierrez, K. (1995). Pedagogies of dissent and transformation: A dialogue with Kris Guteierrez. In P. McLaren (ed.), *Critical pedagogy and predatory culture.* (p. 147). New York: Routledge.

Harding, S. (1986). *The science question in feminism.* Ithaca, NY: Cornell University Press.

hooks, b. (1994). *Outlaw culture.* New York: Routledge.

Kincheloe, J. (1999). Trouble ahead, Trouble behind: Grounding the post-formal critique of educational psychology. In Kincheloe, J., Steinberg, S., and Hinchey, P. (eds.). *The post-formal reader.* New York: Falmer Press.

——. (2002). *The sign of the burger: McDonald's and the culture of power.* Philadelphia: Temple University Press.

Kincheloe, J., Steinberg, S., and Hinchey, P. (1999). *The post-formal reader.* New York: Falmer Press.

Kincheloe, J., Steinberg, S., & Villaverde, L. (1999). *Rethinking intelligence.* New York: Routledge.

Leistyna, P. (1999). The personality vacuum: Abstracting the social from the psychological. In Joe Kincheloe (ed.), *Rethinking intelligence* (pp. 51–68). New York: Routledge.

Los Angeles Times. (1999). 26 July.

McLaren, P. (1995). *Critical pedagogy and predatory culture.* New York: Routledge.

Pinar. W. (1999). Post formal research: A dialogue on intelligence. In Joe Kincheloe et al. (ed.), *Rethinking intelligence* (pp. 247–256). New York: Routledge.

Reich, W. (1948). *The mass psychology of fascism.* New York: Farrar, Straus, & Giroux.

United Nations Development Program. *Human Development Report* (1999). *www.undp.org/hdro*

Weil, D. (1998). *Towards a critical multicultural literacy.* New York: Peter Lang.

Wexler, P. (1996). *Holy sparks: Social theory, education and religion.* New York: St. Martin's Press.

Wood, E. (1999). Unhappy families: Global capitalism in a world of nation states. *Monthly Review, 51* (3), 1–12.

Chapter 12

Kathleen S. Berry

MULTIPLE INTELLIGENCES
ARE NOT WHAT THEY SEEM TO BE

If there are two things most people can agree on these days, they are that free-market capitalism is the only way to organize a modern society and that the key to economic growth is "knowledge."
—JOHN CASSIDY, *"The Price Prophet"*

Contextualizing the Discussion

The connections made between intelligence and educational success or failure have a long history dominated mainly by educational psychology and assigned a position of power that is taken for granted by many participating members of society. The project of critical cultural theorists is to dismantle the way in which constructs such as Gardner's Multiple Intelligences create, circulate, and maintain unequal systems of power relations located, in this case, in educational theories and policies that inform practices and free-market capitalism. Some criticisms of intelligence theory come from within the discipline of cognitive psychology itself. Some critiques of Gardner's MI show how it is relevant or not to teaching and learning. Most criticisms of theories and practices of intelligence classify individuals whether they can or will learn the dominant knowledge of the institution. Very limited, if any, criticism is directed at how intelligence theories like MI are in fact a classification system that reproduces the thought and knowledge of Western civilization (excluding knowledge and values of women, nonwhite races, non-Christian, local, and premodern ways of knowing), legitimizes the inequities of capitalism and engages participants in competition for control and mastery of their world (Bourdieu 1993).

When I think of multiple intelligences, certain individuals come to mind—Rosie, Tony, Bonnie, Jamie, and hundreds of other students. I think of mentors such as S. Steinberg, J. Kincheloe, D. Heathcote, J. Blakey, and D. Dillon. I think of family, friends, and colleagues. I think of the multiple contexts and times I've encountered resistance to my own thinking and actions that required drawing upon some piece of knowledge or values from someone or somewhere else, so much a part of me that I can't separate the warp threads from the woof. Sometimes I create knowledge and solve problems that, no matter how hard I try to locate the source, seem to come from those ancient premodern, rhapsodic intellects of wonder and passion—no names and no shape—constantly shifting, fleeting, and, many times, disappearing. A process so complex, often boring and routine, that it can only be captured in symbolic and phenomenological terms.

In modern education, academic and pedagogical voyeurs such as teachers, parents, governments, and cognitive psychologists have trapped the elusive process of coming to consciousness into a fixed entity called intelligence—or in the case of Gardner (1993a)—multiple intelligences. His works, as scholarly and beguilingly penned as they are, have seduced the field of education into yet another Western logocentric, psychological categorization. Under the guise of educational/school reform, his theory of MI has spawned a host of other supportive theories, practices, disciples, and critics. Informed by the theory of MI, professional educators continue to create and implement curriculum documents, pedagogical practices and materials, and testing and evaluation around the mind as a material location for the promises of a democratic education. Once labelled, however, whether in the singular or the plural, intelligence acts as an economic, social, political, and cultural passport for some and for others, a cage. In formal modern educational circles, the concepts of intelligence have a long-standing history, tenacious political purposes, and formidable implications for limiting democracy and social justice.

Gardner conceptualizes intelligence around what culture values the most in thinking subjects. If we align his theory of MI with postmodern critical theory, however, it can be shown how his classification of intelligences reproduces the dominant, mainstream social, institutional, and civilizational structures of Western culture. In fact, his theory systematically fulfils corporate/capitalist agendas, maps out an apolitical education, supports hegemonic practices, reduces knowledge and value to Western logocentrism, creates homogeneous subjects without agency, and excludes the impact of modern hyperreality on sources and constructs of knowledge. Without serious challenge to theories such as MI, without a counter-hegemonic discourse and resistance to using intelligence as a dominant organizing force of subjects and subjectivity, formalized education is, for many, a debilitating and near-impossible avenue to democratic participation.

The grand narrative of MI is becoming, through a hegemonic process, a dominant organizing framework of modern, formal education. For example, teacher education textbooks and courses (mainly educational psychology) group discussions of intelligence around MI. In science education, form is being substituted for content under the umbrella of doing science as an intelligence. Classroom teachers and professional development days at local and national levels are increasing demanding "practical applications" of MI theory. In one school, learning and timetables are slowly being organized based on a different MI: at 9 AM, social intelligence; at 10 AM, logical-mathematical intelligence, and so on. On the one hand, theorists of intelligence/s have grouped around hierarchies such as intellectual, language, moral, emotional, and social levels of development (Piaget, Kohlberg, and Erickson, to name a few); interactive processes (Vygotsky); or academic-based areas such as sociology, biology, linguistics, social, and cognitive psychology. Gardner, on the other hand, has framed his theory of MI around the major subject disciplines of formalized thinking that reads like a school timetable—language arts(linguistic), health (intrapersonal), mathematics (logical-mathematical), physical education(bodily-kinesthetic), science (logical-naturalist), social studies(interpersonal), music (musical), and art (spatial).

MI as Capitalism

With good intentions to theorize MI as a source of capital, Gardner (1993b) claims them as those specific intelligences that are valued by society. Instead, what is really created is the basis of a work force that fulfils the agenda of symbolic and cultural capitalism in addition to material/economic capitalism. In either case, the different forms of capital are unequally distributed among gender, race, class, religion, sexuality, families, and other cultural groups and institutions. Although the different forms of capital may not be reduced to each other, one form can interact with another to access privilege in another form. MI may be cultural and symbolic capital, as clearly stated by Gardner, but they also serve to access economic and political capital for those few carrying the classification criteria.

Intelligence as a concept in the name of modern democratic education is a creation of a social, cultural, economic, and political history. It was created gradually as an outcome when mass education became the major means to political and economic participation and social justice for all. Without a place for women and children after they were taken off the labor force during the Industrial Revolution, with the withdrawal of apprenticeship education for males, with the decreasing power of the church (the old capitalists) as an educational institution because of the increasing secularization brought about by Western rationality and scientific objectivity, formalized schooling became a location of capital.

Access to the rights and privileges of democracy became the promise of a secular education, and the chief product was knowledge. Questions about the production, circulation, and measurement of knowledge were asked from a capitalist stance: What knowledge? Whose knowledge? How measured? Who produces the best product that becomes capital for Western civilization? Is the money that governments (the capitalists of modernism) are spending to educate the masses (mainly white, European, Christian, colonizing males) being spent efficiently? How do we find out? What participants are producing the best products (knowledge)? And, most important, as an outcome of education framed around MI, society and institutions asked: Who gets to be in charge of, paid the most for, and valued the most for creating/producing, circulating, and maintaining dominant mainstream knowledge and values that will provide the major capital of modern civilization?

Similar to the work force of pre-industrial and industrial times, capital is created by a division of labor based on intelligence and harboured within the normalizing codes and structures of institutions such as education. In addition, MI creates a legitimization of production-line thinking with the compartmentalization of knowledge into academic disciplines. This concurs with Foucault's (1984) theory of power/knowledge and how disciplinary technologies (such as MI) preceded modern capitalism (18). I would argue further that these disciplinary technologies such as MI are discursive discourses and practices that *reproduce* modern structures and techniques of capitalism and thus reproduce systems and practices of exclusion, inequities and social injustices. For example, those students with only one intelligence can access only a limited range of capital. Those with two or three abilities supervise the single-intelligence people. Those who have intelligence in all areas become the leaders and bosses, those with the most power. Thus, MI hegemonically accesses membership to the status quo hierarchy necessary for the generation and maintenance of capitalism. Further analysis of who gets to be considered as intelligent or possess intelligences, who gets to be placed in academic streams and who in labor-intensive streams are crucial questions that challenge the assumptions about the links between MI and the reproduction of inequities through hegemonic practices such as capitalism. As MI acts as an organizing device of subjects and subjectivity in society and institutions, as power/knowledge plays out through the everyday practices of MI, and without critical scrutiny by teachers, parents, and curriculum designers, MI will continue to seduce and reproduce. Important questions about the relationship between the logic of capitalism and the logic of MI challenge the continued pathologizing of students/subjects based on measures and discourses of intelligence.

Although the social and historical process is more complex and circular than I have briefly reviewed, these were the circumstances and questions that created a need, a means, a category, a tool, a language, a test that would measure everything from what we teach to whom we teach, who is the best to teach, who gets to keep participating longer, who gets access to the limited spaces, who gets to be professionals and who laborers, and who gets to have political and economic power and who does not. To encapsulate all of the complexity and purposes, a panacea, created by cognitive psychologists and educational administrators in the early 1900s, became known as "intelligence." And in spite of the expansion of the term to include "multiple," Gardner's theory is still a modernist's reduction of thought to a Western conception of knowledge as capital.

This troping of industrial, technological rationality, and cognitive psychology with intelligence is indeed a tired, overused metaphor of modern education. Education as training or education for liberation has been a long-standing question that underpins the logic of schooling. When the ephemeral dust, however, is cleared on the question, the dynamics of modern education as part of Western Enlightenment's project of progress through reason actually privilege certain systems of knowledge such as those constructed by the theory and practices of MI. Furthermore, the dominant modes of thought/intelligences became legitimized as capital, through the development of standard levels of knowledge known as a singular intelligence quotient (IQ) and measured through tests that placed students on scales ranging from below average, to average, above average, and genius. In combination with a battery of other tests that measured interests, abilities, and academic placements, IQ became a dominant device for directing students into academic, vocational, or remedial streams. Very little difference is demonstrated by the intentions of MI.

A perusal of professional and academic journals, the Internet, educational textbooks, student theses, and books by and about MI indicates a pattern of practices suggesting that, in spite of Gardner's move away from the generalizations of IQ, the foundations of Western capitalism have continued to circulate throughout the field of education. Theorists including Gardner, writers and researchers in fields such as educational psychology and academic disciplines, curriculum planners and implementors, administrators, teachers, textbook publishers, program designers, and evaluators, and a bevy of educators with an investment in studies of intelligence produce works that are indeed a major source of symbolic capital. Each domain is hegemonically sealed within systems of production that act in overt independence yet in fact covertly interact with one another to constitute a system of symbolic capital that in turn increases economic and political capital for both the institutions and the players within. Consumers of the products, including parents, society, media, and other factions are caught in the legitimization of intelligence as capital. There is no mistake that for most people, education still is seen as a major means for "getting a job." Limited attention or interest is given to education as a major means of social justice, liberation, democratic participation, and the establishment of global peace. It unsettles my pedagogical sensibilities to think that educational structures and concerns still assign such an important position to the role of intelligence. Part of the disconcertment is due to the apolitical stance taken by educators and parents toward the discourses and practices of intelligence theories.

Education is a political system, but reducing it to a category such as intelligence, even as a plurality, universalizes knowledge and disables democracy. Most of the literature and research on MI reveals a pattern that avoids the political implications of the inclusion of MI as an educational standard to strive for and as a measure of achievement. A search through the literature available in books, journals, conferences, and the Internet indicates the application of MI to the following general categories:

1. projects and language instruction (Nishijima 1996);
2. implementation (Sternberg 1994; Gardner 1991);
3. school reform (Leiss & Ritchie 1995; Sternberg 1994);
4. evaluation and MI inventory (Donavan & Iovino 1997);
5. MI and assessment;
6. teaching, learning, and cognitive styles (Armstrong 1994; Morgan 1996; Gardner 1982; *Educational Leadership* 1997; Boss 1994; Gardner 1994; Silver, Strong, & Perini 1997);
7. use of MI to meet educational standards;
8. increasing scores in subject disciplines;
9. learning disabled and the gifted (Ericsson & Charness 1994; Gardner 1997; Matthews 1988);
10. classroom practices and activities (Black 1994).

One of the few challenges to the formalism of intelligence theories was the work of Margaret Donaldson (1992) in *Human Minds: An Exploration*. In this book, she continues where she left off in her award-winning book *Children's Minds* (1978), with a challenge to her professor's (Piaget's) formalist classification of intelligence. She combines notions from pre-Enlightenment ages with several dashes of postformalist thinking, including Buddhist thought, to critique the privileging of the scientific (formalist) mode in theories of the human mind. If indeed there are other discussions and applications of MI from a critical theorist's position, they are very few in number and avoid economic and political dynamics.

A major—perhaps the major—organizing device of Western society and institutions, especially in the last throes of modern life, is capitalism. Any theories or practices that are compatible with the agendas of capitalism, including colonial residuals, are welcomed and embraced through a hegemonic process of promises and seduction. Since the material and economic capital of intelligence is the students, local, national and global governments, international industries and corporations, and other institutions structured around capitalism work as a complex network that demand a competitive resource. The "brightest" and the best are selected from graduates based on rankings gathered in large part from quantitative intelligence testing (e.g., SAT, LSAT, MSAT scores) to subject-discipline testing of content and skill, in essence measurements of MI (e.g., math, science, language). Regardless of the sociohistorical context in which the rankings occur, there is an underlying standard against which students are measured. Herein lies the undemocratic base of troping intelligence with educational rationale.

The discourse and practices of intelligence as capital circulate through a number of social-historical levels and act as validation for instituting particular policies and programs. Intelligence becomes capitalism when desire creates a market for its production in such areas as:

- parents' dreams of a good life for their children, including the best jobs;
- governments' need to fulfil platform promises to taxpayers that they are getting the best education system for their dollars;

- educational programmers designing curricula that cover current knowledge, with teachers controlling and measuring the knowledge of curriculum;
- developmental levels of learning that teach and test progression through the ranks;
- placement of students according to academic abilities (never interests or cultural contexts);
- evaluation of students for admission to next grade;
- admission to different levels of postsecondary education;
- societal standards;
- institutional standards;
- corporate influence on what constitutes knowledge to the domination of Western civilization's globalization through the Euro/Amerocentric logic of capitalism

This entire accumulation of interests results in a very powerful "grand narrative" of intelligence which grants a control of knowledge that early in the hegemonic process progressively decides who accesses power and who doesn't.

What ensues from the discussion of the partnership between capitalist agendas and theories of intelligence might appear as a criticism that, in the long run, will not transform the policies and practices of Western education. Attempts at reforms in the early 2000s cannot rely merely on intellectual attacks against capitalism as the root of all evil or on Marxist criticism. I agree that intelligence attached to capitalist power is undemocratic. Recognition of capitalist agendas is progressively liberating when we challenge the mechanisms, such as intelligence theories, that ensure the continued disabling of large segments of the global population. However, what can't be ignored or shuffled to a theoretical sideline is the continuing practice of connecting intelligence as a legitimate means to a capitalist vision of education.

Education as capital is not new, whether in reference to the apprenticeship/ guild/church models of the premodern era or the Fordist state and corporate model of late modernism. In either case, the organization of education around symbolic capital such as intelligence is still a link to the material capital of Western economies and politics. In the globalization of knowledge by Western culture and technology, universalizing consciousness and standardizing education based on a framework such as MI sire a period of profiteering for the West as did the European early colonization of the non-European worlds and the later colonization of the world by American economic, political, cultural, and intellectual means. Throughout these historical cycles of colonization, capitalism has pushed and forced modes of production to include the standardization of the world; the reduction of knowledge to MI is no exception. It "fits" for educational producers and consumers. In the quest for the projected privileges of capitalism in modern society, educational institutions throughout the world, under the guise of globalization, have adopted or wish to adopt the knowledge base that constructed Western powers. Access to the universal ideology of capitalism is a means to that end supplied by educational institutions and demanded by multinational corporations as the newest driving force in the globalization of knowledge. Specific intelligences such as created by MI become one of the major suppliers to the corporate ends. And if freedom and democracy, economic and political power are part of the ends, then globalization of knowledge through intelligences is the right of every society, culture, nation, and civilization. But that's a formidable assumption and, as a postmodern critical theorist must argue cogently, a false assumption to be challenged.

There is perhaps a degree of liberation at the global level when education planners and players institute intelligence theories and practices (which range from organizing relationships within the classroom and society to the testing of intelligence for its market value). To most institutions, including education and corporations, access to the knowledge of the West means access to modernization and modern life. What better way to buy that power than to create a resource that is in demand by the pivotal organizer of modern life, the political and economic systems of capitalism? So intelligence is not merely a commodity in Western society but a resource for globalization, which actually means intelligences that have been created and designed to continue the power of Western civilization; intelligences shaped by Western disciplines that amass power through consent to dominant constructs of what knowledge and whose knowledge is capital.

While neosocialist stances have historically argued against organizing education around capitalist and corporate agendas or focused more on the sociocultural impact of capitalism or positioned the interests of capitalism and education for social justice and democracy in opposition, Ladwig (1995) reminds us that modern mass education historically has always been tied to national economies (212). To ignore this point places discussions of intelligence outside the individual, societal, institutional, and global levels of interest and need. Given that denial, concepts of MI will continue to circulate within personal and public levels without challenge. And without recognition of where and how capitalist agendas and concepts such as MI systematically intersect to legitimize educational practices, will any resistance to the imbalances of power be forthcoming or legislatively possible?

Resistance to the power and privileges given to modern capitalism has an extensive history, beginning with the legacies of overt Marxism and, more covertly, with communism. At the end of the twentieth century, the modernists' project of the Enlightenment which engulfs the world with scientific, objective rationality based in Eurocentric knowledge and values is firmly entrenched in institutional systems and materials. Along with the technological hyperrealities that convince us of the demise of global socialism, critical theorists are presented with limited ground and exhausted intellectual energy to dismantle hegemonic practices such as MI, a handmaiden to social injustices.

Challenges to the theories and practices of MI in educational fields are few. However, critical theorists, informed by discourse from the margins of modern life such as feminism, people of color, and the colonized, are interrupting the "common sense," taken-for-granted discourse and practices of traditional formalist thought constructed by educational psychology—the conceptualizing mother of MI.

Recently, the prefix "post" has been attached to many words in an attempt to question the status quo of the Western world. For example, the literature and discourse on postmodern, poststructural, postformal, postcolonial, and postfeminist theory demand a dismantling of dominance, especially by those fields of production created and maintained by Western history and culture. In the historical process of formalizing thought and knowledge, intelligence remains one of the major organizing devices that have supported the levels of capitalism that have created and maintained unequal power relations in every corner of education. Nonresistance will occur until the discourse and frameworks provided by the postisms enter the discussions and open the field of the formalized production of knowledge and thought under the rubric of intelligence. The scrutiny of formalism presented by postformalism questions the power relations established by grand narratives such as Gardner's MI (Kincheloe & Steinberg 1993).

The field of Western logic is vast, and its offspring are present in many ways, most of which are invisible to an uninformed or differently informed, common-sense consciousness. In order to construct a differently informed consciousness and reveal the taken-for-grantedness of commonsense thinking, postformalism enters the cracks and crevices of formalist systems to alert theorists and practitioners to where, how, and why Western logic exists. The logic of MI is dependent on the logic of capitalism. Although capitalism and intelligence may seem like strange bedfellows, their secret affair needs to be made public for everyone from parents to teachers, from educational administrators to media forums. Until that happens, the field of education remains unfaithful to many in its promise of equality and justice for all.

As systems of education, economics, politics, and communications are globalizing both at the micro and macro levels of society, the homogenization of knowledge and values is a threat. In a rush for individuals, families, schools, and nations to access the power of Western modern life, especially that of the United States, powerful and invisible forces are at play in organizing systems of consent to activities that contribute to homogenization through globalization. More than ever, what is needed in education is the force of differences that retains the creative forces of traditional, modern, postmodern, and postcolonial identity, thought, and values; new realities with social justice, not capitalism, as the organizing force. MI dances seductively in its reduction of thought and knowledge to a homogenous system that privileges Western thought and values. And make no mistake: the seduction is extensive in its intent and travels.

In his book *To Open Minds,* Gardner (1989) documents how China is open to including its past in the economic, political, and cultural move into modernization. What he glosses over, however, is how modernization and his theory of MI are garnered from Western history, systems, and specific Western geniuses. Chinese education that adopts MI as a model of teaching and learning should be aware that MI is developed from the structuralist thought of Europeans such as Piaget and

Levi-Strauss; from Western culture's dominant academic disciplines that support an already established categorization of knowledge; and from people defined as geniuses in their intelligence category, e.g., Martha Graham (body-kinesthetic), Einstein (logical-mathematical), Picasso (spatial), and Ghandi, who was non-European but educated in England (interpersonal).

To adopt MI in education at the global level is flawed in so many dangerous ways that it seems incomprehensible that nations, Western and non-Western, would consider its constructs. Granted, nations want to create and maintain modern educational systems that produce citizens who establish power (mainly economic, as discussed before) and standards (measured by modernization). MI may seem to be one way to do so. But nations must challenge the constructs of MI in order to recognize the oppression of differences and the homogenization of thinking. Theories and practices of intelligences may seem like a passport to modernization and global capital, but creativity is the key to local, national, and global power for all. Creativity is the source of intelligence that produces power and capital—ownership of knowledge and value that shifts in the contexts of time and place, from moment to moment.

Creativity is an elusive process and requires a process of thinking that seems to avoid classification such as MI attempts to do. James Gleick's (1993) extensive study of Richard Feyman reveals that the "intelligence" of genius, for example, is neither a process nor a set of criteria that can be captured in symbolic or methodological approaches. Gleick's metaphoric study of an individual's intelligence, similar to Gardner's appropriation of "geniuses" to develop his classification system of MI, produces quite a different result than Gardner's:

> William Duff, in his 18th century essay, gave birth to the modern meaning of the word "genius". . . and his contemporaries wished to identify genius with godlike powers of invention, of creation, of making what was never before; to do so they had to create a psychology of imagination. . . . Their several centuries of labor [on the study of what makes intelligence] have produced no consensus on the qualities. (Gleick 1993, 313)

Today, the psychology of the imagination has been reduced even further to MI yet seems to provide answers for many educators about teaching, learning, thinking, and evaluating. Indeed if intelligence studies are isolated from their sociohistorical, economic, and political contexts, they appear to be something they aren't.

At the personal, societal, national and global levels where educational institutions search for a future that is democratic, powerful, and sees knowledge as capital, why would nations such as China consider MI as a source of organization and evaluation of curriculum and students, a means to an end? To modernize means to Westernize, and "the tools of the master are what we need" to do so. This is faulty thinking at its best, the feminists (such as Audre Lorde) would argue. The master, in this case Western thought and values, might share the resources of modernization, including theories and practices of intelligence. But be assured, drawing from the personal experiences and histories of subjugated peoples, masters don't release knowledge or power without a cost to the consumers. Generations of women, people of color, the poor, and the colonized can attest to this. Appropriation of intelligence theories, one of the master's tools, cannot be decontextualized either from their source in Western thought or from the capitalist agenda. Recognition of MI as one of the master's tools that suppresses creativity should produce, among educators and the public, a spirit of resistance to classification systems that formalize intelligence. Creative intelligence is borderless and resists formalization as Gleick (1993) and others have found (Kincheloe, Steinberg, & Tippins 1999). Intelligence theories become, discursively, the late modern-day colonizers of consciousness.

Postcolonial, postfeminist, postmodern, deconstruction, and postformal thought, for example, acts as a challenge to Western logic, including cognitive categories of MI, as "the only way to organize a modern society" (Cassidy 2000). While classifications of intelligence may seem like a way to organize teaching, learning, and evaluation, what they really structure is a truth-value and consciousness. How those structures come to be accepted as natural and normal—made to seem real—is part of a historical process that is governed by Western logic and capitalism. Although students/parents/educators/nations may accept intelligence categories (whether the below-above average/average categories or those of MI) as the way to organize education in line with capitalist structures, postformal thought, along with other postisms, does not. In fact, at every level of modern hierarchies, postformalism identifies the economic and political production hegemonically sealed in something that is merely an ideological construct. Without a recognition of the power of Western logic to influence and contain everyday lives, there is no opportunity for social action and diversity within culturally, economically, and political constructed systems and concepts such as MI.

Systems of organization (such as MI) based on Western logic have collected individuals, society, institutions, and modern civilization into such dominant, formalized realities that oppression and differences in the world go unnoticed or are marginalized. Critical theorists deconstruct the power of Western logic and its offspring classifications such as MI that construct discourses and practices of universalism and centres of power. Trying to function and learn within the borders set by MI can become, for many, a process of isolation, loneliness, self-loathing, and exclusion from the centers of power. These are people who:

- do not fit the dominant logic of white, male, Christian, heterosexual, middle-class/upper-class, Western objectivity and rationality (definitions of intelligence);
- do not fit at the intersections of Western logic (where race, class, gender, nationality, etc. intersect);
- act (consciously or unconsciously) against formalist regimes of truth and discourses for a variety of rationales.

Soon the sense of agency to challenge and resist is diminished or impossible. Who does that process leave at the center? You? Me? Your family? Friends? Students? Gardner?

Lumping MI together with capitalism, politics, systems of classification, Western logic, and white, male, heterosexual, and other dominant constructs as the intersecting causes of social injustices and nondemocratic practices in education can be as damaging as ignoring their apolitical, decontextualized forces. It essentializes the subjects; that is, it assumes that all individuals fall naturally, normally, or are forced within those constructs. Furthermore, essentialism reduces the agency of the subjects who inhabit or are classified by those constructs. Deconstructing the logic of MI may decenter dominant power. However, subjects within and outside the mainstream are in a constant state of consenting, negotiating, and resisting the boundaries of classification and dominant logic. In a democratic society, educators, parents, students, and a host of other subjects have the right to challenge binding societal and institutional borders of intelligence, including MI.

When I ask students whether they would rather have a below-average intelligence or a below-average mark in a subject area, they answer the latter: "We can change the marks by studying but not our intelligence." When I question teachers or parents, they reply similarly. In below-average grades there seems to be a sense of agency; in below-average intelligence, none. How did it get to be so? I suggest that the power of MI driven by the Western logic of capitalism plays an overwhelming part in the lack of agency felt in the responses. I agree in part with Best and Kellner, who argue that:

> postmodernism lacks an adequate theory of agency, of an active creative self, mediated by social institutions, discourses, and other people. Here we find Sartre's notion of the self as a project useful in his emphasis that creative subjectivity is an accomplishment of a process of self-creation rather than as a given. Yet theories of subjectivity and political agency must be mediated with theories of intersubjectivity which stress the ways that the subject is a social construct and the ways that sociality can constrict or enable individual subjectivity. In addition, an adequate theory of subjectivity should stress the social construction of the subject, its production in discourses, practices and institutions. (1991, 284)

Agency to challenge is sometimes difficult, sometimes impossible for a variety of reasons. At the borders and intersections between modern and postmodern education, sources of knowledge have changed over the years, from the dominance of oral cultures and book cultures to the current electronic culture of television, film, and Internet. It was an awakening to me last week when, after assigning research topics for report writing, I watched the university students in my writing class rush comfortably and almost naturally to the computer to access knowledge. Where I searched through books, and still do, these students demonstrated to me that, for them, electronic texts are the dominant source of knowledge. I wondered which is the more intelligent source, books or computers? Who is more intelligent? My generation with its "book learning," which is still highly valued, or these students with intelligences shaped by electronic sources? Or my parents and grandparents, who, with very limited formal education, accessed power to negotiate and resist the classifications of class, sexuality, age, gender, language, and intelligence?

Reflection on my own questions, after lengthy abstractions about MI, capitalism, hegemony, education, agency, and democracy, led me back to the title of this chapter—MI are not what they seem to be! In fact intelligence is a sociopolitical construct subject to abuses and not, as cognitive psychologists would like us to believe, a substance of a just and democratic education.

Hindsight or Foresight?

Whatever directions education takes, it seems there is always a clash between the past, present, and future. The establishment of theories of intelligence seems to be no exception. The discussion in this chapter considered the hegemonic processes directed by the logic and politics of Western capitalism. How the hierarchical process siphons itself throughout educational policies and practices demands attention and challenge. How to challenge becomes a concern of critical theorists. Public and practitioners say (sometimes yell): "Show us how, where and when." "Show us how to transform policies and practices." "Practice what you preach." "Give us some ideas to get us started."

The first step is informed practitioners. The context in which I write this is filled with the politics of theory and practices that carry huge assumptions about intelligence. The accumulation of power for certain theories and practices is, through hegemonic practices, a dominant and driving force in subject disciplines and in education faculty. This also means that institutional powers are in play. Government ministries or departments of education assign funding and players to the licensing process for teachers and their upgrading—and what's hot and becoming hotter is MI. Recently minutes of a meeting came across my desk that were filled with a science course for future secondary teachers that connects science teaching and learning with MI and giftedness. The faculty voted overwhelmingly to accept the course, except for the three or four critical theorists who recognized the hegemony of the consensus vote. Yes, MI is indeed capital, in schools and universities, in teacher education faculties, for corporate agendas and parents and other public investors in education. It spreads. It is produced by academic discourse that eventually circulates through publications and by highly profiled players, especially those with Ivy League credentials that seduce secular and educational administrators. MI is sold as capital to a profession generally naive about the nature of intelligence. Both the public and the teaching profession fail to see that intelligence is a socially constructed entity and that Gardner's MI has gained acceptance by the work of funding agencies and publishing companies who only operate in the conceptual confines of the status quo. What is called intelligence becomes a sorting mechanism that operates like the gates of a university which only the rich and "brightest" can pass though or like my years of walking around a local university campus to get to work thinking that, as a temporary secretary, I didn't have the "intelligence" credentials to walk into or through the campus. That walk around the center of intelligence was twenty minutes longer and through some of the roughest areas of society, where gangs waited to rob and rape me. So my self-esteem and consciousness were shaped by the geography and history of intelligence which lie outside the institutional borders of educational criteria based on intelligence.

And the production, circulation, and maintaining of the status quo will remain, leaving creativity and differences far behind. Knowledge as capital will disappear because with the homogenizing, with everyone having the same reduced intelligences, there will be no product to sell, no knowledge worth buying, because it will reproduced by a status quo capital. Capital works on having products to sell, mass produced for quick and efficient marketing and demanding consumers. That is what theories and practices of intelligence will produce—capital for a nation, knowledge as capital that is tied to intelligence. Intelligence means knowledge; knowledge is capital; therefore intelligence is capital. Currently MI is even greater capital in the fields of education: teaching, learning; textbooks, subject disciplines, and so forth. So where does this leave all the other knowledges, such as that of critical theorists, which challenge the principles and practices of teachers and educational institutions that produce and circulate intelligence and knowledge as status quo, subject-disciple capital that perpetuates Western civilization even in the throes of globalization, and market capital that comes from nontraditional structural, cultural, and historical worlds that are different from those entrenched in the Western world? No inventions will emerge to create new capital; no knowledge will be generated that questions and challenges the status quo if intelligence becomes something that reduces the imagination to fit into boxes and categories that can be tested and marketed. Education for opportunity and social justice and equity will disappear.

References

Armstrong, T. (1994). *Multiple intelligences in the classroom*. Alexandria, VT: Association for Supervision and Curriculum Development.

Best, S., & Kellner, D. (1991). *Postmodern theory: Critical interrogations*. New York: Guilford Press.

Black, S. (1994). Different kinds of smart. *The Executive Educator, 16*(1), 24–27.

Boss, J. (1994). The autonomy of moral intelligence. *Educational Theory, 44*(4), 399–416.

Bourdieu, P. (1993). *The field of cultural production: Essays on art and literature*. New York: Columbia University Press.

Cassidy, J. (2000). The price prophet. *New Yorker,* 7 February, pp. 44–51.

Donaldson, M. (1992). *Human minds: An exploration*. New York: Allen Lane.

———. (1978). *Children's minds*. New York: HarperCollins.

Donavan, B., & Iovino, R. (1997). *Approach to expanding and celebrating teacher portfolios and student portfolios*. Paper presented at the annual meeting of the NE Educational Research Association, October, Ellenville, NY.

Educational Leadership (1997). Teaching for Multiple Intelligences—Theme Issue, *55*(1).

Eisner, E. W. (1994). Multiple intelligences: Theory into practice. In Sternberg, R. (1994).

Reforming school reform: Comments on multiple intelligences: The theory in practice. *Teachers College Record, 95*(4), 561–569.

Ericsson, K., and Charness, N. (1994). Expert performance: Its structure and acquisition. *American Psychologist, 49*(8).

Foucault, M. (1984). Polemics, politics, and problematisation. In Rabinow, P. (ed.) *The Foucault reader.* New York: Pantheon, pp. 381–390.

Gardner, H. (1982). *Art, mind, and brain: A cognitive approach to creativity.* New York: Basic Books.

———. (1989). *To open minds: Chinese clues to the dilemma of contemporary education.* New York: Basic Books.

———. (1991). *The unschooled mind: How children think and how schools should teach.* London: Fontana Press.

———. (1993a). *Frames of mind: The theory of multiple intelligences.* New York: Basic Books.

———. (1993b). *Multiple Intelligences: The theory in practice.* New York: HarperCollins.

———. (1994). Intelligences in theory and practice: A response to Elliot W. Eisner, Robert J. Sternberg, and Henry M. Levin. *Teachers College Record, 95*(4), 561–569.

———. (1997). Six afterthoughts: Comments on varieties of intellectual talents. *Journal of Creative Behavior, 31*(2), 120.

Gleick, J. (1993). *Genius: The life and science of Richard Feyman.* New York: Vintage.

Hatch, T., & Gardner, H. (1990). If Binet had looked beyond the classroom: The assessment of multiple intelligences. *International Journal of Educational Research, 14*(5), 415–430.

Kincheloe, J., & Steinberg, S. (1993). A tentative description of post-formal thinking: The critical confrontation with cognitive theory. *Harvard Educational Review, 63*(3), 296–320.

Kincheloe, J., Steinberg, S., and Tippins, D. (1999). *The stigma of genius: Einstein, consciousness, and education.* New York: Peter Lang.

Ladwig, J. (1995). Educational intellectuals and corporate politics. In R. Smith & P. Wexler (eds.), *After post-modernism: Education, politics and identity* (pp. 225–240). London: Falmer Press.

Leiss, E., & Ritchie, G. (1995). Using MI theory to transform a first grade health curriculum. *Early Childhood Education Journal, 23*(2), 71–79.

Light unit activities based on MI. (2002). *www.rockeyview.ab.cal*

Matthews, D. (1988). Gardner's multiple intelligences: An evaluation of relevant research and a consideration of its application to gifted education. *Ropier Review, 11*(2), 11–17.

Morgan, H. (1996). An analysis of Gardner's Multiple Intelligences. *Ropier Review, 18*(4), 15–22.

Nishijima, M. (1996). Using Gardner's multiple intelligences in a Japanese-as-a-foreign-language classroom. Unpublished master's thesis, University of New Brunswick, Fredericton, Canada.

Rabinow, P. (ed). (1984). *Foucault reader: An introduction to Foucault's thought.* New York: Pantheon Books.

Schools using MI to determine strength areas of students. (2002). www.adiz.k12.co.us/skyview/profile.html.

Silver, H., Strong, R., & Perini, M. (1997). Integrating learning styles and multiple intelligences. *Educational Leadership 55*(1), 22–27.

Sternberg, R. (1994). Reforming school reform: Comments on multiple intelligences: The theory in practice. *Teachers College Record, 95*(4), 561–569.

CONTRIBUTORS

Peter Applebaum is associate professor and coordinator of math education at Arcadia University.

Kathleen S. Berry is professor of education and drama at the University of New Brunswick.

Donald S. Blumenthal-Jones is associate professor of ethics and education at Arizona State University.

Gaile S. Cannela is professor of education and psychology at Texas A & M University.

Richard Cary is professor of art and art education at Mars Hill College.

Joe L. Kincheloe is professor of education at the CUNY-Graduate Center and Brooklyn College.

Jay L. Lemke is professor of science education at the University of Michigan-Ann Arbor.

Marla Morris is associate professor of education at Georgia Southern University.

Kathleen Nolan is a doctoral student in education at the CUNY-Graduate Center.

Yusef Progler is professor of international and cultural studies and education at Zayed University in Dubai.

Danny Weil is the Director of the Institute for Critical Thinking in California.

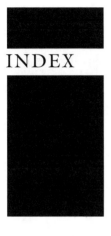

INDEX

Studies in the Postmodern Theory of Education

General Editors
Joe L. Kincheloe & Shirley R. Steinberg

Counterpoints publishes the most compelling and imaginative books being written in education today. Grounded on the theoretical advances in criticalism, feminism, and postmodernism in the last two decades of the twentieth century, Counterpoints engages the meaning of these innovations in various forms of educational expression. Committed to the proposition that theoretical literature should be accessible to a variety of audiences, the series insists that its authors avoid esoteric and jargonistic languages that transform educational scholarship into an elite discourse for the initiated. Scholarly work matters only to the degree it affects consciousness and practice at multiple sites. Counterpoints' editorial policy is based on these principles and the ability of scholars to break new ground, to open new conversations, to go where educators have never gone before.

For additional information about this series or for the submission of manuscripts, please contact:

Joe L. Kincheloe & Shirley R. Steinberg
c/o Peter Lang Publishing, Inc.
275 Seventh Avenue, 28th floor
New York, New York 10001

To order other books in this series, please contact our Customer Service Department:

(800) 770-LANG (within the U.S.)
(212) 647-7706 (outside the U.S.)
(212) 647-7707 FAX

Or browse online by series:
www.peterlangusa.com